T0345050

Internet of Things Vulnerabilities and Recovery Strategies

The Internet of Things (IoT) is a widely distributed and networked system of interrelated and interacting computing devices and objects. Because of IoT's broad scope, it presents unique security problems, ranging from unsecure devices to users vulnerable to hackers. Presenting cutting-edge research to meet these challenges, *Internet of Things Vulnerabilities and Recovery Strategies* presents models of attack on IoT systems and solutions to prevent such attacks. Examining the requirements to secure IoT-systems, the book offers recovery strategies and addresses security concerns related to:

- Data Routing
- Data Integrity
- Device Supervision
- IoT Integration
- Information Storage
- IoT Performance

The book takes a holistic approach that encompasses visibility, segmentation, and protection. In addition to visual approaches and policy-driven measures, the book looks at developing secure and fault-tolerant IoT devices. It examines how to locate faults and presents mitigation strategies, as well as security models to prevent and thwart hacking. The book also examines security issues related to IoT systems and device maintenance.

Faheem Syeed Masoodi is Assistant Professor in the Department of Computer Science, University of Kashmir. Earlier, he served the College of Computer Science, University of Jizan, Saudi Arabia, as an Assistant Professor.

Alwi M. Bamhdi is Associate Professor in the Department of Computer Sciences, Umm Al-Qura University, Saudi Arabia. He received his MSc and Ph.D. in computer science in 2014 from Heriot-Watt University, UK.

Majid A. Charoo has worked as a technology consultant in Global Science & Technology Forum, Singapore, and was an Assistant Professor in Al-Jouf University, Saudi Arabia, in the department of Information Sciences.

Zubair Sayeed Masoodi is Assistant Professor and head of the Computer Applications Department at Government Degree College for Women, Sopore, India. He is currently heading the Department of Computer Applications at this college.

Arif Mohammad is Lead Digital Engineer at Louis Dreyfus Company, The Netherlands.

Gousiya Hussain is currently pursuing a PhD in Cloud Security from the Department of Computer Sciences, Mewar University, India.

Internet of Things Vulnerabilities and Recovery Strategies

Edited by
Faheem Syeed Masoodi, Alwi M. Bamhdi,
Majid A. Charoo, Zubair Sayeed Masoodi,
Arif Mohammad, and Gousiya Hussain

CRC Press
Taylor & Francis Group
Boca Raton London New York

CRC Press is an imprint of the
Taylor & Francis Group, an **informa** business

First edition published 2025
by CRC Press
2385 NW Executive Center Drive, Suite 320, Boca Raton FL 33431

and by CRC Press
4 Park Square, Milton Park, Abingdon, Oxon, OX14 4RN

CRC Press is an imprint of Taylor & Francis Group, LLC

© 2025 Taylor & Francis Group, LLC

ISBN: 9781032473314 (hbk)
ISBN: 9781032756172 (pbk)
ISBN: 9781003474838 (ebk)

DOI: 10.1201/9781003474838

Typeset in Garamond
by Newgen Publishing UK

Contents

Preface

The Internet of Things (IoT) has become a big part of our lives, connecting every-thing from our homes to factories. But with all this connectivity comes some risks to our privacy and security.

In this book, *Internet of Things Vulnerabilities and Recovery Strategies*, we explore these risks and how to make our digital world safer. We look at the latest research and real-life stories to help researchers, people who work with technology, and policymakers understand and solve these problems.

This book is organized into 17 chapters, each covering important topics such as Internet of Things, Data Privacy and Security, Cyber-Physical Threat Intelligence, Privacy Preservation in Cyber Physical Systems, Bio-Inspired Meta-Heuristic Methodologies for Security, Auditing IoT Security Vulnerability, Information Storage in IoT, Internet of Things Cloud Security Challenges, IoT Security with Blockchain Technology, Intrusion Detection and Privacy and Security. Each chapter provides valuable insights and practical strategies for addressing the complex challenges of IoT security and privacy. Whether you're a seasoned researcher, a dedicated practitioner, or a policymaker concerned with safeguarding our digital future, this book offers a comprehensive guide to navigating the intricate landscape of IoT vulnerabilities.

Contributors

Syed Wajid Aalam
Department of Computer Science
Islamic University of Science and
   Technology
Kashmir, India

Praveen Kumar Agarwal
School of Business Management
CSJM University
Kanpur, India

Aamir Salam Ahanger
Department of Computer Sciences
University of Kashmir
Kashmir, India

Yusuf Jibrin Alkali
Federal Inland Revenue Service
Nigeria

Wasia Ashraf
Department of Computer Sciences
University of Kashmir
Kashmir, India

Alwi M. Bamhdi
Computing College Al Qufudah
Umm Al-Qura University
Mecca, Kingdom of Saudi Arabia

Ashima Bhatnagar Bhatia
Vivekananda Institute of Professional
   Studies
New Delhi, India

A. S. N. Chakravarthy
CSE Department
JNTUK
Kakinada, Andhra Pradesh, Indi

Hannah Divyanka Doss
Christ University
Bangalore, India

Bazila Farooq
School of Computer Application
Lovely Professional University
Jalandhar, Punjab, India

Reshma Gulwani
Information Technology Department
RAIT, D.Y. Patil (Deemed to be
   University) Nerul, Navi
Mumbai, India

P. Harikrishna
Department of Computational
   Intelligence
Malla Reddy College of Engineering
   and Technology
Hyderabad, India

Sandeep Joshi
Department of Computer Science and
    Engineering
Manipal University
Jaipur, India

Shubhalaxmi Sanjay Joshi
School of Computer Science &
    Engineering
Dr. Vishwanath Karad, MIT World
    Peace University
Pune, India

Divyashree K.S.
School of Law Christ University
Bangalore, India

R. Kaviarasan
Department of Computer Science and
    Engineering
RGM College of Engineering and
    Technology
Nandyal, India

Asra Khanam
Department of Computer Sciences
University of Kashmir
Kashmir, India

Shama Kouser
Department of Computer Science
Jazan University
Jazan, Saudi Arabia

Nimish Kumar
BK Birla Institute of Engineering and
    Technology
Pilani (Rajasthan), India

Praveen Kumar
Python Lead
Fidelity International
Gurugram, Haryana, India

Faheem Syeed Masoodi
Department of Computer Sciences
University of Kashmir
Kashmir, India

Achyutananda Mishra
School of Law Christ University
Bangalore, India

Rahul Reddy Nadikattu
University of the Cumberland
Williamsburg, Kentucky, USA

Pallavi
Department of Computer Science and
    Engineering
Manipal University
Jaipur, India

Manikandan Rajagopal
Lean Operations and Systems
School of Business and Management
CHRIST (Deemed to be University)
Bangalore, Karnataka, India

Ramkumar S.
Department of Computer Science
    School of Sciences,
CHRIST (Deemed to be University)
Bangalore, Karnataka, India

Deepak Singh
Matter Vision Mechanics
Noida, UP, India

Mohini Preetam Singh
Department of ECE, Meerut Institute
    of Engineering & Technology
Meerut, Uttar Pradesh, India

Sunil Sonawane
Computer Department
Dr. D.Y. Patil University
Ambi, Pune, India

Tawseef Ahmed Teli
Department of Higher Education
Jammu and Kashmir, India

Namita Tiwari
Department of Mathematics
School of Basic Sciences
CSJM University
Kanpur, India

Ashutosh Tripathi
T. Systems
Pune, India

Himanshu Verma
BK Birla Institute of Engineering and
  Technology
Pilani (Rajasthan), India

Amit Virmani
Department of Computer Applications
UIET, CSJM University
Kanpur, India

Pawan Whig
Vivekananda Institute of Professional
  Studies
New Delhi, India

Syed Irfan Yaqoob
School of Computer Science &
  Engineering
Dr. Vishwanath Karad, MIT World
  Peace University
Pune, India

Manas Kumar Yogi
CSE Department
Pragati Engineering College (A)
Surampalem, Andhra Pradesh, India

Chapter 1

The Internet of Things (IoT): A Cripple to Data Privacy and Security

Hannah Divyanka Doss and Achyutananda Mishra

Christ University, Bangalore, India

1.1 Defining the Internet of Things (IoT)

Industrial revolutions have blurred the traditional distinction of the physical, digital and biological worlds. Technology has empowered human tasks to be automated and to function without manual intervention (Sun, 2018). Its influence is seen and felt the world over as an inevitable and overwhelming change. The Internet is undoubtedly one of the greatest inventions of mankind. Initially, the Internet gained popularity across the world for its ease, accessibility, knowledge and the assistance it provided.

The Internet then expanded to enable human communications and correspondence irrespective of geographical and physical boundaries, where personal devices are the 'actors of interaction'. It came to be known as the Internet of People (IoP), where humans and devices became part and parcel of interactions and not merely just end users of the Internet (Conti & Das, 2017). However, with the further advancement of technology in the twenty-first century, the world has transitioned to the Internet of Things.

DOI: 10.1201/9781003474838-1

IoT has changed the perception of human beings towards tasks and also the expectations from physical objects. IoT envelopes technology that creates a network of Internet-enabled physical things or objects that we use in our everyday lives. Such physical things or objects are embedded with sensors that share and analyze data. The ultimate goal of such a network is to increase the quality and simplicity of human life.

According to Kranenburg (2011), the Internet of Things is a forum where 'things' are made smart by giving to each an autonomous identity, personality, intelligence and agency. These things have the competency to share information in a common information space (Pereira & Funtowincz, 2015). Likewise, another dimension of the IoT is given by the Transmission Control Protocol (TCP) and Internet Protocol (IP), which highlight the functioning of such virtual personalities (things) utilizing imbedded intelligent interfaces to connect and communicate with social-user environments (Minerva et al., 2015).

The IoT is one such technology that enables the Internet to connect the physical world through ubiquitous sensors (Bassi et al., 2013). It aims to empower traditional industries and spaces by infusing them with technologies to make them intelligent (Georgios et al., 2019).

With the growth of IoT, people are connected better than before; goods are imported and exported to the maximum level, thus making today's business a part of the world economy. At a personal level, IoT helps objects be tuned to the needs of users. It adapts to their needs and responds to make their everyday life efficient, easy and convenient. As for IoT in businesses, it increases competitiveness by the power to influence company performances by gauging customer preferences (Del Giudice, 2016).

1.2 Role of Data in IoT

1.2.1 Defining Data

The importance of data in today's world means much more than ever before. In layman's terms, data means information. It is something that gives us an understanding of the subject in question, be it a characteristic or a feature. It is raw information that can be processed and analysed for future necessary actions. Such data gives a unique connotation or deciphers such information from the rest.

The *Cambridge Dictionary* defines data to include electronic information and facts or numbers that can be collected and stored in a computer system for the purpose of examination, consideration and further decision-making (Cambridge Dictionary, 1999). The *Merriam-Webster Dictionary* describes data as factual information that can be used for further reasoning, drawing decisions, conclusions and calculations (Merriam-Webster, 1996). In India, the idea of data includes information, knowledge, facts and concepts that are prepared in a formal manner and has the ability to be processed and stored by a computer system or network (Information Technology Act, 2000, Sec. 2(o)).

'Data' and 'Information' are used interchangeably in various legislations and regulations. The data that is not directed or linked to a specific person is regarded to be general data and freely accessible to all. There lies no protection for such data (Rumbold & Pierscionek, 2018). However, protection, legal sanction and enforceability are only extended to the concept of 'personal data'.

Personal data is such information that relates to an identified or identifiable person (General Data Protection Regulation, 2018, Art. 4(1)). It is information that removes the anonymity of a person in a public sphere. Examples of such personal information are name, birth date, residential address (permanent or temporary), e-mail address, contact number and voter identification number. Sensitive personal data is an important aspect of personal data. Examples of sensitive personal data can be financial passwords and any information regarding physical, mental and psychological health and biometrics (Information Technology Rules, 2011, Sec. 3).

Data is, therefore, a valuable asset to every human being. It is exclusive information held and owned by that person himself or herself. Data can be qualified as one's own property. However, the Information Revolution has consistently spurred debate on the concept of data, or rather personal data, being qualified as 'property' and can attract property rights and protection under law.

In general, the right to property is one's right to exclusively enjoy and benefit from a tangible or intangible thing (Merrill, 1998). Thomas Hobbes, John Locke and Jean Jacques Rousseau propounded the Natural Rights Theory that underlined the rights naturally given to a living person by a constitution. Such enforceability and protection of rights include the right to life and liberty as well as property (Paul et al., 2005). Property rights are a bundle of rights inherent, and attached, to the property in question (Mack, 1995). As per Lesig (2002), the world has transcended into acknowledging data as a commodity and, hence, property rights and appropriate protection must be extended to data.

1.2.2 Data-run Technology

The adoption of 'Digital Transformation' by enterprises signifies the integral role digital technologies play in combining the achievement of goals and innovation (Jun et al., 2022). Businesses, governments, educational establishments have reformed their functioning and operations to incorporate technology in meeting their market demands. Digital Transformation is a process to achieve organisational goals based entirely on the data of consumers (Kirchmer, 2021). It is only with certain information that sectors are able to map their road ahead. For example, an e-commerce clothing brand can only achieve success if the owners are aware of current fashion trends and the future needs of customers. If a clothing website collects data of an expectant other, they visually market products for newborn babies as that will be a need in the near future. This benefits the user, but more so the data collected and analysed, have monetarily benefited the website (company) to a greater extent.

Data can include scientific principles or very intrinsic information of persons who are part of the target group to achieve institutional objectives. Revolutionised Image Detection Systems are data-enabled systems used by police departments for faster identification of criminals. Such systems link any personal information procured as evidence, such as facial characteristics or eye color, to the information of habitual offenders saved on databases (Jain and Ross, 2015).

The functioning of IoT depends entirely on a large magnitude of data. For systems to adapt to the needs of the users, IoT requires the data of the user, be it personal or sensitive data. The IoT ecosystem is a large network of devices that continuously transmits data through the Internet, their processors and sensors (Hong, 2020). The information collected is transferred through a IoT gateway to a storage processor, where the information is analyzed and then responds to the environment and situation (Vermesan and Friess, 2013).

The basic patchwork of IoT is the same, irrespective of the field the IoT works in – industrial, business or personal. For example, in an online shopping application, the main form of data carried through IoT is an individual's preferences, likes and choices. The question is why this data is important to a person. This is qualified as personal data, which has the ability to identify a person, either directly or indirectly, including its characteristics, location or any such factor that is particular to physiological, genetic, economic and cultural identities of a natural person (General Data Protection Regulation, 2018, Art. 4). In the manufacturing sector, machinery and other such fixed assets are embedded with sensors. Such equipment can monitor the condition of the machinery in real time. This will ensure that the machinery used is in good condition and can foresee any breakdown or mishap in the future (Javid et al., 2021).

SMART home security systems are common in today's world. The system and the owner/s of the home are constantly connected, irrespective of persons being within the household or away. The only requisite is to have Internet-enabled systems. Translating Figure 1.1, the house is enabled with a Smart Security System and such is tagged to the homeowner's Smartphone. Smart Doorbells can allow data transfer when the doorbell is rung as a notification to the homeowner's phone. Smart cameras can record movement and also interact with those who have entered the premises. This recording and responses are also powered through the homeowner's phone. Smart Exhaust and Smart Sprinklers can be turned on and off through the Smartphone and can send information to the manufacturers when servicing is required.

Prima facie, IoT seems to be extremely convenient to users. It allows them to be physically absent, yet have control over their own castle. However, looking at it from the lens of realism, IoT does have certain red flags that have gone unnoticed. First,

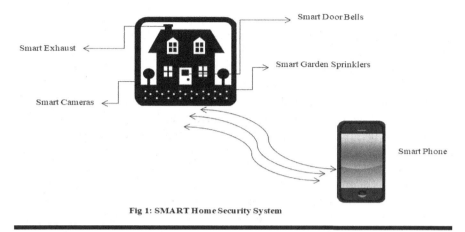

Fig 1: SMART Home Security System

Figure 1.1   SMART Home Security System.
Source: Created by the author.

the extent of protection of data when transferred and, second, where such data is stored and, lastly, who has control of that data, discussed below.

1.3   Data Privacy and Security

1.3.1   Understanding Privacy

'A man's house is his castle', is a deep-rooted principle in Anglo-American jurisprudence (Hafetz, 2001). This principle is embodied in the domestic law of ownership and privacy by nation-states. For example, the Fourth Amendment of the Constitution of the United States is aimed to protect society from unreasonable and unauthorized searches and seizures by the government. The concept of 'home' includes the brick-and-mortar structure of the house against robbery, burglary, trespassing and also political rights and rights against the state like unlawful entry even by government officials (Hafetz, 2001).

Warren and Brandeis (1890) defined the right to privacy as 'the right to be let alone'. William Brennan (1972) brought forward the 'non-intrusion theory of privacy' in a case that describes privacy as "the right of the individual to be free from unwarranted government intrusion" (Eisenstadt versus Baird, 1972). However, since a human is a social animal, the theory seemed impractical, as social beings are to be bound by rules with reasonable restrictions on the right to privacy. The concept of privacy was approached differently by many theorists. Privacy was also interpreted as the 'theory of seclusion', where perfect privacy is, "when one is completely inaccessible to others" (Gavison, 1980).

Over time, the concept of privacy has changed, from having a physical and tangible meaning to now a mental and intangible aspect. Alan Westin, Charles Fried and Arthur Miller brought forward the 'control theory of privacy'. Westin (1968) shaped the definition of the 'right to privacy' as the right of an individual or institution to dictate when, how and to what extent their information should be communicated to others. Fried (1990) propounded that privacy is not absence of information in the minds of others, but the control of one's information with them. Miller propounded that privacy is the ability of an individual to control the circulation of his own information (Christie, 1971).

Privacy has been confused with terms like liberty, autonomy, secrecy and solitude. The right to privacy is understood as anything that can be invaded, intruded, breached, lost, diminished and violated (Tavani, 2007). Every human being is entitled to a life of dignity, which includes privacy and security (Floridi, 2016). Such entitlement places limitations on the actions of governments unless there is call for reasonable restrictions of such entitlement.

Privacy includes informational privacy rights, which is the ability to control the collection, use, and disclosure of one's personal information (Levesque, 2016). Data protection is a legal safeguard established to prevent the misuse of information of private individuals or public entities on any medium, including computers. It forms an integral part of the right to privacy; it is only when the former is present that the latter is assured.

1.3.2 Data Privacy

Data privacy is a right and data protection is the legal mechanism to protect the said right. Privacy and data protection are regarded to be societal concepts that entitle people to autonomy and freedom in regard to their private and personal life (Blume, 2010). Data privacy is also referred to as information privacy, which is defined as an area of data protection concerned with the proper handling of sensitive data, including personal data (Smith et al., 2011).

The dictionary definition of data protection includes a legal framework, regulations and guidelines enforced to deter illegal sharing and storage of data (McIntosh, 1999). A data protection framework is intended for giving individuals a substantial degree of control over their data and the power to make decisions on how it is used. It is the adoption of administrative, technical, or physical deterrents to safeguard personal data.

Data privacy is that area of data protection concerned with the proper handling of personal data (SNIA, 2021). It directs the relationship between the collection and dissemination of data technology, the public expectation of privacy, and the legal and political issues surrounding them (Singh, 2011). Data security is protecting one's pool of data, such as databases, from vulnerability, mishandling and unauthorized access and use (Dhawan, 2014).

1.3.3 Data Protection a Human Right

The 1948 Universal Declaration of Human Rights (UDHR) is equally applicable and enforceable in the physical and digital worlds. Despite the fact that the UDHR was drafted in the pre-digital era, and the changes in online interdependence, expression and assembly, the Declaration is regarded as a milestone document in the protection of human rights (Hariharan, 2017). As the Preamble suggests, the UDHR is applicable, enforceable and in tandem with social and cultural change, innovation and technological progress.

The UDHR entitles every person to the right of privacy and protection from any arbitrary interference by the government and their agencies. This right includes affairs within one's family, home and correspondence. It further includes intangible subjects of honor and reputation (Universal Declaration of Human Rights, 1948, Art. 12). The said Article has broadened its scope to include the concept of data within the meaning of privacy. Though the UDHR expressly binds the actions of governments and ensure the protection of human rights, there lies an equal duty on private institutions and businesses (Ruggie, 2007).

The aim of the UDHR is that human beings are born with certain rights vested in them, which ought to be respected by the state and private institutions. The right to live with dignity is said to be the foremost right one possesses on being born (Universal Declaration of Human Rights, 1948, Art. 1). Human dignity is a foundation of one's human rights. Human dignity recognises equal, inherent and inalienable value of every person (Daly, 2020). In furtherance of the same, and in a world where 'things' communicate and share data, the right to data protection is recognised as a human right. Such principles of law and privacy have been reiterated in other international instruments (International Covenant on Civil and Political Rights, 1976, Art. 17).

1.3.4 Data Protection in Other Jurisdictions

European Union: Data protection is a well-established and recognised right in the European Union. As technology develops, European law has managed to keep pace by responding to it with assurance of the protection of such a right. The Convention for the Protection of Human Rights and Fundamental Freedoms (1950), seeks to reaffirm their profound belief in fundamental freedoms and human rights. The Convention respects the right to private life of an individual and protects it from any unauthorised access (Convention for the Protection of Human Rights and Fundamental Freedoms, 1950, Art. 8).

The Charter of Fundamental Rights of the European Union (2000), is enforced to further enhance and strengthen fundamental rights in light of changes in society, social progress and scientific and technological developments. Article 7 of the Charter declares that every individual has a right to his or her private and family life, home and communications. Article 8 recognises the rights of an individual to their personal data and casts a duty on those utilising such data to fairly and legally do so with the user's consent. Further, the Article suggests that users must have a right to rectify any of their personal data. Such compliance and safeguards are ensured by independent authorities (Charter of Fundamental Rights, 2000, Art.8).

The General Data Protection Regulation, 2018 is the latest and most reliable legislative action of enforcement taken by the European Union in protecting personal data. The regulation grants exclusive data privacy and protection rights to citizens of the European Union and, by virtue of its extra-territorial scope, it attempts to create international law. It regulates the freedom of controllers by four main articles of the General Data Protection Regulation – the rights of consent, withdrawal, to be forgotten and portability.

United States of America: The United States has no explicit or specific general data protection legislation for the whole country. The prerogative is vested in the centre and state governments to formulate their rules with respect to privacy and data protection. At the centre, the US Federal Trade Commission (FTC) is obligated to protect consumers and citizens from any breach of personal data. States have adopted their own data-breach legislations customized to specific sectors that handle personal data (Group, 2021). The onus lies on the FTC with respect to penalizing the wrong-doers. The United States Privacy Act (1974), came into effect to deter the wrongful and illegal use of data and information of individuals held by the government. This is when databases were created and made popular. Although not entirely within the purview of privacy, it is noteworthy that, the US Constitution secures the right of citizens to be protected in their homes, papers and effects against any unreasonable search and seizure, unless such as by legal warrant (Fourth Amendment, 1789).

States have their own laws on various subjects and sectors. For example, The Driver's Privacy Protection Act (1994), governs privacy and disclosure of personal information collected by the department concerned. Information collected can include user's photographs, social security number, driver identification number, telephone number or any information concerning disability (Freidwald, 2012).

India: However, there are certain countries that do not have sufficient laws with respect to data protection. The laws are either redundant, obsolete or loosely drafted and do not guarantee the human right of data privacy, if not in its constitutional form. In India, the concept of privacy has always been a topic of debate. A recent judgment by the Supreme Court of India, Justice K.S. Puttaswamy (Retd.) and Anr. versus Union of India (2017), recognized the right to privacy as an integral and undeniable part of the right to life under the Indian Constitution. The Supreme Court noted that it should be read as a part of the preambular values like liberty, dignity and fraternity in this case.

Currently, the Information Technology Act (2000), is the only legislative action that addresses issues of privacy, but not in its entirety. The Information Technology (Amendment) Act (2008), was enacted by the Indian Parliament to respond to the need for data protection.

Another important question that comes into play is whether 'the current Indian legislation is sufficient to cater to the needs of the Internet of things?' Section 43A was inserted by the 2008 Amendment with the intention of adding a sense of privacy in regard to sensitive personal information held by private intermediaries. It seeks to provide privacy by avoiding or negating any unauthorized disclosure of "sensitive personal data or information".

1.4 Challenges of Data Privacy and Security

Ever since the evolution of IoT, one of the biggest threats to it is the lack of security, thereby infringing the right to data privacy. This debate of IoT being a threat to data privacy has been long standing because of the intensity of user's data that is involved. Though IoT has been said to assist and help users, the threat inherent in it causing harm to one's privacy cannot be ignored or negated.

Each physical object has sensors which have the ability to take in contextual information from their surroundings, whether it seems to be relevant or not. It can be associated with a spy who is constantly keeping watch and hunting for data. Such information can include images, weather conditions, traffic areas, and so forth,. These objects together form the IoT, or the said network of physical objects. By way of algorithms, Big Data and Artificial Intelligence, such data is analysed, and tasks are performed with minimal error which makes it better than if the tasks are manually conducted.

Every day, thousands of people utilize the Internet for various things. Though purposes are different, the primary problem remains the same where data is being taken. Such data is often sold for benefit by data-processing companies. Markets are constantly on the lookout for consumer behavior to enhance their database and build consumer profiles. 'Deepface', an artificially intelligent application on Facebook assists users by recognising certain facial features in pictures and already suggesting certain names to the faces. This in itself reduces the anonymity of a person in a public sphere (Taigan and Yang, 2014). Even public authorities are consistently under surveillance for information for their own public functions of health conditions, family and employment status, and so forth. (Purtova, 2008).

It is said that one's house is one's safety net and fort; a space to be one's own self, to be away from public scrutiny. But imagine one's every action, movement, and words in such a space are being illegally recorded, even when one did not mean it to be so. This is how IoT has crept into our lives unknowingly, unassumingly and sometimes unwillingly. The following few questions expose the challenges posed by IoT with reference to Data Privacy and Security:

a. Has one ever thought about why applications on phones require the location of the user?
b. Can the voice assistant device record voices around it even if the code word/command has not been said?
c. Data lost by corporations cannot be hushed under the carpet of 'accidents'. Can modern policy support the sanctity of one's data that users give in good faith?
d. How does information entered in one application reflect in other applications?

As data is one's own property, one has a right to decide how, why, when, where and by whom it is used. Liberty is defined to be a concreate word that entails one's ability to choose (Shakthi Vahini versus Union of India, 2010). There is information of individuals in public records, as an obligation or through consent, including birth dates, tax details, and so forth. But there is certain information that users voluntarily give to private individuals and social media applications like Instagram, Facebook, and Google Maps, where information is given for a limited purpose of using the services.

The 'I Agree' clause on various websites and applications is the medium through which informed consent is secured. This is the most misunderstood conclusion as users do not read the terms and conditions before clicking on 'I Agree'. Online contracts and 'unreadness' of users promote unfair practices (Ben-Shahar, 2009). In this way, data is taken with explicit consent but without actual consent from the user.

Moreover, the platforms ask for certain unrelated data and compel the user to accept this condition. This information is used for the furtherance of their business motive. These online platforms permanently store such information and profile the user on the basis of their preferences and habits (Dwivedi et al., 2021). Information collected is used for wrongful or unauthorized purposes not intended by the user.

In Figure 1.1 (above), the transmission of data seems to be very basic, from the various appliances of the SmartHome to the Smartphone. However, what happens in the interim, i.e. transmission is highly complex. This is where there is a high chance of data being misused, saved, sold, lost and abused. This is where the data privacy infringement takes place.

Translating Figure 1.2, the particular device (mobile phone) has applications of camera, banking, location, web-search, fitness and SMART Home. This also means that that device has information about the person's facial features, financial information, movement, online presence and searches, health and wellness and home structure. The mobile phone can be used to perform various activities and tasks in regard to these applications. The convenience is evidently high and assistive to the user. The flip side is that all this information is stored in a processor along with other

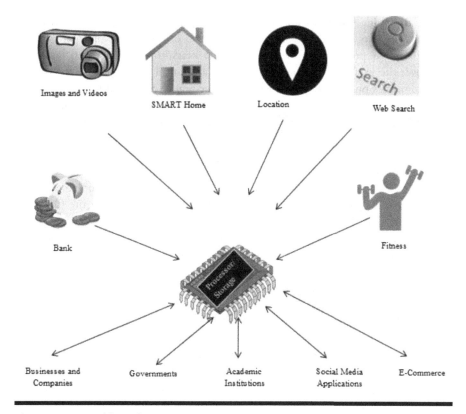

Figure 1.2   Working of IoT.
Source: Created by the author.

data of millions of various users. This information can be accessed, sold, and shared with companies and websites who can use it for their own monetary benefit. A bank can know the extent of loans in one's bank account and make calls regarding it, or an insurance broker can understand the user's health, and make insurance bids or pictures and videos can be sold off for gain; or a robber can enter a house by knowing the location of the user with information from the SMART Home, or web-searches can be tracked to see what the user is currently interested in.

Therefore, even though there are laws and rules to ensure privacy, that privacy is not wholly assured and protected. There is a high chance of such data being abused by the actors involved. It has happened in the recent past where data has been misused, abused and sometimes not used for the purpose it is taken for. Cyber attacks are on the rise, which means the right to privacy is in a more fragile state than any other right. The following few illustrations highlight how the right to privacy is susceptible to attack and violations.

a. **Cambridge Analytica Case:** The data breach scandal of Cambridge Analytica and Facebook is the most talked about because of the involvement of the 2016 US presidential elections and the magnitude of Facebook users all over the world. Cambridge Analytica is a political consultant company that combines productive data analytics, behavioral sciences and innovative technology integrated in a single approach (Mitov, 2021). Methods to collect data were strategically done and executed whereby Aleksandr Kogan, the owner of Global Science Research came up with an application called 'This Is Your Digital Life' (Duarte, 2020). There was a paid survey of 120 questions that sought to probe one's personality, and out of which, results were ascertained on what was referred to as "the big five personality questions": openness, conscientiousness, extroversion, agreeableness, and neuroticism – the OCEAN model (Detrow, 2018). An application was developed in such a way that if people were to answer the survey, it could be done only through logging into their Facebook account – giving free access to their user ID, personal information like gender, birthdate, likes, interests and list of friends. Facebook authorized access to Kogan only for academic purpose, but he partnered with Cambridge Analytica (Detrow, 2018).

The whistleblower, Christopher Wylie, was a former employee of Cambridge Analytica. He explained how data of an individual helped in the US 2016 Elections. The questionnaire became the training set on the basis of which predictions were made (Hern, 2018). The intention of having such questionnaires on Facebook was to analyse the answers procured, gather information such as the likes, shares and comments of the user to create a model that could predict personality. Advertisements were there accordingly put out to persuade their judgment of voting (Rathi, 2019). The Cambridge Analytica case is a classic example of how information willfully acquired can be routed for abusive practices, not authorized by the user.

b. **Echo Murder Case:** The Amazon Echo is a hands-free speaker that functions on voice commands and comes to life with the word, "Alexa". In 2015, at Bentonville, Arkansas, James Bates and Victor Collins watched a football game at the house of Bates. Unfortunately, the next morning Collins was found dead in the bathroom. Bates was arrested on charges of first degree murder. One of the invitees that evening remembered that music was streamed on the Amazon Echo (Chavez, 2017). The police sought to retrieve electronic data of audio recordings captured by the Echo. After much debate and long drawn-out litigation, Bates had allowed and given consent for Amazon to release such recordings. Having done so, the court in 2017, based their judgment partly on the contents of the audio retrieved from Amazon Echo and dropped charges (De La Garza, 2017).

Privacy settings of Alexa state that the device is constantly on the watch for the code word/command and starts to record only after that. However, privacy clauses on their website further state that there is a possibility of an "accidental wake-up", where the Echo may mistake hearing a wake word and start recording (Amazon.com, 2021). This in itself creates a lacuna.

The Arkansas case had the Amazon Echo's recording work in favor of Bates. However, the real question is whether Bates had actually given consent for the Echo to record all of what transpired on that day.

c. **Verkada Inc.**: Verkada Inc. is a Silicon Valley company incorporated in the United States with the aim of developing cloud-based building security systems. They integrate security equipment – video cameras, access control systems and environmental sensors with artificial intelligence (Verkanda.com, 2021).

On its website, Verkada Inc. expressed that on March 8 and 9, 2021, their platform was compromised, exposing 97 customers' data, including video and images (Verkanda.com, 2021). The system hacked 150,000 surveillance cameras, which include women's health clinics, hospitals and offices. Apart from that, few cameras have facial-recognition, which has the ability to identify people, taking away their anonymity in the public platform (Turton, 2021). This security breach has grossly infringed the privacy of individuals.

d. **Selling Identity Information**: In today's world, companies collect and sell the detailed information of individuals based on their online and offline presence, enough to create a benchmark or a trace of one's life and its preferences (Gordon et al., 2013). Often they dig into the personal lives of people for their own profit motive. Information so collected has the ability to define who the individual is, even their character of being preferential, ambitious, political, and so forth (Webster, 2006). Information such as birth date, postcode and gender can be traded freely without one's permission, as they are considered pseudonymous and not personal information. This means that such data cannot be used to specifically trace back to a person without additional information. However, this also shows that one's information is given away without consent.

e. **Voice Assistant Malfunctions**: The Amazon Echo Dot is a hands-free speaker that functions with voice commands. A Londoner reached his home to be surprised by his Amazon Echo Dot saying fragmentary commands that were identified to be from the previous interactions with the device. This happened even though the wake command/word was not used. The information included requests to book train tickets and other information like recording television shows (Lynskey, 2019). It showcases how the device has stored information that is personal to the user; the location of the user on a specific date/period, his preferences, and so forth. This is a clear-cut privacy infringement and could have been misused if it had fallen on the wrong ears.

f. In 2018, a customer of Amazon located in Germany reached out to the Amazon center to review his archived data. Unfortunately, amongst the other data, he received 1700 audio recordings by Alexa that were of another customer. By way of information, he could place the name and location of the rightful owner of the audio notes; he believed that he had entered into the intimate sphere of another without permission, knowledge and consent (Ingber, 2018).

1.5 Conclusion

In light of the above discussion, it can be safely concluded that IoT has a built-in tendency to breach the right of the data privacy and security of its users. The very fact that it is consented for a purpose does not sanctify permanent storage of data and transfer through IoT networks. Such unauthorized use needs to be recognized as an infringement of the right to data privacy.

The 'I Agree' clause must be regulated to limit the terms and conditions so that there is no transfer or sharing of personal data as a compulsion in lieu of utilizing the website/application.

For the effective enforcement of the right to data privacy and security of an individual, IoT must not be allowed to store any information permanently. There must be a check to see whether the data of a person is still available after they have chosen to be 'forgotten'. This mechanism will ensure accountability and transparency.

Further, unrelated information must not be collected by applications. For applications to function, only the information actually required in real time may be taken. Information must not be transferred to, shared with or sold to businesses. It is important that the express or explicit consent of the subject is taken into consideration for any such data to be transferred. Moreover, there should be a mechanism in place to create sensitization amongst individuals/citizens to use their personal information in a diligent way, and they should be informed of their rights while using IoT.

IoT having cross-border ramification and impacting the valuable human right to privacy need to be regulated by an internationally agreed legal framework mandating the nation-states to make provisions for its regulation protecting the right to privacy of the individual.

References

4th Amendment, United States Constitution, Passed by Congress September 25, 1789. Ratified December 15, 1791.

Amazon.com. (2021). Is alexa always listening?. www.amazon.com/is-alexa-always-listening/b?ie=UTF8&node=21137869011 18.05.2023

Bassi, A., Bauer, M., Fiedler, M., Kramp, T., Van Kranenburg, R., Lange, S., & Meissner, S. (2013). *Enabling things to talk* (pp. 379). Springer Nature.

Ben-Shahar, O. (2009). *The myth of the 'opportunity to read' in contract law*. University of Chicago Law & Economics.

Blume, P. (2010). Data protection and privacy–basic concepts in a changing world. *Scandinavian Studies in Law. ICT Legal Issues, 56*, 151–164.

Brandeis, L., & Warren, S. (1890). The right to privacy. *Harvard Law Review, 4*(5), 193–220.

Chavez, N. (2017). Arkansas judge drops murder charge in amazon echo case. *CNN International Edition*. https://edition.cnn.com/2017/11/30/us/amazon-echo-arkansas-murder-case-dismissed/index.html

Christie, G. C. (1971). The right to privacy and the freedom to know: A comment on professor Miller's "The Assault on Privacy". *University of Pennsylvania Law Review, 119*(6), 970–991.

Conti, M., Passarella, A., & Das, S. K. (2017). The Internet of People (IoP): A new wave in pervasive mobile computing. *Pervasive and Mobile Computing, 41*, 1–27.

Convention for the Protection of Human Rights and Fundamental Freedoms, 1950.

Daly, E. (2020). *Dignity rights: Courts, constitutions, and the worth of the human person*. University of Pennsylvania Press.

Data Protection. In C. McIntosh (1999), Cambridge University Press. (4th Edition) https://dictionary.cambridge.org/dictionary/english/data 18.05.2023

Data. In F. Mish (1996), Merriam-Webster Dictionary (12th Edition) www.merriam-webster.com/dictionary/data 18.05.2023

De La Garza, E. (2017). Charges dropped in amazon echo murder case'. Courthouse News Service. www.courthousenews.com/charges-dropped-in-amazon-echo-murder-case/

Del Giudice, M. (2016). Discovering the Internet of Things (IoT): Technology and business process management, inside and outside the innovative firms. *Business Process Management Journal, 22*(2), 263–270.

Detrow, S. (2018, March 20). What did Cambridge Analytica do during the 2016 election?. *NPR*. www.npr.org/2018/03/20/595338116/what-did-cambridge-analytica-do-during-the2016-election

Dhawan, S. (2014). Information and data security concepts, integrations, limitations and future. *International Journal of Advanced Information Science and Technology (IJAIST), 3*(9), 9.

Duarte, R. P. G. M. (2020). *Case Study: Facebook in face of crisis* (Doctoral dissertation).

Dwivedi, Y. K., Ismagilova, E., Hughes, D. L., Carlson, J., Filieri, R., Jacobson, J., … & Wang, Y. (2021). Setting the future of digital and social media marketing research: Perspectives and research propositions. *International Journal of Information Management, 59*, 102168.

Eisenstadt v. Baird. (1972) 405 U.S. 438.

Floridi, L. (2016). On human dignity as a foundation for the right to privacy. *Philosophy & Technology, 29*, 307–312.

Freiwald, S. (2012). Do lawyers violate the driver's privacy protection act when they obtain drivers' motor vehicle records to solicit the drivers' participation in litigation without obtaining the drivers' express consent-maracich v. spears (12–25). *Preview US Supreme Court Case, 40*, 68.

Fried, C. (1990). Privacy: A rational context. In *Computers, ethics, & society* (pp. 51–63). https://dl.acm.org/doi/abs/10.5555/77685.77822

Gavison, R. (1980). Privacy and the limits of law. *The Yale Law Journal, 89*(3), 421–471.

General Data Protection Regulation, 2018.

Georgios, L., Kerstin, S., & Theofylaktos, A. (2019). Internet of Things in the context of industry 4.0: An overview. *International Journal of Entrepreneurial Knowledge*, Center for International Scientific Research of VSO and VSPP, *7*(1), 4–19.

Gordon, J., Perrey, J., & Spillecke, D. (2013). Big data, analytics and the future of marketing and sales. McKinsey: Digital Advantage. www.forbes.com/sites/mckinsey/2013/07/22/big-data-analytics-and-the-future-of-marketing-sales/?sh=1056b0e55587

Group, G. (2021). Data protection 2020 laws and regulations USA, ICLG. [online] International Comparative Legal Guides International Business Reports. https://iclg.com/practice-areas/data-protection-laws-and-regulations/usa 18.05.2023

Hafetz, J. L. (2001). A man's home is his castle: Reflections on the home, the family, and privacy during the late nineteenth and early twentieth centuries. *William & Mary Journal of Women and the Law, 8*, 175.

Hariharan, G. (2017). Understanding international standards for online freedom of expression. https://giswatch.org/year/2017-unshackling-expression-study-law-criminalising-expression-online-asia 18.05.2023

Hern, A. (2018). Cambridge Analytica: How did it turn clicks into votes. *The Guardian, 6*. www.theguardian.com/news/2018/may/06/cambridge-analytica-how-turn-clicks-into-votes-christopher-wylie

Hong, S. (2020). An efficient Iot application development based on integrated IOT knowledge modules. *Issues in Information Systems, 21*(3), 72–82.

Information Technology (Reasonable Security Practices and Procedures and Sensitive Personal Data or Information) Rules, 2011.

Information Technology Act, 2000.

Ingber, S. (2018). Amazon customer receives 1,700 audio files of a stranger who used alexa. NPR. www.npr.org/2018/12/20/678631013/amazon-customer-receives-1-700-audio-files-of-a-stranger-who-used-alexa 18.05.2023

International Covenant of Civil and Political Rights, 1976.

Jain, A. K., & Ross, A. (2015). Bridging the gap: From biometrics to forensics. *Philosophical Transactions of the Royal society B: Biological sciences, 370*(1674), 20140254.

Javaid, M., Haleem, A., Singh, R. P., Rab, S., & Suman, R. (2021). Upgrading the manufacturing sector via applications of industrial internet of things (IIoT). *Sensors International, 2*, 100129.

Jun, S., Kim, J. Y., & Park, J. (2022). Methodology for data analysis of digital transformation.

Kirchmer, M. (2021). Digital transformation: Value-driven, process-led and data-based.

Lessig, L. (2002). Privacy as property. *Social Research: An International Quarterly, 69*(1), 247–269.

Levesque, R. J. (2016). *Adolescence, privacy, and the law: A developmental science perspective.* Oxford University Press.

Lynskey, D. (2019). Alexa are you invading my privacy?. *The Dark Side of Our Voice Assistants. The Guardian, 9.* www.theguardian.com/technology/2019/oct/09/alexa-are-you-invading-my-privacy-the-dark-side-of-our-voice-assistants

Mack, E. (1995). The self-ownership proviso: A new and improved Lockean proviso. *Social Philosophy and Policy, 12*(1), 186–218.

Merrill, T. W. (1998). Property and the right to exclude. *Nebraska Law Review, 77,* 730.

Minerva, R., Biru, A., & Rotondi, D. (2015). Towards a definition of the Internet of Things (IoT). *IEEE Internet Initiative, 1*(1), 1–86.

Mitov, A. (2021). *Ethical use of artificial intelligence through the Utilitarianism perspective* (Bachelor's thesis, University of Twente).

Paul, E. F., Miller Jr, F. D., & Paul, J. (Eds.). (2005). *Natural rights liberalism from Locke to Nozick: Volume 22, Part 1* (Vol. 22). Cambridge University Press.

Pereira, A. G., & Funtowicz, S. (2015). *Science, Philosophy and Sustainability. The End of the Cartesian dream. London.*

Purtova, N. (2008). Property in personal data: A European perspective on the instrumentalist theory of propertisation. *Eur. J. Legal Stud., 2,* 193.

Puttaswamy, Justice K.S. (Retd.) & Anr. vs. Union of India & Ors (2017) 10 SCC 1

Rathi, R. (2019). Effect of Cambridge analytica's facebook ads on the 2016 US presidential election. Towards Data Science.

Ruggie, J. G. (2007, December). Corporate responsibility to respect human rights. In Report from the SRSG's multistakeholder meetings held in.

Rumbold, J. M., & Pierscionek, B. K. (2018). What are data? A categorization of the data sensitivity spectrum. *Big data research, 12,* 49–59.

Shakthi Vahini *v.* Union of India, Writ Petition (Civil) No. 231 of 2010

Singh, S. S. (2011). Privacy and data protection in India: A critical assessment. *Journal of the Indian Law Institute, 53*(4), 663–677.

Smith, H. J., Dinev, T., & Xu, H. (2011). Information privacy research: An interdisciplinary review. *MIS quarterly, 34*(4), 989–1015.

Snia.org. 2021. What is data privacy? | SNIA. [online] Available at: www.snia.org/education/what-is-data-privacy 18.05.2023

Sun, M. (2018). The impacts of the fourth industrial revolution on jobs and the future of the third sector.Taigan, Y., Yang, M., Ranzato, M., Wolf, L. (2014) Deepface: Closing the gap to human-level performance in face verification–meta research. In *Proceedings of the IEEE conference on computer vision and pattern recognition* (pp. 1701–1708).

Tavani, H. T. (2007). Philosophical theories of privacy: Implications for an adequate online privacy policy. *Metaphilosophy, 38*(1), 1–22.

Turton, W. (2021). Hackers breach thousands of security cameras, exposing Tesla, jails, hospitals. Bloomberg. www.bloomberg.com/news/articles/2021-03-09/hackers-expose-tesla-jails-in-breach-of-150-000-security-cams 18.05.2023

Universal Declaration of Human Rights, 1948.

Van Kranenburg, R. (2011). The internet of things. *World Affairs: The Journal of International Issues, 15*(4), 126–141.

Verkada.com. (2021). *Verkada Security Update–Incident Report.* www.verkada.com/security-update/report/#:~:text=From%20March%208%2D9%2C%202021,data%20acces sed%2C%20including%20badge%20credentials%20 18.05.2023

Verkada.com. (2021). Why Verkada? hybrid cloud solution. www.verkada.com/why-verk ada/video-security/ 18.05.2023

Vermesan, O., & Friess, P. (Eds.). (2013). *Internet of things: Converging technologies for smart environments and integrated ecosystems.* River publishers.

Webster, M. (2006). *Data protection in the financial services industry.* Gower Publishing, Ltd.

Westin, A. F. (1968). Privacy and freedom. *Washington and Lee Law Review, 25*(1), 166.

Chapter 2

Cyber-Physical Threat Intelligence for IoT Using Machine Learning

Sunil Sonawane[1] and Reshma Gulwani[2]

[1]Computer Department, Dr. D.Y. Patil University,
Ambi, Pune, India

[2]Information Technology Department, RAIT, D.Y. Patil (Deemed
to be University), Nerul, Navi Mumbai, India

2.1 Introduction

The Internet of Things (IoT) has transformed methods in a variety of fields. The IoT paradigm seeks to connect individuals anywhere and at any time. The IoT is distinguished through a three-layer design comprised of connection, application, and awareness levels. Safety guidelines must be adhered to at every layer to preserve the reliability of the IoT [1]. Furthermore, as technology advances, embedded subsystems' vulnerability increases. As a result, embedded security is a necessary component while designing intelligent systems. With a technical transformation, it permits interaction between people and device connectivity. The Internet of Things may help to implement innovative Internet services as well as applications across all life forms through efforts to improve the quality of our lives. IoT devices and services, trust is crucial. Furthermore, systems and connections for IoT protection need to be watched and studied to avoid system component impact from providing intolerable dangers as well as to guarantee efficient protection by assessing social activity and moral use of IoT advanced technologies [2].

Vulnerabilities in devices for the IoT have been discovered, making them secure against numerous sorts of assaults. Further safety challenges like security, confidentiality, and accessibility, constitute a hazard in addition to the possibility of losing pertinent data. It is feasible to predict what sorts of attacks will happen with inexpensive IoT gadgets by keeping an eye on vulnerable services and IoT gadgets [3]. The quantity of IoT gadgets in houses and lifestyles has grown substantially in recent years. Technology is fast evolving, and there are an increasing number of machines connected online. This number is predicted to increase and become considerably greater than it is currently during the next few years. There will be more devices, but they will all be unique. The danger is that hackers would use the advancement of this technology to conduct assaults. They will depend heavily on newly revealed deficiencies and insufficient customers' privacy preferences. It indicates that other connected gadgets are also vulnerable in addition to this particular machine. IoT device flaws could be a problem concern because they expose devices to a variety of attacks, including denying services and safety problems such as secrecy, reticence, accessibility, and assault susceptibility [4–5].

MQTT is a protocol that can be subject to many types of assaults and is employed in this work to solve IoT and embedded system vulnerabilities [6]. It aids with transmission, verification, and negotiation, including the dismissal of limited broadband connections, along with the platform-independent paradigm [7]. The problem occurs until the MQTT protocol receives signals and demands them through forwarding packets in a certain connection area, especially within systems where no authentication is implemented. The "HELLO deluge assault" wherein an IoT system is targeted or inundated by connection queries until the facility is cancelled, is the most well-known of these assaults [8]. It is possible to evaluate overall "basic" and "bad" performance by the Internet-of-Things systems and applications within relevant settings using strong data exploration algorithms (ML) [9].

To develop a hardened cybersecurity defense methodology, we identify key areas within the system where vulnerabilities may occur, analyze various DDoS (Distributed Denial of Service) attack recognition classifications, such as SVM, RF, KNN, and LR, including in an ANN model, MLP, NB, and DT, and provide a cybercrime corrective action strategy that can help. Procedure assessment, data activity analysis, access control, penetration testing, mitigation against cyberattacks, as well as remaining stable operation are among the essential features of the experiment. The experimental findings are compared to previous research [9–12] for validation.

Because malicious attacks on images containing personal confidential information (such as document images) pose significant threats to property privacy and security, there is a high demand for dependable detection techniques against various photo manipulation methods. Direct modifications to the original image file are currently well encountered by analyzing file-based forensic traces, such as EXIF format

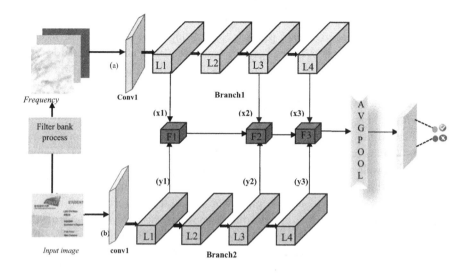

Figure 2.1 Pipeline of the proposed architecture.

Source: Created by the author.

and content [13–14], and the traces of multiple compressions [15–16], but such forensic traces can be effectively erased by recapturing the distorted images using another device, thus increasing the authenticity of the images that are made up [17].

Figure 2.1 displays our entire approach's pipeline. When given an input image, the first branch (referred to as *branch1* in Figure 2.1) extracts detail loss artifacts using a filter bank pre-process module. Simultaneously, the second branch (labeled branch 2 in Figure 2.1) collects instances of color distortion artifacts caused by the red, green and blue (RGB) input. The final forecasts are created by combining discriminative information from both frequency-based and RGB models. Our recommended model can go through full end-to-end training using cross-entropy loss. In the following sections, we will go through the specifics of our proposed system's two main components, which include data preprocessing and the integration of multi-scale cross-attention fusion.

2.2 Related Work

The IoT connects practically all environmental gadgets to build innovative computer-based solutions that enable someone's life via the web, whether they are mechanical as well as digital. Numerous Internet of Things technologies, including wearables, related aged care, including driverless cars, are now having a direct influence on people's daily activities. Even while the Internet of Things provides several benefits, this creates numerous security concerns. To ensure the continued success of IoT applications, IoT makers should prioritize addressing these difficulties. Owners of IoT devices should verify that their gadgets have adequate security safeguards. With the advent of IoT, the number of security risks and cybercrimes has expanded substantially [18].

IoT struggles with a number of problems, including inadequate gadget updates, actuation tracking, inadequate as well as vulnerable standards, and client denial [19]. The authors [20] discuss the background of IoT authentication and encryption precautions, employing strategies towards the development of IoT elements, scenarios, as well as networks, existing network approaches, ideal confidentiality concepts, or the need for various degrees of the Internet of Things.

Researchers examined DDoS prediction in SDN performed utilizing the suggested algorithm DDAML, and the outcomes were contrasted with those of KNN and SVM approaches. Experiment findings showed that the suggested algorithms outperformed other methods [9]. In the next paper, the performance study measures for SVM, ANN, NB, DT, and unsupervised learning were used to detect UNBS-NB 15 and KDD99 Botnet DDoS attacks (USML) (accuracy, sensitivity, and specificity) [10]. To identify DDoS assaults in software-defined networks [11], researchers applied machine learning (SVM, KNN) and neural network (ANN) methods. SVM recognized 92.6 percent of DDoS assaults, KNN detected 95.67 percent, ANN detected 91.07 percent, and NB detected 94.48 percent. Researchers employed computer vision (SVM) for SDN self-defence networks [12], as well as recognition rate, was judged to be between 98–99 percent .

Based on the analysis of existing literature, enhancing the security measures within both integrated components and Internet of Things (IoT) devices is of paramount importance. Numerous researchers have explored diverse approaches, strategies, and data analysis techniques to address this concern. These efforts encompass both technical and procedural considerations. By contrast, the present study adopts an information extraction and analysis methodology that encompasses the interconnected circuits incorporating integrated components. This approach offers distinct advantages for researchers compared to any other findings highlighted in the survey. Several scholars have delved into this subject utilizing a range of methodologies, strategies, and investigative tools. Furthermore, this chapter includes a comprehensive examination of the technical and physical challenges associated with the discussed topics.

2.2.1 MQTT: Threat Model

Since MQTT is characterized as a lightweight, fundamental, and general protocol, it lacks inherent provisions for authentication or payload encryption. This absence of robust security measures has proven to be a significant oversight, as it introduces vulnerabilities that could potentially allow unauthorized access to intercepted data transmissions. Regrettably, the development of the MQTT protocol appears to have neglected these security considerations [6, 21].

For the establishment of seamless connectivity and effective navigation within the Internet of Things (IoT), the integration of middleware-based network interfaces for IoT has been deemed essential. Notably, MQTT has emerged as a prominent application protocol within the IoT domain. Nevertheless, prior to implementing any countermeasures in MQTT-based IoT systems, it becomes imperative to thoroughly assess potential risks.

This study extensively explores the vulnerability landscape of MQTT, shedding light on the mechanics of assaults targeting MQTT providers. The protocol employs a publish–subscribe model, which plays a pivotal role in understanding the roles of various MQTT entities: the "broker" (the central MQTT element), the "publisher" (an entity transmitting information), and the "subscriber" (an entity receiving said information). The broker assumes the responsibility of receiving information from publishers and subsequently disseminating it to subscribers. A graphical representation of the MQTT threat model is depicted in Figure 2.2.

Figure 2.2 depicts the threat model for MQTT, a widely used IoT application protocol. This chapter thoroughly examines the consequences of DoS (Denial of

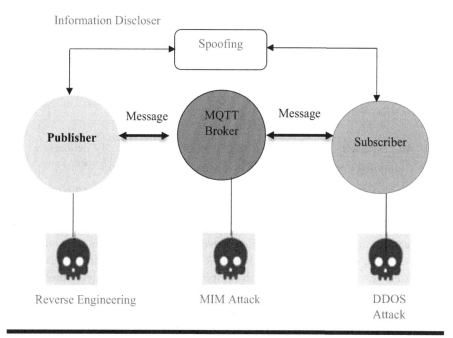

Figure 2.2   MQTT Threat Model.

Source: Created by the author.

Service) attacks on MQTT brokers. A virtual machine-based testbed is methodically built to analyze the impact of DDoS attacks on the operational efficiency of a MQTT broker network.

In order to devise effective strategies against potential MQTT vulnerabilities, it becomes essential to accurately discern and recognize possible threats. When attacks are linked to the attacker's understanding, they can be structured in terms of information parameters. This establishes a connection between the attack configurations and the Moving Target Defense (MTD) configuration settings. Notably, this connection is often explored to unveil the interplay between attackers and the MQTT Threat Model illustrated in Figure 2.1.

The identification of potential threats and the establishment of effective countermeasures against MQTT vulnerabilities are intrinsically interconnected. Specifically, when attacks are intrinsically tied to the knowledge possessed by potential attackers, these attacks can be articulated in terms of information parameters. This interrelation is consistently employed to uncover the relationships existing between assault configurations and the MTD setup. Notably, this linkage aids in elucidating the intricate dynamics between attackers and the MQTT Threat Model, as represented in Figure 2.1.

Furthermore, to ascertain a correlation between attackers and the MTD network, an examination of the interplay between assault inputs and MTD application programs is often employed [22]. This approach is frequently utilized to probe the interconnectedness of attackers with the broader MTD network by scrutinizing the interdependencies between assault inputs and MTD application processes.

The proposed device's constituent data elements can be aptly depicted using a combination of name-value pairs.

An information parameter (ψ) can be expressed as $\psi = (n, v)$ and can accept a value (v) dependent on its type (n).

1. An expected data constant $\left(\widehat{\Psi} = \Psi_1, \Psi_2, \Psi_2, \cdots, \Psi_n, \cdots\right)$ denotes a set containing every probability (v) given to m, denoted by m $= (\Psi.v)$.

2. An amalgamated factor (Ψ) is an assortment among all informational sub-parameters denoted by $g_i \Psi = n, \{\Psi_1, \Psi_2, \cdots, \Psi_n\}$.

Attacker: Through the utilization of restricted access authorization and computer-aided methods, an unauthorized individual can potentially breach the security of your system. Even without an in-depth comprehension of its underlying mechanics, the concept of reverse engineering revolves around the exploration of the process by which a pre-existing object, method, device, tool, or computer program executes its designated functions. Essentially, it involves dismantling and dissecting technological entities to uncover their functioning principles, with the intention of replication or enhancement. The insights derived from the decoding process can prove instrumental in comprehending its operations, repurposing obsolete components, conducting maintenance tasks, and even facilitating further investigations based on the network and technology in question.

Eavesdropping is used to manipulate data in the context of Man in the Middle (MITM) attacks. Attackers use brute force to launch DoS or DDoS attacks against both the broker and the subscriber. These actions entail the attacker having vital information, such as the host's IP address, server port, and operating system. This relevant information is frequently obtained through the attacker's acquaintance with the system's subtleties, which include what are known as information parameters.

Additionally, the assailant must possess a profound understanding, coupled with specialized knowledge, of specific techniques like the utilization of the POSIX-compliant Unix system's mmap method, which enables the mapping of objects and devices onto memory storage. The strategy of memory-mapped storage I/O is applied in this context. In cases where data formats aren't directly retrieved from storage disks and hence don't occupy any physical memory, request splitting methods are deployed to address this challenge.

Type of Attack: In our analysis, we operate under the assumption that past attacks have furnished the attacker with awareness regarding the operating system version, Source IP, and the identifier of the analyzer device. An array of attack categories exists, encompassing Distributed Denial of Service, Man-in-the-Middle (MitM), brute-force, and Denial of Service (DoS) threats. Those attacks which exert an influence on network data are categorized as impactful assaults. Such an attack's presence can be effectively detected by monitoring the ramifications arising from alterations to the information flow.

An attack (a) becomes a pair containing raw data $\Omega = \left(\Omega_{pre,} \Omega_{post} \right)$ that, when performed, transfers to convert 2 into 1, as shown by $\left(\Psi_1 \cdot v = \Psi_2 \cdot v \right)$. Formally, the execute action is written as execute $(a) \Leftrightarrow \left(a \cdot \Psi_1 \cdot v = a \cdot \Psi_2 \cdot v \right)$. Table 2.1 depicts the many sorts of attack requirements discussed in [22].

Table 2.1 displays the network attack specification kinds. Inside the proposed model, it's often thought that x's purpose is to abuse permissions upon that victim machine, which it may do by executing a series of various sorts of assaults, $\varphi = \varphi_1, \varphi_2, \cdots, \varphi_5$ were

φ_1 – obtains the target's IP address;
φ_2 – captures the application's port number;
φ_3 – captures the characteristics of the operating system;
φ_4 – takes use of the application's dynamic nature;
φ_5 – exploits the target by deploying an agent.

Table 2.1 Defining the Many Varieties of Threats

Type	Ω_{pre}	Ω_{post}
φ_1	$\Psi_{d1} \cdot ip \neq \Psi^x_{d1}.ip$	$\langle \Psi^x_{d1}.ip, \Psi_{d1} \cdot ip \rangle$
φ_2	$\Psi^x_{d1}.ip \neq \Psi_{d1} \cdot ip \wedge \Psi^x_{d1}.port \cdot \neq \Psi_{d1} \cdot port$	$\langle \Psi^x_{d1}.port, \Psi_{d1} \cdot port \rangle$
φ_3	$\Psi^x_{d1}.ip = \Psi_{d1} \cdot ip \wedge \Psi^x_{d1}.port \cdot$ $= \Psi_{d1} \cdot port \wedge \Psi^x_{d1}.os \neq \Psi^x_{d1}.os$	$\langle \Psi^x_{d1}.os, \Psi_{d1} \cdot os \rangle$
φ_4	$\Psi^x_{d1}.ip = \Psi_{d1} \cdot ip \wedge \Psi^x_{d1}.port \cdot = \Psi_{d1} \cdot port \wedge \Psi^x_{d1}.os$ $= \Psi^x_{d1}.os \wedge \Psi^x_{d1}.vul \neq \Psi^x_{d1}.vul$	$\langle \Psi^x_{d1}.vul, \Psi_{d1} \cdot vul \rangle$
φ_5	$\Psi^x_{d1}.ip = \Psi_{d1} \cdot ip \wedge \Psi^x_{d1}.port \cdot = \Psi_{d1} \cdot port \wedge \Psi^x_{d1}.os$ $= \Psi^x_{d1}.os \wedge \Psi^x_{d1}.vul = \Psi^x_{d1}.vul$	$\langle \Psi^x_{d1}.exa, \Psi^x.exa,$ $\Psi^x_{d1}.exa, \Psi^x.exa \rangle$
φ_6	$\Psi^x_{d1}.ip = \Psi_{d1} \cdot ip \wedge \Psi^x_{d1}.port \cdot = \Psi_{d1} \cdot port \wedge \Psi^x_{d1}.exa$ $= \Psi^x_{d1}.exa \wedge \Psi^x_{d1}.root = \Psi^x_{d1}.root$	$\langle \Psi^x_{d1}.root, \Psi_{d1} \cdot root \rangle$

Source: Created by the author.

2.3 Research Methodology

This study employs a combination of quantitative and qualitative methodologies. The primary objective of this investigation is to address inquiries pertaining to cybersecurity challenges within the digital realm, specifically focusing on threats to the Internet of Things (IoT) ecosystem. These concerns encompass potential risks that target IoT nodes and span diverse network technologies. Moreover, this study incorporates identification approaches that rely on the utilization of modelling techniques within distributed systems, a theme gleaned from our comprehensive analysis of prior research works. For a visual representation of the proposed research methodology, refer to Figure 2.3.

The research procedure is outlined as follows:

1. Establish a virtual network designed to systematically monitor both typical and irregular network behaviours.
2. Traffic flow simulation:

   ■ Initially, distributed authentic nodes are across the network, engaging in regular communication patterns. Various data points are gathered through the tool's functionalities, encompassing factors like temperature fluctuations, charging mechanisms, transmission utilization, and overall transmission delays.

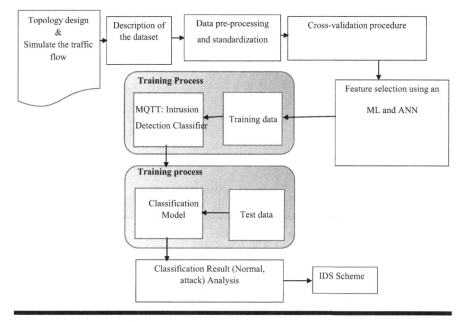

Figure 2.3 Methodology.
Source: Created by the author.

■ The second scenario introduces a flooding attack by deploying a malicious node. This attacking node targets adjacent nodes, initiating an attack scenario.

The gathered data is then harnessed to facilitate the Intrusion Detection System (IDS) in identifying abnormal activities within compromised IoT communications.

3. Analyze routes and extract relevant features
4. Packet inspection
5. Configure the system for detection and defense against attacks
6. Perform analysis of performance and categorization
7. Implement the IDS Strategy

In essence, the research methodology involves creating a virtual network with a specific focus on monitoring network behaviors. It also includes simulating traffic patterns, analyzing communication routes, inspecting data packets, preparing the system to implement defense mechanisms, conducting assessments of performance and categorization, and ultimately operationalizing the Intrusion Detection System (IDS) strategy.

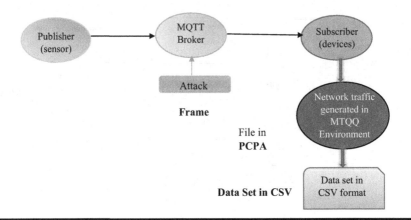

Figure 2.4 Steps to create the attack dataset.

Source: Created by the author.

A. Intrusion Detection Classifier: The methodology for acquiring the dataset and identifying Internet of Things (IoT) features is elaborated upon below. In one instance, another machine executes an attack on the server. Recordings are generated to compile pertinent CSV information, which is then analyzed and categorized for each network activity. Refer to Figure 2.4 for a visual representation of the procedures involved in creating the assault dataset.

To address the security challenges inherent in MQTT, a classifier approach was implemented by introducing one-classification algorithms.

- **Dataset Overview and Pre-processing:** The collection consists of Internet surveillance attacks as well as a MQTT brute-force diligence. The training dataset [23] consists of 4998 entries categorized into eight classes and characterized by 34 attributes. Prior to beginning the categorization task, baseline data processing tasks were done. Columns that had a strong correlation of 0.9 were eliminated. In the absence of data, mean imputation was used, followed by attribute scaling [24–25].
- **Cross-Validation Process:** The predictive models were evaluated using cross-validation techniques (CV) [26]. This involved looking into both k-fold and leave-one-out cross-validation methods. In the instance of the k-fold method, 80 percent of the dataset served as the training set, while the remaining 20 percent functioned as the testing set with no renewal. This approach employed 5-fold cross-validation.
- **Artificial Neural Network (ANN):** Multilayer Perceptron's (MLPs) are a feedforward Artificial Neural Network (ANN) variation. MLPs, which have three layers (input, hidden, and output), work as a supervised learning system that uses backpropagation to distinguish between data that does not follow linear

separability. ReLU (Rectified Linear Units) is used as the activation function in both the input and hidden layers, with the Adam (Adaptive Moment Estimation) optimizer [27].

■ **Performance Evaluation:** The performance of each model is assessed using a variety of metrics, such as sensitivity, precision, and overall efficiency. Other metrics, such as precision, recall, and the F1 score, are critical in assessing correctness, and completeness, and creating a balanced perspective between precision and recall [28].

Filter Bank for Input Image Processing Module for Pre-processing: Previous study [17] found that due to resolution mismatches between screens and cameras, the recapture procedure frequently results in the loss of delicate features. In response to this worry, it was proposed [17] to recover these artifacts from high-frequency image data using multi-wavelet decomposition. A following study [29] created a learnable pre-processing filter, whose spectral response was detected as a high-pass filter, indicating the presence of distinguishing features in the high-frequency domain. Based on these findings, a filter bank comprised of three bandpass filters was designed to extract modality-specific data from input images. Figure 2.5 depicts the overall transformation process.

The original RGB input image is converted to grayscale. This grayscale representation is then transformed using a two-dimensional Discrete Cosine Transform (DCT) [30], yielding a matrix of DCT coefficients. Following that, three separate bandpass filters are produced. For example, the following formula describes how to make a low bandpass filter:

$$B_{low}(i,j) = \begin{cases} 1 & if \ 0 \le (i+j) < k, \\ 0 \ if \ k \le (i+j) < 2 \cdot k, \\ 0 & if \ 2 \cdot k \le (i+j) \end{cases} \tag{2.1}$$

where k is the value used to divide the frequency range into low, moderate, and elevated concentrations, and i, j(1,224) signify element location indices. When

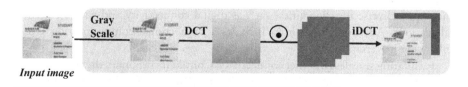

Figure 2.5   The Complete Frequency Filter Bank Preprocessing.
Source: Created by the author.

the first term is satisfied, the value of B_low (i,j), which reflects the element value of the low filter at the position (i,j), is set to 1. When the second and third conditions are met, respectively, the value of the filter element can be changed to construct the B_mid and B_high filters. Three different filters are then used to element-wise multiply the frequency matrix, with each of the output matrices containing DCT coefficients from a different frequency range. The inverted dct conversion will then be used to restore the three distinct result frequency matrices to the feature space.

After that, the three distinct output grayscale images are synthesized in the following order: low, middle, and high. Our approach retrieves lossless frequency information of the input image divided by frequency band, in contrast to earlier techniques like [31] and [17] that only return restricted high-frequency information.

Complementary RGB Image Input: It has been shown in [17] that the recapture process will also produce a color distortion, altering the correlation between various color channels, which can be seen as another discriminative artifact. We advise utilizing an image in RGB color space as the input to branch 2 to examine the distortion artifact for recapture identification.

2.4 Experimental Setup and Analysis

The author's distinct contribution to this domain emerges from a rigorous exploration aimed at understanding and characterizing the issue, culminating in the formulation of a proposed solution.

The Wireless Sensor Network (WSN) operating system, renowned for its simplicity, serves as a foundational component supporting this lightweight and compact operating framework. Operating at the system level, this platform facilitates pre-emptive multitasking. Noteworthy aspects of Contiki OS encompass typical ROM and RAM requirements, with setups typically necessitating 40 kilobytes of ROM and 2 kilobytes of RAM. An extensive configuration of Contiki comprises a spectrum of features, encompassing IPv6 integration, anticipatory multiprocessing, TCP/IP communication, prototype tasks, and even inclusive components like an integrated Web browser and private Web server. The array of utilities extends to encompass diverse functionalities, such as digital connectivity and window-saving calculations. Additionally, Contiki includes a bidirectional communication layer, enhancing its versatility.

Facilitating seamless Internet connectivity, Contiki incorporates the uIP protocol stack, a compact TCP/IP solution adhering to RFC standards. Furthermore, for communication needs within the Rime domain, a dime-powered radios solution is adopted. This solution, known for its efficiency, opens up fundamental avenues for interaction.

Table 2.2   Experimental Variables

Experimental variables	Value
Generated period	2 Min
Region for modeling	200×200 meter
Mac method	IEEE 802.11
Amount of objects	12
Several sorts of motes	3
Radio frequency	Length Loss Communication limit for UDGM
Communication frequency	50 m
The interfering zone	101 m
Several links	10
Numerous locations	1

Source: Created by the author.

In the realm of executing flooding attacks at the transport layer, the attacker initiates contact with neighboring nodes through DODAG Data Dissemination (DIS) messages. This interaction triggers actions such as a restart of the trickle timer or the transmission of responses in the form of DODAG Data (DIO) Attribute messages to address unicast DIS signals.

Table 2.2 presents the simulation parameters, providing a comprehensive overview of the specifications governing the conducted simulations.

Dataset. Our study is based on a dataset made available by [32], a document image library. It consists of two datasets: Dataset 1 (84 real photographs, 588 recaptured images), and Dataset 2 (48 real photos, 384 recaptured images). Both datasets were collected using various tools and were saved in TIFF format. To evaluate the quality cross-performance, we also create duplicate datasets that are JPEG compressed for the two datasets on its foundation.

In order to ensure that the training dataset does not already know anything about the validating and testing datasets, we partitioned the database into 12 separate documents rather than images for these two datasets. After training the models on high-quality dataset 1, we will examine the approaches on dataset 2 (cross-dataset evaluation), dataset 1 with JPEG image compression (cross-quality evaluation), and dataset 2 with JPEG image compression (cross-dataset and cross-quality assessment). Figure 2.6 below shows the multi-scale fusion mechanism:

The number N represents the number of multi-scale fusions. In our study, we set N = 3.

Baseline Models and Training Planning: Our suggested architecture is compared to four standard generic CNN architectures with different layer

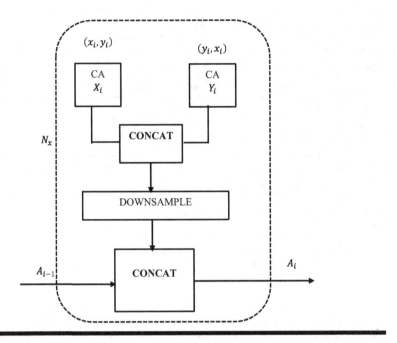

Figure 2.6 The multi-scale fusion mechanism.

Source: Created by the author.

configurations: resnet34, resnet50, resnet152 [33], densenet121, densenet169, densenet201 [34], resnext50 [35], and efficientb4 [36, 37]. To alter the binary classification job, the classifier in all generic CNNs is replaced with two fully connected layers, layer1 with 256 nodes and layer2 with two nodes. Furthermore, we contrast our strategy with the essential distinction between convolution design and the Siamese network [32]. The resnet50 is chosen as the cornerstone of our proposed model because it can deliver the desired performance with a reasonably small model size based on intra-domain assessment.

The k value of the proposed filter bank is set to 10 throughout the training phase, and all models are trained with input resolution 224224. The batch size is 64, the training epochs are 20, and the learning rate is 104 when the Adam optimizer and cross-entropy loss are used. PyTorch 1.12.0 provides the foundation for our implementation.

Table 2.3 shows the evaluation of cross-dataset, Table 2.4 shows the Cross-quality (JPEG Compression) Evaluation and Table 2.5 shows the Cross-dataset and Cross-quality Evaluation.

Table 2.3   Evaluation of Cross-dataset

Model	AUC (%) ↑	AP (%) ↑	HTER (%) ↓	ACC (%) ↑	EER (%) ↓
siamese network	88.39	89.23	18.5	81.2	16.59
resnet34	81.07	89.56	24.34	72.57	26.28
efficientnetb4	88.78	94.29	22.7	82.82	19.69
resnet50	81.1	89.32	25.8	69.52	25.58
densenet169	84.85	89.53	26.39	70.12	23.89
resnext50	80.25	89.52	24.65	71.63	26.58
densenet201	88.89	91.17	24.45	71.2	21.74
resnet101	75.55	86.79	28.48	63.06	31.23
resnet152	92.07	93.1	22.12	71.58	16.95
densenet121	81	89.45	27.4	73.01	26.87
cdc network	86.75	92.06	24.35	78.52	22.33
branch1	89.59	93.87	17.23	80.84	16.33
proposed	95.02	95.82	14.13	85.65	14.29

Source: Created by the author.

Table 2.4   Cross-quality (JPEG Compression) Evaluation

Model	AUC (%) ↑	EER (%) ↓	HTER (%) ↓	AP (%) ↑	ACC (%) ↑
densenet121	98.85	3.56	37.89	99.62	89.56
efficientnetb4	96.28	4.47	36.23	99.48	89.21
resnet50	94.67	12.48	25.15	99.36	91.15
densenet169	94.50	11.23	29.25	98.89	90.52
densenet201	98.29	2.89	22.96	98.23	93.92
resnet101	99.12	4.53	19.53	98.54	94.63
resnet152	93.40	11.23	21.26	99.56	93.92
resnet34	94.28	9.56	25.56	99.19	92.46
resnext50	84.35	22.89	33.25	94.56	92.62
cdc network	95.24	12.36	38.23	98.48	90.32
siamese network	88.20	14.16	18.63	88.23	84.48
branch1	96.20	8.52	17.62	99.59	93.32
proposed(3scale)	99.30	1.56	9.23	98.32	96.36

Source: Created by the author.

Table 2.5 Cross-dataset and Cross-quality Evaluation

Model	ACC (%) ↑	AUC (%) ↑	EER (%) ↓	AP (%) ↓	HTER (%) ↓
densenet121	70.23	81.21	28.28	88.31	42.52
efficientnetb4	70.56	82.65	24.96	83.54	38.64
resnet50	75.31	80.25	23.64	88.98	23.56
densenet169	78.65	85.64	19.96	92.23	26.12
densenet201	72.89	85.79	27.65	88.54	28.10
resnet101	71.56	78.15	27.84	89.54	26.05
resnet152	75.65	81.35	20.65	88.46	22.54
resnet34	72.68	81.09	28.65	85.58	27.98
resnext50	70.54	79.28	28.86	86.25	35.52
cdc network	73.46	84.65	25.89	88.05	32.57
siamese network	71.27	73.21	35.87	78.60	31.82
branch1	75.41	85.37	20.19	89.48	33.07
proposed (3scale)	85.16	92.37	14.50	97.62	15.89

Source: Created by the author.

2.5 Results

2.5.1 Scenario 1: The Network is in a Normal State (Transmission Delay and Energy Use)

Other networks were receiving networks acting as conventional monitors, whereas Node-1 is a green colored sink node that operated as an edge network. Take Endpoints 2, 4, and 5 all are visible inside node 12's range. Figure 2.7 depicts the network in its typical state, whereas Figure 2.8 depicts the typical energy usage. Connection 1 as well as the yellow nodes continue to play similar responsibilities as previously. Network 12 evolved into a malevolent network that launched a swamping assault on nodes 2, 4, and 5. The processes for creating the assault dataset are depicted in Figure 2.9.

2.5.2 Scenario 2: Attack on a System (WSN Operations to Find Anomalies)

Figure 2.7 depicts the attacked system, while Figure 2.10 depicts the typical energy usage during the assault. Every transmitter connection (2–12) utilized about the same amount of actual, it had a weak signal at a 1.2 mW level. When vertices (4,

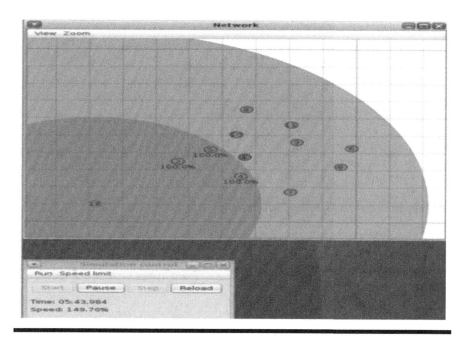

Figure 2.7 A system in its typical condition.

Source: Created by the author.

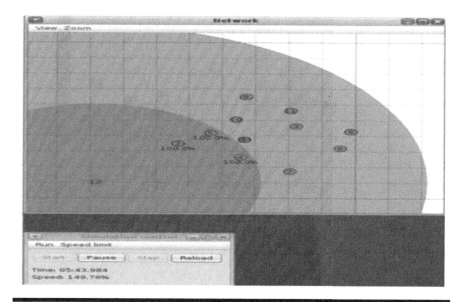

Figure 2.8 A system in its typical condition. (Average power consumption.)

Source: Created by the author.

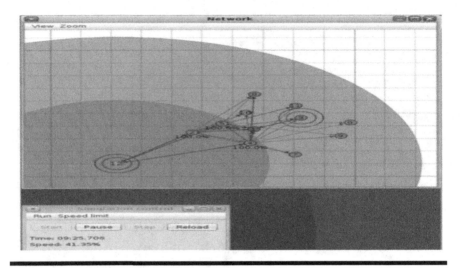

Figure 2.9 Unusual system condition.

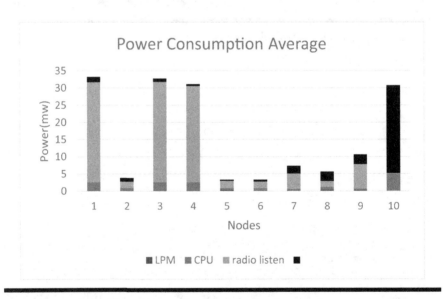

Figure 2.10 Average power consumption during the attack.

Source: Created by the author.

2, 12, and 5) are compared to various vertices, we can observe they can have a substantially greater energy usage of roughly 30 mW. The other nodes' energy usage is also higher than previously, at around 2.5 mW or even higher. We discovered that a radio broadcast is responsible for a major portion of the energy usage for node 12 (attacker) since it is continually sending messages to vertices 4, 2, and 5. The experiment demonstrates that hearing is responsible for a considerable amount of energy usage for nodes 2, 4, and 5 because they are continually receiving requests from node 12.

In Figure 2.11, results of the assault as a consequence of keeping an eye on the channel's power and energy throughout the assault scenario. Figure 2.12 depicts the number of as time passes, missing parcels, whereas Figure 2.13 depicts the status within the packages throughout the assault.

Tables 2.6 and 2.7 display node information under normal and assault settings. We can find out how long was every destination in the below regions visited for using Contiki. Table 2.7 shows that the equivalent power usage (LPM transmission power, CPU power, and listening power) is significant throughout the assault.

Cooja as an Operating System: Cooja emerges as a user-friendly operating system, tailored for streamlined experimentation, setting it apart from alternative tools like Wireshark and Omnet+. Its simplicity renders it particularly suitable for conducting experiments and evaluations.

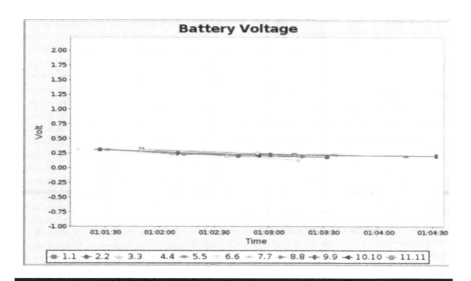

Figure 2.11 Abnormality in voltage level.

Source: Created by the author.

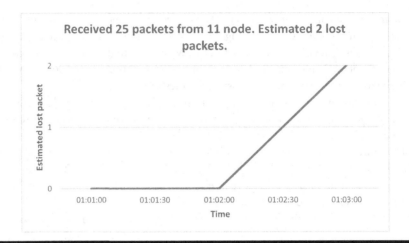

Figure 2.12 Packets lost overtime.

Source: Created by the author.

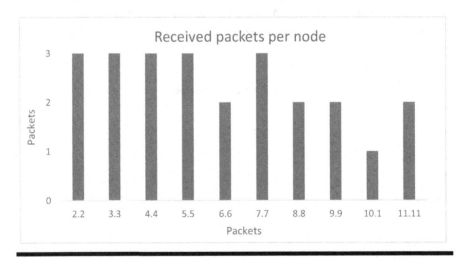

Figure 2.13 Packet states under the attack.

Source: Created by the author.

Summarizing the Investigation: The paramount importance of detecting attacks to safeguard IoT networks from potential intruders is a salient takeaway from the conducted study. It is imperative to recognize that every malicious hacker endeavors to infiltrate IoT devices, capitalizing on vulnerabilities that consistently arise within integrated systems and IoT connections. Drawing from the amassed research, the

Table 2.6   Link Data in Typical Circumstances

Node	Received	Dups	Lost	Hops	Rtmetric	Ext	Churn	Beacon Interval	Reboot	CPU Power	(LPM) Power
1.1	0.02	0.02	0.02	0.02	0.02	0.02	0.02	0 minutes, 07 seconds	0.02	0.02	0
2.2	4.01	0.02	0.02	1.10	522	15.10	0.02	2 minutes, 31 seconds	0.02	2.02	0.104
3.3	3.01	0.02	0.02	1.10	561	15.10	0.02	0 minutes, 07 seconds	0.02	0.53	0.146
4.4	3.01	0.02	0.02	1.10	513	15.10	0.02	0 minutes, 07 seconds	0.02	2.03	0.103
5.5	3.01	0.02	0.02	1.10	511	15.10	0.02	0 minutes, 07 seconds	0.02	2.10	0.102
6.6	1.10	0.02	0.02	1.10	1004	15.10	0.02	1 minutes, 22 seconds	0.02	0.51	0.147
7.7	2.10	0.02	0.02	1.10	1038	15.10	0.02	1 minutes, 37 seconds	0.02	0.51	0.148
8.8	1.10	0.02	1.10	2.10	1497	31	0.02	0 minutes, 23 seconds	0.02	0.92	0.135
9.9	2.10	0.02	0.02	1.10	1047	15.10	0.02	2 minutes, 31 seconds	0.02	0.54	0.146
10.10	1.10	0.02	1.10	2.10	1935	31	0.02	2 minutes, 42 seconds	0.02	1.03	0.131
11.11	1.10	0.02	1.10	1.51	1387	23	1.10	0 minutes, 47 seconds	0.02	0.71	0.141
Average	1.81	0.02	0.26	1.13	911	17.17	0.08	1 minutes, 13 seconds	0.02	1.07	0.118

Source: Created by the author.

Table 2.7 Network Details in Assault Circumstances

Node	CPU Power	LMP Power	Listening Power	Transmission Power	Power	On-time	Listen Duty Cycle	Transmit Duty Cycle
1	2.457	0.074	0.001	0.001	0.001		0.001	0.001
2	1.107	1.892	26.322	2.022	30.401	1 m	40.204	2.922
3	2.542	1.846	2.637	1.706	4.034	0 m	3.72	2.330
4	1.218	1.511	25.815	1.889	28.801	1 m	42.358	2.678
5	1.801	1.622	26.536	1.970	29.601	1 m	43.561	2.828
6	2.501	1.342	2.512	2.027	4.191	0 m	3.521	3.935
7	2.494	1.546	0.416	1.708	3.768	0 m	3.361	2.334
8	2.505	1.437	1.372	2.501	5.912	0 m	2.950	7.589
9	1.945	1.343	0.720	2.178	4.592	0 m	3.868	3.221
10	2.638	1.634	1.842	4.811	8.826	0 m	3.738	8.178
11	2.822	1.443	1.166	3.208	6.242	0 m	4.611	5.161
Average	2.632	1.518	9.121	2.456	11.671	0 m	12.536	3.743

Source: Created by the author.

Table 2.8 Packet Analysis in Different Snort Modes

Snort Mode	No. of Packets	Protocol by Breakdown										
		TCP	UDP	ICMP	ARP	EAPOL	IPv6	Ethloop	IPX	FRAG	Other
Packet Capture	72	2	65	0	3	0	0	0	0	5	0
	%	0	89	0	2.87	0	0	0	0	8.57	0
Logging Mode	17	0	17	0	0	0	0	0	0	0	0
	%	0	100	0	0	0	0	0	0	0	0
Alert mode	4	2	0	0	2	0	0	0	0	0	0
	%	50	0	0	50	0	0	0	0	0	0
Sniffer Mode	14	0	11	0	3	0	0	0	0	0	0
	%	0	78.5	0	21.5	0	0	0	0	0	0

Source: Created by the author.

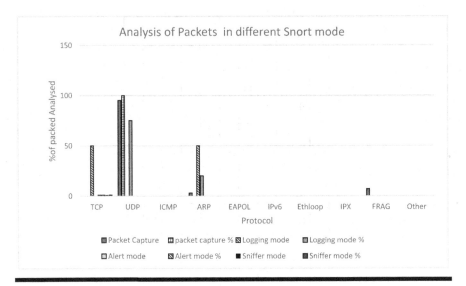

Figure 2.14 Examination of packets using various Snort modes.

Source: Created by the author.

authors outline a multitude of patterns that influence the diverse skill sets required for executing this comprehensive research. This could potentially pose a challenge for researchers, especially those not well-versed in program minutes. Hence, the study leverages digital forensic methodologies to unearth anomalies within systems, gather pertinent information, and pinpoint contributing factors. A pivotal step involves scrutinizing the outcomes to discern whether the Internet traffic adheres to typical patterns. Ultimately, in the context of a hypothetical scenario, the identification of the vulnerable channel through which the perpetrator operates comes to the fore.

Although bandwidth utilization and throughput rise, the attack detection rate drops as the number of packets or nodes increases. Snort captures packets and saves them in a directory while in packet logger mode. When in IDS mode, it detects suspicious network activity using the rules specified in the snort.conf file and generates an alert if the rules are broken. Table 2.8 and Figure 2.14 show several Snort packet processing options. The detection rate of attacks decreases as the number of packets or nodes increases, as does bandwidth utilization and throughput. Snort creates a directory for each packet it collects while in packet logger mode. It recognizes unusual internet behavior by using the recommendations set in the snort.conf file and issues a warning whenever the criteria and observed activity match. Data transit is evaluated using sFlow-RT. It is used to analyze traffic, evaluate networking performance, and determine capacity. Figure 2.15 shows that a higher peak implies flooding traffic from any IP address. The volume of illegal data that had flooded the

Figure 2.15   Attack and mitigation flow IO graph.
Source: Created by the author.

victim's network dropped once the network was trained. Lower peaks after 00.24.50 seconds indicate that mitigation was successfully achieved.

2.6 Conclusions

Proposed Methodology for Vulnerability Detection: This study introduces an original methodology for the investigation and identification of vulnerabilities within integrated and IoT systems operating on Contiki OS. This method encompasses data collection and subsequent analysis utilizing the capabilities of Cooja. Through a comparative analysis, the study reveals numerous attacks linked with the employed strategies, with a notable focus on flood attacks.

Numerical Exploration and Example Scenario: Illustrating the numerical inquiry, a well-defined scenario is presented, featuring the monitoring of Machine-to-Machine (M2M) communications through MQTT. This process is undertaken twice: initially under standard conditions and subsequently to gauge the implications of malicious actions following a standard attack. Hierarchical clustering technology employed in M2M communications within the IoT context empowers authorized users to scrutinize connection patterns. The structure of the information signal in the IoT landscape is vigilantly observed and documented through a numerical experiment. The scenario's outcome entails the accumulation of records pertaining to flooding attack incidents, particularly RPL triage assaults. This influences various network facets, including luminosity, speed, energy utilization, and battery capacity. The amalgamation of regular network data, traffic, and attack information furnishes a comprehensive dataset. Consequently, a specialized dataset tailored for intrusion detection system applications is generated, facilitating the identification and assessment of vulnerabilities within IoT devices. The core objective of this study revolves around the detection of flooding occurrences. However, a controlled approach was selected, as the process of anomaly detection during virtualized network analysis consumed considerable time, potentially leading to substantial losses.

Future Prospects and Deep Convolutional Neural System: Future research efforts will try to broaden the dataset to include attributes such as attack times, attack payloads, and various attack kinds. In addition, the dataset's properties will be improved, increasing its usability. A unique Deep Convolutional Neural System with two branches is introduced in the scope of this work. This innovation recognizes image recovery attacks and addresses fine detail loss as well as color distortion issues. The fine detail loss artifact is specifically repaired utilizing a specialized filter bank technique in conjunction with a novel two-branch deep neural network with a multi-scale cross-modal attention fusion mechanism. The research findings confirm that the suggested architecture consistently gives superior performance across a variety of paper recapture scenarios.

References

[1] G. Fersi, Fog Computing and Internet of Things in One Building Block: A Survey and an Overview of Interacting Technologies. *Cluster Computing*, 24, 2757–2787, 2021. https://doi.org/10.1007/s10586-021-03286-4

[2] E. Nehme, R. El Sibai, J. Bou Abdo, et al. Converged AI, IoT, and Blockchain Technologies: A Conceptual Ethics Framework. *AI Ethics*, 2, 129–143, 2022. https://doi.org/10.1007/s43681-021-00079-8

[3] N. Torres, P. Pinto, S.I. Lopes, Security Vulnerabilities in LPWANs – An Attack Vector Analysis for the IoT Ecosystem. *Applied Sciences*, 11, 3176, 2021. https://doi.org/10.3389/app11073176

[4] W. Ben Arfi, I. Ben Nasr, T. Khvatova, Y. Ben Zaied, Understanding Acceptance of eHealthcare by IoT Natives and IoT Immigrants: An Integrated Model of UTAUT, Perceived Risk, and Financial Cost, *Technological Forecasting and Social Change*, 163, 120437, 2021. ISSN 0040-1625, https://doi.org/10.1016/j.techfore.2020.120437

[5] N. Ho-Sam-Sooi, W. Pieters, M. Kroesen, Investigating the Effect of Security and Privacy on IoT Device Purchase Behaviour, *Computers & Security*, 102, 102132, 2021. ISSN 0167-4048, https://doi.org/10.1016/j.cose.2020.102132.

[6] C. Patel, N. Doshi", A Novel MQTT Security Framework in Generic IoT Model", *Procedia Computer Science*, 171, 1399–1408, 2020. ISSN 1877-0509, https://doi.org/10.1016/j.procs.2020.04.150

[7] F. De Rango, G. Potrino, M. Tropea, P. Fazio, Energy-Aware Dynamic Internet of Things Security System Based on Elliptic Curve Cryptography and Message Queue Telemetry Transport Protocol for Mitigating Replay Attacks, *Pervasive and Mobile Computing*, 61, 101105, 2020. ISSN 1574-1192, https://doi.org/10.1016/j.pmcj.2019.101105

[8] S. Cakir, S. Toklu, N. Yalcin, "RPL Attack Detection and Prevention in the Internet of Things Networks Using a GRU Based Deep Learning", in *IEEE Access*, 8, 183678–183689, 2020. DOI: 10.1109/ACCESS.2020.3029191

[9] S. Mishra, "Network Traffic Analysis Using Machine Learning Techniques in IoT Networks", *IJSI*, 9(4), 107–123, 2021. http://doi.org/10.4018/IJSI.289172

[10] K. Kumari, M. Mrunalini, "Detecting Denial of Service Attacks Using Machine Learning Algorithms", *J Big Data*, 9, 56, 2022. https://doi.org/10.1186/s40 537-022-00616-0

[11] H. Polat, O. Polat, A. Cetin, Detecting DDoS Attacks in Software-Defined Networks through Feature Selection Methods and Machine Learning Models. *Sustainability*, 12, 1035, 2020. https://doi.org/10.3389/su12031035

[12] S. Mishra, S. Kumar Sharma, M. A. Alowaidi, "Multilayer Self-Defense System to Protect Enterprise Cloud", *Computers, Materials & Continua*, 66(1), 71–85, 2021. https://doi.org/10.32604/cmc.2020.022475

[13] J. Li et al. (2022). "Two-Branch Multi-Scale Deep Neural Network for Generalized Document Recapture Attack Detection." *ICASSP 2023-2023 IEEE International Conference on Acoustics, Speech and Signal Processing (ICASSP)*. IEEE, 2023.

[14] S. Sumathi, R. Rajesh, S. Lim, "Recurrent and Deep Learning Neural Network Models for DDoS Attack Detection", *Journal of Sensors*, 2022, Article ID 8530312, 21, 2022. https://doi.org/10.1155/2022/8530312

[15] N. Xu, X. Wang, Y. Xu, T. Zhao, X. Li, "Deep Multi-Scale Residual Connected Neural Network Model for Intelligent Athlete Balance Control Ability Evaluation", *Computational Intelligence and Neuroscience*, 2022, Article ID 8912709, 11, 2022. https://doi.org/10.1155/2022/8912709

[16] J. Ahn, Y. Lee, M. Kim, J. Park, "Vision-Based Branch Road Detection for Intersection Navigation in Unstructured Environment Using Multi-Task Network", *Journal of Advanced Transportation*, 2022, Article ID 9328398, 13, 2022. https://doi.org/10.1155/2022/9328398

[17] C. Chen, L. Wei, L. Zhang, Y. Peng, J. Ning, "DeepGuard: Backdoor Attack Detection and Identification Schemes in Privacy-Preserving Deep Neural Networks", *Security and Communication Networks*, 2022, Article ID 2985308, 20, 2022. https://doi.org/10.1155/2022/2985308

[18] T. Janarthanan, M. Bagheri, S. Zargari, (2021). IoT Forensics: An Overview of the Current Issues and Challenges. In: Montasari, R., Jahankhani, H., Hill, R., Parkinson, S. (eds) *Digital Forensic Investigation of Internet of Things (IoT) Devices. Advanced Sciences and Technologies for Security Applications*. Springer, Cham. https://doi.org/10.1007/978-3-030-60425-7_10

[19] B. Hammi, S. Zeadally, R. Khatoun, J. Nebhen, Survey on Smart Homes: Vulnerabilities, Risks, and Countermeasures, *Computers & Security*, 117, 102677, 2022. ISSN 0167-4048, https://doi.org/10.1016/j.cose.2022.102677

[20] E. Ismagilova, L. Hughes, N. P. Rana, et al. Security, Privacy and Risks within Smart Cities: Literature Review and Development of a Smart City Interaction Framework. *Information Systems Frontiers*, 24, 393–414, 2022. https://doi.org/10.1007/s10 796-020-10044-1

[21] A. Hue, G. Sharma, J.-M. Dricot, Privacy-Enhanced MQTT Protocol for Massive IoT. *Electronics*, 11, 70, 2022. https://doi.org/10.3389/electronics11010070

[22] Y. Zheng, Z. Li, X. Xu, Q. Zhao, Dynamic Defenses in Cyber Security: Techniques, Methods and Challenges, *Digital Communications and Networks*, 8(4), 422–435, 2022. ISSN 2352-8648, https://doi.org/10.1016/j.dcan.2021.07.006

[23] M. Labonne. Anomaly-Based Network Intrusion Detection Using Machine Learning. *Cryptography and Security [cs.CR]*. Institut Polytechnique de Paris, 2020. English. ffNNT: 2020IPPAS011ff. fftel02988296f

[24] N. Lin, Y. Chen, H. Liu, H. Liu, A Comparative Study of Machine Learning Models with Hyperparameter Optimization Algorithm for Mapping Minuteseral Prospectivity. *Minuteserals*, 11, 159, 2021. https://doi.org/10.3389/minutes1 1020159

[25] M. Aledhari, R. Razzak, R. M. Parizi, Machine Learning for Network Application Security: Empirical Evaluation and Optimization, *Computers & Electrical Engineering*, 91, 107052, 2021. ISSN 0045-7896, https://doi.org/10.1016/j.comp eleceng.2021.107052

[26] D. Chou, M. Jiang. 2021. A Survey on Data-Driven Network Intrusion Detection. *ACM Computing Surveys*, 54(9), Article 182 (December 2022), 36. https://doi.org/10.1145/3472753

[27] A. E. Ibor, F. A. Oladeji, O. B. Okunoye, C. O. Uwadia, Novel Adaptive Cyberattack Prediction Model Using an Enhanced Genetic Algorithm and Deep Learning (AdacDeep), *Information Security Journal: A Global Perspective*, 31(1), 105–124, 2022. DOI: 10.1080/19393555.2021.1883777

[28] K. M. Ghori, M. Imran, A. Nawaz, et al. Performance Analysis of Machine Learning Classifiers for Non-Technical Loss Detection. *Journal of Ambient Intelligence Humanized Computing*, 2020. https://doi.org/10.1007/s12652-019-01649-9

[29] I. Ahmad, W. U. Rehman Khan, S. Ullah, N. Mufti, A. G. Alharbi, N. Hussain, M. Alibakhshikenari, M. Dalarsson, "Highly Compact GCPW-Fed Multi-Branch Structure Multi-Band Antenna for Wireless Applications", *International Journal of Antennas and Propagation*, 2022, Article ID 1917807, 9, 2022. https://doi.org/10.1155/2022/1917807

[30] G. Y. Kim, J. Y. Kim, S. H. Lee, S. M. Kim, "Robust Detection Model of Vascular Landmarks for Retinal Image Registration: A Two-Stage Convolutional Neural Network", *BioMed Research International*, 2022, Article ID 1705338, 14, 2022. https://doi.org/10.1155/2022/1705338

[31] M. Wang, C. Lee, W. Wang, Y. Yang, C. Yang, "Early Warning of Infectious Diseases in Hospitals Based on Multi-Self-Regression Deep Neural Network", *Journal of Healthcare Engineering*, 2022, Article ID 8989897, 13, 2022. https://doi.org/10.1155/2022/8989897

[32] A. Ullah, N. Javaid, A. Sani Yahaya, T. Sultana, F. Ahmad Al-Zahrani, F. Zaman, "A Hybrid Deep Neural Network for Electricity Theft Detection Using Intelligent Antenna-Based Smart Meters", *Wireless Communications and Mobile Computing*, 2021, Article ID 9933111, 19, 2021. https://doi.org/10.1155/2021/9933111

[33] Z. Liu, C. Wang, W. Wang, "Online Cyber-Attack Detection in the Industrial Control System: A Deep Reinforcement Learning Approach", *Mathematical Problems in Engineering*, 2022, Article ID 2280871, 9, 2022. https://doi.org/10.1155/2022/2280871

[34] S. Du, Z. Chen, H. Wu, Y. Tang, Y. Li, "Image Recommendation Algorithm Combined with Deep Neural Network Designed for Social Networks", *Complexity*, 2021, Article ID 5196189, 9, 2021. https://doi.org/10.1155/2021/5196189

[35] D. Han, S. Yun, B. Heo, Y. Yoo, "Rethinking Channel Dimensions for Efficient Model Design", *2021 IEEE/CVF Conference on Computer Vision and Pattern Recognition (CVPR)*, 732–741, 2021. DOI: 10.1109/CVPR46437.2021.00079

[36] L. Wang, X. Wang, A. Hawbani, Y. Xiong, X. Zhang, "Rethinking Separable Convolutional Encoders for End-to-End Semantic Image Segmentation", *Mathematical Problems in Engineering*, 2021, Article ID 5566691, 12, 2021. https://doi.org/10.1155/2021/5566691

[37] C. Nykvist, M. Larsson, A. H. Sodhro, A. Gurtov, A Lightweight Portable Intrusion Detection Communication System for Auditing Applications. *International Journal of Communication Systems*, 33, e4327, 2020. https://doi.org/10.1002/dac.4327

Chapter 3

Privacy Preservation in Cyber Physical Systems Using Entropy-Based Techniques

Manas Kumar Yogi[1] and A. S. N. Chakravarthy[2]

[1]*CSE Department, Pragati Engineering College (A),
Surampalem, Andhra Pradesh, India*

[2]*CSE Department, JNTUK, Kakinada, Andhra Pradesh, India*

3.1 Introduction

In our modern-day world smart technologies are taking over the traditional computing systems in every domain of life. Cyber physical systems are considered to be a mixture of cyber systems and hardware systems [1]. The main purpose of the cyber physical system is to combine the dynamic property of hardware devices with the state of art communication technology. Cyber physical systems have found their role in various areas of application such as smart transportation, smart healthcare, smart industrial and manufacturing units, smart energy systems, and so forth. It has been observed that majority of the cyber physical systems are part of an eco-system where the utility of a computing system increases the performance of the computing system. The best example for this is the role of the cyber physical system in life support machines or any other infrastructures which are critical to human beings. The privacy aspect related to any IoT (Internet of Things) system is based on the careful usage of the participating elements [2]. For this aspect, mainly technology is

DOI: 10.1201/9781003474838-3

involved because the trust factor in human beings can be compromised to a greater extent. Thus, in this context, arrives the PET (Privacy Enhancing Technologies). In the digital world, privacy has become a human right which gives faith and goodwill in the users to become a part of the smart ecosystem in various domains of life. The main challenge for researchers is to devise a mechanism such that the sensitive data of a legal user is not compromised in the hands of a malicious user. In this area of research, the main challenge is to develop a privacy metric which is measurable, effective, and distinguishable from other privacy metrics. Both data mining and statistical approaches currently are ruling this area of research. But adversarial machine learning techniques are posing a threat to the current popular privacy-preserving techniques due to their learning ability and understanding user behaviour.

Salient features of privacy metrics in Cyber Physical Systems (CPS):

■ A good privacy metric increases the uncertainty of identifying a user by the adversary

■ A good privacy metric has a high probability of hiding a user's sensitive information

■ A good privacy metric should mirror how difficult it is for the adversary to succeed

■ A good privacy metric should denote non-sensitive data and its utility in the final application

■ A good privacy metric should increase in its strength when the adversary's strength also increases.

The role of privacy preservation in cyber physical systems is becoming a challenge day by day .The main reason is that, in a cyber physical system, sensors are a vital part of the ecosystem, which can be manipulated to alter the functionality of the hardware devices. Information leakage through the sensors gives rise to serious damage in society. The main research challenge in this field is due to the complex architecture of the cyber physical systems, making it difficult to develop a privacy model and security model. Yet another challenge is that in a cyber-physical system it is laborious to trace and validate the privacy threads due to multiple participating entities, which have numerous sensors that relay the data to various private and public data servers [3]. For instance we can consider a scenario whereby a wearable smart device is continuously feeding data to a medical institution server that is used by the doctor to monitor the patient's health reports. But if this data is hacked then the health of the patient can be strongly compromised. Consequently, we can observe that, due to the probability of privacy leakage in a CPS ecosystem in the absence of a privacy threat, the model will render the CPS application useless. Privacy attacks can be passive as well as active. Passive attacks take more time to carry out, but their consequence is very harmful due to the fact that over time the sensitive data being shared in a network accumulates to a considerable size. In recent years researchers have developed many models and measures to counter this challenge [4]. But the main problem lies in the application of these models because not all the aspects of a real-life scenario can be modeled during the design of such privacy threat models. Most of the privacy preservation techniques have drawn strength from the below principles.

Encryption – This mechanism involves usage of public and private keys for data transmission. The main limitation is that its computational complexity is very high and not suitable for public databases.

Anonymization – This technique removes the private and sensitive data before query evaluation by a user. The limitation of this mechanism is the probability of re-identification is high for a public database which is very large in size.

Differential Privacy – Currently the most popular privacy-preserving strategy due to its low computational complexity and strong mathematical foundations. The weakness is that its trade-off with data utility is difficult to maintain and suffers from dimensionality curse when applied to high dimensional application data [5].

Due to the ease in implementation of differential privacy in advanced CPS, this technique has been accepted by most of the organizations throughout the world. Also, looking from an adversary's point of view, this mechanism will prevent the attacker from using methods of carrying out linkage attacks, inferencing attacks or other techniques of re-identification. In this work, the principles of differential privacy will be used as basis to develop a novel information theoretical framework for privacy preservation.

3.2 Privacy Domains

In the below domains the privacy enhancing technologies are essential to safeguard the sensitive information of the users and instill more confidence in the stakeholders.

1. Systems of Communication network: Not just the identity of sender and receiver can be compromised, but also the context and content of the channel of communication can come under attack from adversaries in this type of communication systems.
2. Social Networks: Adversaries can try to extract sensitive private data from the profile of the users in a social network.
3. Genome Privacy: The genome construction and re-construction technologies have opened a dangerous door of privacy at the gene level where the adversary can find opportunity to alter the genetic data and cause damage to a person's identity.
4. Location-based Services: Attackers try to get hold of the movement of users and generate travel profiles which may have adverse effect in smart transportation purposes.
5. Smart Billing Systems: Adversaries can infer usage of service based on the bills and bill patterns and can cause harm to the users.

3.3 Related Work

The privacy protection techniques have been well researched in CPS as well as IoT systems. The popular methods are the spatial cloaking method, dummy location method, and cryptography primitive-based method. The spatial cloaking technology constructs a hidden region containing K users thereby decreasing the attack probability to 1/K [6] .The limitation of this method is poor quality of service. Also, if the concentration of users in a region is sparse then the anonymous region will not be built by the algorithm and mechanism involved fails. In dummy location technique multiple dummy locations are combined before sending them to the service provider. The multi-objective algorithm achieves k-anonymity by formulating k-1 dummy areas through the mobile clients. The challenge is to decrease the computing power and storage of local mobile clients. In cryptographical approaches, encryption and decryption facilities are used for safeguarding the security and privacy of both the sender and receiver parties [7]. But the problem with such a mechanism is the high computational overhead involved in maintaining the keys and the effort required for encryption and decryption process. In the domain of information based entropy, researchers have developed measure for guessing the user identity with entropy [8]. The basic principle is that, if the sensitive information in an anonymized table is diverse than the average privacy loss can be minimized. But the main challenge is that the entropy-based privacy metrics can only justify the uncertainty of a private data in a dataset but cannot increase the degree of anonymity [9]. Entropy methods don't address the aspect of how rich the attacker is in terms of computing power and bandwidth and storage needs.

Entropy-based privacy measures are highly suitable for location privacy as from time to time the user does not remain in the same region [10]. In such cases the attacker has knowledge about user location at specific time duration. By using belief tables based on Bayes theorem and knowledge bases for hiding user location and activity during a time interval the adversary can be defeated in their purpose [11]. User centric privacy is yet another direction which supports the usage of entropy-based mechanism for privacy preservation [12]. This concept advocates the policy that user privacy reduces in linear proportion over time with a speed factor. Assuming a base privacy metric which has lower limit of zero for privacy boundary, this metric holds the notion that every cycle of a privacy preservation mechanism is independent of each other.

As observed from the Figure 3.1 illustration, the majority of the research work has been carried out in the area of Reyni entropy [13]. The main reason is that it suits for an ideal privacy scenario for a user. Even if the attacker has the highest degree of determining the user identity, this method has the probability of minimizing that attack. Next comes the technique of normalized entropy where differential privacy also poses an equal challenge in terms of application and popularity [14]. Most of the applications related to smart technologies like e-healthcare systems work with normalized entropy. The only limitation is its mathematical representation

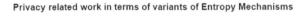

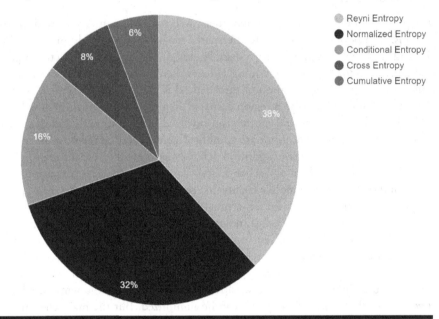

Figure 3.1 Current related work in the area of privacy related to variants of entropy technique.

Source: Created by the author.

which hinders its application in other domains of IoT [15]. Table 3.1 below shows the approximation of research applications carried out by Entropy techniques for Privacy preservation.

3.4 Proposed Mechanism

We are motivated to use the measure-preserving dynamical system where the measure is privacy of a user in a cyber-physical system [11]. So, our model is converted to a privacy preserving dynamical system. We regard the various sensor related functions in a CPS as representation of dynamic aspects of a complex CPS. We model the CPS as a tuple as shown below:

$$CPS = (Y, B, \mu, T) \tag{3.1}$$

In above equation, Y represents the set of values of sensitivity of a user data,

B represents 6-algebra over Y, i.e. the probability values of Y.

μ represents values from [0, 1].

T represents a transformation $Y \rightarrow Y$ which preserves the privacy.

Table 3.1 Approximation of Research Applications Carried Out by Entropy Techniques for Privacy Preservation

Sl.no.	Reference	Entropy Technique	Application Area
1	[1][2][3][4]	Reyni Entropy	Medical Cyber-physical systems, smart healthcare system, smart energy systems, smart agriculture
2	[1][5][6]	Normalized Entropy	Smart industrial systems
3	[2][3][4]	Conditional Entropy	Smart military systems, smart electricity grids
4	[4][7][8]	Cross Entropy	Precision agriculture
5	[9][10]	Cumulative Entropy	Smart transportation

Source: Created by the author.

The main goal is to derive the set Y after transformation which has high values of privacy for the user that will be possible only when the sensitivity values in Y are optimal. So, for obtaining the optimal values of Y we now introduce the concept of measure theoretic entropy.

Given a set of queries, represented by

$$Q= \{q_1, q_2, q_3, \ldots q_n\} \tag{3.2}$$

The entropy of the set of queries denoted by Q can be represented as,

$$M(Q) = -\sum_Q \mu(Q)\log\mu(Q) \tag{3.3}$$

Once we obtain the entropy of set of queries represented by Q, we observe that the negative sign will try to balance out the successful attacks of an adversary to extract the privacy values. Hence, the process tries to minimize the values for $M(Q)$. Once we observe that the entropy reaches highest negative value, we consider it as optimal value for B. So, we replace the value of B with M (Q) value. The below equation is now the new state for the dynamic CPS. We should observe that the M (Q) values will change over state transitions due to the sensor data and also due to the set of adversarial queries, Q. To handle this challenge, the transformation, T is tuned in such a fashion that the sensitivity values of Y are never violated beyond values of μ.

The privacy-preserving dynamical system can now be defined as

$$CPS=(Y,M(Q) \mu,T) \tag{3.4}$$

The anti-classification theorem adds strength to our proposed mechanism by stating that the set of queries Q over a transformation of the original CPS cannot measure with certainty the difference between the values of the original dataset versus the values in the modified dataset. So, our mechanism is safe from inferencing attacks as well as linkage attacks.

Algorithm PPEM (Privacy Preservation with Entropy Method)

> Step 1. Initialise the mathematical model of the CPS with a tuple representation. Initialize the values for all the tuples of the CPS.
> Step 2. Carry out a suitable transformation for the Y vector, which contains the privacy sensitivity values.
> Step 3. For a set of queries Q, compute the entropy measure given with below equation

$$M(Q) = -\sum_{Q} \mu(Q) \log \mu(Q)$$

> Step 4. Derive the mathematical model for the CPS with a tuple which preserves the privacy of a user in the CPS ecosystem.
> Step 5. Check the value of $M(Q)$ is optimal or not.
> Step 6. If M (Q) value is not optimal then repeat the above process. Go to Step 2.
> Step 7. Exit.

3.5 Experimental Results

For experimental results, we have used python language to implement the proposed method and dataset of heart failure prediction is obtained from kaggle. The dataset has 918 records. We assume the private attributes are Age and Sex. The other eight attributes indicate the values which may lead to heart failure. Figure 3.2 indicates a snapshot of the dataset used in the experiments.

The patient whose value is 1 for the Heart Disease column are having other attributes which result in heart disease and patients whose value is 0 don't have any heart issues. In case the adversary wants to know the gender and age of patients whose Heart Disease value is 1, the proposed method hides the data by application of entropy-based technique.

From the plot of Figure 3.3, it can be observed that the proposed method outperforms other popular methods in terms of privacy preservation even though the number of queries from the attacker increases substantially. In the plot, it is shown that the technique of partial differential privacy has the lowest increase in the

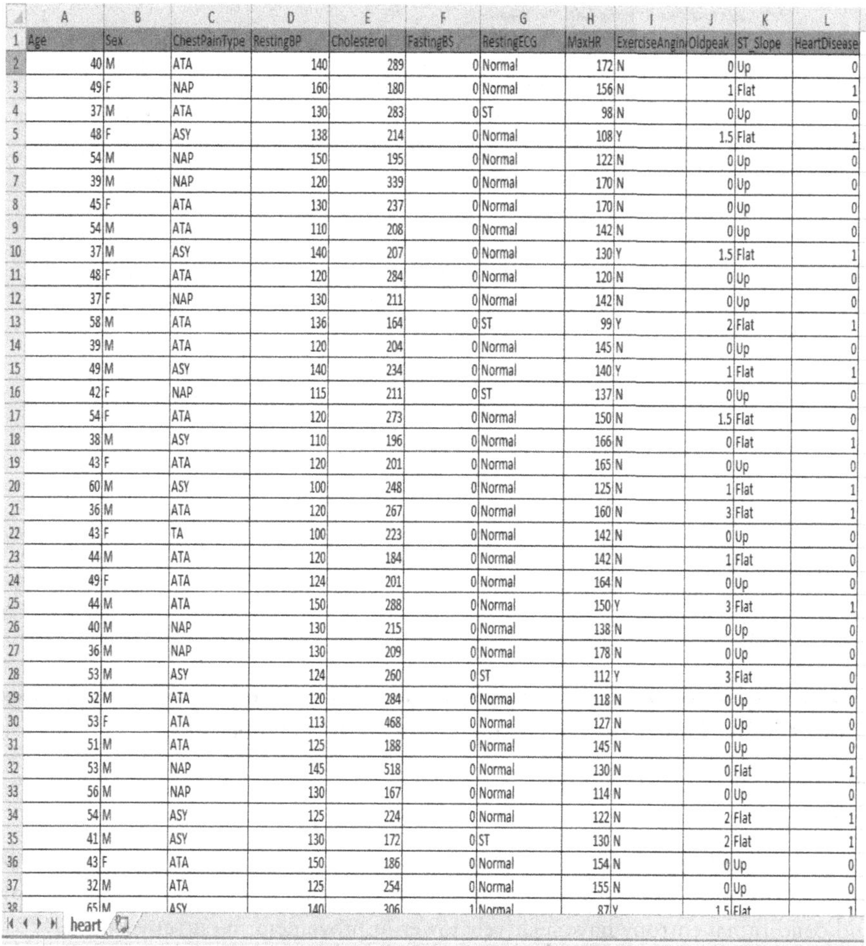

	A	B	C	D	E	F	G	H	I	J	K	L
1	Age	Sex	ChestPainType	RestingBP	Cholesterol	FastingBS	RestingECG	MaxHR	ExerciseAngin	Oldpeak	ST_Slope	HeartDisease
2	40	M	ATA	140	289	0	Normal	172	N	0	Up	0
3	49	F	NAP	160	180	0	Normal	156	N	1	Flat	1
4	37	M	ATA	130	283	0	ST	98	N	0	Up	0
5	48	F	ASY	138	214	0	Normal	108	Y	1.5	Flat	1
6	54	M	NAP	150	195	0	Normal	122	N	0	Up	0
7	39	M	NAP	120	339	0	Normal	170	N	0	Up	0
8	45	F	ATA	130	237	0	Normal	170	N	0	Up	0
9	54	M	ATA	110	208	0	Normal	142	N	0	Up	0
10	37	M	ASY	140	207	0	Normal	130	Y	1.5	Flat	1
11	48	F	ATA	120	284	0	Normal	120	N	0	Up	0
12	37	F	NAP	130	211	0	Normal	142	N	0	Up	0
13	58	M	ATA	136	164	0	ST	99	Y	2	Flat	1
14	39	M	ATA	120	204	0	Normal	145	N	0	Up	0
15	49	M	ASY	140	234	0	Normal	140	Y	1	Flat	1
16	42	F	NAP	115	211	0	ST	137	N	0	Up	0
17	54	F	ATA	120	273	0	Normal	150	N	1.5	Flat	0
18	38	M	ASY	110	196	0	Normal	166	N	0	Flat	1
19	43	F	ATA	120	201	0	Normal	165	N	0	Up	0
20	60	M	ASY	100	248	0	Normal	125	N	1	Flat	1
21	36	M	ATA	120	267	0	Normal	160	N	3	Flat	1
22	43	F	TA	100	223	0	Normal	142	N	0	Up	0
23	44	M	ATA	120	184	0	Normal	142	N	1	Flat	0
24	49	F	ATA	124	201	0	Normal	164	N	0	Up	0
25	44	M	ATA	150	288	0	Normal	150	Y	3	Flat	1
26	40	M	NAP	130	215	0	Normal	138	N	0	Up	0
27	36	M	NAP	130	209	0	Normal	178	N	0	Up	0
28	53	M	ASY	124	260	0	ST	112	Y	3	Flat	0
29	52	M	ATA	120	284	0	Normal	118	N	0	Up	0
30	53	F	ATA	113	468	0	Normal	127	N	0	Up	0
31	51	M	ATA	125	188	0	Normal	145	N	0	Up	0
32	53	M	NAP	145	518	0	Normal	130	N	0	Flat	1
33	56	M	NAP	130	167	0	Normal	114	N	0	Up	0
34	54	M	ASY	125	224	0	Normal	122	N	2	Flat	1
35	41	M	ASY	130	172	0	ST	130	N	2	Flat	1
36	43	F	ATA	150	186	0	Normal	154	N	0	Up	0
37	32	M	ATA	125	254	0	Normal	155	N	0	Up	0
38	65	M	ASY	140	306	1	Normal	87	Y	1.5	Flat	1

⏮ ◀ ▶ ⏭   heart

Figure 3.2   Snapshot of Dataset used for application of proposed method.

Source: Created by the author.

property of privacy preservation. The nearest competitor for the proposed method is the group differential privacy which has still around 1.5% less performance degree. The graph shows an increasing trend due to the fact that all the privacy preservation techniques are designed to scale in performance as the attacker increases the attempt to extract private values from the dataset by extensive querying.

The graph in Figure 3.4 shows the comparative analysis of proposed method with other popular methods involving variants of entropy based techniques. The entropy of the system for privacy preservation has an increasing trend when the number of queries by the attacker also increases. It can be observed with ease that the proposed

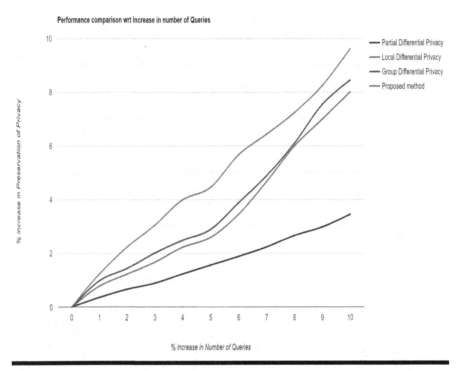

Figure 3.3 Performance comparison wrt increase in number of queries.
Source: Created by the author.

method outperforms the other methods with nearly 2% margin of its nearest competitor method, which is Reyni entropy. The other methods of normalized entropy and conditional entropy have relatively lower improvement in entropy values.

3.6 Future Directions

Currently, this proposed method is used with the principle of measure theoretic entropy and does not consider the batches of similar queries. In some cases the adversary generates a group of queries which are similar and only the query structure is dissimilar. The group queries also known as batch queries try to put more pressure on the proposed method to break its logic. So, in future work, the intension is to use ergodic privacy-preserving transformations, so that the anti-classification theorem is equipped with the robustness of facing batch queries generated to carry out their malicious intensions. Yet another aspect to look into the future research is the length of the attributes in a dataset which are considered to be private. Our method

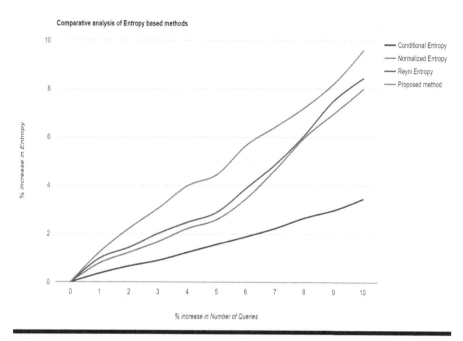

Figure 3.4   Comparative Analysis of current popular methods.
Source: Created by the author.

scales well up to five or six private attributes but more than that the performance of the proposed method may not be suitable. The main reason is that the logarithmic calculations are not so much costly for short records but as number of records in a dataset increases, the computational costs over these records also scale to become costly.

3.7 Conclusion

In this research work, the focus is placed on the effect of entropy-based methods to increase the uncertainty of inferencing the private data of a user in a cyber-physical system. Due to this increase in uncertainty, linkage attacks and re-identification attacks cannot be carried out and subsequently, the sensitivity of private data is also saved. The experimental results show the proposed method is better in performance when compared to current methods of privacy preservation in a CPS. Moreover, the proposed method is also facing the challenge of increase in the number of queries by the adversary by always trying to find the optimal values of privacy sensitivity values.

References

1. Farokhi, Farhad. "Development and analysis of deterministic privacy-preserving policies using non-stochastic information theory." *IEEE Transactions on Information Forensics and Security* 14.10 (2019): 2567–2576.
2. Zhang, Zeyu, Zhiyang Lu, and Youliang Tian. "Data privacy quantification and de-identification model based on information theory." *2019 International Conference on Networking and Network Applications (NaNA)*. IEEE, 2019.
3. Ding, Wenxin, et al. "Calibration with privacy in peer review." *2022 IEEE International Symposium on Information Theory (ISIT)*. IEEE, 2022.
4. Sfar, Arbia Riahi, et al. "A game theoretic approach for privacy preserving model in IoT-based transportation." *IEEE Transactions on Intelligent Transportation Systems* 20.12 (2019): 4405–4414.
5. Kim, Dongyeon, et al. "Willingness to provide personal information: Perspective of privacy calculus in IoT services." *Computers in Human Behavior* 92 (2019): 273–281.
6. Ahmad, Imtiaz, et al. "Tangible privacy: Towards user-centric sensor designs for bystander privacy." *Proceedings of the ACM on Human-Computer Interaction, CSCW2* 1 (2020): 1–28.
7. Chong, Michelle S., Henrik Sandberg, and André MH Teixeira. "A tutorial introduction to security and privacy for cyber-physical systems." *2019 18th European Control Conference (ECC)*. IEEE, 2019.
8. Wang, Jinbao, Zhipeng Cai, and Jiguo Yu. "Achieving personalized k–anonymity-based content privacy for autonomous vehicles in CPS." *IEEE Transactions on Industrial Informatics* 16.6 (2019): 4242–4251.
9. Li, Shancang, Houbing Song, and Muddesar Iqbal. "Privacy and security for resource-constrained IoT devices and networks: Research challenges and opportunities." *Sensors* 19.8 (2019): 1935.
10. Keshk, Marwa, et al. "Privacy-preserving big data analytics for cyber-physical systems." *Wireless Networks* 1 (2022): 1–9.
11. Lu, Yang, and Minghui Zhu. "A control-theoretic perspective on cyber-physical privacy: Where data privacy meets dynamic systems." *Annual Reviews in Control* 1 (2019): 423–440.
12. Abie, Habtamu. "Cognitive cybersecurity for CPS-IoT enabled healthcare ecosystems." *2019 13th International Symposium on Medical Information and Communication Technology (ISMICT)*. IEEE, 2019.
13. Lv, Pin, et al. "An IoT-oriented privacy-preserving publish/subscribe model over blockchains." *IEEE Access* 7 (2019): 41309–41314.
14. Pan, Qianqian, et al. "Side-channel analysis-based model extraction on intelligent CPS: An information theory perspective." *2021 IEEE International Conferences on Internet of Things (iThings) and IEEE Green Computing & Communications (GreenCom) and IEEE Cyber, Physical & Social Computing (CPSCom) and IEEE Smart Data (SmartData) and IEEE Congress on Cybermatics (Cybermatics)*. IEEE, 2021.
15. Cogliati, Dario, et al. "Intelligent cyber-physical systems for industry 4.0." *2018 First International Conference on Artificial Intelligence for Industries (AI4I)*. IEEE, 2018.

Chapter 4

Securing IoT Environment Using Bio-Inspired Meta-Heuristic Methodologies

P. Harikrishna[1] and R. Kaviarasan[2]

[1]Department of Computational Intelligence, Malla Reddy College of Engineering and Technology, Hyderabad, India

[2]Department of Computer Science and Engineering, RGM College of Engineering and Technology, Nandyal, India

4.1 Introduction

In 1999, Procter and Gamble computer scientist Kevin Ashton coined the term Internet of Things, often abbreviated as IoT [1]. IoT consists not only of computers but devices that can either transmit or receive data like an animal in the forest that has a biochip embedded in it to track its location, or a human who has an implant that can be used to monitor his/her heart rate per second/real time or a set of sensors that are present in the wheels of a car and relays the tire pressure to the driver via an application. So, if a device needs to connect to IoT [2], it should be a Web-based smart device. These smart devices have sensors to collect the data, a processor to act on the data collected from the sensor and communications to transmit the data to others in the network. Several organizations make use of the IoT in order to increase brand value and revenue, as well as to revamp the user's experience. IoT is used in several applications like home automation, healthcare, energy harvesting [3] and other industries [4].

With the use of several networking technologies IoT devices can communicate with other IoT devices in its network as well as run its services on cloud computing. Bluetooth technology is considered to be at the lower end of the stack of technologies on which the network is built. There are several protocols present in the IoT that are helpful in creating, managing and maintaining the network along with the data that is being transmitted across these networks.

The IoT has a three-tier architecture (Figure 4.1a), which consists of Application Layer, Network Layer and Perception Layer. The function of the Application Layer is that it is responsible for dispensing the application-specific services to the user(s). It is also accountable to describe the different applications in which the IoT can be utilized properly – such as smart health, smart city and smart homes and so forth. The second layer, namely the network layer, is helpful in connecting with and communicating to other networking devices, computers/servers and smart devices. It is also responsible for processing and transmitting the data collected from the various sensors in the devices. Perception layers, also considered as the physical layer, are made up of sensors that are helpful in collecting information regarding the environment. This layer is also helpful in identifying the other smart objects present in its environment.

Most of the researchers in the field of IoT are of the opinion that the three-layer architecture is insufficient, so they have proposed a five-layer architecture as seen in Figure 4.1b, which additionally has the business and processing layers. The processing layer is called as a middleware layer and is used to store, analyze and process the data sent from the transport layer. The transport layer is helpful in transferring the data from the sensor between the perception and processing layers.

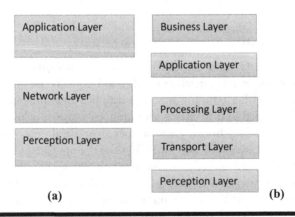

(a)   (b)

Figure 4.1   Three-Tier and Five-Layer IoT Architecture.

Source: Created by the author.

4.1.1 Security Issues in IoT

Even though IoT has several advantages like automation, proper resource utilization and accessibility, which simplifies the work of its user as it is constantly plagued with drawbacks, such as lack of international standards, complexity, dependence and security concerns [5–6]. Out of these, security [7] is a most-important concern in IoT. Some security issues that involve IoT are poor testing, outdated software, open-source code vulnerabilities, malware risk, weak passwords, lack of privacy and encryption [8]. In poor testing, the developers of IoT concentrate on the effectiveness of the devices and its ability to communicate, but the developers are not worried about identifying the weakness of IoT from a security point of view. Similar to that of other software in the computer, there is a need to ensure that the software that runs IoT devices are kept up to date to ensure that new vulnerabilities do not penetrate the system. A stark feature of the IoT system is its ability to work efficiently on open source software. But this feature is also an issue, since most of the open source software has unknown vulnerabilities [9] and bugs.

The attacker can make use of malware and gain access to the IoT devices and damage them. Prowli and Mira are some of the malwares that affect the performance of IoT devices. Cyberattacks [10] occur commonly in IoT due to weak passwords, outdated software and lack of encryption. Denial of service (DoS) attacks [11], spoofing, data theft and DNS poisoning are the most commonly occurring cyberattacks that concern the IoT system. A DoS attack is a type of cyber attack that ensures that a particular computing resource is unavailable to an authentic user at any given time.

A distributed denial of service (DDoS) is a powerful variant wherein the attacker, with the help of other infected computers (namely bots), attack the victim. In IoT, spoofing [12] attacks are a simple kind of cyberattack wherein the attacker acts as a legitimate user while stealing the authentic user's IP address or the MAC address. The legitimate user's credentials can be stolen by the attacker by sending some fake messages which are very hard to differentiate from normal messages. In Mid-2022, a DNS [13] poisoning attack was detected in an IoT which affected some millions of devices connected via the IoT. These attacks were due to uClibe and UClibc-ng, which were popular C libraries that had allowed attackers to perform DNS attacks on victim IoT devices. After successfully performing the attack, the perpetrators had full control of the IoT device and also had deceived the victim device to accept a forged response. So, from this example it is quite evident that there is a scope in research to pursue mechanisms that can be deployed to prevent unauthorized users any access to the IoT network.

4.1.2 Literature Survey

As mentioned previously, there are several security issues in IoT that need to be addressed. The best methods to address these issues is by using meta heuristics algorithms like Ant Colony Optimization (ACO) [14], Particle Swarm Optimization (PSO) [15], Grey Wolf Optimization (GWO) [16] and so forth. This section sheds light on the how researchers have devised different security mechanisms to thwart security issues in IoT as well as recent security issues that were prevented by using different metaheuristics algorithms [17–18].

The authors [19] presented security-aware modelling and verification techniques that can be used on Control Interpreted Petri Nets (CIPN)-based sequential control applications. They have also demonstrated how to transform CIPN-based models for a network industrial controller into Time PetriNet (TPN)-based models. Also, steps have been discussed to design a channel-specific attack model to capture the anomaly behavior with the help of non-determinism.

IoTGuard [20] is used in IoT as a policy-based enforcement system that is dynamic in nature. IoTGuard has three distinct phases. The first phase deals with code instrumentor implementation that can be used to add additional logic to the application's code used to collect its information during runtime. The second phase has a dynamic model that is used to store the app's information. The model is helpful in representing the app's runtime execution behavior. The final phase is used to identify the various safety and security policies along with its enforcement on the individual app's dynamic model. The main goal of this system is for protecting the user from insecure and unsafe device states that can be achieved by constantly monitoring the behavior of the IoT.

Wenbo Ding et.al [21] have proposed IoTSAFE, which can be used as enforcement systems for protecting the safety and security of the system. The IoTSAFE system is helpful in envisaging risky situations as well as to block any hazardous device states by generating the device's physical model. This system had been implemented on a SmartThings platform. The IoTSAFE system was found to be around 96 percent accurate and was able to prevent around 53 highly risky conditions for a given 36-user policies.

The authors [22] have proposed FELIDS (Federated Learning-based Intrusion Detection System) to thwart attacks on agriculture based IoT. This system makes use of three deep learning-based classifiers, namely CNN (Convolutional Neural Networks), RNN (Recurrent Neural Networks) and DNN (Deep Neural Networks). This system was proved to be effective in preserving privacy as well as providing higher accuracy levels in detecting attacks in IoT.

Peeves [23] was designed to automatically verify all the smart home events by considering the event's physical signature. These events can be detected with the help of various sensors that are already present in the smart home or can be purchased off the shelf. Various events like door, fridge and window can be spoofed in real time, but due to the fact that the detection rate of Peeves is high, the probability of the attack occurring is much diminished. The authors [24] have generated a DDoS dataset with the help of 33 types of scans and as many as 60 types of DDoS attacks. This is then followed by combining the generated dataset with three publicly available datasets just for maximizing the attack coverage as well as to train the machine learning (ML) algorithms. They have proposed a twofold ML approach to detect and prevent IoT-based botnet attacks.

Yuan Tian et al. [25] have proposed SmartAuth, which can be used to gather security-related information from an IoT app's description and code as well as to generate a user interface for authorization. This system can be used to dodge apps that are being over-privileged. M.J. Murillo [26] has proposed a novel approach that can be compared to the two-factor authentication used worldwide these days. This approach makes use of an operational authority that can provide a real time two-factor authorization for the requests made by the service provider on behalf of pervasive users.

RF-IoT [27] was proposed by the author to prevent various attacks in the IoT-based networking environment. RF-IoT has been designed as a security framework which provides a balancing act between security and network latency. This framework can be used in various applications, such as health and environment monitoring as well as in smart transportation. The authors [28] have proposed a framework that is used to transmit sensitive data, such as personal information and face identifier in fog and cloud. They also ensure that the CIA (confidentiality, integrity and availability) properties are well preserved by developing a data encryption scheme, authentication and key agreement schemes as well as to check the integrity. By this proposed framework the security of the system is increased but there is also a slight increase in the communication overhead.

ITACS (IP traceback Ant Colony System) [29] can be used to identify the source of the network attacks in specific DoS attacks. The main goal of this system is to pursue the attack path. This is achieved by taking the traffic flow and the time as metrics for consideration. The efficiency and effectiveness are calculated at each phase. The authors [30] have proposed an efficient ABC algorithm to improve the security as well as QoS aware scheduling in a cloud-based platform. Here the algorithm assigns a task to an optimal VM (virtual machine) depending on the QoS policy and the security levels of the user. For the purpose of balancing the load of the VM, reduce cost,and accommodate security and risk, a hive table is generated and maintained.

The authors [31] have made use of hybrid modified bPSO (Binary Particle Swarm Optimizer) and bGWO (Binary Gray Wolf Optimization) to make improvement in intrusion detection systems. To provide effective classification and attack detection in an IDS, there are different feature selection techniques. The proposed hybrid IDS technique makes use of benchmark datasets like UNSW-NB15 and NSL KDD'99. The system has been found to be effective in detection accuracy and reduction in false alarm rates. Patrizia Ribino et al. [32] have proposed a novel decentralized cyber security model for securing the data in the health-care sector. There are two types of agents, primary agents and supervisor agents. Primary agents are lightweight agents designed to monitor a certain space of the health-care system, whereas supervisor agents are used for protecting the whole health care system as a whole. This is achieved by cyber-security awareness and also by activating cooperative intelligence.

SFLA-QIM (Shuffled Frog Leaping Algorithm-Quantization Index Modulation) [33] is used for providing watermarking of images. SFLA is used to find out the right position to embed, and QIM is used as a fitness function, which is developed based on SNR (Signal to Noise Ratio). By using the proposed SFLA-QIM the authors were able to provide proof that there were able to prevent attacks like Noise addition, cropping, amplitude scaling etc..

4.2 Overview of the Proposed Work

This section conveys the proposed method for detecting the attack. The IoT-23 dataset is used in the proposed method, as the datasets are yardsticks for IoT traffic and possess 20 internments of malware in IoT devices. This dataset is a collection of 500 hours of network traffic and contains 760 million additional packets.

The dataset is preprocessed, and the feature extraction will be carried out using Recursive Feature Elimination. Once the data are extracted the proposed methodology is used for detecting the attacks. Figure 4.2 highlights the steps involved in the proposed work.

4.2.1 Data Preprocessing

The data preprocessing is an activity done after the input has been collected. It is the process of identifying and removing unwanted noise and eliminating the missing data from the dataset.

■ **Data Cleaning:** This is an approach to identifying incorrect and corrupt data from the datasets and also removing incorrect and corrupt data found within the dataset. The missing data are handled by dropping the observations.

■ **Normalization:** This is the pre-processing stage, where a new range is attained from the present range. It is quite evident that datasets will contain incomplete, irrelevant and missing data. These kinds of data have to be removed to enhance the quality. The min max algorithm will be used to do integration and normalization activity. The normalization approach is used for predicting the new range based on the forecasted and the predicted ranges. The normalization is the processes of scaling the data such that the values are normalized data and should fall between 0 and 1. The effects of variation can be eliminated by comparing with the values from more than two datasets.

■ **Data Transformation:** It is a technique to convert the raw dataset into a specific format that is used to retrieve the data in an efficient way. The raw data

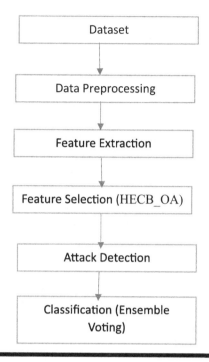

Figure 4.2   Block Diagram of the Proposed Work in Detecting the Attack.
Source: Created by the author.

has to be converted into suitable format before retrieving the data. The data transformation is vital to provide patterns by which it is easy to understand the strategy that is used in data conversion. Various transformation methods like smoothing, aggregation and generalization.

■ **Data Integration:** This is one of the preprocessing approaches that combines the data from different sources and gives the user a unique perspective on the data. Data are collected from databases or flat files. The data received from different sources is stored in a heterogeneous database that is used by the client in accessing the files.

4.2.2 *Recursive Feature Elimination*

Feature selection is an approach that selects the most relevant features from the dataset. When minimal number of features are present it makes the machine learning algorithm run more efficiently. If the input features are irrelevant it may mislead the machine-learning algorithm, resulting in worst predictive performance.

The Recursive Feature Elimination is a feature selection algorithm. It is a completely different machine-learning algorithm and is used in fundamentals of the method, and wrapped by Recursive Feature Elimination which is helpful in selecting the features. It is completely in contrast with filter-based selection as it selects the features based on whatever score is largest.

The RFE eliminates the weakest features from the dataset until the needed feature is obtained. It eradicates the collinearity and the dependencies found to be prevalent in the proposed method, and it keeps a specified number of features. After extraction of the feature it is not possible to determine the number of features that are valid or invalid. To determine the valid features a cross validation is used with RFE using a scoring method to identify which features have the best score. The RFE trains the entire system with an identified entire set of features to find the cause for least decrement that designates the reason for stopping.

4.2.3 Feature Selection

The meta-heuristic algorithm is used in the feature selection, which improves the rate of detecting the attacks. The unselected features identified and extracted using RFE is not used for classification of the attack. The meta-heuristic approach is used for selecting the appropriate features in the search space. The proposed work is created by hybridizing two bio-inspired meta-heuristic approaches.

4.2.4 Elephant Search Optimization

This algorithm [34] is used by mimicking the behavior of elephants when searching for food. There will be a clan of female elephants led by a male elephant. The matriarch leads the group towards the food source. The matriarch is responsible for finding the food source outside the group and the members do a local search that is nearer to the matriarch. The group is composed of female and baby elephants.

Some predefined assumptions must be considered based on the biological behavior of the elephants: (a) Every elephant has a visual range, which helps in identifying any other elephants that might threaten them when they are in search of food. The visibility of the elephant is calculated using Euclidean distance. The visibility range of the male elephant is higher than the female elephants present in the clan. The Euclidean distance is helpful is identifying threatening elephants during the search of food. (b) In case two elephant groups coming into visual contact with each other, the fitness value of the two male elephants is evaluated. Based on the calculated fitness, the male elephant with the lowest fitness value will leave the territory, and the male with the highest fitness value will take over the clan. The weakest elephant will abscond in random direction. (c) Every elephant in the group has a maximum life time. After the death of an elephant a newborn will proceed in assuming the gender of the dead elephant.

The matriarch is considered to be the eldest with the best fitness value, and carries forward the clan during the food search and in protecting the clan represented using equation 4.1.

$$MT_{best,clan} = \alpha.MT_{center,clan} \tag{4.1}$$

Where $MT_{best.clan}$ denotes the matriarch of the clan who has the best fitness value, and α is a parameter that controls the movement which ranges between 0 to 1 and to keep the matriarch in center of the clan using equation 4.2.

$$MT_{center,clan,d} = \frac{1}{n_{clan}} \sum_{i=1}^{n_{clan}} MT_{center,clan,d} \tag{4.2}$$

Where d is the dimension, in the total dimension Dn, n_{clan} highlights the total number of elephants in the clan. The center is the average of all the present solutions in the obtained in the clan.

The female elephants present in the clan always follow the rules levied by the matriarch. They carry out a local search to fetch add more details to the matriarch of the clan. The movement of the female elephants is given by equation 4.3.

$$FE_{new,clan,j} = FE_{clan,j} + \beta\left(FE_{best,clan} - FE_{clan,j}\right).r \tag{4.3}$$

Where $FE_{new,clan,j}$ is the new position of the female elephant j in clan and $FE_{clan,j}$ denotes the previous position of the elephant, $FE_{best,clan}$ is the best solution of the female elephant and r indicates the influence of the leader in determining the best solution and the value of r ranges between 0 to 1.

The male elephants are responsible for exploring the space during food search. The male elephants with the lowest fitness value are moved in random directions using equation 4.4. This will happen when two male elephants come within close visibility range and the elephant with best fitness value will take over the clan and defeated male will flee from the territory.

$$MT_{worst,clan} = MT_{min}\left(MT_{max} - MT_{min}\right). ran \tag{4.4}$$

Where MT_{max} & MT_{min} represent the lower and upper bounds of the solution and *ran* is the number that changes randomly between 0 and 1.

4.2.5 Chaotic Map Bat Optimization Algorithm

This algorithm is created based on the prey hunting behavior of bats [35] using echo location. In nature there are many categories of bats, which differ in size and weight. But all of them possess similar characteristics during navigation and hunting for prey. The bats when hunting emit higher ultrasonic waves and decrease their loudness when the prey is in close proximity.

The velocity vector of bats is updated using equation 4.5.

$$Vel_i(t+1) = Vel_i(t) + \left(X_i(t) - G_{best}\right)Freq_i \tag{4.5}$$

$$X_i(t+1) = X_i(t) + Vel(t+1) \tag{4.6}$$

The position vector is updated with respect to velocity of the bat over a period of time 't' which is obtained from equation 4.6 and G_{best} is the best solution obtained for the bat 'i'.

The frequency of the bat is determined with equation 4.7.

$$Freq_i = Freq_{min} + \left(Freq_{max} - Freq_{min}\right)\beta \tag{4.7}$$

Where β is a random number for uniform distribution and it value fall in range [0,1].

Equations 4.1–4.3 help in better exploration of the food source in the search space and the best solution can be obtained.

To perform better exploration a random walk has to be carried out to attain the global optima using equation 4.8. Thus, the bat starts to increase the loudness emitted and starts to perform exploration instead of performing the exploitation process.

$$X_n = X_o + \varepsilon \text{Å} \tag{4.8}$$

Where ε is the random number between 0 and 1 Å and tells about the loudness emitted by the bat.

The balancing of the equations is well-ordered by two factors, loudness ( ) and pulse rate (r) using equations 4.9 and 4.10.

$$\text{Å}_i(t+1) = \alpha \, \text{Å}_i(t) \tag{4.9}$$

$$r_i = (t+1) = r_i(0)\left[1 - \exp(-\gamma t)\right] \tag{4.10}$$

The constant α and γ are the cooling factors used in simulated annealing. The simulated annealing method is derived from the physical annealing process and works well in scenarios where there are numerous local optima that the algorithms may encounter. It is also employed to achieve global optima. The value of loudness and pulse rate are updated and improved over a period of time, which indicates the bats are obtaining the best solution with respect to predicting the prey.

In a traditional bat algorithm, the randomness can be replaced with a chaotic map because of its better properties (statistics and dynamic). The chaotic map replaces the random variables and it is called chaotic optimization. The chaotic maps can increase the iterative steps at higher speed when compared with standard probability distribution.

4.2.6 *Hybrid Elephant and Chaotic Bat Optimization Algorithm (HECB_OA)*

In this algorithm the populations are randomly initialized in the search space. The velocity vector and frequency associated with the Chaotic Bat algorithm is used in Elephant Algorithm Objective Function. The frequency and velocity of the elephants vary with respect to the distance of the prey. The rest of the elephant population is randomly divided into clans led by a matriarch. Every clan consists of female elephants and is led by a male elephant. During the food search the matriarch will lead the clan in search of food and is followed by the clan. The clan does a local search and matriarch does a global search in larger search space. The position of the food source is updated over a period of time by varying the velocity and frequency. The best position of the food source is obtained. When the matriarch comes in close contact with other male elephant within the same territory, the male elephants with best fitness value will lead the clan and the defeated elephant will flee in random direction.

4.2.7 *Ensemble Voting Classifier*

The voting classifier algorithm classifies the attacks present in the dataset. The voting classifier algorithm predicts the result based on the highest probability as the algorithm trains on numerous ensemble model. This model works based on the prediction of other models. It aggregates the findings of classifiers like Random Forest and Decision Tree algorithm and predicts based on the highest voting. The advantage of this classifier is despite creating separate models and finding the accuracy better to create a single accuracy. There are two types of voting (a) Hard Voting and (b) Soft Voting

4.2.7.1 Hard voting

In hard voting the output is based on the highest vote that is been obtained from other classifiers. Let's consider two: Random Forest classifier and Decision Tree algorithm. If the random forest algorithm is the highest then random forest output will be the final prediction.

Weighted majority vote can be computed using equation 4.11.

$$y = \arg max_i = \sum_{n=1}^{m} w_n x_a \left(C_n(x) = i \right) \tag{4.11}$$

x_a is the characteristics function and $C_n(x) = i \in A$, where A is class labels

4.2.7.2 Soft voting

In this type the output is based on the average of probabilities given to the class. The average of random form is computed and the average of decision tree is computed, and the highest average is the final output obtained.

The class labels are predicted based on the probabilities p, and w_j is the weight assigned to the jth classifier using equation 4.12.

$$y = \arg max_i \sum_{j=1}^{m} w_j P_{ij} \tag{4.12}$$

4.3 Experimental Results

The proposed HECB_OA is carried out against the IoT 23 dataset [36–37] and analyzed using the benchmarks identified during the literature, and it is evaluated against the performance metrics. The metrics such as Recall, Precision, Bandwidth, Life time of devices, Drop Rate and Detection Rate have been used for evaluating the proposed work. From the results it is inferred that the proposed work HECB_OA is found to have par excelled when compared with the benchmarks identified.

The Figure 4.3 highlights the proposed work HECB_OA in detecting the attack that is present in the dataset as a result of IoT devices used in the communication. It is evident from the results that the proposed has far excelled in detecting the attack when compared with the existing methods SFLA, ITACS and BPSO_BGWO. The detection rate is an important parameter in the IoT. The HECB_OA has a better detection rate when compared to SFLA, ITACS and BPSO_BGWO by 14 percent, 12 percent and 6 percent.

Figure 4.4 depicts the drop rate when an attack occurs and gives the insight of the proposed word when number of attacks increases. During communication the

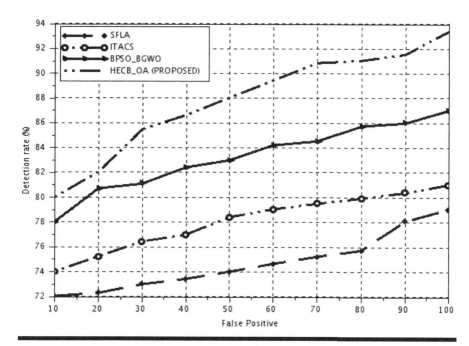

Figure 4.3   False Positive against Detection Rate.

Source: Created by the author.

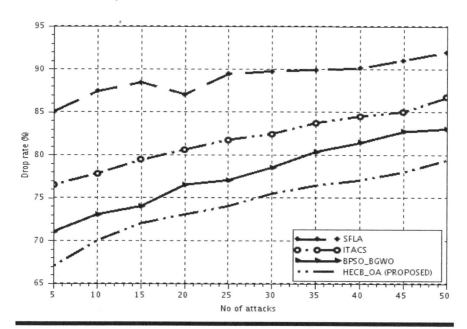

Figure 4.4   Drop Rate versus No. of Attacks.

Source: Created by the author.

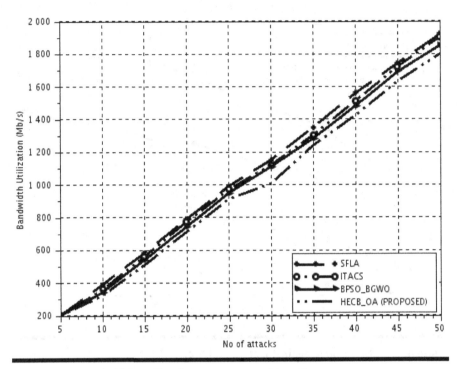

Figure 4.5   Bandwidth Utilization versus No. of Attacks.

Source: Created by the author.

packet drop is quite common in IoT devices, and when more packet drop happens it will hard to reconstruct the messages that is been sent from the IoT devices. The graph highlights the drop rate is found to minimum for HECB_OA when compared to other existing works SFLA, ITACS and BPSO_BGWO by 13 percent, 7 percent and 3 percent.

Figure 4.5 highlights the bandwidth utilization and has been used effectively by the proposed work when compared with other benchmarks that are identified. The bandwidth is being depleted by the attacker nodes, and it decreases the life time of the IoT devices. The graph portrays effective utilization of bandwidth despite the presence of attacks. The proposed HECB_OA is found to have utilized minimal bandwidth when compared to existing works SFLA, ITACS and BPSO_BGWO by 120 mb/s, 100 mb/s and 35 mb/s at an average.

Figure 4.6 highlights the overall life time of the IoT devices in the presence of attacks. The life time of the IoT is important for communication. The life time may be depleted when attacks happen in the network, as many attacks target draining the energy level of the nodes. The proposed work HECB_OA has an improved life time even in the presence of attacks when compared to SFLA, ITACS and BPSO_BGWO by 270 mAh, 220 mAh, 80 mAh at an average.

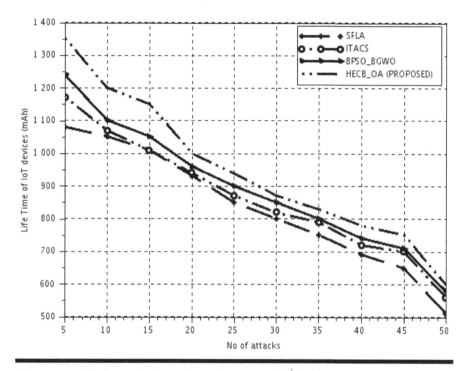

Figure 4.6   Lifetime of IoT Devices versus No. of Attacks.
Source: Created by the author.

The Figure 4.7 highlights the dominance of the proposed work on Precision as conveys about true positive in detecting the occurred attack that had happened in the IoT devices. Precision tell about overall number of predicted positives by overall predicted positives. The proposed work HECB_OA has better performance when compared to SFLA, ITACS and BPSO_BGWO by 17 percent, 15 percent and 12 percent.

4.4 Conclusion

The Internet of Things (IoT) consists of several physical entities: humans, devices and sensors. And IoT is used in different domains, including medical, agricultural and traffic-monitoring systems. In the last decade there has been a substantial rise in the use of the IoT Network because of several advantages in the above-mentioned domains. But there have been some concerns regarding the robustness of the IoT Network, hence we have proposed a novel meta-heuristics algorithm, namely HECB_OA, which makes use of Elephant Search Optimization and Chaotic Map

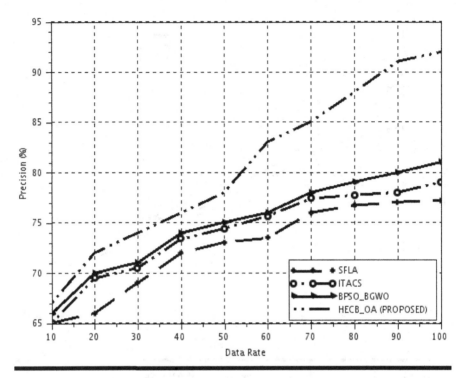

Figure 4.7 Precision versus Data rate.

Source: Created by the author.

Bat Optimization algorithm. The proposed algorithm HECB_OA is compared with several existing benchmark techniques like SFLA, ITACS and BPSO_BGWO inorder to test the efficiency of the proposed system with metrics like False Positive, Drop Rate, Bandwidth utilization etc. In drop rate, the proposed system is found to be 13 percent, 7 percent and 3 percent better when compared with SFLA, ITACS and BPSO_BGWO respectively. In the future, different types of meta heuristics algorithms can be incorporated to increase the efficiency of our system.

References

[1] Baskoro Azis et.al, "IoT human needs inside compact house," *Journal of Open Innovation: Technology, Market, and Complexity*, Vol. 9, no. 1, p. 100003, Mar. 2023

[2] Vipul Moudgil, Kasun Hewage, Syed Asad Hussain and Rehan Sadiq, "Integration of IoT in building energy infrastructure: A critical review on challenges and solutions," *Renewable and Sustainable Energy Reviews*, Vol. 174, p. 113121, Mar. 2023.

[3] Sherali Zeadally, Faisal Karim Shaikh, Anum Talpur and Quan Z. Sheng, "Design architectures for energy harvesting in the Internet of Things," *Renewable and Sustainable Energy Reviews*, Vol. 128, Aug. 2020.

[4] Adam Trendowicz et.al, "User experience key performance indicators for industrial IoT systems: A multivocal literature review," *Digital Business*, Vol. 3, no. 1, June 2023.

[5] M. Vijayakumar and T. S. Shiny Angel, "A survey on IoT Security: Security threads and analysis of botnet attacks over IoT and avoidance," *Lecture Notes in Networks and Systems*, Vol. 370, pp. 141–154, May 2022.

[6] H. Pillutla and A. Arjunan, "A Survey of security concerns, mechanisms and testing in cloud environment," *2018 Second International Conference on Electronics, Communication and Aerospace Technology (ICECA)*, pp. 1519–1524, Sept. 2018.

[7] Apostolos Gerodimos, Leandros Maglaras, Mohamed Amine Ferrag, Nick Ayres and Ioanna Kantzavelou, "IoT: Communication protocols and security threats," *Internet of Things and Cyber-Physical Systems*, Vol. 3, 2023.

[8] Padmalaya Nayak and G. Swapna, "Security issues in IoT applications using certificateless aggregate signcryption schemes: An overview," *Internet of Things*, Vol. 21, Apr. 2023.

[9] Jesús E. Díaz-Verdejo, Rafael Estepa Alonso, Antonio Estepa Alonso and German Madinabeitia, "A critical review of the techniques used for anomaly detection of HTTP-based attacks: Taxonomy, limitations and open challenges," *Computers & Security*, Vol. 124, Jan. 2023.

[10] Yusuf Alaca and Yüksel Çelik, "Cyber attack detection with QR code images using lightweight deep learning models," *Computers & Security*, Vol. 126, Mar. 2023.

[11] Pillutla Harikrishna and A. Amuthan, "Rival-model penalized self-organizing map enforced DDoS attack prevention mechanism for software defined network-based cloud computing environment," *Journal of Parallel and Distributed Computing*, Vol. 154, pp. 142–152, Aug. 2021.

[12] Haixia Wang et.al., "Anti-spoofing study on palm biometric features," *Expert Systems with Applications*, Vol. 218, May 2023.

[13] Chris Marrison, "Understanding the threats to DNS and how to secure it," *Network Security*, Vol. 2015, no. 10, pp. 8–10, Oct. 2015.

[14] N.K. Sreeja, "A hierarchical heterogeneous ant colony optimization based fingerprint recognition system," *Intelligent Systems with Applications*, Vol. 17, Feb. 2023.

[15] A. Amuthan and R. Kaviarasan,"Weighted inertia-based dynamic virtual bat algorithm to detect NLOS nodes for reliable data dissemination in VANETs," *Journal of Ambient Intelligence and Humanized Computing*, Vol. 10, no. 11, Nov. 2018.

[16] Jesus Aguila-Leon et.al., "Solar photovoltaic maximum power point tracking controller optimization using Grey Wolf optimizer: A performance comparison between bio-inspired and traditional algorithms," *Expert Systems with Applications*, Vol. 211, Jan. 2023.

[17] Absalom E. Ezugwu et.al., "Metaheuristics: A comprehensive overview and classification along with bibliometric analysis," *Artificial Intelligence Review*, Vol. 54, pp. 4237–4316, Mar. 2021.

[18] Zhongqiang Ma et.al., "Performance assessment and exhaustive listing of 500+ nature-inspired metaheuristic algorithms," *Swarm and Evolutionary Computation*, Vol. 77, Mar. 2023.

[19] Vuk Lesi, Zivana Jakovljevic and Miroslav Pajic, "Security analysis for distributed IoT-based industrial automation," *IEEE Transactions on Automation Science and Engineering*, Vol. 19, no. 4, pp. 3093–3108, Oct. 2022.

[20] Z. Berkay Celik, Gang Tan and Patrick McDaniel, "IOTGUARD: Dynamic enforcement of security and safety policy in commodity IoT," *Proceedings 2019 Network and Distributed System Security Symposium*, Feb. 2019.

[21] Wenbo Ding, Hongxin Hu and Long Cheng, "IOTSAFE: Enforcing safety and security policy with real IoT physical interaction discovery," *Network and Distributed System Security Symposium*, Feb. 2021.

[22] Othmane Friha et.al., "FELIDS: Federated learning-based intrusion detection system for agricultural Internet of Things," *Journal of Parallel and Distributed Computing*, Vol. 165, pp. 17–31, Jul. 2022.

[23] Simon Birnbach, Simon Eberz and Ivan Martinovic, "Peeves: Physical event verification in smart homes," *ACM SIGSAC Conference on Computer and Communications Security*, Nov. 2019.

[24] F. Hussain et al., "A two-fold machine learning approach to prevent and detect IoT Botnet attacks," *IEEE Access*, Vol. 9, pp. 163412–163430, Nov. 2021.

[25] Yuan Tian et.al., "SmartAuth: User-centered authorization for the Internet of Things," *26th USENIX Security Symposium*, Aug. 2017.

[26] M. J. Murillo, "A two-factor authorization approach for increasing the resiliency of IoT-based autonomous consumer-oriented systems," *IEEE Internet of Things Journal*, Vol. 5, no. 5, pp. 4132–4141, Oct. 2018.

[27] G. N. Anil, "RF-IoT: A robust framework to optimize Internet of Things (IoT) security performance," *Software Engineering Methods in Intelligent Algorithms*, May 2019.

[28] Pengfei Hu et.al., "Security and privacy preservation scheme of face identification and resolution framework using fog computing in Internet of Things," *IEEE Internet of Things*, Vol. 4, no. 5, Oct. 2017.

[29] H. -H. Chen and W. Yang, "The design and implementation of a practical Meta-Heuristic for the detection and identification of denial-of-service attack using hybrid approach," *2010 Second International Conference on Machine Learning and Computing*, May 2010.

[30] M. Roshni Thanka, P. Uma Maheswari and E. Bijolin Edwin, "An improved efficient: Artificial Bee Colony algorithm for security and QoS aware scheduling in cloud computing environment," *Cluster Computing*, Vol. 22, no. S5, pp. 10905–10913, Oct. 2017.

[31] Qusay M. Alzubi et. al, "Intrusion detection system based on hybridizing a modified binary grey wolf optimization and particle swarm optimization," *Expert Systems with Applications*, Vol. 204, Oct. 2022.

[32] Patrizia Ribino, Mario Ciampi, Shareeful Islam and Spyridon Papastergiou, "Swarm intelligence model for securing healthcare ecosystem," *Procedia Computer Science*, Vol. 210, pp. 149–156, Nov. 2022.

[33] Xia Li,Lingjun Liu,Na Wang and Jeng-Shyang Pan, "A new Robust Watermarhing scheme based on shuffled frog leaping algorithm," *Intelligent Automation & Soft Computing*, Vol. 17, 2011, no. 2, Mar. 2013.

[34] Mrutyunjaya Panda, "Elephant search optimization combined with deep neural network for microarray data analysis," *Journal of King Saud University–Computer and Information Sciences*, Vol. 32, no. 8, pp. 940–948, Oct. 2020.

[35] H. Liang, Y. Liu, Y. Shen and F. Li, "A multiobjective chaotic bat algorithm for economic and emission dispatch," *2017 Chinese Automation Congress (CAC)*, pp. 4684–4689, IEEE. Oct. 2017.

[36] F. Jeelani, D. S. Rai, A. Maithani and S. Gupta, "The Detection of IoT Botnet using machine learning on IoT-23 dataset," *2nd International Conference on Innovative Practices in Technology and Management (ICIPTM)*, Vol. 2, pp. 634–639, Apr. 2022.

[37] Sebastian Garcia, Agustin Parmisano and Maria Jose Erquiaga. (2020). IoT-23: A labeled dataset with malicious and benign IoT network traffic (Version 1.0.0) [data set]. Stratosphere Lab., Praha, Czech Republic, Tech. Rep (2020).

Chapter 5

Security of IoT and Its Solutions

Pallavi[1] and Sandeep Joshi[2]

[1]Department of Computer Science and Engineering,
Manipal University Jaipur, Jaipur

[2]Department of Computer Science and Engineering,
Manipal University Jaipur, Jaipur

5.1 Introduction

The Internet of Things (IoT) is conceptualized as a network that is both linked and dispersed, comprised of embedded systems that communicate with one another via either wired or wireless communication methods. It is also defined as the network of physical objects or things that are empowered with limited computation, storage, and communication capabilities. These objects are also embedded with electronics (such as sensors and actuators), software, and network connectivity that enables these objects to collect data, sometimes process the data, and exchange data with other objects. The rate at which physical devices in our immediate environment are being connected to the Internet is picking up speed. A recent report by Gartner estimates that there will be approximately 8.4 billion connected things across the globe in the year 2020. It is anticipated that by the year 2022, this number will have increased to 20.4 billion. The use of IoT applications is increasing in all parts of the world. The major driving countries in this include Western Europe, North America, and China. The fast expansion of the Internet of Things has been beneficial to enterprises and has boosted market research and commercial strategy in a variety of ways. In a similar vein, with the introduction of automated services the

DOI: 10.1201/9781003474838-5

Internet of Things has enhanced the quality of life of individuals. On the other hand, such an uncontrolled explosion presents greater difficulties regarding privacy and security. The architecture of the IoT is depicted in its past, present, and future states in Figure 5.1. In the not-too-distant future, it is anticipated that the gadgets will not only be connected to the Internet and other local devices, but they will also be able to directly interact with other devices that are connected to the Internet. In addition to the devices and objects that are being linked, a new notion known as the Social Internet of Things (SIoT) is coming into existence. SIoT will make it possible for users of various social networking platforms to connect to the devices, after which those users would be able to share the gadgets via the Internet. The issue of security and privacy is brought up by the extensive range of applications for the Internet of Things. Emerging IoT apps are unable to meet the high demand and risk losing all of their potential if an ecosystem for the internet of things is not reliable and interoperable. In addition to the basic security concerns that are experienced by the Internet, cellular networks, and WSNs, the IoT also has its unique security obstacles. Some of these challenges include problems with authentication, administration, information storage, and privacy.

The Internet of Things has become an integral part of our daily lives, and it continues to expand rapidly. IoT refers to a network of physical devices, vehicles, home appliances, and other items embedded with sensors, software, and connectivity that allow them to collect and exchange data. The security of IoT is a growing concern, as the devices are vulnerable to cyber-attacks that could compromise user data, privacy, and safety. This chapter will discuss the security challenges of IoT and the solutions to mitigate them.

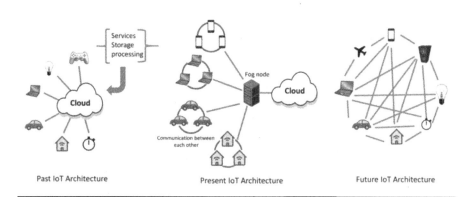

Figure 5.1   Present and Future Architecture of IoT.
Source: Google Images.

5.2 IoT Security-Critical Application Zones

The Internet of Things (IoT) has fundamentally altered the way in which we engage with technology, which has opened the door to a wealth of new opportunities and prospects for individuals as well as for enterprises. Yet, this broad use of Internet of Things devices has also brought forth a new set of security challenges and hazards. In this chapter, we will discuss the security-critical application areas of the Internet of Things, as well as the possible risks and problems that are connected with each of these application areas.

■ Healthcare

Internet of Things devices for healthcare are increasingly being utilised to monitor patients' vital signs, track patients' adherence to medicine, and enhance patient outcomes. Yet, the use of these gadgets also results in the introduction of brand new security dangers. For instance, if Internet of Things medical equipment were to be hacked, it may result in a patient receiving the incorrect dosage of medication or being monitored in an inappropriate manner. Hackers may also acquire access to sensitive patient data such as medical records and then exploit that data for malicious reasons if they got their hands on them.

■ Smart Houses

In recent years, there has been a rise in demand for intelligent household devices such as smart door locks, smart thermostats, and smart security cameras. Yet, new concerns regarding safety and protection are raised by these technologies. For instance, if a smart lock were to be hacked, it may enable a burglar to enter a residence that had been protected by the lock. In addition, the equipment in a smart house may be used to spy on the people, which would raise worries about their privacy.

■ Control Systems for Industrial Establishments

The management of essential infrastructure, such as electricity grids, water treatment facilities, and transportation networks is carried out with the assistance of industrial control systems (ICS). The integration of IoT devices into ICS systems introduces additional potential vulnerabilities. For instance, if a hacker were to obtain access to an IoT device that was being used to operate a power system, they could possibly create major power outages and put people in danger. In addition, the devices that make up ICS might be susceptible to cyberattacks, which would raise issues over the integrity of critical infrastructure.

■ Transportation

The application of devices connected to the Internet of Things in the transportation sector has the potential to enhance both safety and efficiency. For instance, IoT sensors might be used to monitor the operation of vehicles and determine which ones require maintenance before the problem becomes urgent. Yet, the usage of Internet of Things devices in transportation creates additional vulnerabilities in terms of safety. If a hacker were to obtain access to an Internet of Things device that was being used to drive a vehicle, for instance, this might possibly cause the vehicle to crash or create another safety concern.

■ **Challenges and Mitigation Measures**

The security-sensitive application domains of the Internet of Things provide a one-of-a-kind set of difficulties that need to be tackled in order to protect the safety and security of humans as well as vital infrastructure. Among these difficulties are the following:

- The difficulty of implementing IoT systems: Because of their potentially high level of complexity, Internet of Things systems can make it challenging to locate and fix security flaws.
- The lack of standardisation that exists in IoT devices can make it challenging to deploy security measures in a manner that is consistent across a variety of devices.
- Because of their limited processing power and memory, many of the devices that make up the IoT provide a challenge when it comes to the implementation of robust security measures.

Many other preventative measures, can be taken into effect in order to solve these challenges, such as the following:

- Usage of robust encryption and authentication: In order to safeguard data both while it is in transit and while it is at rest, IoT devices should be encrypted. In addition, in order to stop unwanted access to IoT devices, robust authentication procedures, such as two-factor authentication, should be utilised.
- Updating and patching on a regular basis: In order to address any security flaws, Internet of Things devices should be frequently updated with the most recent security patches and firmware upgrades. Application of security best practises The design and implementation of IoT devices should take into account security best practises such as least privilege and defence in depth. The security-sensitive application areas of the Internet of Things create new difficulties and hazards that need to be addressed in order to protect the safety and security of persons as well as vital infrastructure. It is possible to lessen the impact of these dangers and make full use of the Internet of Things' potential advantages by putting in place stringent safety precautions and industry standards.

5.3 Vulnerability Sources in IoT Applications

The Internet of Things is an industry that is expanding at a breakneck pace and that comprises a wide variety of linked applications and devices. Yet, as the number of devices and apps connected to the IoT continues to grow, so too do the security risks associated with them. In this chapter, we will talk about the many different places where security vulnerabilities may be found in IoT applications.

Risks to Information Technology Presented by Internet of Things Applications5

5.3.1 Adware, Spyware, and Other Viruses

Malware and viruses are one of the Internet of Things' most prevalent and widespread security risks. One definition of malware is "malicious software" with the intent to cause disruption or harm to computer systems, networks, or other devices. Viruses are a special kind of malware that may replicate themselves and spread to other programmes and files on a system by attaching themselves to other programmes and files. Downloads that are malicious, unprotected networks, or devices that have been infiltrated are all potential entry points for malware and viruses into Internet of Things applications. Figure 5.2 below shows the layers in IoT:

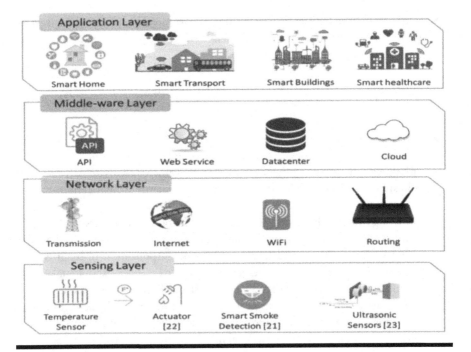

Figure 5.2   Layers in IoT System.

Source: Google Images.

5.3.2 Insufficient Efforts Made for Authentication and Authorization

Authentication and permission are essential elements of security for the internet of things. Poor authentication and authorization methods can result in illegal access to Internet of Things devices and apps. This is something that attackers can take advantage of to get access to sensitive information or control over devices. Common causes of inadequate authentication and authorization in Internet of Things applications include passwords that are easy to guess, authentication mechanisms that have become obsolete, and communication routes that are not secure.

5.3.3 Interference with the Body

Because Internet of Things devices are frequently installed in accessible public areas or other locations, they are susceptible to being physically tampered with. To acquire illegal access to or control over Internet of Things devices, it may be necessary to physically manipulate or damage those devices. This is an example of physical tampering. Physical tampering is another method that might be used by attackers to put malware or spyware on Internet of Things devices.

5.3.4 Communication Routes that Are Not Protected

Communication channels allow devices connected to the Internet of Things to exchange information with one another and with centralised servers. Attackers have the capability of intercepting these communication channels in order to steal sensitive information or obtain unauthorised access to Internet of Things devices or apps. Unprotected communication channels are frequently the result of insufficient encryption or the use of unprotected network protocols.

5.3.5 Insecure Data Storage

Oftentimes, apps for the IoT will store sensitive information such as personal details, financial details, and authentication credentials. Attackers have the potential to steal or otherwise take advantage of this information if it is not stored in a secure manner. Inadequate encryption, outmoded security standards, or the use of unprotected storage devices can all contribute to the storing of data in an insecure manner.

5.3.6 IoT Device Vulnerabilities

Threats to data security may also be posed by the gadgets that make up the internet of things. It's possible that manufacturers don't properly protect IoT devices, which leaves them vulnerable to exploitation by malicious actors. Unpatched software, obsolete firmware, and default passwords are examples of common vulnerabilities in Internet of Things devices.

5.4 Security Challenges of IoT

Lack of Standardization: IoT devices are produced by a wide variety of vendors and may be distinguished from one another by their usage of distinct operating systems, communication protocols, and security functions. As a result of this variability, the development and implementation of common security measures across all devices is a tough task. IoT devices are manufactured by different vendors with different security protocols, making it difficult to create universal security standards for IoT. As a result, many IoT devices are not designed with security in mind, making them vulnerable to attacks.

Inadequate Authentication: A significant number of IoT devices lack robust authentication protocols, making it impossible to authenticate the user or device's identity. Because of the system's lack of strength, it is simple for malicious actors to assume the identity of authorized users or devices and get access to the network.

Vulnerability to Attacks: IoT devices are susceptible to various types of cyber-attacks, such as denial-of-service (DoS) attacks, malware attacks, and man-in-the-middle attacks. Attackers can exploit vulnerabilities in the devices' software or hardware to gain unauthorized access to the system.

Lack of Encryption: Many IoT devices do not encrypt the data they transmit, making it vulnerable to interception and eavesdropping. This lack of encryption can compromise user privacy and data security. Encryption is essential to secure data transmitted between IoT devices. However, many IoT devices use weak encryption algorithms or do not encrypt data at all, making them easy targets for hackers.

Inadequate Firmware and Software Updates: IoT devices often lack a reliable way to update firmware and software, which means that vulnerabilities discovered after the device is manufactured may never be addressed. As a result, attackers can exploit these vulnerabilities to gain unauthorized access to IoT devices.

Data Privacy: With the sheer amount of data generated by IoT devices, it is crucial to ensure that this data is collected, stored, and used in a way that respects users' privacy. However, many IoT devices are designed to collect and transmit data by default, without user consent or knowledge. This data can include personal information such as location, health, and even biometric data.

IoT Privacy Challenges: Lack of User Control: IoT devices often operate without user interaction, which means that users may not be aware of the data that is being collected or transmitted. This lack of control can make it difficult for users to understand the privacy implications of using IoT devices.

Cross-Device Tracking: With IoT devices being interconnected, attackers can track users across multiple devices, creating a comprehensive profile of their habits and behavior. This information can be used to launch targeted attacks or to sell user data to third parties.

Third-Party Data Sharing: Many IoT devices collect and transmit data to third-party companies, such as advertisers, without user consent or knowledge. This sharing of data can result in sensitive information being leaked to unauthorized parties, resulting in identity theft or financial fraud.

Legal Challenges: As IoT continues to evolve, there are few legal frameworks in place to regulate IoT devices' privacy and security. This creates uncertainty for users and manufacturers alike, making it difficult to determine who is responsible for protecting users' privacy.

5.5 Solutions for IoT Security

Standardization: IoT security can be improved through standardization. This involves developing and implementing standard security measures across all devices. Standardization can make it easier for manufacturers to build secure devices, and for users to manage and secure their devices. Standardization of security protocols and frameworks can help ensure that IoT devices are designed with security in mind. This can include the development of universal security standards for IoT devices and the implementation of regulations that require manufacturers to meet these standards.

Strong Authentication: Strong authentication mechanisms, such as multi-factor authentication and biometric authentication, can help verify the identity of users and devices. This can prevent unauthorized access to the system and improve data security.

Regular Software Updates: Regular software updates can help fix vulnerabilities and improve security. Manufacturers should provide timely and regular updates to their devices to ensure that they are secure.

Encryption: IoT devices should use encryption to protect data transmission. Strong encryption mechanisms, such as Advanced Encryption Standard (AES), can ensure that data is transmitted securely and is not vulnerable to interception. IoT devices must use strong encryption algorithms to secure data transmitted between devices. Additionally, all sensitive data must be encrypted both in transit and at rest.

Network Segmentation: Network segmentation involves dividing a network into smaller subnetworks. This can help isolate IoT devices from other devices on the network, reducing the attack surface for attackers.

5.6 Conclusion

IoT devices have become an integral part of our daily lives, but their security is a growing concern. IoT devices are vulnerable to various types of cyber-attacks, and their heterogeneity makes it challenging to implement standard security measures. To improve IoT security, manufacturers should develop and implement standard security measures, provide regular software updates, use strong authentication mechanisms, encrypt data transmission, and segment networks. These solutions can help mitigate the security challenges of IoT and ensure that users' data and privacy are protected. The security and privacy challenges facing IoT are significant and require careful consideration from manufacturers, policymakers, and users. As IoT continues to evolve, it is important to prioritize security and privacy to ensure that the potential benefits of this technology can be realized without compromising users' safety and privacy. By working together, we can create a more secure and private IoT ecosystem that benefits everyone. IoT has revolutionized the way we live and work, but security concerns must be addressed to ensure the safety and privacy of users. Standardization, encryption, password management, updatability, and physical security are essential components of a comprehensive IoT security strategy. By implementing these measures, manufacturers can create IoT devices that are secure and reliable, enabling users to reap the benefits of IoT technology without compromising their security.

IoT applications offer many benefits, but they also come with significant security risks. Understanding the sources of security threats in IoT applications is essential for developers, manufacturers, and end-users to protect themselves against attacks. By implementing best practices for security, such as strong authentication and authorization, secure communication channels, and secure data storage, IoT applications can be made more resilient against security threats.

Chapter 6

A Gradational Approach for Auditing IoT Security Vulnerability: Case Study of Smart Home Devices

Manikandan Rajagopal[1] and Ramkumar S.[2]

[1]Lean Operations and Systems, School of Business and Management, CHRIST (Deemed to be University), Bangalore, Karnataka, India

[2]Department of Computer Science, School of Sciences, CHRIST (Deemed to be University), Bangalore, Karnataka, India

6.1 Introduction

The Internet of Things (IoT) is a rapidly growing technology that has transformed the way we live our lives. IoT has made our homes smarter, our cars more connected, and our businesses more efficient. With the growing number of IoT devices in use, the need for IoT security has become more important than ever before[1]. The security of IoT devices is vital because these devices have the potential to be hacked, which could lead to serious consequences, such as loss of privacy and identity theft. Therefore, it is essential to conduct an IoT security audit to ensure that the IoT devices are secure and safe to use. IoT is a complex network comprising of various devices and sensors for information exchange. IoT devices can be controlled remotely, and they can be accessed through the Internet. The most common IoT devices include smart thermostats, smart lights, smart locks, smart cameras, smart TVs, and wearable devices.

DOI: 10.1201/9781003474838-6

The Internet of Things has become a pervasive technology that is transforming the way we live and work. IoT devices are becoming increasingly common in homes, businesses, and cities, and are being used for a wide range of purposes, from smart homes and wearables to industrial automation and smart cities[2]. While IoT has the potential to bring many benefits, including improved efficiency, reduced costs, and enhanced convenience, it also poses significant security risks. These risks can have serious consequences, ranging from privacy violations to physical harm. Given the risks posed by IoT devices, it is essential to conduct regular audits of these systems [3–4]. An IoT audit is a systematic review of the security and privacy of IoT devices, networks, and applications. The audit is conducted to identify potential security vulnerabilities and to recommend measures to address these vulnerabilities.

As IoT devices are becoming more popular, the need for IoT security has also increased. The security of IoT devices is crucial because they are vulnerable to attacks from hackers. An IoT security audit is necessary to ensure that the devices are secure and safe to use. The audit helps to identify vulnerabilities in the devices, such as weak passwords, outdated firmware, and unencrypted data transmission. The audit also helps to identify potential threats to the devices, such as malware, viruses, and cyber attacks.

There are several reasons why an IoT audit is essential. First and foremost, IoT devices are inherently vulnerable to cyber-attacks. These devices are often connected to the Internet, which makes them susceptible to hacking and other forms of cyber-crime[5]. This vulnerability is compounded by the fact that many IoT devices lack basic security features, such as password protection and encryption. In addition, many IoT devices are built on outdated or insecure software platforms, which can make them vulnerable to attacks.

Second, IoT devices are often used to collect and store sensitive data. This data can include personal information, such as names, addresses, and social security numbers, as well as financial and medical data. If this data falls into the wrong hands, it can be used for identity theft, fraud, and other malicious purposes. An IoT audit can help identify potential data breaches and recommend measures to prevent them.

Third, IoT devices are often used in critical infrastructure, such as power grids, transportation systems, and healthcare facilities. A security breach in these systems can have serious consequences, ranging from financial losses to physical harm. An IoT audit can help identify potential vulnerabilities in these systems and recommend measures to address them.

Fourth, IoT devices are often used in complex ecosystems that involve multiple vendors and technologies. This complexity can make it difficult to ensure the security of these systems. An IoT audit can help identify potential weaknesses in these ecosystems and recommend measures to address them.

Hence, an IoT audit is essential for several reasons. It can help identify potential security vulnerabilities, recommend measures to address these vulnerabilities, prevent data breaches, ensure the security of critical infrastructure, and address the complexities of IoT ecosystems.

There are several steps involved in an IoT security audit. These steps include:

1. Identify IoT Devices: The first step in an IoT security audit is to identify all the IoT devices that are connected to the network. This includes both hardware and software devices.
2. Map IoT Devices: The next step is to map the IoT devices on the network. This helps to identify the location of each device and how it is connected to the network.
3. Assess Device Security: The third step is to assess the security of each IoT device. This involves checking the firmware, passwords, and encryption protocols used by each device.
4. Check Network Security: The fourth step is to check the security of the network. This involves checking the firewalls, routers, and other network devices for any vulnerabilities.
5. Test Security: The fifth step is to test the security of the IoT devices and the network. This involves using penetration testing tools to simulate an attack and identify any weaknesses in the security.

Implement Security Measures: The final step is to implement security measures to address any vulnerabilities identified in the audit. This includes updating firmware, changing passwords, and implementing encryption protocols. IoT has transformed the way we live our lives, and it has become an integral part of our daily routines. However, the security of IoT devices is crucial because they are vulnerable to attacks from hackers. Therefore, it is essential to conduct an IoT security audit to ensure that the devices are secure and safe to use. The audit helps to identify vulnerabilities in the devices and potential threats to the network. By implementing security measures to address these vulnerabilities, we can ensure that our IoT devices are safe and secure. This chapter a framework for IoT security audit is proposed. The guidelines provided in standards across the globe were taken as the base for IoT auditing. The efficiency of the proposed model is also tested using experiments for its scalability and timeliness and found to be effective.

6.2 IoT Security Standards

The increasing adoption of IoT technologies in various sectors such as healthcare, transportation, and industrial control systems has raised serious concerns about security and privacy risks. To address these issues, several organizations have developed security standards for IoT devices and systems. In this section, a comparative analysis of the most popular Internet of Things security standards and frameworks is presented. IoT devices have become ubiquitous in modern society, with everything from cars to refrigerators now connected to the Internet. However, this increased connectivity has also brought about new security challenges. In order to address these challenges, various IoT security standards have been developed. In this chapter, we will explore some of the different IoT security standards that have been established.

The first-ever standard proposed for IoT security is ISO 27001 [6]. Here, a framework is recommended for sensitive information protection and information availability from the sensors. The standard gives a set of robust controls and good practices to ensure the U.S. Central Intelligence Agency (CIA) that the information is accurate. Further, guidelines on risk identification, assessment and mitigation are also provided for better security management of IoT devices.

Another important IoT security standard is the IEC 62443 series [7]. This series of standards focuses specifically on industrial control systems (ICS), which are commonly used in manufacturing and other critical infrastructure applications. The IEC 62443 series provides a framework for securing ICS networks and devices, including requirements for network segmentation, access control, and threat detection.

The NIST Cybersecurity Framework is another important IoT security standard. Developed by NIST [8], it provides a comprehensive framework to handle risks and incidents in a IoT environment. It includes a set of core functions, categories, and subcategories that organizations can use to develop their own cybersecurity programs. The framework also emphasizes the importance of continuous monitoring and risk management.

The Cloud Security Alliance (CSA) [9] has also developed a set of IoT security standards. The CSA IoT Working Group has developed several guidelines and best practices for securing IoT devices and networks. These include recommendations for device authentication, data encryption, and network segmentation. The CSA also offers a security certification program for IoT devices and services.

Finally, the Open Web Application Security Project (OWASP) [10] has developed a set of IoT security guidelines. The OWASP IoT Project provides a list of the top-ten security risks associated with IoT devices, as well as recommendations for mitigating these risks. The guidelines include recommendations for securing device communication, protecting sensitive data, and implementing secure authentication.

To wrap up, IoT security is a critical issue that must be addressed to protect users' privacy and data. Various IoT security standards have been developed to provide guidance and best practices for securing IoT devices and networks. These standards include the ISO/IEC 27001:2013, the IEC 62443 series, the NIST Cybersecurity Framework, the CSA IoT security guidelines [11], and the OWASP IoT security guidelines. By following these standards, organizations can help to ensure the security and integrity of their IoT ecosystems.

As the use of IoT devices continues to grow, concerns about their security and privacy have become more prominent. While there are several standards and guidelines available for securing IoT devices, there are still significant gaps in the current security standards. One of the major gaps is the lack of a comprehensive security framework for IoT devices. Many IoT devices are designed to be low-power, low-cost, and resource-constrained, which makes it difficult to implement strong security measures. Additionally, the wide range of IoT devices, each with their unique functionality and requirements, makes it challenging to create a one-size-fits-all security standard. As a result, many IoT devices are released with limited security measures or are designed to rely on security features provided by other components in the network, leaving them vulnerable to attacks. Another gap in IoT security standards is the lack of regulation and enforcement. While there are standards and guidelines available, they are often voluntary and not legally binding. This makes it difficult to ensure that IoT device manufacturers comply with the established security standards. Additionally, the lack of regulation makes it challenging to hold manufacturers accountable for security breaches caused by their devices.

Another significant gap in IoT security standards is the lack of attention given to firmware updates and patch management. Many IoT devices are designed to operate for long periods without maintenance, and firmware updates are often infrequent or non-existent[12]. This creates a situation where vulnerabilities are left unaddressed, leaving devices open to attacks. Moreover, many IoT devices have embedded systems with outdated software that may not be compatible with newer security standards. While there are several standards and guidelines available for securing IoT devices, there are significant gaps in the current security standards. Addressing these gaps is critical for ensuring the security and privacy of IoT devices and the data they collect[13]. Manufacturers, regulators, and security experts must work together to develop comprehensive security frameworks, enforce security standards, and provide regular firmware updates and patch management.

6.3 Literature Study

The purpose of this section is to highlight the distinctiveness of the research presented in this chapter in comparison to other approaches aimed at securing IoT devices. While other approaches use various methods – executing source code, creating provenance graphs, or performing static and dynamic code analysis to assess security and safety policies – they do not offer a concrete solution for conducting security audits of IoT device logs and configurations, as presented in this chapter. Although there are security solutions specifically designed for smart homes, none of them provide an auditing solution for IoT devices.

Moreover, this chapter introduces a proactive technique for auditing IoT devices, which is distinct from retroactive or incremental approaches used in other studies. Retroactive approaches, such as the one used in [14], are limited in their ability to prevent damage and only audit systems after an incident has occurred. Incremental approaches, such as those in [15–16], may cause a delayed response. On the other hand, the prematured approach as in [17], shall lead to pre-computation, which leads to inconsistencies and they are not applicable to IoT devices due to their computational and storage constraints, heterogeneity, and limited logging functionality.

6.4 Framework for Security Audit of IoT

Security audits are critical for ensuring the security and integrity of Internet of Things devices and networks. A security audit involves a systematic evaluation of an organization's IoT infrastructure to identify vulnerabilities and risks. In this chapter, we will outline a step-by-step process for conducting a security audit in IoT.

Step 1: Define the Scope and Objectives of the Audit
The first step in conducting a security audit in IoT is to define the scope and objectives of the audit. This involves identifying the IoT devices and networks that will be audited, as well as the goals and expectations of the audit. The scope of the audit should be well-defined to ensure that all relevant areas of the IoT infrastructure are evaluated.

Step 2: Identify the Threat Landscape
Here, the threat environment is identified by involving the potential and expected risks the organization's IoT infrastructure may face. Threats can include hackers, malware, and physical attacks. It is important to consider all possible threats and risks, as well as their likelihood and impact.

Step 3: Assess the Current Security Controls
The next step is to assess the current security controls that are in place to protect the organization's IoT infrastructure. This involves reviewing security policies, procedures, and technologies to determine their effectiveness in mitigating identified threats and risks. It is important to identify any weaknesses or gaps in the existing security controls.

Step 4: Conduct Vulnerability Assessments
Once the current security controls have been assessed, vulnerability assessments should be conducted to identify potential weaknesses in the IoT infrastructure. This involves using automated and manual techniques to identify vulnerabilities in devices, networks, and applications. Vulnerability assessments can include port scanning, network mapping, and penetration testing.

Step 5: Analyze the Results
The results of the vulnerability assessments should be analyzed to identify the most critical vulnerabilities and risks. This involves prioritizing the identified vulnerabilities based on their likelihood and impact. It is important to consider the potential consequences of each vulnerability and prioritize the most critical ones for remediation.

Step 6: Develop Remediation Plan
Once the analysis is completed, the plan for remedial activity has to take place for addressing the risks. This remedial plan must also incorporate appropriate action for mitigating all the vulnerability. The organization's comprehensive plan for IoT security shall also be arrived at using the remedial plan.

Step 7: Implement Remediation Plan
Once the remediation plan has been developed, it should be implemented to address the identified vulnerabilities and risks. This involves deploying patches and updates, configuring security controls, and updating security policies and procedures. It is important to ensure that all remediation actions are completed in a timely manner.

Step 8: Monitor and Review
Finally, the organization should monitor and review the effectiveness of the remediation plan. This involves regularly testing the IoT infrastructure to ensure that vulnerabilities have been addressed and that security controls are effective. The organization should also continue to assess the threat landscape and make adjustments to their security posture as needed. The process involves defining the scope and objectives of the audit, identifying the threat landscape, assessing the current security controls, conducting vulnerability assessments, analyzing the results, developing a remediation plan, implementing the plan, and monitoring and reviewing the effectiveness of the remediation. By following this step-by-step process, organizations can improve their overall IoT security posture and protect their sensitive data and assets. Figure 6.1 shows an conceptual view of the steps involved.

6.5 Proposed Framework

At a high level, the security auditing framework for IoT devices is illustrated in Figure 6.2. Its primary functions include collecting audit data from IoT devices and storing it on a cloud server where auditing computations, such as verification, are delegated. In addition, the proposed framework must also communicate with diverse users like subject matter experts, owners of IoT-based smart homes for gathering the requirements for auditing and to issue them with final reports on auditing. The proposed framework is specifically for smart homes, and other landscapes are not

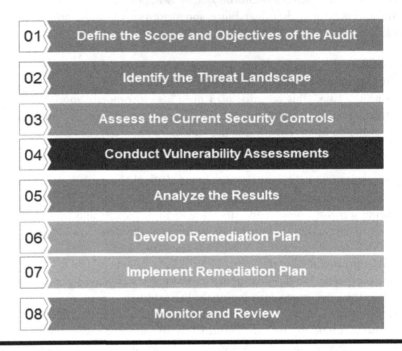

Figure 6.1 Steps in IoT Security Audit.

Source: Figure created by the author.

considered in this chapter. Collection of Data, verification and a user dashboard are the important components of the proposed framework. The collection of data is responsible for collecting audit data from IoT devices and processing it before sending it to the cloud server for verification. The verification engine is responsible for verifying the security policies obtained from users against the audit data collected. Finally, the dashboard provides users with a comprehensive view of the audit results in the form of reports.

6.5.1 Data Collection

The engine for collecting and processing data consists of two sub-engines: one for collecting data and the other for processing it. The data collection engine acquires the necessary audit data from smart home platforms, such as Google Nest, in batch mode. Furthermore, to obtain the audit data necessary, an IoT hub or cloud server

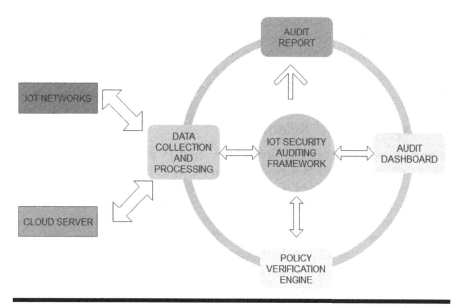

Figure 6.2   Proposed Framework.
Source: Figure created by the author.

may also be used, considering the implementation nature of the smart home [18].
Data extraction and filtering are taken care by the data processing engine. The data
thus collected and processed are normalized to follow a uniform pattern and are
then translated to rules. The rules generated are based on the type of processing
engine used.

6.5.2 Verification

The engine responsible for verifying security policies and detecting security breaches
uses verification and validation algorithms when it receives audit requests or updated
inputs. Conventional data are made used for expressing the models with policies
for facilitating the reasoning of model automatically, which are found to be more
effective than manual process [19]. In case a security policy gets violated, the evidence will be provided by back-end verification. After the completion of validation,
the results of the audit are stored in the repository which can be accessed by the processing engine. Based on the policies, different verification shall be used.

6.5.3 Dashboard

The user dashboard provides an option for choosing from various standards and from
the specific policy, standards that are being derived from conventional standards.

Once the user submits a request for auditing, the processing takes place for the selected rules, and results are presented to the user. Users are given information about any violations that have occurred, including detailed evidence to support the findings. The audit reports are saved for a specific duration of time.

6.6 Experimental Results

Experiments were carried out in test beds. A set of 14 products of a smart home were considered. Rasberry Pi were used for simulating the computing environment. The experiment also consisted of virtual setup having six different IoT devices. It is ensured that both the setup produces output in a consistent format. Minimal system configuration was used to test the performance. The idea behind having two test beds is to ensure that the data are generated. The physical set up produced real time data while the virtual set up helped in scaling up the data to a thousand different smart home, thus helping to assure scalability.

6.6.1 Experimental Results

Efficiency is concentrated on the first level of experiments. The Figure 6.3 indicates the comparison of time taken to identify a threat. Here the threat taken for

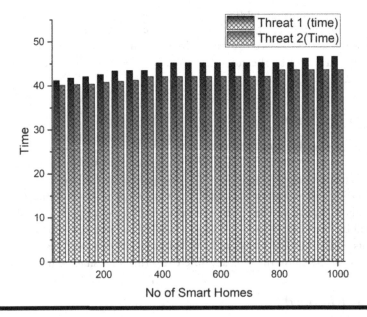

Figure 6.3   Execution Time Analysis.

Source: Figure created by the author.

Table 6.1   Execution Time Analysis

No of Smart Homes	Time complexity	
	Threat 1 (time)	Threat 2(Time)
50	41.2	40.1
100	41.8	40.3
150	42.1	40.4
200	42.6	40.8
250	43.4	41
300	43.5	41.3
350	43.5	42.1
400	45.2	42.1
450	45.2	42.1
500	45.2	42.1
550	45.2	42.1
600	45.2	42.1
650	45.2	42.1
700	45.2	42.1
750	45.2	42.1
800	45.2	43.6
850	45.2	43.6
900	46.2	43.6
950	46.6	43.6
1000	46.6	43.6

Source: Table created by the author.

consideration is the "unauthorized door opening" scenario and "smoke detection" for a thousand smart homes. As is seen from the results, the sum of time required to complete the verification process is not increasing with an increase in the number of smart homes, which shows the consistency in performance. Table 6.1 shows the experimental results:

The next set of experiments was conducted to detect the computational complexity. Figure 6.4 and Figure 6.5 show the CPU and memory usage for two scenarios previously discussed. It is seen from the figures that the usage of CPU and Memory were kept well below 21 percent until the number of smart homes exceeded nine hundred. Also, the reason is identified as the amount of data that gets accumulated is the cause of more CPU usage and not the experimental environment. Table 6.2 shows the experimental results

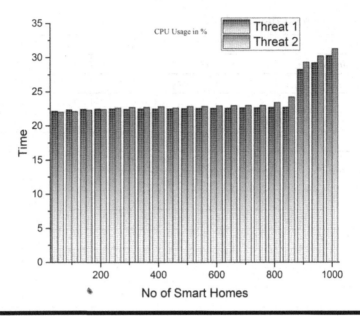

Figure 6.4 CPU Usage Analysis.

Source: Figure created by the author.

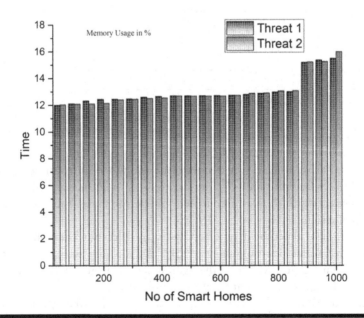

Figure 6.5 Memory Usage Analysis.

Source: Figure created by the author.

Table 6.2   CPU and Memory Usage Analysis

	CPU Usage in %		Memory Usage in %	
No of Smart Homes	Threat 1	Threat 2	Threat 1	Threat 2
50	22.13	22.0	12.01	12.04
100	22.34	22.1	12.11	12.09
150	22.42	22.3	12.32	12.11
200	22.45	22.4	12.45	12.16
250	22.47	22.6	12.46	12.41
300	22.41	22.7	12.48	12.45
350	22.45	22.7	12.61	12.51
400	22.46	22.8	12.67	12.56
450	22.48	22.6	12.71	12.70
500	22.51	22.84	12.71	12.69
550	22.54	22.83	12.72	12.69
600	22.56	22.91	12.73	12.69
650	22.58	22.94	12.75	12.74
700	22.61	22.96	12.81	12.89
750	22.61	22.98	12.89	12.91
800	22.68	23.41	12.98	13.06
850	22.70	24.21	13.01	13.09
900	28.23	29.31	15.21	15.24
950	29.21	30.21	15.39	15.27
1000	30.26	31.26	15.51	16.01

Source: Table created by the author.

6.7 Discussions

The formal verifications used in the study are expressive [20] and hence, the framework was capable enough to deal with variety of security constraints. Here, any kind of rule generated through the processing engine shall be accommodated for auditing, which proves the scalability of the model. The general challenge of the study was to how to find the data when a new rule is generated. The use of external tools may help to solve the issue, but it will also lead to time and memory overheads. The proposed model is designed for functioning with a range of IoT devices and can easily be extended to other domains, also apart from the smart home. The challenge in adopting this framework to other domains lies in data collection and rule specification. Overheads in consistent format of data are also foreseen. The challenges are left as open research issues, which shall be addressed by community researchers.

6.8 Conclusion

A gradient approach proposed for the security audit of IoT devices is proposed in this chapter. The proposed framework used conceptual verification and also experimental verification. It is seen from the results that the proposed framework is robust in terms of time and CPU usage. Future directions are on the domain of privacy while performing security audits. One of the great challenge in the method is as to how the raw data can be converted to rules. The idea of implementing it through Association Rule mining is also considered. The chapter is intended to show the possible framework, and the results are obtained from pre-described environments. Future directions will also include proposing a holistic framework that includes the recent IoT security standards for bringing in a universal approach.

References

1. H. Lin, and N. W. Bergmann, "IoT privacy and security challenges for smart home environments," *Information*, vol. 7, no. 3, pp. 44, 2016.
2. N. M. Karie, N. M. Sahri, and P. Haskell-Dowland, "IoT threat detection advances, challenges and future directions," in *Proc. IEEE Workshop Emerg. Technol. Secur. IoT (ETSecIoT)*, Sydney, NSW, Australia, Apr. 2020, pp. 22–29.
3. L. Cédric, D. Eleni, T. Guillaume, D. Guillaume, and A. Mouhannad. (Dec. 2015). Security and resilience of smart home environments. *Good Practices and Recommendations.* Accessed: Mar. 30, 2021
4. V. R. Kebande, N. M. Karie, and H. S. Venter, "Adding digital forensic readiness as a security component to the IoT domain," *Int. J. Adv. Sci., Eng. Inf. Technol.*, vol. 8, no. 1, pp. 1–11, 2018.
5. W. M. S. Stout, and V. E. Urias, "Challenges to securing the Internet of Things," in *Proc. IEEE Int. Carnahan Conf. Secur. Technol. (ICCST)*, Orlando, FL, USA, Oct. 2016, pp. 1–8. doi: 10.1109/CCST.2016.7815675
6. Z. A. Solangi, Y. A. Solangi, S. Chandio, M. B. S. A. Aziz, M. S. B. Hamzah, and A. Shah, "The future of data privacy and security concerns in Internet of Things," in *Proc. IEEE Int. Conf. Innov. Res. Develop. (ICIRD)*, Bangkok, Thailand, May 2018, pp. 1–4. doi: 10.1109/ICIRD.2018.8376320
7. D. Geneiatakis, I. Kounelis, R. Neisse, I. Nai-Fovino, G. Steri, and G. Baldini, "Security and privacy issues for an IoT based smart home," in *Proc. 40th Int. Conv. Inf. Commun. Technol., Electron. Microelectron. (MIPRO)*, Opatija, Croatia, May 2017, pp. 1292–1297. doi: 10.23919/MIPRO.2017.7973622
8. W. Ali, G. Dustgeer, M. Awais, and M. A. Shah, "IoT based smart home: Security challenges, security requirements and solutions," in *Proc. 23rd Int. Conf. Autom. Comput. (ICAC)*, Huddersfield, U.K., Sep. 2017, pp. 1–6, doi: 10.23919/IConAC.2017.8082057
9. V. R. Kebande, J. Bugeja, and J. A. Persson, "Internet of threats introspection in dynamic intelligent virtual sensing," in *Proc. 1st Workshop CyberPhys. Social Syst. (CPSS)*, Bilbao, Spain, 2020, pp. 1–8.

10. L. Tawalbeh, F. Muheidat, M. Tawalbeh, and M. Quwaider, "IoT privacy and security: Challenges and solutions," *Appl. Sci.*, vol. 10, no. 12, pp. 4102, Jun. 2020.
11. M. A. Razzaq, S. H. Gill, M. A. Qureshi, and S. Ullah, "Security issues in the Internet of Things (IoT): A comprehensive study," *Int. J. Adv. Comput. Sci. Appl.*, vol. 8, no. 6, pp. 383, 2017.
12. V. R. Kebande, and I. Ray, "A generic digital forensic investigation framework for Internet of Things (IoT)," in *Proc. IEEE 4th Int. Conf. Future Internet Things Cloud (FiCloud)*, Vienna, Austria, Aug. 2016, pp. 356–362.
13. Jurcut, T. Niculcea, P. Ranaweera, and N.-A. Le-Khac, "Security considerations for Internet of Things: A survey," *Social Netw. Comput. Sci.*, vol. 1, no. 4, pp. 1–19, Jul. 2020.
14. H. M. T. Gadiyar, G. S. Thyagaraju, and T. P. Bhavya, "Privacy and security issues in IoT based smart home applications," *Int. J. Eng. Res. Technol.*, vol. 6, no. 15, pp. 1–3, 2018.
15. D. J. MacInnis, V. M. Patrick, and C. W. Park, "Looking through the crystal ball," in *Review of Marketing Research*, vol. 2. Bingley, U.K.: Emerald Group Publishing, 2006, pp. 43–80.
16. S. Nagarkar, and V. Prasad, "Evaluating privacy and security threats in IoT-based smart home environment," *Int. J. Appl. Eng. Res.*, vol. 14, no. 7, pp. 1–4, 2019.
17. J. Bugeja, A. Jacobsson, and P. Davidsson, "On privacy and security challenges in smart connected homes," in *Proc. IEEE Eur. Intell. Secur. Informat. Conf. (EISIC)*, Uppsala, Sweden, Aug. 2016, pp. 172–175.
18. M. Seliem, K. Elgazzar, and K. Khalil, "Towards privacy preserving IoT environments: A survey," *Wireless Commun. Mobile Comput.*, vol. 2018, pp. 15, Nov. 2018. doi: 10.1155/2018/1032761
19. F. Hall, L. Maglaras, T. Aivaliotis, L. Xagoraris, and I. Kantzavelou, "Smart homes: Security challenges and privacy concerns," 2020, arXiv:2010.15394. [Online]. Available: http://arxiv.org/abs/2010.15394
20. Cook, M. Robinson, M. A. Ferrag, L. A. Maglaras, Y. He, K. Jones, and H. Janicke, "Internet of cloud: Security and privacy issues," in *Cloud Computing for Optimization: Foundations, Applications, and Challenges*. Cham, Switzerland: Springer, 2018, pp. 271–301.

Chapter 7

Managing and Securing Information Storage in the Internet of Things

Aamir Salam Ahanger, Faheem Syeed Masoodi, Asra Khanam, and Wasia Ashraf

Department of Computer Sciences, University of Kashmir, India

7.1 Introduction to Managing and Securing Information Storage in IoT

Data collected and processed by IoT devices need to be managed and secured to ensure their integrity, confidentiality, and availability. In light of the proliferation of IoT across various industries, such as smart homes, healthcare, manufacturing, and transportation, effective storage and security mechanisms become increasingly important. In IoT, information storage refers to the collection, retention, and organization of data generated by devices [1]. These Internet connected devices, furnished with sensors, adeptly accumulate extensive volumes of data from their immediate surroundings. This data can include sensor readings, user interactions, environmental conditions, and more. Effectively managing this data is crucial for extracting valuable insights, enabling informed decision-making, and enhancing the functionality of IoT systems [2]. In summary, managing and securing information storage in IoT involves implementing appropriate data governance practices, ensuring scalable storage infrastructure, employing encryption and access control measures, validating data integrity, using secure protocols and APIs, staying up to date with

DOI: 10.1201/9781003474838-7

security patches, complying with privacy regulations, implementing backup and disaster recovery plans, and monitoring for threats and incidents. By addressing these aspects, organizations can safeguard the valuable data generated by IoT devices and maintain the trust and integrity of their IoT systems [3].

7.1.1 Importance of Information Storage in IoT

Information storage plays a crucial role in the Internet of Things (IoT) for several reasons:

Data Analysis and Decision Making: A data analyst inspects, cleans, transforms, and models data with the goal of discovering useful information, drawing conclusions, and supporting decision-making. It involves various techniques and methodologies to extract insights, patterns, and trends from raw data, making it more understandable and actionable. Data analysis plays a crucial role in informing strategies, solving problems, and making informed decisions across a wide range of domains, from business and science to healthcare and social sciences. On the other hand, decision-making involves selecting a course of action from multiple alternatives based on available information and desired outcomes. Making the right decision involves evaluating different options, weighing potential risks and benefits, and aligning objectives with goals. Data analysis greatly contributes to decision-making by providing quantitative and qualitative insights that enable individuals and organizations to make more informed and rational choices. By leveraging data analysis, decision-makers can reduce uncertainty, optimize resource allocation, and improve overall outcomes [4].

Real-time Control and Monitoring: Information storage facilitates immediate monitoring and control of IoT devices. Through the storage of data produced by IoT sensors, organizations can engage in real-time data analysis, oversee device functionality, identify irregularities, and initiate relevant responses [5].

Historical Data Analysis: Storing IoT data allows organizations to analyze historical data trends and patterns. By examining historical data, businesses can identify long-term patterns, perform predictive analytics, and gain insights that can lead to improved operational efficiencies, proactive maintenance, and better resource planning [6]. Historical data analysis can help organizations optimize processes, detect anomalies, and predict future events or trends.

Compliance and Regulatory Requirements: Information storage is crucial for meeting compliance and regulatory requirements. Many industries, such as healthcare and finance, have strict regulations regarding data retention, privacy, and security. By properly storing and managing IoT data, organizations can demonstrate compliance, respond to audits, and meet legal obligation.

Machine Learning and AI Applications: Storing IoT data is essential for training machine learning models and deploying artificial intelligence (AI) applications.

Machine learning algorithms require large amounts of data for training, and the availability of historical IoT data enables the development of accurate and robust models. By storing data, organizations can continuously refine and improve their AI applications, making them more intelligent and effective over time [7].

Troubleshooting and Forensics: Information storage facilitates troubleshooting and forensic analysis in the event of system failures, security breaches, or incidents. By storing relevant data, organizations can investigate the root cause of issues, perform post-incident analysis, and identify vulnerabilities or weaknesses in their IoT infrastructure [8]. This information can help improve system reliability, enhance security measures, and prevent future incidents.

Data-driven Innovation: Storing IoT data provides a valuable resource for driving innovation. By leveraging stored data, organizations can explore new use cases, develop new products or services, and identify opportunities for business growth. The availability of historical IoT data enables organizations to experiment, iterate, and innovate based on insights gained from the stored information [9].

In conclusion, information storage is of paramount importance in the IoT ecosystem. It enables data analysis, real-time monitoring, historical data analysis, compliance, machine learning, troubleshooting, and fosters data-driven innovation. Through adept management and robust security of information storage, organizations can unleash the complete potential of IoT, acquire invaluable insights, and extract substantial business worth from their IoT endeavors.

7.1.2 Challenges and Risks in IoT Data Storage

While information storage in the Internet of Things (IoT) offers numerous benefits, there are several challenges and risks associated with managing and storing IoT data [10][11][12]. These include:

1. Vast Volume of Data: The copious data generated by IoT devices through a variety of sources and sensors presents substantial challenges in terms of storage capacity, scalability, and expenses, making the task of storage and management quite complex. Organizations must invest in scalable storage infrastructure to handle the ever-increasing volume of IoT data.

2. Data Variety and Complexity: IoT data comes in diverse formats, structures, and types. It includes sensor readings, multimedia files, time-series data, and more. Storing and organizing such varied data requires appropriate data models, storage formats, and indexing mechanisms. Handling the complexity of diverse data sources and formats can be a technical challenge.

3. Data Velocity: Internet of Things (IoT) data is frequently produced instantly or almost instantly, necessitating rapid storage and processing capacities. Conventional storage methods might encounter difficulties managing the rapid pace at which data is created. It is crucial for businesses to guarantee

that their storage framework is capable of meeting the rapidity and timeliness criteria of IoT data.

4. Data Privacy and Security: IoT data storage introduces significant privacy and security risks. The distributed nature of IoT, along with multiple data collection points, increases the potential attack surface. Protecting data from unauthorized access, ensuring data integrity, and addressing privacy concerns become critical. Encryption, access controls, and secure communication protocols must be implemented to mitigate these risks.

5. Data Quality and Reliability: IoT data quality and reliability can be challenging to ensure due to factors such as sensor inaccuracies, network issues, and data transmission errors. Poor data quality can affect the accuracy and reliability of analytics and decision-making processes. Organizations need to implement data validation techniques and error handling mechanisms to maintain data quality and reliability.

6. Storage and Bandwidth Limitations: IoT devices commonly function in settings with limited resources, including restricted storage and bandwidth capacities. Storing large amounts of data locally on devices may not be feasible due to these limitations. Therefore, organizations must carefully consider data retention policies, balancing the need for local storage and cloud-based storage solutions.

7. Data Lifecycle Management: IoT data has a lifecycle from the time it is generated to when it becomes obsolete or is no longer needed. Handling the complete data lifecycle, which involves tasks like retaining, archiving, and removing data, can present intricate challenges. Organizations must establish clear data governance policies and processes to manage data effectively throughout its lifecycle.

8. Interoperability and Standards: IoT ecosystems involve a variety of devices, platforms, and protocols. Achieving interoperability and ensuring seamless data storage across different systems can be challenging. The absence of standardized formats, protocols, and interfaces can impede endeavors related to data storage and integration.

9. Regulatory Compliance: Compliance with data protection and privacy regulations, such as GDPR or CCPA, is crucial for IoT data storage. Organizations need to ensure that their storage practices align with the applicable regulatory requirements. Compliance with data retention periods, consent management, and data subject rights adds complexity to IoT data storage.

10. Vendor Lock-In: Organizations relying on third-party IoT platforms or cloud providers for data storage may face vendor lock-in risks. Switching storage providers or platforms can be difficult due to proprietary formats or lack of data portability. Organizations need to carefully evaluate vendor lock-in risks and consider data migration strategies upfront.

To tackle these challenges and mitigate associated risks, a holistic strategy for IoT data storage is necessary. This encompasses the implementation of strong security protocols, investment in expandable infrastructure, adoption of data governance methodologies, assurance of data accuracy, and adherence to regulatory requirements. Organizations must stay vigilant, continuously assess risks, and update their storage strategies to mitigate potential issues and optimize the value derived from IoT data [13][14].

7.1.3 Overview of Security Concerns in IoT Storage

Security concerns in IoT storage are of paramount importance due to the sensitive nature of the data generated and stored by IoT devices [15][16]. The following are key security concerns that need to be addressed when it comes to IoT storage:

1. Data Privacy: IoT devices amass a considerable volume of personal and sensitive data, encompassing health details, location information, and user actions. Safeguarding data privacy becomes imperative to safeguard individual rights and conform to privacy mandates. It is imperative to establish effective safeguards for data encryption, access management, and the integration of techniques that uphold privacy.

2. Data Integrity: Preserving the consistency of data in the realm of IoT is crucial for upholding its precision, dependability, and credibility. Unauthorized alterations, meddling, or data damage could result in erroneous conclusions, erosion of confidence, and impaired operational effectiveness.

3. Unauthorized Access and Authentication: IoT storage setups must implement stringent protocols for access control to thwart unauthorized entry to confidential information. Robust authentication techniques, like two-factor authentication (2FA) or biometric verification, should be utilized to guarantee that solely approved users or devices can retrieve stored data.

4. Insider Threats: The security of IoT storage is notably jeopardized by insider risks. These risks involve individuals within the organization, such as employees, contractors, or partners, who are either malicious or have been compromised, and may intentionally exploit or disclose confidential data. To address this concern, enforcing rigorous access controls, closely monitoring user activities, and implementing role segregation can aid in reducing the impact of insider threats.

5. Network Security: IoT gadgets communicate data through networks, rendering them susceptible to attacks originating from the network. It is imperative to safeguard the storage framework against unapproved entry, covert monitoring, and Man-in-the-Middle (MITM) assaults. Strengthening network security can be achieved by introducing secure network protocols like Transport Layer Security (TLS), dividing the network into segments, and integrating systems for detecting and preventing intrusions (IDS/IPS).

6. Cloud Storage Security: Numerous enterprises utilize cloud-based storage options to manage IoT data, underscoring the vital importance of safeguarding data stored in the cloud. This entails implementing strong access management, encrypting data both when it is stored and during transmission, employing secure authentication methods, and conducting routine security assessments of the cloud service providers. When selecting a cloud storage provider, organizations should also take into account factors like data jurisdiction and adherence to regulatory mandates.

7. Physical Security: Physical security measures should not be overlooked, especially when IoT storage devices are deployed in remote or vulnerable locations. Securing the physical infrastructure, restricting physical access, and protecting storage devices from theft, tampering, or unauthorized physical manipulation are essential aspects of IoT storage security.

8. Security of Firmware and Software: IoT devices and storage systems rely on firmware and software to function. Ensuring the security of these components is critical to prevent unauthorized access, exploitation of vulnerabilities, or unauthorized modifications. Regular updates, patch management, and secure coding practices should be followed to mitigate software-related security risks.

9. Data Backup and Disaster Recovery: Adequate data backup and disaster recovery mechanisms are crucial in the event of data loss, system failures, or security incidents.

10. Compliance with Regulations: Organizations should be aware of the regulatory requirements, implement necessary controls, and ensure proper data handling practices to avoid legal and compliance issues.

Addressing these security concerns requires a multi-layered approach encompassing encryption, access controls, authentication mechanisms, network security, regular updates and patches, employee awareness training, and adherence to best practices in IoT security. By implementing robust security measures and staying proactive in addressing emerging threats, organizations can safeguard IoT storage and protect the integrity and confidentiality of the stored data.

7.2 Storage Alternatives for IoT Data

When it comes to storing IoT data, organizations have several alternatives to choose from based on their specific requirements [17][18].

1. Cloud Storage: Cloud storage is a popular choice for storing IoT data due to its scalability, flexibility, and accessibility. Cloud service providers offer infrastructure and platforms that can handle large volumes of data generated by

IoT devices. Organizations can take advantage of cloud storage solutions such as object storage, data lakes, or databases specifically designed for IoT data. Cloud storage also provides features like high availability, data replication, and built-in security measures.

2. Edge Storage: Edge storage involves storing IoT data locally on edge devices or gateways rather than transmitting it to a centralized cloud server. This approach reduces latency and network bandwidth requirements, making it suitable for real-time applications. Edge storage is particularly useful in scenarios where low-latency data processing, immediate response, or inter-mittent connectivity is crucial. It allows for local data analysis and selective transmission of relevant data to the cloud for further processing or long-term storage.

3. Fog Storage: Fog computing, an extension of edge computing, combines local edge devices and cloud resources to store and process IoT data. In fog storage, data is stored and processed in distributed fog nodes located closer to the IoT devices, reducing latency and network congestion. Fog storage enables real-time analytics, local decision-making, and efficient use of network band-width. It offers a balance between local storage and cloud connectivity, making it suitable for applications that require a mix of edge and centralized data processing.

4. Hybrid Storage: Hybrid storage combines both local storage (edge or fog) and cloud storage to leverage the benefits of both approaches. IoT data is stored locally for immediate processing and response, while selected data or aggregated insights are periodically transmitted to the cloud for long-term storage, further analysis, or archival purposes. Hybrid storage provides a flex-ible and scalable solution, allowing organizations to optimize data storage and processing based on their specific needs and constraints.

5. On-Premises Storage: Some organizations prefer to store IoT data on their own infrastructure, commonly referred to as on-premises storage. This approach provides full control over data management and security but requires investment in hardware, maintenance, and data center facilities. On-premises storage can be suitable for sensitive applications or industries with strict regulatory requirements where data sovereignty and physical control are critical.

6. Distributed Storage Networks: Distributed storage networks leverage decentralized architectures, such as blockchain or peer-to-peer networks, for storing IoT data across a network of nodes. This approach provides enhanced data resilience, security, and eliminates the need for a central authority. Distributed storage networks are suitable for applications that prioritize data immutability, transparency, and fault tolerance.

It is important to note that organizations can adopt a combination of storage alternatives based on their specific use cases and requirements. The choice of storage solution depends on factors such as data volume, velocity, latency requirements, security considerations, cost, scalability, and regulatory compliance. Careful evaluation of these factors can help organizations determine the most suitable storage alternative for their IoT data [19][20].

7.2.1 Cloud Storage Solutions for IoT Data

Cloud storage solutions play a crucial role in managing and storing the vast amounts of data generated by Internet of Things (IoT) devices [21][22]. Depending on the specific requirements and security considerations, organizations can choose from three different types of cloud storage models: public cloud, private cloud, and hybrid cloud. Let is explore each of these options in the context of IoT data storage.

- **Public Cloud Storage:** Public cloud storage involves leveraging third-party service providers to store and manage data in their infrastructure. This option offers several benefits for IoT data storage, such as scalability, cost-effectiveness, and ease of use. Public cloud providers like Amazon Web Services (AWS), Microsoft Azure, and Google Cloud Platform (GCP) offer dedicated services and APIs for storing and processing IoT data. Organizations can take advantage of the provider is infrastructure and services to store, analyze, and retrieve IoT data.
- **Private Cloud Storage:** Private cloud storage refers to dedicated infrastructure that is owned and operated by the organization itself or a trusted third-party vendor. In the case of IoT data storage, private clouds offer greater control, security, and compliance compared to public cloud solutions. Organizations can deploy private cloud storage systems within their own data centers or opt for managed private cloud solutions provided by vendors. Private cloud solutions are suitable for sensitive IoT data or applications that require strict data governance and compliance.
- **Hybrid Cloud Storage:** Hybrid cloud storage merges the advantages of public and private clouds. In this way, organizations can leverage the scalability and cost-effectiveness of the public cloud while maintaining control over sensitive or critical IoT data. Hybrid cloud setups allow organizations to store non-sensitive IoT data in the public cloud, while keeping sensitive data private. The approach allows organizations to optimize storage and processing resources based on security requirements.

When selecting a cloud storage solution for IoT data, it is crucial to consider factors such as data security, compliance regulations, scalability, performance, and cost. Organizations should assess their specific requirements and evaluate different providers and solutions to choose the option that best meets their needs [23].

7.2.2 Edge Storage Solutions for IoT Data

Edge storage solutions provide local storage capabilities at the edge of the network, closer to the source of IoT data generation [24][25]. Here are some notable edge storage solutions for IoT data:

1. Local Storage on IoT Devices: IoT devices themselves can have built-in storage capabilities, allowing them to store data locally. These devices can range from sensors, actuators, gateways, or edge servers. Local storage on IoT devices is particularly useful in scenarios where real-time processing, low latency, or intermittent connectivity is critical. It enables data collection, local analytics, and immediate decision-making without relying on cloud or centralized storage. However, the storage capacity of individual IoT devices may be limited, and data must be periodically offloaded to other storage solutions for long-term retention and further analysis.

2. Edge Servers or Gateways with Storage: Edge servers or gateways are devices deployed at the edge of the network that act as intermediaries between IoT devices and the cloud. These devices often include local storage capabilities, allowing them to temporarily store and process IoT data before transmitting it to the cloud or central storage. Edge servers or gateways can perform edge analytics, data aggregation, and filtering, reducing the amount of data that needs to be sent to the cloud. They can store relevant data locally for immediate access and transmit aggregated or summarized data to the cloud for long-term storage and in-depth analysis.

3. Network-Attached Storage (NAS) at the Edge: Network-Attached Storage (NAS) devices can be deployed at the edge of the network to provide local storage capabilities for IoT data. NAS devices offer scalable storage capacity and can serve as centralized storage points for multiple IoT devices in proximity. IoT devices can write data directly to the NAS, enabling local storage, retrieval, and subsequent processing or analysis. NAS at the edge provides faster access to data, reduces latency, and minimizes reliance on cloud or centralized storage.

4. Solid-State Drives (SSDs) or Flash Storage:

    Solid-state drives (SSDs) or flash storage solutions provide high-performance and reliable storage for edge computing environments. These storage technologies offer fast read/write speeds, low power consumption, and high durability, making them suitable for edge storage requirements. SSDs or flash storage can be integrated into edge servers, gateways, or even IoT devices to provide local storage capabilities for IoT data. They allow for quick data access and efficient storage operations at the edge, enabling rapid processing and decision-making.

5. Edge-Optimized Storage Solutions:

Some vendors offer specialized edge storage solutions specifically designed for IoT environments. These solutions are tailored to handle the unique requirements of edge computing, such as limited resources, intermittent connectivity, and harsh environments. Edge-optimized storage solutions often provide features like data compression, caching, data deduplication, and efficient data transfer protocols to optimize storage operations at the edge. They are designed to support local data storage, processing, and analytics, while ensuring reliable data synchronization with centralized storage when connectivity is available.

Organizations should consider factors such as data volume, latency requirements, local processing needs, connectivity limitations, and environmental conditions when selecting edge storage solutions for IoT data. It is important to strike a balance between local storage capabilities and the need for centralized storage or cloud connectivity to ensure data availability, resilience, and efficient utilization of network resources [26].

■ Edge Computing and Local Storage

Edge computing and local storage are closely intertwined when it comes to processing and storing IoT data. Let is explore their relationship and benefits: Edge computing refers to the paradigm of processing and analyzing data at or near the edge of the network, closer to the source of data generation. It involves deploying computational resources, such as edge servers, gateways, or edge devices, at the edge to perform data processing tasks locally [27][28]. Local storage plays a crucial role in edge computing as it enables the storage of data in proximity to where it is generated, reducing latency and dependency on centralized storage or cloud resources. Here are the key aspects of edge computing and local storage:

1. Reduced Latency: Reduced latency refers to the decreased time delay or lag between the initiation of an action and the corresponding response or result. In various technological contexts, including computer systems, networks, and communication processes, minimizing latency is important to enhance performance, improve user experience, and enable real-time interactions. Here are a few domains where reduced latency is crucial:

2. Bandwidth Optimization: By processing and filtering data at the edge, edge computing improves the use of network capacity. The amount of data that must be transported over the network is decreased since only pertinent or aggregated data is sent to the main cloud or storage.Local storage facilitates the temporary storage of data, allowing edge devices or servers to store, analyze, and process data locally without overwhelming the network. This helps in bandwidth conservation and cost optimization.

3. Offline Operation: IoT devices often operate in environments with intermittent or limited connectivity. Local storage enables edge devices to continue operating and storing data even when network connectivity is disrupted. Data can be stored locally until connectivity is restored, allowing for offline operation and ensuring data continuity. Once connectivity is available, stored data can be synchronized with centralized storage or transmitted to the cloud for further analysis.

4. Data Privacy and Security: Data privacy refers to the control individuals have over their personal information, including how it is collected, stored, processed, and shared. It involves ensuring that individuals personal data is handled in a way that respects their rights and preferences. Data security involves safeguarding data from unauthorized access, breaches, and other malicious activities. It includes measures to protect data integrity, confidentiality, and availability.

5. Scalability and Resilience: Edge computing, coupled with local storage, enables distributed and scalable architectures. Multiple edge devices or servers can be deployed in a network, each equipped with local storage capabilities. This decentralized approach ensures redundancy, fault tolerance, and high availability. If one edge device fails or loses connectivity, data can still be stored and processed on other edge devices, maintaining the resilience of the system.

6. Cost Optimization: Local storage at the edge reduces the need for extensive cloud storage resources, resulting in cost savings. Instead of transmitting and storing all IoT data in the cloud, organizations can leverage local storage to retain relevant or valuable data locally and transmit only aggregated or summarized data to the cloud for long-term storage or further analysis. This optimizes the utilization of cloud resources and reduces data transfer costs.

By combining edge computing and local storage, organizations can achieve real-time data processing, reduced latency, enhanced privacy and security, offline operation, scalability, resilience, and cost efficiency. It empowers organizations to leverage the power of IoT data at the edge while effectively managing storage and processing requirements [29].

■ Fog Computing and Distributed Storage

Fog computing and distributed storage are closely related concepts that work together to enable efficient processing, storage, and management of IoT data [30] [31]. Let is explore their connection and benefits:

Fog Computing: A decentralized computing model known as fog computing brings cloud computing capabilities closer to the networks edge, or to the locations where data is produced and consumed. In fog computing, processing and data storage are dispersed among a network of gadgets, such as routers, gateways, edge servers, and IoT (Internet of Things) gadgets, which are placed nearer to the data source rather than in a centralized data center.

Distributed Storage: Distributed storage involves the distribution of data across multiple storage nodes or devices, creating a decentralized storage architecture. Data is replicated or distributed across these nodes to ensure redundancy, fault tolerance, and scalability. Distributed storage provides higher availability, improved data resilience, and efficient utilization of storage resources.

The connection between Fog Computing and Distributed Storage: Fog computing and distributed storage work together to create a cohesive and efficient IoT ecosystem:

1. Localized Data Processing: Localized data processing refers to the practice of performing data processing tasks in close proximity to the source of the data, typically at or near the point where the data is generated. This approach contrasts with centralized data processing, where data is transmitted to a remote data center or server for analysis and computation. Localized data processing has gained significance with the rise of edge computing and the need for real-time, responsive, and resource-efficient data analysis.

2. Local Storage on Fog Nodes: Fog nodes in a fog computing environment often include local storage capabilities. These local storage resources enable the storage of IoT data closer to the edge devices, reducing the reliance on centralized cloud storage. Local storage on fog nodes allows for quick access to data, supports offline operation, and facilitates local data storage and retrieval.

3. Distributed Storage on Fog Nodes: Distributed storage techniques can be employed on fog nodes to create a distributed storage architecture. Data can be replicated or distributed across multiple fog nodes, ensuring redundancy, fault tolerance, and improved data resilience. Distributed storage on fog nodes enhances data availability, enables load balancing, and provides scalability as the number of edge devices and data sources increase.

4. Efficient Data Management: Fog computing, combined with distributed storage, allows for efficient data management. Data can be processed, analyzed, and stored in a distributed manner across fog nodes. Relevant or aggregated data can be selectively stored on fog nodes, reducing the need to transmit all data to the cloud. This minimizes network congestion, optimizes bandwidth, and reduces the storage requirements in the centralized cloud infrastructure.

5. Dynamic Resource Allocation: Fog computing and distributed storage enable dynamic resource allocation in the IoT environment. Fog nodes can intelligently distribute computational and storage resources based on the proximity to data sources, processing requirements, and available resources. This allows for efficient utilization of resources, improved performance, and scalability.

The combination of fog computing and distributed storage provides benefits such as reduced latency, efficient data processing, improved data availability, fault tolerance, scalability, and optimized resource utilization. It empowers organizations to perform real-time analytics, make faster decisions, enhance data reliability, and alleviate the load on centralized cloud infrastructure [32][33].

7.2.3 Hybrid Storage Approaches for IoT Data

Hybrid storage approaches combine the benefits of different storage solutions to optimize the storage and management of IoT data [34][35]. These approaches leverage a combination of cloud storage, edge storage, and on-premises storage to meet specific requirements. Here are some hybrid storage approaches for IoT data:

1. Cloud-Edge Hybrid Storage: In this approach, IoT data is stored both in the cloud and locally at the edge. Edge devices or gateways store data locally for immediate processing, real-time analytics, or offline operation. Relevant or aggregated data is then selectively transmitted to the cloud for long-term storage, further analysis, or archival purposes. Cloud storage provides scalability, accessibility, and global data availability, while edge storage reduces latency, optimizes bandwidth, and ensures local processing capabilities.
2. Cloud-On-Premises Hybrid Storage: This approach combines cloud storage with on-premises storage infrastructure. IoT data is stored in the cloud for scalable storage capacity, disaster recovery, and global accessibility. However, certain sensitive or critical data is stored on-premises for enhanced security, compliance, or low-latency access. This hybrid storage approach allows organizations to leverage the cost-effectiveness and scalability of the cloud while maintaining control over sensitive data.
3. Cloud-Edge-On-Premises Hybrid Storage: In this comprehensive hybrid storage approach, IoT data is distributed across cloud storage, edge storage, and on-premises storage. Edge devices store data locally for immediate processing, real-time analytics, and offline operation. Relevant data or insights are transmitted to the cloud for long-term storage and centralized analysis. Additionally, certain sensitive or critical data is stored on-premises for security, compliance, or specialized processing requirements. This hybrid approach offers a balance between edge processing, cloud scalability, and on-premises control.
4. Multi-Cloud Hybrid Storage: Multi-cloud hybrid storage involves using multiple cloud service providers to store and manage IoT data. Organizations distribute data across different cloud storage platforms to mitigate vendor lock-in, optimize costs, and enhance data redundancy. IoT data is stored across multiple clouds, providing fault tolerance, disaster recovery capabilities, and

ensuring data availability in case of service disruptions. Multi-cloud hybrid storage allows organizations to take advantage of different cloud providers strength and services while maintaining flexibility and data portability.

5. Edge-Cloud-Fog Hybrid Storage: This hybrid storage approach combines edge, cloud, and fog storage to create a comprehensive storage infrastructure. Edge devices store data locally for immediate processing, real-time analytics, and local decision-making. Fog nodes, located between the edge and the cloud, provide intermediate storage and processing capabilities. Relevant data is selectively transmitted to the cloud for long-term storage, advanced analytics, and global accessibility. This approach optimizes storage and processing at each layer of the IoT architecture, leveraging the strengths of edge, fog, and cloud storage solutions.

Hybrid storage approaches provide organizations with flexibility, scalability, data control, and cost optimization. They allow organizations to tailor their storage infrastructure to meet specific requirements, taking into account factors such as data sensitivity, latency, compliance, scalability, and cost considerations. By combining different storage solutions, organizations can achieve an optimized storage architecture that balances local processing, global accessibility, data resilience, and efficient resource utilization.

■ Edge-to-Cloud Data Offloading Strategies

Edge-to-cloud data offloading strategies involve the transfer of IoT data from edge devices or edge computing infrastructure to centralized cloud storage or processing systems. These strategies help optimize data storage, processing, and analytics by leveraging the capabilities of both edge and cloud environments [36][37]. Here are some commonly used edge-to-cloud data offloading strategies:

1. Real-Time Streaming: Real-time streaming involves transmitting IoT data from edge devices to the cloud in near real-time. Data is continuously streamed over the network, enabling immediate processing, analysis, and storage in the cloud. This strategy is suitable for applications that require real-time monitoring, instant decision-making, or centralized data storage. Real-time streaming often utilizes protocols such as MQTT (Message Queuing Telemetry Transport) or Apache Kafka to ensure efficient and reliable data transmission.

2. Periodic Batch Processing: In this strategy, edge devices accumulate IoT data locally over a period of time and periodically transmit batches of data to the cloud for processing and storage. Data is collected, aggregated, and compressed at the edge, reducing the frequency of data transmission. Batch processing reduces network overhead and optimizes bandwidth utilization. It

is useful when the volume of data generated by edge devices is high and continuous real-time transmission is not necessary.

3. Threshold-based Offloading: Threshold-based offloading involves setting thresholds on specific data parameters or events at the edge. When data surpasses a predefined threshold, it is offloaded to the cloud for further analysis or storage. This strategy helps filter and prioritize relevant data, reducing the amount of data that needs to be transmitted to the cloud. Threshold-based offloading optimizes network bandwidth and reduces cloud storage costs by selectively sending critical or anomalous data for in-depth analysis.

4. Edge Analytics with Cloud Aggregation: In this strategy, edge devices perform initial data processing and analytics locally, generating insights or summarized data. Only the aggregated or relevant data is transmitted to the cloud for further analysis, long-term storage, or integration with other data sources. Edge analytics reduce latency and enable faster decision-making, while cloud aggregation provides centralized processing and comprehensive analysis capabilities. This strategy balances local processing and cloud resources, optimizing storage and computation across the edge-to-cloud continuum.

5. Intelligent Data Routing: Intelligent data routing involves making data offloading decisions based on specific criteria or context. Edge devices analyze data locally and make intelligent decisions about whether to process and store the data locally or offload it to the cloud. This strategy leverages machine learning algorithms, rule-based engines, or AI models to determine the most appropriate destination for data based on factors such as data type, size, urgency, or resource availability. Intelligent data routing optimizes storage, processing, and network utilization dynamically based on changing conditions.

Organizations should consider factors such as data volume, processing capabilities, network bandwidth, latency requirements, data sensitivity, and resource availability when selecting edge-to-cloud data offloading strategies. The choice of strategy depends on the specific IoT use case, the importance of real-time processing, cost considerations, and the desired balance between edge and cloud resources. By implementing effective edge-to-cloud data offloading strategies, organizations can optimize storage, processing, and analytics in their IoT ecosystem.

■ Tiered Storage Architectures for IoT Data

Tiered storage architectures for IoT data involve organizing data into multiple tiers based on its characteristics, access frequency, and storage requirements [38][39]. This approach allows organizations to optimize storage resources, cost, and performance. Here are the components and benefits of tiered storage architectures for IoT data:

1. Hot Tier: The hot tier, also known as the primary tier, includes the most frequently accessed and critical IoT data. This tier is typically stored in high-performance storage systems, such as solid-state drives (SSDs) or in-memory databases. The hot tier enables fast data retrieval, real-time analytics, and immediate access to the most relevant and valuable data. Storing frequently accessed data in the hot tier minimizes latency and ensures rapid response times for time-sensitive applications.

2. Warm Tier: The warm tier consists of data that is accessed less frequently than the hot tier but is still important for historical analysis, trend identification, or periodic reporting. This data is stored in storage systems with a balance of performance and capacity, such as traditional hard disk drives (HDDs) or network-attached storage (NAS). The warm tier offers cost-effective storage for data that is not immediately needed but may be accessed periodically for insights or long-term analysis.

3. Cold Tier: The cold tier comprises data that is infrequently accessed or has low-value for immediate analysis but may still have long-term value for compliance, archival, or historical purposes. This data is typically stored in cost-efficient and high-capacity storage systems, such as magnetic tape libraries or offline storage. The cold tier enables organizations to store large volumes of IoT data at a lower cost, optimizing storage expenses while ensuring data retention and compliance requirements are met.

4. Data Lifecycle Management: Tiered storage architectures often incorporate data lifecycle management techniques. This involves automatically moving data between different tiers based on predefined policies and data characteristics. For example, data may be promoted from the warm tier to the hot tier if its access frequency increases, or demoted from the hot tier to the warm or cold tier if it becomes less frequently accessed. Data lifecycle management ensures that data is stored in the most appropriate tier based on its relevance, access patterns, and storage requirements.

5. Intelligent Caching and Tiering: To further optimize storage performance, intelligent caching and tiering mechanisms can be employed. Caching involves temporarily storing frequently accessed data in faster storage layers, such as SSDs or memory, to accelerate data retrieval. Tiering involves automatically moving data between different tiers based on real-time usage patterns or data access characteristics. These mechanisms dynamically adapt to changing data access patterns, ensuring that frequently accessed data is readily available in the faster storage layers while less frequently accessed data is moved to lower-cost tiers.

6. Integration with Cloud Storage: Tiered storage architectures can be extended to include cloud storage as one of the tiers. Organizations can leverage cloud storage services for offloading less frequently accessed or cold data, thereby reducing on-premises storage costs and scaling storage capacity as needed.

Cloud storage integration allows for seamless data movement between on-premises storage tiers and cloud-based tiers, providing flexibility, scalability, and cost optimization.

By implementing tiered storage architectures for IoT data, organizations can achieve a balance between performance, cost, and scalability. Frequently accessed and critical data resides in high-performance storage tiers, while less frequently accessed or cold data is stored in cost-effective tiers [40]. This approach optimizes storage resource utilization, reduces costs, improves data access efficiency, and aligns storage capabilities with the value and access requirements of IoT data.

7.3 Security Measures for IoT Data Storage

Security measures for IoT data storage are crucial to protect the sensitive information collected and stored by Internet of Things (IoT) devices. As IoT devices are increasingly being used in various domains, such as healthcare, transportation, and smart homes, it becomes essential to ensure that the data generated and stored by these devices is adequately protected from unauthorized access, tampering, and other security threats [41][42]. Here are several security measures commonly employed for IoT data storage:

1. Encryption: Encryption is a fundamental security measure that ensures data confidentiality. IoT data should be encrypted both during transit and at rest. Enhanced encryption algorithms, such as AES, are typically used to encrypt data. This prevents unauthorized parties from accessing and understanding the data even if they manage to intercept or gain access to it.
2. Access Control: Implementing robust access control mechanisms is essential for IoT data storage security. Access control ensures that only authorized individuals or systems can access the stored data. This is achieved through techniques like user authentication, role-based access control (RBAC), and strong password policies. Access control also helps in limiting the privileges and actions that different users or entities can perform on the data.
3. Secure Communication: IoT devices often transmit data over networks to storage systems or other devices. Securing the communication channel is crucial to prevent eavesdropping, data tampering, and unauthorized access. TLS and SSL protocols are commonly utilized to create secure communication link by encrypting the data during transit.
4. Data Integrity: Ensuring the integrity of IoT data is important to detect any unauthorized modification or tampering attempts. Techniques such as cryptographic hashes, digital signatures, and message authentication codes (MACs) are employed to verify the integrity of data. By comparing the hash or

signature of the received data with the original, any alterations or corruption can be detected.

5. Secure Storage: IoT data is often stored in databases, cloud platforms, or other storage systems. These storage systems should be designed with security in mind. Measures like data segregation, access controls, and regular security updates help in safeguarding the stored data. Additionally, employing encryption for data-at-rest and using secure storage protocols further enhances the security of the stored data.

6. Secure Firmware and Software Updates: IoT devices rely on firmware and software to function properly. However, vulnerabilities or weaknesses in these components can be exploited by attackers. It is essential to ensure that devices receive regular security updates and patches. Implementing a secure update mechanism that verifies the integrity and authenticity of firmware and software updates helps in mitigating potential security risks.

7. Secure Protocols and Standards: Implementing secure communication protocols and industry-standard security frameworks is crucial for IoT data storage. Protocols like MQTT (Message Queuing Telemetry Transport), CoAP (Constrained Application Protocol), and security frameworks such as OAuth (Open Authorization) and OAuth 2.0 provide secure communication channels and standardized security practices for IoT devices.

8. Data Backup and Recovery: Implementing a robust data backup and recovery strategy is essential to mitigate the risk of data loss due to system failures, disasters, or cyberattacks. Regular backups of IoT data should be performed, and backup data should be stored securely to prevent unauthorized access. Testing the recovery process periodically ensures that the data can be restored in case of any incidents.

Implementing these security measures collectively helps in ensuring the confidentiality, integrity, and availability of IoT data throughout its lifecycle, from collection to storage. It is important to note that security should be approached holistically, considering the entire ecosystem of IoT devices, networks, and storage systems, and continually adapting security practices to address emerging threats and vulnerabilities [43].

■ Data Encryption Techniques for Secure Storage

Data encryption techniques are crucial for ensuring the security and confidentiality of sensitive information when it is stored on various storage devices or systems. Data is encoded throughout the encryption process so that only authorized persons with the right decryption key can decode it [44][45]. Here are a few popular data encryption methods for safe storage: Here are some common data encryption techniques used for secure storage:

1. Symmetric Encryption: When encrypting and decrypting data, symmetric encryption, commonly referred to as private-key encryption, employs the same secret key. Both data encryption and decryption use the same key. Although effective, this strategy faces a hurdle in securely distributing the secret key to those parties that need it. Standard for Advanced Encryption AES is a popular symmetric encryption technique that offers high security and effectiveness. Numerous key lengths (128, 192, or 256 bits) are supported, and it is regarded as secure for a variety of applications.

2. Asymmetric Encryption: One key is used for encryption and the other is used for decryption in asymmetric encryption, also known as public-key encryption. While the private key is kept private, the public key can be freely disseminated. The key distribution issue that symmetric encryption faces is resolved by this method. Rivest-Shamir-Adleman: For the protection of data storage and transmission, many people employ the well-known asymmetric encryption technique RSA. It works well for digital signatures and key exchange as well.

3. Hybrid Encryption: In order to benefit from each type of encryption advantages, hybrid encryption mixes symmetric and asymmetric encryption. This method encrypts data with a symmetric key, which is subsequently encrypted with the recipients public key.

It is important to choose encryption techniques that align with your specific security requirements and compliance regulations. Proper encryption implementation, key management, and secure storage practices are essential components of a robust data security strategy [46].

■ **Access Control Mechanisms for Protecting Data**

Access control mechanisms are important elements of data security plan, designed to protect sensitive information by regulating who can access, modify, or interact with data. These mechanisms ensure that only authorized individuals or entities can perform specific actions on data while preventing unauthorized access and potential breaches [47][48]. There are several access control models and techniques used to enforce data protection:

1. Role-Based Access Control (RBAC): In RBAC, access is allowed in accordance with previously allocated roles to users. Users are given roles based on the duties they are responsible for, and each position has a set of associated permissions. This streamlines access management and guarantees uniformity across user rights.

2. Attribute-Based Access Control (ABAC): Access rights are decided by ABAC using attributes (characteristics or qualities). User attributes, resource

attributes, and environmental attributes are examples of attributes. Decisions regarding access are based on the policies that specify the guidelines pertaining to these attributes.

3. Discretionary Access Control (DAC): DAC grants access based on the discretion of the data owner. Data owners can define access permissions for individual users or groups. This model allows for flexibility but can lead to inconsistencies and potential misuse.

4. Mandatory Access Control (MAC):MAC enforces access permissions based on predefined security labels or levels. Users and data objects are assigned labels, and access is determined by comparing labels and predefined rules. This model is often used in high-security environments.

5. Role-Based Hierarchical Access Control (RB-HAC):RB-HAC extends RBAC by incorporating hierarchical relationships among roles. Users in higher-level roles inherit the permissions of roles lower in the hierarchy. This model helps manage complex access scenarios in organizations.

6. Rule-Based Access Control (RBAC): In RBAC, access is determined by a set of rules defined by administrators. These rules can consider various factors, such as user attributes, time of access, and location.

7. Time-Based Access Control: Time-based access control restricts access to certain time periods. This can be useful for granting temporary access, enforcing business hours, or ensuring that sensitive data is only accessible during specific windows.

Access control mechanisms are implemented through software and hardware solutions, often integrated into identity and access management (IAM) systems. Effective access control strategies require careful planning, regular review, and continuous monitoring to adapt to changing security requirements and potential threats.

▪ Authentication and Authorization in IoT Storage

Authentication and authorization are fundamental concepts in ensuring the security of data stored within Internet of Things (IoT) environments. IoT storage involves handling data generated by various IoT devices and sensors, and it is crucial to implement robust authentication and authorization approach to protect this data from illegitimate access and misuse [49][50]. Authentication in IoT Storage:

Authentication is the process of verifying the identity of a user, device, or application before granting access to the system or data. In the context of IoT storage, authentication ensures that only legitimate and authorized entities can interact with the stored data.For IoT storage, authentication can involve the following aspects:

1. Device Authentication: devices in IoT need to authenticate themselves before accessing or transmitting data. This prevents unauthorized devices from interacting with the storage system.
2. User Authentication: Users who access IoT storage platforms should be authenticated using strong authentication methods, such as username/password combinations, biometrics, or two-factor authentication (2FA).
3. Application Authentication: Applications or services that interact with IoT storage should also be authenticated to ensure that only trusted applications can access and manipulate the data.
4. Mutual Authentication: This involves both parties such as an IoT device and a storage system authenticating each other before data transfer. It prevents attacks from fake devices or malicious storage endpoints.

Authorization in IoT Storage: An authenticated user, device, or application can only access data or operate within a system after being authorized to do so. It makes sure that only authorized parties can carry out particular operations on the stored data [51][52]. Authorization in IoT storage includes:

1. Role-Based Access Control (RBAC): Assigning roles to users, devices, or applications and defining permissions based on these roles. This restricts access and operations based on the users or devices role.
2. Attribute-Based Access Control (ABAC): Granting access based on attributes like device type, location, time, or other contextual information. ABAC allows for more fine-grained control over access.
3. Access Policies: Defining rules and policies that dictate which entities can perform certain actions on the data. For instance, an IoT device might have read-only access to certain data while having write access to others.
4. Conditional Access: Modifying access permissions based on specific conditions. For example, granting temporary access during maintenance or allowing access only from specific locations.
5. Least Privilege Principle: Providing the minimum level of access necessary for a user, device, or application to perform its intended tasks. This minimizes the risk of unauthorized access or data leakage.

Combining strong authentication and appropriate authorization mechanisms helps ensure that only authorized entities can access, modify, or interact with IoT-stored data [53][54]. As the IoT landscape continues to grow, implementing effective security measures becomes even more critical to prevent data breaches and protect sensitive information [55][56].

7.4 Backup and Disaster Recovery in IoT Storage

Backup and disaster recovery strategies are essential for IoT storage systems to ensure data resilience, minimize the impact of potential data loss or system failures, and enable timely restoration of IoT data [57][58][59]. Here is an overview of backup and disaster recovery considerations for IoT storage:

1. Backup Planning: Developing a comprehensive backup plan is crucial to protect IoT data. Consider the following aspects when planning backups:
    a. Data Identification: Identify the critical IoT data that needs to be backed up. Prioritize data based on its importance, sensitivity, and business impact.
    b. Backup Frequency: Determine how frequently backups should be performed based on the rate of data generation, data volatility, and acceptable recovery point objectives (RPO). RPO defines the maximum tolerable data loss.
    c. Backup Methodology: Choose the appropriate backup methodology based on your IoT storage system characteristics. Common methods include full backups, incremental backups, and differential backups.
    d. Data Retention Policy: Define the retention period for backup data. Consider regulatory requirements, data lifecycle, and business needs. Retention periods should be aligned with legal and compliance obligations.
    e. Backup Storage: Determine the storage medium and location for backup data. Multiple copies of backups should be stored in secure and geographically diverse locations to protect against physical disasters and unauthorized access.
2. Redundancy and Replication: Implementing redundancy and data replication strategies can enhance data availability and minimize downtime. Consider:
    a. Redundant IoT Storage Systems: Deploy redundant storage systems with synchronized data replication. This ensures that data remains accessible even if one system fails.
    b. Geographically Distributed Replication: Replicate data across geographically diverse locations to protect against regional disasters and improve disaster recovery capabilities.
3. Disaster Recovery Planning: To maintain business continuity in the case of a disaster, a thorough disaster recovery strategy must be developed. Consider the following:
    a. Impact Assessment: Conduct a thorough assessment to identify potential risks and their impact on IoT storage systems. Evaluate both natural and man-made disasters that could affect the availability and integrity of the data.
    b. Recovery Time Objective (RTO): Define the maximum tolerable downtime for recovery after a disaster. RTO indicates the time within which IoT storage systems and data should be restored.

    c. Recovery Point Objective (RPO): Define the maximum tolerable data loss after recovery. RPO indicates the point in time to which data should be recovered.

    d. Disaster Recovery Site: Establish a separate physical or cloud-based disaster recovery site that can host replicated IoT storage systems. Ensure the site has the necessary infrastructure, connectivity, and security measures.

    e. Disaster Recovery Testing: Regularly test the disaster recovery plan to validate its effectiveness. Conduct simulated disaster scenarios to identify weaknesses, improve recovery processes, and train personnel.

4. Regular Backup Testing and Validation: Perform regular testing and validation of backups to ensure their integrity and effectiveness. This includes:

    a. Backup Data Restoration: Regularly restore backup data to test its integrity and ensure successful restoration.

    b. Data Consistency Checks: Verify the consistency of backup data and ensure it aligns with the original data. Use checksums, hashes, or other validation methods to ensure data integrity.

    c. Backup System Monitoring: Continuously monitor backup systems to detect any failures, errors, or anomalies. Implement automated alerts for backup job failures or abnormal backup behavior.

5. Personnel Training and Documentation: Ensure that personnel responsible for backup and disaster recovery processes are adequately trained. Maintain detailed documentation of backup and recovery procedures, including step-by-step instructions, contact information, and escalation processes.

6. Data Encryption: Consider encrypting backup data to protect it from unauthorized access during storage and transit. Encryption safeguards sensitive IoT data and ensures compliance with data protection regulations.

7. Continuous Improvement and Updates: Regularly review and update backup and disaster recovery strategies to adapt to evolving technology, business requirements, and emerging threats. Stay up-to-date with industry best practices and implement improvements accordingly.

By implementing robust backup and disaster recovery strategies, IoT storage systems can minimize the impact of data loss and system failures, maintain data integrity, and ensure business continuity. Regular testing, monitoring, and refinement of these strategies are crucial to their effectiveness.

■ Importance of Data Backup and Recovery in IoT

Data backup and recovery are of paramount importance in IoT (Internet of Things) environments due to the following reasons [60][61]:

1. Data Resilience: IoT generates vast amounts of valuable data that drive critical processes and decision-making. Data backup ensures its resilience against potential loss due to hardware failures, software errors, cyberattacks, natural disasters, or human errors. By having reliable backups, organizations can recover and restore the data promptly, minimizing the impact on operations.

2. Business Continuity: IoT deployments often support mission-critical operations in various sectors, including healthcare, manufacturing, transportation, and utilities. In case of data loss or system failures, having backups enables swift recovery and restoration of services, ensuring uninterrupted business continuity. This reduces downtime, mitigates financial losses, and preserves customer trust and satisfaction.

3. Compliance and Legal Requirements: Many industries have strict compliance and legal requirements governing data protection, retention, and recovery. For instance, regulations like the General Data Protection Regulation (GDPR) and industry-specific standards such as HIPAA (Health Insurance Portability and Accountability Act) in healthcare require organizations to implement adequate data backup and recovery measures. Compliance with these regulations helps avoid penalties, reputational damage, and legal consequences.

4. Disaster Recovery: Various crisis situations, such as natural disasters including floods, fires, earthquakes, and power outages, might affect IoT deployments. Organizations can efficiently recover from such calamities by putting in place reliable data backup and recovery systems. Critical systems and services can be restored after a disaster with the help of backups kept in multiple locations with different topographies and thorough disaster recovery procedures.

5. Data Integrity and Accuracy: Data integrity is crucial in IoT, as accurate and reliable data is vital for decision-making and operational efficiency. Backing up data helps maintain its integrity by ensuring that it remains uncorrupted and can be restored to its original state. This is particularly important in scenarios where data tampering or corruption could have severe consequences, such as healthcare devices or critical infrastructure systems.

6. Protection against Cybersecurity Threats: IoT systems face an increasing number of cybersecurity threats, including ransomware attacks, data breaches, and unauthorized access attempts. Regular data backups act as an insurance against these threats. In case of a successful attack, organizations can restore data from backups, preventing data loss and reducing the leverage cybercriminals have.

7. Recovery from Human Errors: Human errors, such as accidental deletion, improper configuration, or unintended modifications, can lead to data loss or corruption in IoT environments. Backups provide a safety net to recover from such errors, allowing organizations to revert to a known good state and minimize the impact of human mistakes.

8. Efficient System Upgrades and Testing: Backups also facilitate system upgrades, updates, and testing in IoT environments. Organizations can perform tests and pilot deployments using backups without affecting the live production environment. This ensures a smooth transition and minimizes the risk of disruptions or errors during system updates or upgrades.

9. Historical Data Analysis and Trend Identification: Backed-up data serves as a valuable resource for historical analysis, trend identification, and predictive modeling. Organizations can leverage historical IoT data to gain insights, make informed decisions, identify patterns, and improve business strategies. Without reliable backups, valuable historical data could be permanently lost.

Overall, data backup and recovery play a critical role in ensuring the availability, integrity, and resilience of IoT data. By implementing robust backup strategies, organizations can safeguard their operations, comply with regulations, protect against disasters and cybersecurity threats, and maintain business continuity in the face of unexpected events [62].

■ Backup Strategies for IoT Data

Implementing effective backup strategies for IoT data is crucial to ensure its availability, integrity, and recoverability. Here are some key considerations and strategies for backing up IoT data:

1. Determine Critical Data: Identify the critical IoT data that requires backup based on its importance, sensitivity, and business impact. Prioritize data that is essential for operations, decision-making, compliance, and customer service.

2. Define Backup Frequency: Determine how frequently backups should be performed based on factors such as the rate of data generation, data volatility, and acceptable Recovery Point Objectives (RPO). RPO defines the maximum tolerable data loss in case of a failure or data loss event.

3. Select Backup Methodology: Choose the appropriate backup methodology based on your IoT data characteristics and requirements.

4. Backup Storage Options: Choose appropriate storage options for backup data. Consider factors such as capacity, scalability, accessibility, security, and cost. Common backup storage options include:
   a. On-Premises Storage: Backup data can be stored on local storage systems within your organizations infrastructure. This provides direct control over the data but requires adequate storage capacity and protection against local disasters.
   b. Cloud Storage: Cloud-based backup solutions provide scalable and cost-effective storage options. Data is securely stored in remote data centers,

offering easy accessibility, redundancy, and disaster recovery capabilities. However, data security and compliance considerations should be addressed.

c. Hybrid Storage: A hybrid approach combines on-premises and cloud storage. It allows organizations to benefit from both local control and the flexibility of the cloud. Organizations can perform regular backups to local storage and replicate critical data to the cloud for added resilience.

5. Secure Backup Data: Implement encryption mechanisms to protect backup data from unauthorized access. Encryption ensures the confidentiality and integrity of backup data, particularly when stored in off-site or cloud environments. Use strong encryption algorithms and securely manage encryption keys.

6. Test and Validate Backups: Regularly test and validate backup data to ensure its integrity and recoverability. Perform periodic restoration tests to verify that backup data can be successfully restored and accessed when needed. Validate the consistency and quality of backup data through periodic data integrity checks.

7. Off-Site and Redundant Storage: Store backups in off-site locations to protect against local disasters or physical damage. Off-site storage ensures data resilience in case of on-premises incidents. Additionally, maintain multiple copies of backups to guard against data loss due to hardware failures or corruption.

8. Automation and Monitoring: Implement automated backup processes to ensure regular and consistent backups. Leverage backup management solutions that provide scheduling, monitoring, and alerting capabilities. Monitor backup jobs, verify their completion, and promptly address any failures or errors.

9. Versioning and Retention Policies: Consider implementing versioning and retention policies for backup data. Versioning allows you to maintain multiple historical copies of data, enabling restoration to specific points in time. Retention policies define how long backup data should be retained based on regulatory, legal, and business requirements.

10. Disaster Recovery Planning: Integrate backup strategies into a comprehensive disaster recovery plan. Test the disaster recovery plan periodically to validate its effectiveness.

Implementing a well-defined backup strategy for IoT data helps ensure data availability, reliability, and recoverability. Consider the specific requirements of your IoT environment, regulatory obligations, and business continuity needs when designing and implementing backup strategies. Regularly review and update the backup strategy to align with evolving IoT data management practices and technology advancements [57][59].

■ **Disaster Recovery Planning for IoT Storage**

Disaster recovery planning for IoT storage involves developing strategies and procedures to ensure the availability, integrity, and recovery of data stored within Internet of Things (IoT) environments in the event of a disaster, such as hardware failures, data corruption, cyberattacks, natural disasters, or other disruptive incidents. An effective disaster recovery plan for IoT storage is crucial to minimize downtime, data loss, and potential negative impacts on IoT operations [62][63]. Here is an overview of the key elements involved in disaster recovery planning for IoT storage:

1. Business Impact Analysis (BIA): Understand the criticality of various IoT applications and data. Identify which IoT devices and data are most crucial to your business operations. This assessment helps prioritize disaster recovery efforts.
2. Risk Assessment: Identify potential risks and threats that could impact IoT storage. This includes hardware failures, software glitches, cybersecurity breaches, natural disasters, and more. Evaluate the likelihood and potential impact of each risk.
3. Data Backup and Replication: Implement regular and automated backups of IoT data to secure storage locations. Utilize techniques such as continuous data replication to ensure near real-time data synchronization between primary and backup systems.
4. Redundancy and Failover: Design IoT storage systems with redundancy and failover capabilities. Implement redundant hardware components, such as redundant servers and storage devices, to ensure continuous availability.
5. Data Recovery Strategies: Describe the many forms of disaster recovery plans. As part of this, recovery time objectives (RTOs) and recovery point objectives (RPOs) are defined to specify how quickly data must be retrieved and how much data loss is acceptable.
6. Incident Response Plan: Develop a plan to respond to different types of disasters. Outline the roles and responsibilities of team members, procedures to follow, and communication protocols to ensure a coordinated response.
7. Testing and Training: Regularly test the disaster recovery plan to ensure its effectiveness. Conduct simulations and drills to evaluate the response time, recovery process, and coordination among teams. Provide training to relevant personnel on their roles and responsibilities.
8. Cybersecurity Measures: Integrate cybersecurity measures into the disaster recovery plan to safeguard data during recovery. Ensure that recovered systems are free from malware and vulnerabilities.

9. Communication Plan: Establish communication channels and protocols to keep stakeholders informed during and after a disaster. This includes notifying employees, customers, partners, and regulatory authorities if necessary.

Disaster recovery planning for IoT storage is an ongoing process that requires coordination, resources, and attention to detail. A well-prepared disaster recovery plan helps minimize downtime, ensures data integrity, and supports the continuity of IoT operations even in the face of unexpected disruptions.

■ Data Replication and Redundancy Techniques

Data replication and redundancy techniques are vital for ensuring data availability, fault tolerance, and resilience in IoT storage systems. These techniques involve creating and maintaining multiple copies of data across different locations or storage systems [64][65]. Here are some commonly used data replication and redundancy techniques:

1. Full Replication: Full replication involves creating complete and identical copies of data across multiple storage systems or devices. Any changes made to the original data are propagated to all the replicas. Full replication provides high availability and allows for seamless failover in case of a system or component failure. However, it can be resource-intensive and requires adequate storage capacity.
2. Partial Replication: Partial replication involves selectively replicating subsets of data based on predefined criteria. This approach is suitable when not all data needs to be replicated across all storage systems. For example, frequently accessed or critical data can be replicated in real-time, while less critical or less frequently accessed data can be replicated at a lower frequency or on-demand.
3. Geographical Redundancy: Geographical redundancy, also known as geographic dispersion, involves storing data copies in geographically diverse locations. This technique protects against regional disasters, ensuring data availability even if an entire site or region is affected. Geographical redundancy can be achieved by replicating data to multiple data centers located in different regions or by utilizing cloud-based storage services with global data centers.
4. Erasure Coding: Erasure coding is a data redundancy technique that breaks data into small fragments, adds redundant information (parity), and distributes them across multiple storage devices or nodes. This technique allows data recovery even if some fragments or devices are lost or unavailable. Erasure coding provides higher storage efficiency compared to traditional replication methods.
5. Hybrid Replication: Hybrid replication combines multiple replication techniques to achieve desired levels of data availability and resilience. This

approach allows organizations to use a combination of full replication, partial replication, geographical redundancy, or erasure coding based on the specific requirements of different data sets or applications within the IoT storage system.

6. Active-Active Replication: Active-active replication involves maintaining multiple active copies of data that are simultaneously updated and accessible. This technique enables load balancing and improves performance by distributing data access across multiple replicas. In case of a failure, the remaining active replicas can continue serving requests, ensuring uninterrupted availability.

7. Peer-to-Peer Replication: Peer-to-peer replication leverages the capabilities of distributed systems, where each node can act as both a data source and a replica. Data is shared and synchronized across multiple nodes in a decentralized manner, allowing for scalability, fault tolerance, and efficient data distribution. Peer-to-peer replication is commonly used in distributed storage systems and blockchain-based architectures.

8. Snapshot Replication: Snapshot replication involves creating point-in-time copies, or snapshots, of data. Snapshots capture the state of the data at a specific moment, allowing for quick recovery or rollback to a previous state if necessary. Snapshots can be used as a backup mechanism or as a basis for replication to other storage systems.

9. Synchronous and Asynchronous Replication: Synchronous replication ensures that data changes are immediately propagated to all replicas before acknowledging a write operation. This provides strong consistency but can introduce latency due to the need for synchronous communication. Asynchronous replication, on the other hand, allows for more flexibility by allowing data changes to be propagated to replicas with a slight delay. Asynchronous replication provides higher performance but may result in temporary data inconsistencies.

The choice of replication and redundancy techniques depends on factors such as data criticality, performance requirements, storage capacity, geographical considerations, and budget constraints. Organizations should carefully assess their specific needs and design a replication strategy that provides the desired level of data availability, fault tolerance, and recovery capabilities for their IoT storage systems.

7.5 Data Integrity and Verification in IoT Storage

Data integrity and verification in IoT storage refer to the processes and techniques used to ensure the accuracy, reliability, and consistency of data stored within Internet of Things (IoT) environments. Massive volumes of data are produced and exchanged by IoT devices, maintaining data integrity and verifying its authenticity is crucial to prevent errors, corruption, and unauthorized modifications [66][67]. Here is an overview of these concepts:

Data Integrity: Data integrity refers to the assurance that data remains accurate, consistent, and unaltered throughout its lifecycle. Ensuring data integrity involves preventing unintentional changes, corruption, or loss of data, as well as identifying and addressing any discrepancies that may occur. Several factors contribute to data integrity:

1. Checksums and Hashing: Checksums and cryptographic hashing algorithms generate unique strings of characters based on the data content. These checksums or hashes can be used to verify the integrity of data by comparing them before and after storage or transmission. Any change in data will result in a different checksum or hash value.
2. Cyclic Redundancy Check (CRC): CRC is an error-checking technique used to detect changes in data. It calculates a checksum based on the data is binary representation and compares it to the received or stored checksum to identify errors.
3. Data Validation: Implement data validation mechanisms to ensure that data adheres to predefined formats, rules, and constraints. This prevents inaccurate or incomplete data from being stored.
4. Digital Signatures: Digital signatures use asymmetric encryption to create a unique signature that verifies the origin and integrity of the data. They provide strong assurance of data authenticity and integrity.
5. Write Verification: After writing data to storage, perform a read operation to verify that the data was written correctly. This helps identify write errors or storage issues that could affect data integrity.

Data Verification: Data verification involves confirming the authenticity and correctness of data by comparing it to a trusted source or using specific validation techniques. In the context of IoT storage, data verification helps ensure that the data being stored or retrieved is reliable and valid.

1. Time Stamping: Use time stamps to record the time when data was generated, transmitted, or stored. This helps establish the sequence of events and supports data verification.
2. Chain of Custody: Maintain a secure chain of custody for data to ensure that data has not been tampered with or altered during storage or transmission.
3. Secure Communication Protocols: Implement secure communication protocols (such as HTTPS, MQTT over TLS) to prevent data tampering during transmission between IoT devices and storage systems.
4. Data Auditing: Regularly audit stored data to detect any unauthorized changes or discrepancies. This involves comparing stored data to expected values or historical records.

Data integrity and verification mechanisms provide assurance that the data stored in IoT environments is accurate, reliable, and untampered. By implementing these techniques, organizations can maintain the trustworthiness of their data and make informed decisions based on high-quality information.

■ **Techniques for Ensuring Data Integrity**

Ensuring data integrity involves employing various techniques to maintain the accuracy, consistency, and reliability of data throughout its lifecycle. These techniques are essential to prevent data corruption, unauthorized modifications, and errors that could compromise the quality and trustworthiness of the data [68][69]. Here are some techniques for ensuring data integrity:

1. Checksums and Hashing:Checksums and cryptographic hashing algorithms create unique strings of characters based on the content of data. By comparing checksums or hashes before and after data storage or transmission, you can verify if the data has been altered. Even minor changes in the data will result in significantly different checksum or hash values.
2. Cyclic Redundancy Check (CRC):CRC is a widely used error-checking technique. It involves calculating a checksum based on the binary representation of the data and then comparing it to a precomputed checksum to identify errors. It is commonly used in storage devices and network communications.
3. Digital Signatures: Asymmetric encryption is used in digital signatures to produce a distinctive signature that confirms the data provenance and integrity. The signature is created with a private key and can be validated with the associated public key. Digital signatures are particularly useful for verifying the authenticity of messages and documents.
4. Data Validation and Constraints: Implement data validation mechanisms to ensure that data adheres to predefined formats, rules, and constraints. This prevents incorrect, incomplete, or inconsistent data from being stored.
5. Time stamping: Time stamping records the time when data was generated, transmitted, or stored. This helps establish the chronological sequence of events and supports data verification. Accurate timestamps are crucial for audit trails and maintaining the order of events.
6. Write Verification: After writing data to a storage medium, perform a read operation to verify that the data was written correctly. This helps identify write errors or storage issues that could impact data integrity.
7. Chain of Custody: Chain of custody ensures that data has not been tampered with or altered during storage or transmission. It involves securely tracking and documenting the movement and handling of data to maintain its integrity.

8. Secure Communication Protocols: Make use of secure communication protocols like HTTPS, SSL/TLS, and cryptographic protocols like IPsec, to protect data during transmission. These protocols prevent data tampering and eavesdropping.

By implementing these techniques, organizations can ensure the integrity of their data, build trust among users, and minimize the risk of data corruption or unauthorized modifications. Data integrity is a cornerstone of data quality and forms the basis for informed decision-making.

▪ Blockchain Technology for Immutable Storage

Blockchain technology is a decentralized and distributed ledger system that is widely known for its ability to provide secure, transparent, and tamper-resistant record-keeping. In the context of data storage, blockchain offers a solution for ensuring immutable storage, where data once stored cannot be altered, deleted, or tampered with without leaving a trace. This is achieved through the unique properties of blockchain, including decentralization, cryptographic hashing, consensus mechanisms, and data transparency [70][71]. Here is how blockchain technology ensures immutable storage:

1. Decentralization: Unlike traditional centralized systems, blockchain operates on a distributed network of nodes. Each participant in the network maintains a copy of the entire ledger, eliminating single points of control and vulnerability.
2. Cryptographic Hashing: Data stored on a blockchain is hashed using cryptographic algorithms. Hashing generates a fixed-length string of characters unique to the input data. Even a slight change in the data will result in a completely different hash value.
3. Blocks and Chaining: Data is organized into blocks, each containing a set of transactions or data records. Each block includes a reference (hash) to the previous block, creating a chronological chain of blocks. This chaining ensures that any change to a previous block would require changing all subsequent blocks, making tampering extremely difficult.
4. Proof of Work and Proof of Stake: Consensus mechanisms like PoW and PoS ensure that participants in the network invest resources (computational power or cryptocurrency stakes) to validate transactions. This makes it computationally expensive and economically impractical to alter data retroactively.
5. Data Immutability: When data is put to a block and the block is uploaded to the blockchain, it is nearly impossible to change the data without changing the contents of all succeeding blocks. This calls for the majority of the network to reach consensus, which is quite challenging in a decentralized network.

Block chaining properties make it an ideal technology for ensuring the immutable storage of data. It is particularly beneficial for applications requiring trustworthy record-keeping, such as supply chain tracking, digital identities, provenance tracking, and financial transactions, where data integrity is critical and trust is paramount.

■ Auditing and Verification Mechanisms

Auditing and verification mechanisms are important components for guaranteeing the integrity and trustworthiness of data stored in IoT systems [72][73]. These mechanisms allow for the monitoring, validation, and verification of data to detect any anomalies, errors, or unauthorized activities. Here are some common auditing and verification mechanisms used in IoT storage:

1. Data Logging and Monitoring: Data logging involves capturing and recording relevant information about system activities, events, and user interactions. It enables the retrospective analysis of data to identify potential issues or anomalies. Real-time monitoring of system logs allows for immediate detection and response to suspicious activities, ensuring data integrity and security.

2. Timestamping: Timestamping involves assigning a specific time value to data or events, indicating when they occurred. Timestamps can be used to track the sequence of events, detect unauthorized modifications, and verify the chronological order of data entries. Trusted time sources, such as network time protocols or blockchain-based timestamping services, enhance the reliability and integrity of timestamps.

3. Data Auditing: Data auditing involves periodic reviews and assessments of data to ensure compliance, accuracy, and integrity. Audits can be conducted internally or by external entities to verify the correctness of data, adherence to data policies, and regulatory compliance. Auditing helps identify and rectify any data discrepancies, errors, or unauthorized modifications.

4. Hash Functions and Checksums: Hash functions and checksums can be used to verify the integrity of data. By generating hash values or checksums for data and comparing them with the original values, any modifications or corruption can be detected. Hash functions and checksums provide a fast and efficient way to verify data integrity, especially during data transfers or storage.

5. Digital Signatures: The authenticity, integrity, and non-repudiation of electronic documents, messages, or transactions are provided by digital signatures, which are a type of cryptographic technology. It acts as the digital equivalent of a handwritten signature, assuring that a messages sender or a documents author can be identified and that the messages or documents contents have not been changed since the signature was added.

6. Data Validation and Quality Checks: Implementing data validation mechanisms ensures that data adheres to predefined rules, formats, and constraints. It involves checking data for completeness, accuracy, and

consistency. Data validation techniques, such as format validation, range checks, referential integrity checks, or business rule enforcement, help identify and prevent the storage of invalid or inconsistent data.

7. Access Controls and User Authentication: In order to guarantee data integrity and security, strong access controls and user authentication techniques are essential. By utilizing authentication methods like passwords, fingerprints, or multi-factor authentication, only authorized users are able to access and edit the data. Access controls enforce proper permissions, restrictions, and segregation of duties, preventing unauthorized access or modifications.

8. Peer Reviews and Code Analysis: Peer reviews and code analysis are essential practices for ensuring the integrity and quality of software applications or firmware used in IoT systems. Peer reviews involve having other developers review code for potential vulnerabilities, logic errors, or unauthorized data access. Code analysis tools can automatically scan code for security flaws, ensuring adherence to coding standards and best practices.

9. Regulatory Compliance and External Audits: Compliance with industry regulations and standards plays a significant role in ensuring data integrity. External audits conducted by third-party entities help verify adherence to regulatory requirements, data protection laws, and industry-specific standards. These audits validate the effectiveness of security controls, data handling processes, and overall data integrity practices.

By implementing a combination of these auditing and verification mechanisms, organizations can enhance data integrity, detect anomalies or unauthorized activities, and maintain the trustworthiness of data stored in IoT systems. Regular monitoring, analysis, and improvement of these mechanisms are essential to address emerging threats and vulnerabilities.

▪ Tamper-proof Data Storage Solutions

The integrity and immutability of stored data are ensured by tamper-proof data storage solutions, which are intended to offer a high level of security [74][75]. These solutions use various techniques and technologies to protect against unauthorized access, tampering, or modification of data. Here are some common tamper-proof data storage solutions:

1. Blockchain Technology: Blockchain technology provides a decentralized and immutable storage solution. It uses cryptographic hashing, consensus mechanisms, and distributed ledger technology to ensure the integrity and transparency of data. Data stored on a blockchain is resistant to tampering due to the consensus required from multiple nodes to validate and add new blocks to the chain.

2. Write-Once-Read-Many (WORM) Storage: WORM storage systems allow data to be written once and become read-only afterward. This prevents any subsequent modifications or deletions, ensuring the integrity and immutability of the data. WORM storage is commonly used in compliance-driven industries where data retention and tamper-proof records are required.

3. Content Addressable Storage (CAS): CAS is a storage architecture that assigns a unique identifier, often a cryptographic hash, to each piece of data stored. The identifier is calculated based on the content of the data itself, making it tamper-evident. Any modification to the data would result in a different identifier, ensuring the integrity of the stored information.

4. Hardware Security Modules (HSM): Specialized hardware units known as HSMs offer secure storage and cryptographic functions. They store cryptographic keys and perform operations such as encryption, decryption, and digital signing within a secure environment. HSMs help protect against unauthorized access and tampering of sensitive data and cryptographic materials.

5. Immutable Storage Systems: Immutable storage systems prevent any modification or deletion of data once it is stored. These systems use strict access controls, write-once mechanisms, and data protection measures to ensure data integrity and prevent tampering. Immutable storage systems are often used in regulated industries where data retention, compliance, and auditability are critical.

6. Secure Logging and Audit Trails: Implementing secure logging and audit trails helps capture detailed records of data access, modifications, and system activities. These logs are tamper-evident and can be used to monitor and detect any unauthorized or suspicious activities. Secure logging ensures data integrity and enables forensic analysis in case of security incidents.

7. Tamper-evident Seals and Physical Security: In some scenarios, physical security measures are necessary to ensure tamper-proof data storage. This may involve using tamper-evident seals, locks, or surveillance systems to protect physical storage devices or data centers. Physical security measures complement digital security measures to provide a comprehensive tamper-proof solution.

8. Data Encryption: Encrypting data before storing it adds an extra layer of protection against unauthorized access and tampering. Encryption ensures that data remains confidential and maintains its integrity throughout its lifecycle. Even if an attacker gains access to the stored data, they would be unable to decipher or modify it without the encryption keys.

9. Secure Access Controls: Implementing robust access controls ensures that only authorized users or entities can access and modify the stored data. This involves authentication mechanisms, role-based access controls, and strong user permissions. Secure access controls help prevent unauthorized tampering or modifications by enforcing strict user privileges.

10. Data Backups and Disaster Recovery: Regularly backing up data and implementing effective disaster recovery strategies are essential components of tamper-proof storage. Backups provide a clean and valid copy of the data in case of data loss or corruption. Implementing off-site backups and comprehensive disaster recovery plans ensures the availability and integrity of data even in the event of a major incident.

Organizations should assess their specific requirements, compliance obligations, and risk profiles to choose the appropriate tamper-proof data storage solutions. By implementing these solutions, organizations can protect their data from unauthorized access, tampering, or modification, ensuring data integrity and maintaining trust in their systems.

7.6 Future Trends and Challenges in IoT Storage

Future trends and challenges in IoT storage are influenced by advancements in technology, evolving data management practices, and the increasing scale and complexity of IoT deployments [75][76]. Here are some key trends and challenges to consider:

1. Big Data and Analytics: As the volume, variety, and velocity of IoT data continue to grow, there is a need for scalable and efficient storage solutions capable of handling big data. Storage systems will need to support real-time processing and analytics to derive valuable insights from the vast amount of IoT data generated.

2. Edge Computing and Storage: With the rise of edge computing, data processing and storage are moving closer to IoT devices at the network edge. Edge storage solutions enable faster response times, reduced data transfer, and improved privacy by processing and storing data locally. However, managing distributed edge storage and ensuring data consistency and integrity pose challenges.

3. Distributed Storage Architectures: The increasing scale of IoT deployments requires distributed storage architectures that can handle massive amounts of data across multiple locations. Distributed file systems, object storage, and content delivery networks (CDNs) enable efficient data distribution, replication, and availability in geographically dispersed IoT environments.

4. Data Security and Privacy: Data privacy and security in the IoT continue to be major issues. To guard against unwanted access, tampering, and breaches, IoT storage systems must implement strong encryption, access controls, and authentication protocols. It will also be essential to ensure compliance with data protection laws and resolve privacy issues.

5. Hybrid Cloud and Multi-cloud Storage: Organizations are adopting hybrid cloud and multi-cloud strategies, leveraging both public and private cloud storage for IoT data. This approach offers flexibility, scalability, and cost efficiency. However, managing data across different cloud environments, ensuring data consistency, and addressing data sovereignty and compliance challenges are key considerations.

6. Data Lifecycle Management: Efficient data lifecycle management is essential to optimize storage resources and manage data from creation to deletion. This includes strategies for data retention, archiving, backup, and deletion, while considering regulatory requirements, business needs, and data access patterns.

7. AI and Machine Learning for Storage Optimization: AI and machine learning techniques can be applied to optimize IoT storage systems. These technologies can analyze data usage patterns, predict storage needs, automate data classification and tiering, and optimize storage resources for improved performance and cost efficiency.

8. Interoperability and Standards: Achieving interoperability and adopting common standards in IoT storage is critical to enable seamless integration and data exchange between different IoT devices, platforms, and storage systems. Standardization efforts across IoT protocols, data formats, and storage interfaces are necessary to simplify integration and ensure compatibility.

9. Data Governance and Compliance: With the increasing regulatory focus on data governance and privacy, organizations need to establish robust data governance frameworks and policies. This includes data provenance, data lineage, data quality, and compliance with regulations such as GDPR, CCPA, and industry-specific requirements.

10. Scalability and Cost Optimization: As the number of IoT devices and data sources continues to grow exponentially, scalability and cost optimization become important factors. Storage systems must be able to scale horizontally and vertically to handle the increasing data load while managing costs effectively.

Addressing these future trends and challenges in IoT storage requires a comprehensive approach that considers technology advancements, security measures, data management strategies, and compliance considerations [77]. Organizations should continuously evaluate and adapt their IoT storage architectures, data management practices, and security frameworks to stay ahead in the rapidly evolving IoT landscape.

■ **Evolving Storage Technologies for IoT**

Evolving storage technologies for IoT are continually being developed and refined to address the specific requirements of IoT deployments [78]. These technologies aim to provide scalable, efficient, and reliable storage solutions that can handle the increasing volume, variety, and velocity of IoT data. Here are some evolving storage technologies for IoT:

1. Solid-State Drives (SSDs): SSDs are increasingly replacing traditional hard disk drives (HDDs) in IoT storage systems. SSDs offer higher performance, lower latency, and better reliability due to their lack of moving parts. They provide faster read and write speeds, making them well-suited for real-time data processing and analytics in IoT applications.

2. Non-Volatile Memory Express (NVMe): NVMe is an interface protocol designed specifically for solid-state storage devices. It provides a high-speed, low-latency communication channel between the storage device and the IoT system, enabling faster data transfers and improved storage performance. NVMe is particularly beneficial for IoT applications that require quick access to data, such as real-time monitoring or control systems.

3. Storage Class Memory (SCM): SCM, also known as persistent memory or storage-class memory, combines the speed of memory and the persistence of storage. It provides near-DRAM access speeds with non-volatility, allowing for fast data storage and retrieval. SCM can significantly improve IoT application performance and reduce data latency, making it ideal for time-sensitive IoT workloads.

4. Cloud Storage and Object Storage: Cloud storage platforms offer scalable and flexible storage solutions for IoT applications. Cloud storage provides virtually unlimited storage capacity and enables seamless integration with other cloud-based services, analytics platforms, and AI capabilities. Object storage, in particular, is well-suited for unstructured data in IoT, allowing efficient storage and retrieval of large volumes of data.

5. Software-Defined Storage (SDS): SDS decouples storage hardware from software management, allowing for greater flexibility and scalability. It enables the pooling of storage resources and provides centralized management and automation capabilities. SDS can adapt to the changing demands of IoT deployments, making it easier to scale storage capacity, improve data management, and optimize performance.

6. Edge Storage and Fog Storage: Edge storage refers to the storage capabilities present at the network edge, closer to IoT devices. It enables local data processing and storage, reducing the need for extensive data transfers to centralized cloud storage. Fog storage builds on the concept of edge storage and extends it to a larger distributed network, enabling storage capabilities in fog computing environments. Edge and fog storage help reduce latency, bandwidth requirements, and enable real-time processing in IoT applications.

7. Hyperconverged Infrastructure (HCI): Storage, computing, and networking are all combined into one system by HCI. By offering a uniform and scalable

platform, it streamlines the deployment and maintenance of IoT storage infrastructure. HCI enables efficient resource utilization, seamless scalability, and streamlined data management for IoT applications.

8. Data Deduplication and Compression: Data deduplication and compression technologies optimize storage efficiency by identifying and eliminating redundant or duplicate data. Deduplication reduces storage requirements by storing only unique data, while compression reduces the size of data without loss of information. These techniques help optimize storage capacity and improve data transfer efficiency in IoT storage systems.

9. Quantum Storage: Quantum storage technologies are still in the early stages of development but hold promising potential for future IoT applications. Quantum storage leverages quantum properties to store and process data, offering significant improvements in storage capacity, security, and computational capabilities. Quantum storage has the potential to revolutionize IoT storage by addressing challenges related to data volume, security, and processing power.

10. Storage Orchestration and Data Management Platforms: Storage orchestration platforms and data management solutions are emerging to address the complexity of managing distributed storage systems in IoT deployments. These platforms provide centralized management, monitoring, and automation capabilities, allowing organizations to efficiently manage and optimize storage resources across IoT environments.

As the IoT landscape evolves, storage technologies will continue to advance to meet the evolving demands of IoT applications. Organizations should evaluate and select the most appropriate storage technologies based on their specific requirements, scalability needs, performance expectations, and cost considerations.

■ Scalability and Performance Enhancement

Scalability and performance enhancement are critical considerations for IoT storage systems as they need to handle large volumes of data generated by numerous connected devices [79][80]. Here are some techniques and approaches to achieve scalability and enhance performance in IoT storage:

1. Distributed Storage Architecture: Implementing a distributed storage architecture allows for horizontal scalability by distributing data across multiple storage nodes. Each node can handle a subset of the data and perform parallel processing, resulting in improved storage capacity and performance. Distributed storage systems can be designed using technologies like distributed file systems, object storage, or NoSQL databases.

2. Data Partitioning and Sharding: Data partitioning involves dividing the data into smaller subsets and distributing them across multiple storage nodes. Sharding is a specific partitioning technique where each shard contains a subset of data. This approach enables parallel processing and improves query performance by reducing the amount of data accessed in each operation. Data partitioning and sharding can be based on various criteria such as device ID, data type, or geographical location.

3. Caching: Caching involves storing frequently accessed or hot data in fast and readily available memory, such as solid-state drives (SSDs) or in-memory databases. Caching reduces the latency associated with retrieving data from slower storage media, enhancing overall system performance. Different levels of caching can be used, such as client-side caching, server-side caching, or content delivery network (CDN) caching.

4. Compression and Data Deduplication: Compressing data reduces storage requirements and improves data transfer efficiency. Compression techniques like lossless compression algorithms can reduce the size of data without loss of information. Data deduplication eliminates redundant data by identifying and storing only unique data instances, further reducing storage needs and improving overall system performance.

5. Load Balancing: Load balancing distributes the workload evenly across multiple storage nodes, preventing any single node from becoming a performance bottleneck. Load balancing algorithms monitor the systems resource utilization and dynamically route requests to available nodes, optimizing performance and ensuring scalability. Load balancing can be achieved at the network level or within the storage system itself.

6. Parallel Processing: Leveraging parallel processing techniques allows for concurrent execution of data processing tasks, leading to improved performance. By breaking down tasks into smaller subtasks that can be executed simultaneously, parallel processing reduces the time required to complete operations. Techniques like parallel query processing, parallel file systems, or parallel database architectures can be employed to achieve parallelism.

7. Data Replication and Distribution: Replicating data across multiple storage nodes enhances both scalability and performance. Replication improves data availability and fault tolerance by ensuring redundant copies of data. Additionally, distributing data closer to the point of consumption or processing reduces network latency and improves response times.

8. Scalable Storage Infrastructure: Building a scalable storage infrastructure involves leveraging technologies that can accommodate growing data volumes and handle increased processing requirements. This includes utilizing scalable storage devices, such as cloud storage, object storage, or distributed file systems, that offer the ability to add or remove storage capacity dynamically.

Scalable storage infrastructure ensures the system can handle increased data loads without compromising performance.

9. Data Tiering and Storage Virtualization: Data tiering is the process of grouping data into categories according to usage patterns and distributing it among various storage tiers with various cost and performance parameters. Less often used data can be shifted to slower, less expensive storage while frequently used data might be stored on faster, more expensive storage medium. Storage virtualization provides a layer of abstraction that allows different storage resources to be managed as a single virtualized pool, simplifying scalability and performance management.

10. Performance Monitoring and Optimization: Regular monitoring of system performance metrics, such as response times, throughput, and resource utilization, is crucial for identifying bottlenecks and optimizing performance. Performance monitoring tools can help detect performance issues, provide insights into system behavior, and guide optimization efforts to ensure the system is operating at peak efficiency.

By implementing these scalability and performance enhancement techniques, IoT storage systems can effectively handle the increasing data volumes and processing demands of IoT applications. It is important to assess specific requirements, consider the nature of the data and workload, and continually monitor and optimize the system to meet evolving needs.

■ **Privacy and Security Challenges in Next-generation IoT Storage**

Next-generation IoT storage presents various privacy and security challenges due to the increasing scale, complexity, and interconnectedness of IoT systems [81][82]. Here are some key challenges that need to be addressed:

1. Data Encryption and Protection: Protecting data stored in IoT systems is crucial to maintaining privacy and security. Encryption techniques, such as end-to-end encryption, secure key management, and strong cryptographic algorithms, should be employed to ensure that data is encrypted both during transmission and storage. Additionally, measures such as access controls, data anonymization, and data masking can further protect sensitive information.

2. Secure Access Controls: For the purpose of preventing illegal access and data breaches, effective access controls must be established. To guarantee that only approved people or devices can access and modify the stored data, access control mechanisms such as role-based access control (RBAC), attribute-based access control (ABAC), or multi-factor authentication (MFA) should be implemented.

3. Data Privacy and Consent Management: Large volumes of personal data are gathered and stored by IoT equipment. It is necessary to gain user consent for data collecting and put in place methods for data anonymization, pseudonymization, and privacy-enhancing technologies (PETs) in order to ensure compliance with privacy laws like the General Data Protection Regulation (GDPR).Privacy policies should be transparently communicated to users, and mechanisms for data subject rights, such as data erasure or rectification, should be implemented.

4. IoT Device Security: IoT devices themselves can be vulnerable to security threats, which can impact the integrity and privacy of the stored data. Ensuring the security of IoT devices involves implementing secure boot processes, regular security updates, strong authentication mechanisms, and secure communication protocols. Security measures should be implemented at the device level to protect against device tampering, unauthorized access, and malware attacks.

5. Secure Data Sharing and Interoperability: IoT systems often involve data sharing and interoperability between various devices and platforms. Secure data sharing mechanisms should be implemented to ensure that data is exchanged securely and only with authorized parties. Standardization efforts to establish secure communication protocols, data formats, and interoperability frameworks are essential to mitigate security risks associated with data sharing.

6. Physical Security: Physical security measures for IoT storage infrastructure, including data centers and edge computing environments, are crucial to prevent unauthorized physical access, theft, or tampering. These measures include physical access controls, surveillance systems, environmental monitoring, and secure disposal of storage media to protect against physical attacks or breaches.

7. Supply Chain Security: Ensuring the security of the entire IoT storage supply chain is critical to prevent tampering, counterfeiting, or the introduction of compromised components. Implementing secure supply chain practices, including rigorous vetting of suppliers, secure component sourcing, and hardware/software integrity checks, helps mitigate risks and enhance the security of IoT storage solutions.

8. Regulatory Compliance: Next-generation IoT storage systems must comply with relevant privacy and security regulations. Organizations should stay updated on applicable regulations and standards, such as GDPR, California Consumer Privacy Act (CCPA), or industry-specific requirements, and ensure that their storage practices and security measures align with the regulatory frameworks.

Addressing these privacy and security challenges requires a multi-faceted approach that encompasses technological measures, policy frameworks, and organizational practices. Collaboration between stakeholders, including IoT device manufacturers, storage providers, policymakers, and end-users, is essential to create a secure and privacy-enhancing ecosystem for next-generation IoT storage.

■ Interoperability and Standardization Efforts

The difficulties posed by IoT storage are greatly helped by attempts towards interoperability and standardization. They seek to provide uniform frameworks, protocols, and norms to assure seamless data interchange, device interoperability, and integration between various IoT platforms, storage systems, and devices [83][84]. Here is how interoperability and standardization efforts contribute to the advancement of IoT storage:

1. Protocol Standardization: Interoperability is enhanced by standardizing communication protocols used in IoT storage systems. Protocols like MQTT (Message Queuing Telemetry Transport), CoAP (Constrained Application Protocol), and HTTP (Hypertext Transfer Protocol) provide standardized ways for devices and storage systems to communicate and exchange data. Standardized protocols enable interoperability between different devices and storage platforms, allowing them to work together seamlessly.

2. Data Formats and Schema Standardization: Data transmitted between IoT devices and storage systems can be read and handled uniformly by standardizing data formats and schemas. Across heterogeneous IoT systems, data integration, storage, and processing are made easier by common data formats like JSON (JavaScript Object Notation) or XML (eXtensible Markup Language) and defined schemas like SensorML or OPC UA (Unified Architecture).

3. Metadata and Semantic Interoperability: Metadata standards provide a common set of descriptors and properties for IoT data, facilitating data discovery, interpretation, and integration. Semantic interoperability standards, such as Semantic Web technologies (RDF, OWL), enable data to be described in a machine-readable format, enhancing the understanding and interoperability of data across different systems and domains.

4. API Standardization: Standardizing application programming interfaces (APIs) enables interoperability and integration between IoT devices, storage systems, and applications. Common APIs for accessing and manipulating data stored in IoT storage platforms simplify development, integration, and interoperability efforts. For example, OGC (Open Geospatial Consortium) provides standardized APIs for accessing geospatial data stored in IoT systems.

5. Security and Privacy Standards: Standardization efforts also focus on security and privacy aspects of IoT storage systems. Guidelines for safeguarding IoT storage systems and managing privacy concerns are provided by standards like the ISO/IEC 27000 series for information security management and the NIST (National Institute of Standards and Technology) Cybersecurity Framework. Standardized security protocols, authentication mechanisms, and encryption techniques ensure interoperability and compatibility across different IoT storage solutions.

6. Interoperable Data Models: Developing interoperable data models and ontologies enables seamless integration and exchange of data between diverse IoT systems. Standards like one M2M, Fiware, or Hypercat provide common data models, information models, and ontologies that define the structure and semantics of IoT data. These standardized models facilitate data interoperability and integration across different IoT storage systems.

7. Industry Consortia and Alliances: Collaborative efforts through industry consortia and alliances play a crucial role in driving interoperability and standardization. Organizations such as the Industrial Internet Consortium (IIC), Open Connectivity Foundation (OCF), Thread Group, and AllSeen Alliance work towards developing and promoting interoperability standards for IoT storage and other IoT domains. These collaborative initiatives bring together stakeholders from various industries to establish common frameworks and guidelines.

8. Testing and Certification Programs: Testing and certification programs ensure compliance with interoperability standards and verify the compatibility of IoT storage systems. These programs provide independent validation of conformance to standards, improving trust and confidence in the interoperability of IoT storage solutions. Certification programs, such as the Wi-Fi Alliance or Zigbee Alliance, validate compliance with wireless communication standards and promote interoperability between devices and storage systems.

By promoting interoperability and standardization in IoT storage, organizations can achieve seamless integration, data exchange, and collaboration across diverse IoT ecosystems. Interoperability standards facilitate the integration of different devices, platforms, and storage systems, enabling organizations to choose and combine solutions that best meet their needs while ensuring compatibility and scalability.

References

[1] Shafagh, H., Burkhalter, L., Hithnawi, A. and Duquennoy. S., 2017, November. Towards blockchain-based auditable storage and sharing of IoT data. In Proceedings of the 2017 on Cloud Computing Security Workshop (pp. 45 to 50).

[2] Chervyakov, N., Babenko, M., Tchernykh, A., Kucherov, N., Miranda-Lopez, V. and Cortes-Mendoza, J.M., 2019. AR-RRNS: Configurable reliable distributed data storage systems for Internet of Things to ensure security. Future Generation Computer Systems, 92, pp.1080 to 1092.

[3] Sasirekha, S.P., Priya, A., Anita, T. and Sherubha, P., 2020, December. Data processing and management in IoT and wireless sensor network. In Journal of Physics: Conference Series(Vol. 1712, No. 1, pp. 012002). IOP Publishing.

[4] Soumyalatha, S.G.H., 2016, May. Study of IoT: Understanding IoT architecture, applications, issues and challenges. In 1st International Conference on Innovations in Computing & Net-working (ICICN16), CSE, RRCE. International Journal of Advanced Networking & Applications (Vol. 478).

[5] Zhang, Z.K., Cho, M.C.Y., Wang, C.W., Hsu, C.W., Chen, C.K. and Shieh, S., 2014, November. IoT security: Ongoing challenges and research opportunities. In *2014 IEEE 7th International Conference on Service-Oriented Computing and Applications*(pp. 230 to 234). IEEE.

[6] Kulkarni, P.H., Kute, P.D. and More, V.N., 2016, January. IoT based data processing for automated industrial meter reader using Raspberry Pi. In*2016 International Conference on Internet of Things and Applications (IOTA)*(pp. 107 to 111). IEEE.

[7] Niyato, D., Lu, X., Wang, P., Kim, D.I. and Han, Z., 2016. Economics of Internet of Things: An information market approach. *IEEE Wireless Communications, 23*(4), pp.136 to 145.

[8] Covington, M.J. and Carskadden, R., 2013, June. Threat implications of the internet of things. In *2013 5th International Conference on Cyber Conflict (CYCON 2013)* (pp. 1 to 12). IEEE.

[9] Kopanakis, I., Vassakis, K. and Mastorakis, G., 2016, June. Big data in data-driven innovation: The impact in enterprises performance. In Proceedings of 11th Annual MIBESInternational Conference(pp. 257 to 263).

[10] Yadav, E.P., Mittal, E.A. and Yadav, H., 2018, February. IoT: Challenges and issues in indian perspective. In *2018 3rd International Conference On Internet of Things: Smart Innovation and Usages (IoT-SIU)* (pp. 1 to 5). IEEE.

[11] Surya,L., 2016. Security challenges and strategies for the IoT in cloud computing. *International Journal of Innovations in Engineering Research and Technology ISSN,* pp.2394 to 3696.

[12] Tawalbeh, L.A., Muheidat, F., Tawalbeh, M. and Quwaider, M., 2020. IoT Privacy and security: Challenges and solutions. *Applied Sciences, 10*(12), pp.4102.

[13] Patel, K.K., Patel, S.M. and Scholar, P., 2016. Internet of Things-IOT: Definition, characteristics, architecture, enabling technologies, application & future challenges. *International Journal of Engineering Science and Computing, 6*(5).

[14] Patel, K.K., Patel, S.M. and Scholar, P., 2016. Internet of Things-IOT: definition, characteristics, architecture, enabling technologies, application & future challenges. *International Journal of Engineering Science nd Computing, 6*(5).

[15] Sharma, L., Sengupta, S. and Lohan, N., 2022. An overview of security issues of internet of things. *Computer Vision and Internet of Things: Technologies and Applications*, pp.29 to 40.

[16] Mohanta, B.K., Jena, D., Ramasubbareddy, S., Daneshmand, M. and Gandomi, A.H., 2020. Addressing security and privacy issues of IoT using blockchain technology. *IEEE Internet of Things Journal, 8*(2), pp.881 to 888.

[17] Loria, M.P., Toja, M., Carchiolo, V. and Malgeri, M., 2017,September. An efficient real-time architecture for collecting IoT data. In *2017 Federated Conference on Computer Science and Information Systems (FedCSIS)*(pp. 1157 to 1166). IEEE.

[18] Cerbulescu, C.C. and Cerbulescu,C.M., 2016, May. Large data management in IOT applications. In *2016 17th International Carpathian Control Conference (ICCC)* (pp. 111 to 115). IEEE.

[19] Lu, J., Shen, J., Vijayakumar, P. and Gupta, B.B., 2021. Blockchain-based secure data storage protocol for sensors in the industrial Internet of Things. *IEEE Transactions on Industrial Informatics, 18*(8), pp.5422 to 5431.

[20] Van Capelleveen, G., Pohl, J., Fritsch, A. and Schien, D., 2018, May. The footprint of things: A hybrid approach towards the collection, storage and distribution of life cycle inventory data. In Birgit Penzenstadler, Steve Easterbrook, Colin Venters and Syed Ishtiaque Ahmed (Eds.), *ICT4S2018. 5th International Conference on Information and Communication Technology for Sustainability* (pp. 350 to 364).

[21] Bokefode, J.D., Bhise, A.S., Satarkar, P.A. and Modani, D.G., 2016. Developing a secure cloud storage system for storing IoT data by applying role based encryption. *Procedia Computer Science, 89*, pp.43 to 50.

[22] Sindhuja, P. and Balamurugan, M.S., 2015. Smart power monitoring and control system through Internet of Things using cloud data storage. *Indian Journal of Science and Technology, 8*(19), pp.1.

[23] Xu, S., Yang, G., Mu, Y. and Liu, X., 2019. A secure IoT cloud storage system with fine-grained access control and decryption key exposure resistance. *Future Generation Computer Systems, 97*, pp.284 to 294.

[24] Shen, S., Zhang, K., Zhou, Y. and Ci, S., 2020. Security in edge-assisted Internet of Things: Challenges and solutions. *Science China Information Sciences, 63*, pp.1 to 14.

[25] Zhou, L. and Liu, J., 2021, September. IOT Data storage solution based on hybrid blockchain edge architecture. In *Proceedings of the 2021 4th International Conference on Artificial Intelligence and Pattern Recognition* (pp. 466 to 471).

[26] Lee, J., Lee, K., Yoo, A. and Moon, C., 2020. Design and implementation of edge-fog-cloud system through HD map generation from LiDAR data of autonomous vehicles. *Electronics, 9*(12), pp.2084.

[27] Hassan, N., Yau, K.L.A. and Wu, C., 2019. Edge computing in 5G: A review. *IEEE Access,7*, pp.127276 to 127289.

[28] Cao, K., Liu, Y., Meng, G. and Sun, Q., 2020. An overview on edge computing research. *IEEE Access, 8*, pp.85714 to 85728.

[29] Satyanarayanan, M., 2017. The emergence of edge computing. *Computer, 50*(1), pp.30 to 39.

[30] Ni, J., Zhang, K., Lin, X. and Shen, X., 2017. Securing fog computing for internet of things applications: Challenges and solutions. *IEEE Communications Surveys & Tutorials,20*(1), pp.601 to 628.

[31] Hu,P., Dhelim, S., Ning, H. and Qiu, T., 2017. Survey on fog computing: Architecture, key technologies, applications and open issues. *Journal of Network and Computer Applications, 98*, pp.27 to 42.

[32] Bonomi, F., Milito, R., Natarajan, P. and Zhu, J., 2014. Fog computing: A platform for Internet of Things and analytics. *Big Data and Internet of Things: A Roadmap for Smart Environments*, pp.169 to 186.

[33] Chen, S., Zhang, T. and Shi, W., 2017. Fog computing. *IEEE Internet Computing, 21*(2), pp.4 to 6.

[34] Mahajan, K., Kumar, S. and Kumar, D., 2023. Hybrid methods for increasing security of IoT and cloud data. In *Machine Vision and Augmented Intelligence: Select Proceedings of MAI 2022* (pp. 571 to 586). Singapore: Springer Nature Singapore.

[35] Xu, X., Fu, S., Qi, L., Zhang, X., Liu, Q., He, Q. and Li, S., 2018. An IoT-oriented data placement method with privacy preservation in cloud environment. *Journal of Network and Computer Applications, 124*, pp.148 to 157.

[36] Sosa, R., Kiraly, C. and Rodriguez, J.D.P., 2018, December. Offloading execution from edge to cloud: A dynamic node-red based approach. In *2018 IEEE International Conference on Cloud Computing Technology and Science (CloudCom)*(pp. 149 to 152). IEEE.

[37] Liu,H., Xin, R., Chen, P. and Zhao, Z., 2022,July.Multi-objective robust workflow offloading in edge-to-cloud continuum. In *2022 IEEE 15th International Conference on Cloud Computing (CLOUD)*(pp. 469 to 478). IEEE.

[38] Mrabet, H., Belguith, S., Alhomoud, A. and Jemai, A., 2020. A survey of IoT security based on a layered architecture of sensing and data analysis. *Sensors, 20*(13), pp.3625.

[39] Kumar,P.M. and Gandhi, U.D., 2018. A novel three-tier Internet of Things architecture with machine learning algorithm for early detection of heart diseases. *Computers & Electrical Engineering, 65*, pp.222 to 235.

[40] Bao, Z., Shi, W., He, D. and Chood, K.K.R., 2018. IoTChain: A three-tier blockchain-based IoT security architecture. *arXiv preprint arXiv:1806.02008.*

[41] Mohiyuddin, A., Javed, A.R., Chakraborty, C., Rizwan, M., Shabbir, M. and Nebhen, J., 2022. Secure cloud storage for medical IoT data using adaptive neuro-fuzzy inference system. *International Journal of Fuzzy Systems, 24*(2), pp.1203 to 1215.

[42] Mahmoud, R., Yousuf, T., Aloul, F. and Zualkernan, I., 2015, December. Internet of things (IoT) security: Current status, challenges and prospective measures. In *2015 10th international conference for internet technology and secured transactions (ICITST)* (pp. 336 to 341). IEEE.

[43] Rao, T.A. and Haq, E.U., 2018. Security challenges facing IoT layers and its protective measures. *International Journal of Computer Applications, 179*(27), pp.31 to 35.

[44] Sindhura, S.,Praveen, S.P., Syedbi, S., Pratap, V.K. and Krishna, T.B.M., 2021. An effective secure storage of data in cloud using ISSE encryption technique. *Annals of the Romanian Society for Cell Biology*, pp.5321 to 5329.

[45] Sugumar, R. and Imam, S.B.S., 2015. Symmetric encryption algorithm to secure outsourced data in public cloud storage. *Indian Journal of Science and Technology*, *8*(23), pp.1.

[46] Nagesh, H.R. and Thejaswini, L., 2017, March. Study on encryption methods to secure the privacy of the data and computation on encrypted data present at cloud. In *2017 International Conference on Big Data Analytics and Computational Intelligence (ICBDAC)* (pp. 383 to 386). IEEE.

[47] Qiu, M., Gai, K., Thuraisingham, B., Tao, L. and Zhao, H., 2018. Proactive user-centric secure data scheme using attribute-based semantic access controls for mobile clouds in financial industry. *Future Generation Computer Systems*, *80*, pp.421 to 429.

[48] Samarati, P. and de Vimercati, S.C., 2000. Access control: Policies, models, and mechanisms. In *International School on Foundations of Security Analysis and Design* (pp. 137 to 196). Berlin, Heidelberg: Springer Berlin Heidelberg.

[49] Ali, G., Ahmad, N., Cao, Y., Khan, S., Cruickshank, H., Qazi, E.A. and Ali, A., 2020. xDBAuth: Blockchain based cross domain authentication and authorization framework for Internet of Things. *IEEE Access*, *8*, pp.58800 to 58816.

[50] Tahir, M., Sardaraz, M., Muhammad, S. and Saud Khan, M., 2020. A lightweight authentication and authorization framework for blockchain-enabled IoT network in health-informatics. *Sustainability*, *12*(17), pp.6960.

[51] Istiaque Ahmed, K., Tahir, M., HadiHabaebi, M., Lun Lau, S. and Ahad, A., 2021. Machine learning for authentication and authorization in IoT: Taxonomy, challenges and future research direction. *Sensors*, *21*(15), pp.5122.

[52] Patel, A., Taghavi, M., Bakhtiyari, K. and Junior, J.C., 2013. An intrusion detection and prevention system in cloud computing: A systematic review. *Journal of Network and Computer Applications*, *36*(1), pp.25 to 41.

[53] Ahanger, A.S., Khan,S.M. and Masoodi,F., 2021, April. An effective intrusion detection system using supervised machine learning techniques. In *2021 5th International Conference on Computing Methodologies and Communication (ICCMC)*(pp. 1639 to 1644). IEEE.

[54] Ahanger, A.S., Khan, S.M. and Masoodi, F., 2022. Building an intrusion detection system using supervised machine learning classifiers with feature selection. In *Inventive Systems and Control: Proceedings of ICISC 2022* (pp. 811 to 821). Singapore: Springer Nature Singapore.

[55] Ashoor, A.S. and Gore, S., 2011. Difference between intrusion detection system (IDS) and intrusion prevention system (IPS). In *Advances in Network Security and Applications: 4th International Conference, CNSA 2011, Chennai, India, July 15 to 17, 2011 4* (pp. 497 to 501). Springer Berlin Heidelberg.

[56] De Araujo-Filho, P.F., Pinheiro, A.J., Kaddoum, G., Campelo, D.R. and Soares, F.L., 2021. An efficient intrusion prevention system for CAN: Hindering cyber-attacks with a low-cost platform. *IEEE Access*, *9*, pp.166855 to 166869.

[57] Chang, D., Li, L., Chang, Y. and Qiao, Z., 2021. Cloud computing storage backup and recovery strategy based on secure IoT and spark. *Mobile Information Systems*, *2021*, pp.1 to 13.

[58] Tsubaki,T.,Ishibashi, R., Kuwahara, T. and Okazaki, Y., 2020, January.Effective disaster recovery for edge computing against large-scale natural disasters. In *2020 IEEE*

17th Annual Consumer Communications & Networking Conference (CCNC) (pp. 1 to 2). IEEE.

[59] Ghani,A., Badshah, A., Jan, S., Alshdadi, A.A. and Daud, A., 2020. Issues and challenges in cloud storage architecture: A survey. *arXiv preprint arXiv:2004.06809.*

[60] Chang, D., Li, L., Chang, Y. and Qiao, Z., 2021. Cloud computing storage backup and recovery strategy based on secure IoT and spark. *Mobile Information Systems, 2021*, pp.1 to 13.

[61] Shaukat, K.,Alam, T.M., Hameed, I.A., Khan, W.A., Abbas, N. and Luo, S., 2021, September. A review on security challenges in Internet of Things (IoT). In *2021 26th International Conference on Automation and Computing (ICAC)* (pp. 1 to 6). IEEE.

[62] Chang, D., Li, L., Chang, Y., & Qiao, Z. (2021). Cloud computing storage backup and recovery strategy based on secure IoT and spark. Mobile Information Systems, 2021, 1 to 13.

[63] Shah,S.A., Seker, D.Z., Hameed, S. and Draheim, D., 2019. The rising role of big data analytics and IoT in disaster management: Recent advances, taxonomy and prospects. *IEEE Access, 7*, pp.54595 to 54614.

[64] Karakus, C., Sun, Y., Diggavi, S. and Yin, W., 2019. Redundancy techniques for straggler mitigation in distributed optimization and learning. *The Journal of Machine Learning Research,20*(1), pp.2619 to 2665.

[65] Bhalaji, D.N., 2020. Efficient and secure data utilization in mobile edge computing by data replication. *Journal of IoT in Social, Mobile, Analytics, and Cloud, 2*(1), pp.1 to 12.

[66] Yue, D., Li, R., Zhang, Y., Tian, W. and Huang, Y., 2020. Blockchain-based verification framework for data integrity in edge-cloud storage. *Journal of Parallel and Distributed Computing, 146*, pp.1 to 14.

[67] Lu, N., Zhang, Y., Shi, W., Kumari, S. and Choo, K.K.R., 2020. A secure and scalable data integrity auditing scheme based on hyperledger fabric. *Computers & Security, 92*, p.101741.

[68] Zhu, H., Yuan, Y., Chen, Y., Zha, Y., Xi, W., Jia, B. and Xin, Y., 2019. A secure and efficient data integrity verification scheme for cloud-IoT based on short signature. *IEEE Access, 7*, pp.90036 to 90044.

[69] Pandey, A.K., Khan, A.I., Abushark, Y.B., Alam, M.M., Agrawal, A., Kumar, R. and Khan, R.A., 2020. Key issues in healthcare data integrity: Analysis and recommendations. *IEEE Access, 8*, pp.40612 to 40628.

[70] Khan, A.A., Laghari, A.A., Shaikh, Z.A., Dacko-Pikiewicz, Z. and Kot, S., 2022. Internet of Things (IoT) security with blockchain technology: A state-of-the-art review. *IEEE*

[71]Rahardja, U., Hidayanto, A.N., Lutfiani, N., Febiani, D.A. and Aini, Q., 2021. Immutability of distributed Hash model on blockchain node storage. *Scientific Journal of Informatics, 8*(1), pp.137 to 143.

[72] Barati, M., Aujla, G.S., Llanos, J.T., Duodu, K.A., Rana, O.F., Carr, M. and Ranjan, R., 2021. Privacy-aware cloud auditing for GDPR compliance verification in online healthcare. *IEEE Transactions on Industrial Informatics, 18*(7), pp.4808 to 4819.

[73] Zhang, C., Xu, Y., Hu, Y., Wu, J., Ren, J. and Zhang, Y., 2021. A blockchain-based multi-cloud storage data auditing scheme to locate faults. *IEEE Transactions on Cloud Computing*, *10*(4), pp.2252 to 2263.

[74] Rahman, M.S., Khalil, I., MahawagaArachchige, P.C., Bouras, A. and Yi, X., 2019, July.A novel architecture for tamper proof electronic health record management system using blockchain wrapper. In *Proceedings of the 2019 ACM International Symposium on Blockchain and Secure Critical Infrastructure* (pp. 97 to 105).

[75] Ahmad, L., Khanji, S., Iqbal, F. and Kamoun, F., 2020, August. Blockchain-based chain of custody: Towards real-time tamper-proof evidence management. In *Proceedings of the 15th international conference on availability, reliability and security* (pp. 1 to 8).

[76] Atlam, H.F., Alenezi, A., Alassafi, M.O. and Wills, G., 2018. Blockchain with internet of things: Benefits, challenges, and future directions. *International Journal of Intelligent Systems and Applications*, *10*(6), pp.40 to 48.

[77] Bansal, M., Chana, I. and Clarke, S., 2020. A survey on iot big data: Current status, 13 vs challenges, and future directions. *ACM Computing Surveys (CSUR)*, *53*(6), pp.1 to 59.

[78] Rahim, M.A., Rahman, M.A., Rahman, M.M., Asyhari, A.T., Bhuiyan, M.Z.A. and Ramasamy, D., 2021. Evolution of IoT-enabled connectivity and applications in automotive industry: A review. *Vehicular Communications*, *27*, p.100285.

[79] Yan, Q., Lou, J., Vuran, M.C. and Irmak, S., 2021. Scalable privacy-preserving geo-distance evaluation for precision agriculture IoT systems. *ACM Transactions on Sensor Networks (TOSN)*, *17*(4), pp.1 to 30.

[80] Li, Y., Su, X., Ding, A.Y., Lindgren, A., Liu, X., Prehofer, C., Riekki, J., Rahmani, R., Tarkoma, S. and Hui, P., 2020. Enhancing the Internet of Things with knowledge-driven software-defined networking technology: Future perspectives. *Sensors*, *20*(12), pp.3459.

[81] Zhou, J., Cao, Z., Dong, X. and Vasilakos, A.V., 2017. Security and privacy for cloud-based IoT: Challenges. *IEEE Communications Magazine*, *55*(1), pp.26 to 33.

[82] Bhattasali, T., Chaki, R. and Chaki, N., 2013. Study of security issues in pervasive environment of next generation internet of things. In *Computer Information Systems and Industrial Management: 12th IFIPTC8 International Conference, CISIM 2013, Krakow, Poland, September 25 to 27, 2013. Proceedings* (pp. 206 to 217). Springer Berlin Heidelberg.

[83] Blackstock, M. and Lea, R., 2014,October. IoT interoperability: A hub-based approach. In *2014 International Conference on the Internet of Things (IOT)*(pp. 79 to 84). IEEE.

[84] Wagle, S. and Pecero, J.E., 2019. Efforts towards iot technical standardization. In *Ad-Hoc, Mobile, and Wireless Networks: 18th International Conference on Ad-Hoc Networks and Wireless, ADHOC-NOW 2019, Luxembourg, Luxembourg, October 1–3, 2019, Proceedings 18* (pp. 524–539). Springer International Publishing.

Chapter 8

Mitigation of Internet of Things: Cloud Security Challenges by Using Adaptive Security Principles

Syed Irfan Yaqoob,[1] Shubhalaxmi Sanjay Joshi,[1] and Syed Wajid Aalam[2]

[1]*School of Computer Science & Engineering, Dr. Vishwanath Karad, MIT World Peace University Pune, India*

[2]*Department of Computer Science, Islamic University of Science and Technology, Kashmir, India*

8.1 Introduction

IoT-Cloud refers to the integration of the Internet of Things (IoTs) and cloud computing technologies to enable the seamless flow of data between connected devices and cloud-based services (Kumar et al., 2022; Manyika et al., 2015). IoT devices, such as sensors, wearables, and other smart devices generate massive amounts of data that need to be processed and analyzed in real time to enable decision-making and to extract insights (Bhat, M. I., Yaqoob, S. I., and Imran, M. , 2023).. Cloud computing provides a flexible and scalable platform for storing and processing this data, which can be accessed and managed remotely over the Internet (Kumar et al.,

DOI: 10.1201/9781003474838-8

2022; Manyika et al., 2015). By leveraging the power of the cloud, IoT-Cloud offers numerous benefits, such as reduced costs, improved scalability, enhanced data security, and increased accessibility. In IoT-Cloud, data is transmitted from IoT devices to cloud-based platforms using various connectivity options, such as, *Wi – Fi* , cellular networks, and Bluetooth technology (Atanasova, 2019). Once the data is received, it can be processed and analyzed in real time using advanced analytic tools, artificial intelligence (AI) techniques, that is, computer vision, natural language processing, and other machine and deep learning algorithms.

Broadly speaking, IoT-Cloud is transforming the way organizations collect, process, and analyze data, leading to improved decision-making, enhanced operational efficiency, and the creation of new business opportunities (Chen and Wu, 2021; Guillen, 2019; Gupta et al., 2022; Soldatos, 2017; T et al., 2022). IoT is one of the technologies that have been used exponentially in various applications from the last two decades. In most applications, for example, in real-time communication, processing, computing, and monitoring the artifacts are either wired or wirelessly connected (Chen and Wu, 2021; Guillen, 2019; Gupta et al., 2022; Soldatos, 2017; T et al., 2022). To overcome such a demand, traditional protocols are inadequate in securing IoT devices and, hence, present several security and privacy issues (Chen and Wu, 2021; Guillen, 2019; Gupta et al., 2022; Soldatos, 2017; T et al., 2022). In fact, the situation becomes more complicated when IoT is integrated with Cloud.

As stated, IoT-Cloud is vast network that supports IoT applications and devices, consisting of servers, storage, and infrastructure for real-time operations and processing. It also includes services and standards that facilitate the connection, management, and security of various IoT applications. For companies with limited resources, an IoT-Cloud provides a flexible, scalable, and efficient approach for delivering the necessary infrastructure and services required. In general, by integrating IoT with Cloud, organizations can take advantage of the vast potential of IoT without the need to create the underlying infrastructure and services from scratch. In brief, IoT-Cloud offers a cost-effective, on-demand, and hyper scale capabilities, such as, for example, Google Cloud, Amazon Web Services (AWS), and Microsoft Azure (Atanasova, 2019; Sethi and Sarangi, 2017).

Strictly speaking, in large-scale development and deployment, IoT-Cloud integrates devices equipped with numerous sensors (see Figure 8.1). As a result, security and privacy risks are rampant. While IoT-cloud offers many benefits such as scalability, flexibility, and cost-effectiveness, there are also several risks associated with it, including *security, privacy, reliability, integration* and *cost.* Therefore, in this chapter, we explore how adaptive security principles can be used to mitigate these challenges. That is, we examine these challenges minutely and propose adaptive security measures that can be used to address them. We also highlight the benefits of adaptive security principles and how they can improve security in IoT-Cloud integration. We hope organizations, after adapting these principles, can ensure the

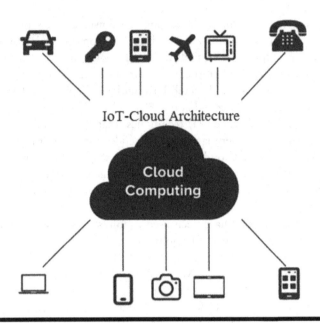

Figure 8.1 Typical Internet of Things Cloud (IoT-Cloud).

Source: Architecture; Sudeep Srivastava, 2023.

security of their IoT-Cloud integration, protect sensitive data, and prevent cyber attacks.

8.2 Security Challenges Faced by IoT-Cloud

With the increasing use of cloud technology for data storage, data security has become a major concern for individuals and businesses alike. In order to maintain data security, cloud service providers follow various data security principles such as confidentiality, integrity, authorization, availability, and privacy. However, misman-agement of data in the cloud can lead to data risks, including data breaches, loss, integrity, and unauthorized access. Keeping this in view, in literature (Atanasova, 2019; Sethi and Sarangi, 2017), different data-related challenges are categorized, as follows:

8.2.1 Data Breaches

Data breaches occur when unauthorized users gain access to the data belonging to individuals or organizations, either through deliberate actions or accidentally. This can be attributed to insufficient authentication/audit procedures, operational errors,

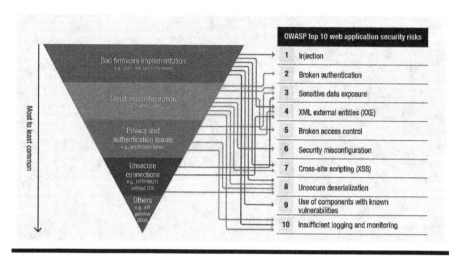

Figure 8.2   Illustration of data breaches.

Source: Shin Li., 2010.

and infrastructure vulnerabilities. Data loss, on the other hand, occurs when malicious attackers gain unauthorized access to the system or network with the intent of altering data, malware, and viruses. See *Figure 8.2* for brief illustration.

8.2.2 Effective Data Management

Effective data management poses challenges in project management, particularly with regard to maintaining the cleanliness of the data. Therefore, IoT-Cloud requires network security to protect against attacks such as denial of service (DoS) and man-in-the-middle attacks. Furthermore, account hacking is a type of attack where an unauthorized user gains access to the victim account by obtaining their login credentials, disrupting the nodes ability to communicate with each other. See Figure 8.3 for brief illustration.

8.2.3 Cloud Security

Cloud security requires application programming interface (API) security, since APIs enable communication between an application and a server. A bad set of APIs increases the likelihood of security vulnerabilities. Abuse of cloud services occurs when cloud users violate their agreements with the cloud platform. Malicious attackers may use brute force attacks, malware, structured query language (SQL) injection, botnets, phishing, and DoS attacks. Service providers are unable to detect attacks conducted against their networks since they are unable to launch or halt them.

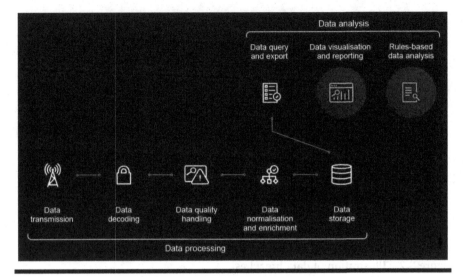

Figure 8.3 Data Management.

Source: Deepshikha Shukla, 2020.

8.2.4 Malicious Intruders

Malicious intruders use the cloud platform, have access to user information and resources, and have the ability to change data. Since IoT depends on cloud computing for the storage of data and resources, security issues in the two computing technologies are a major issue. It is essential to reduce security threats to maintain the trust and integrity of clients. The rapid development of IoT and cloud computing technologies need real-world security. To maintain trust and integrity, it is crucial to address these security threats and implement robust security measures. In the following we have categorized these security challenges with respect to IoT and Cloud computing separately.

8.2.4.1 IoT Security Issues

1. **Device Vulnerabilities:** IoT devices often have limited computational power and storage, making them more susceptible to attacks. Weak authentication mechanisms, default or hardcoded passwords and outdated firmware can provide entry points for intruders.
2. **Communication Security:** IoT devices frequently rely on wireless communication protocols, which can be intercepted or tampered with by attackers. Lack of encryption, insecure data transmission, and unauthorized access to communication channels can compromise the confidentiality and integrity of data.

3. **Data Privacy:** IoT devices generate vast amounts of sensitive data. Inadequate data encryption, insecure storage, and improper handling of personal information can lead to data breaches and privacy violations.
4. **Physical Security:** IoT devices deployed in public spaces or remote locations can be physically tampered with, allowing attackers to gain unauthorized access or manipulate the devices.

8.2.4.2 Cloud Computing Security Issues

1. **Data Breaches**: Cloud platforms store large volumes of user data, making them attractive targets for cybercriminals. Inadequate access controls, weak encryption, and misconfigured permissions can lead to unauthorized access and data breaches.
2. **Insider Threats**: Cloud service providers have access to user data, raising concerns about insider threats. Malicious or negligent employees with privileged access can abuse their privileges, leak sensitive information, or manipulate data.
3. **Data Loss and Availability**: Cloud platforms are susceptible to data loss due to hardware failures, natural disasters, or service disruptions. Without proper backup mechanisms and redundancy, data can become inaccessible or permanently lost.
4. **Multi-Tenancy Risks**: Cloud services are often shared among multiple users, creating potential risks. Inadequate isolation between tenants can enable attackers to access other users' data or exploit shared resources.

8.3 Suggestive Model

As the proliferation of IoT and cloud computing technologies continues, the security of the IoT-Cloud ecosystem must be a top priority. By adopting the suggested model and implementing robust security measures, we can strengthen the protection of user information, resources, and data integrity. We hope this will foster trust, encourage innovation, and ensure the continued growth of these transformative technologies in a secure and reliable manner.

8.3.1 Use of Secure Communication Protocols

One of the most important aspects of securing IoT-Cloud systems is to ensure that all communication between IoT devices and the cloud is encrypted. This can be achieved using secure protocols, such as transport layer security and secure socket layer (TLS/SSL). Encrypting data ensures that even if unauthorized users access the data, they are unable to read it. Encryption also helps prevent eavesdropping and other types of attacks that involve intercepting and listening to network traffic.

8.3.2 Implement Access Control

Implementing access control is a crucial step in securing IoT-Cloud systems. It involves restricting access to the IoT-Cloud system and devices to only authorized personnel. This can be achieved by using role-based access control (RBAC). With RBAC, users are assigned roles, and access to resources is granted based on the role assigned. This helps to prevent unauthorized access and reduces the risk of attacks.

8.3.3 Use Strong Authentication

Strong authentication mechanisms such as two-factor authentication and biometric authentication can prevent unauthorized access to the IoT-Cloud system. Two-factor authentication involves using two different authentication methods, such as a password and a token, to ensure that only authorized personnel can access the system. Biometric authentication involves using physical characteristics such as fingerprints or facial recognition to authenticate users. These mechanisms add an additional layer of security to the system, making it harder for attackers to gain access.

8.3.4 Implement Secure Updates

Ensuring that IoT devices receive secure updates and patches is essential to prevent vulnerabilities and improve security. Attackers often exploit vulnerabilities in IoT devices to gain unauthorized access to the system. Secure updates and patches can address these vulnerabilities and prevent attackers from exploiting them.

8.3.5 Monitor and Analyze Data

Data analytics can help to identify and monitor potential security threats and anomalies in the IoT-Cloud system. By analyzing data, security personnel can detect abnormal behavior and take proactive measures to prevent security breaches. For example, they can set up alerts for suspicious activities and monitor network traffic to detect any unusual patterns.

8.3.6 Secure Storage and Backup

Ensuring that all data is securely stored and backed up in the cloud can prevent data loss from hardware failures, disasters, or security breaches. It is essential to store data in an encrypted format to prevent unauthorized access. Regular backups also ensure that data can be easily restored in the event of a disaster or system failure.

8.3.7 Consistent Security Audits

Performing regular security audits is essential to identify flaws and vulnerabilities in the IoT-Cloud system. This helps to ensure that the system is secure and that any vulnerabilities are addressed before they can be exploited. Security audits should be performed regularly to ensure that the system remains secure over time. These recommendations can help to secure IoT-Cloud systems and prevent attacks. By using secure communication protocols, implementing access control, using strong authentication, implementing secure updates, monitoring and analyzing data, securing storage and backup, and performing regular security audits, the risk of security breaches can be greatly reduced.

8.3.8 Prior Steps to Secure IoT-Cloud

Cloud security does not necessarily have to be the sole domain of information technology (IT) managers. Corporate IT may implement and maintain strict IoT security with the help of the tools and resources provided by cloud IoT providers. The secret is to choose the best IoT cloud provider that can work with a business to achieve IoT security goals. Figure 8.4 provides brief illustration.

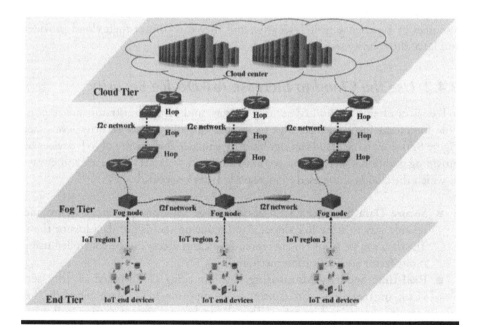

Figure 8.4   Internet of Things (IoT) CloudNetwork.

Source: Deepshikha Shukla, 2020.

8.4 Consult with Cloud IoT Providers about Their Most Recent Security Audits

It is crucial to consult with cloud IoT providers about their most recent security audits before signing any cloud IoT agreements. This helps businesses to understand the security measures the provider has in place and any vulnerabilities they have identified. Based on the audit, the provider may have made enhancements to their systems to prevent potential security breaches. By understanding these measures, businesses can make informed decisions about whether to trust the provider with their IoT devices and data.

8.4.1 Use the Security Choices that Cloud Service Providers Supply

Cloud service providers offer various security measures to protect IoT devices and data. These measures include network communication security, monitoring and security for IoT devices, encryption of IoT data in transit and at rest, and security audits to identify vulnerabilities that IT administrators can plug before a security breach. However, it is up to the businesses utilizing cloud resources to determine these security parameters. In some cases, businesses may not have the necessary resources or experience in IoT security, and they can consult their cloud provider and leave the security setup in the hands of vendor.

8.4.2 Use the Cloud to Increase IoT Device Security

IoT devices often have limited security presets, and IT administrators are responsible for modifying device settings to impose the appropriate security levels (see Figure 8.5). Using the cloud can significantly enhance the security of IoT devices by providing additional layers of protection and security features. Here are some ways in which the cloud can be used to increase IoT device security:

- **Secure Data Storage:** Cloud-based storage solutions provide a secure and reliable way to store IoT device data, reducing the risk of data loss or theft. The data can be stored in encrypted form, and access can be controlled using multi-factor authentication mechanisms.
- **Real-time Security Monitoring:** By leveraging cloud-based security services, organizations can continuously monitor IoT device networks for security threats and breaches. This allows for real-time detection and mitigation of security risks, preventing them from escalating into larger security incidents.
- **Automated Security Updates:** Cloud-based platforms can be used to automate the delivery of security updates to IoT devices. This ensures that devices

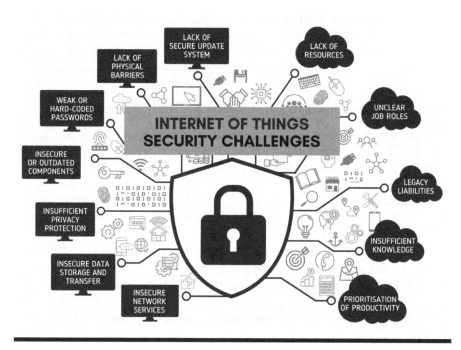

Figure 8.5   Internet of Things (IoT) Security Challenges.
Source: Society, 2020.

are always running the latest security patches and updates, reducing the risk of vulnerabilities being exploited.

- **Advanced Security Analytics:** Cloud-based analytics tools can be used to analyze IoT device data for anomalies and suspicious activity. This can help identify potential security threats before they become serious security incidents.
- **Device Authentication:** Cloud-based authentication services can be used to authenticate and authorize IoT devices, ensuring that only authorized devices can access cloud-based services and data.

8.4.3 Fix the Roles and Responsibilities of the Cloud Vendor and Enterprise IT

An agreement between an enterprise IT department and a cloud IoT vendor results in the creation of a contract outlining the responsibilities of each side (Fernandez-Carames, 2020). The obligations of the cloud provider and the organization's IT team with regard to IoT security should be explicitly stated in the service contract. For instance, the contract should specify who is responsible for monitoring all IoT activities and intervening when security alerts are triggered; who is responsible for implementing software security updates and ensuring they are working correctly; who is responsible for encrypting data while it is at rest and in motion; and who is responsible for defining user levels of IoT authorization. Both the IT teams and the cloud IoT provider must agree on some of these clouds IoT security obligations.

8.4.4 Use the Cloud to Implement Security Measures

The cloud can be used to implement various security measures to protect against cyber threats and safeguard data (Guillen, 2019). Here are some ways in which the cloud can be used to implement security measures:

- **Encryption:** The cloud can be used to implement encryption of data at rest and in transit. Encryption ensures that data is protected even if it is intercepted by an unauthorized party.
- **Access Control:** Cloud-based access control mechanisms can be implemented to ensure that only authorized users have access to data and services. This can include multi-factor authentication, role-based access control, and user activity monitoring.
- **Firewall and Intrusion Detection**: Cloud-based firewalls and intrusion-detection systems can be deployed to protect against cyber attacks. These systems can monitor network traffic and identify potential security threats, alerting security teams to take appropriate action.
- **Vulnerability Scanning:** Cloud-based vulnerability scanning can be used to identify security weaknesses in systems and applications. This enables organizations to address these vulnerabilities before they can be exploited by attackers.
- **Backup and Disaster Recovery:** The cloud can be used to implement backup and disaster recovery solutions. This ensures that data is backed up and can be quickly restored in the event of a security incident or system failure.

8.4.5 Channel Networks

In this connected world era, the Internet of Things (IoT) has become an integral part of businesses, allowing for increased efficiency and productivity. However, IoT devices also pose significant security concerns. Due to the vast number of devices connected to the internet, IoT networks are vulnerable to cyber attacks, data breaches, and other security risks (Manyika et al., 2015).

One of the ways to address these concerns is by using channel networks. A channel network is a technique that isolates internal corporate networks and networks of external business partners or customers to prevent security concerns from spreading from one network to another. This technique helps limit and isolate any IoT security concerns that may develop within a specific network. By isolating internal networks, businesses can ensure that all IoT devices within the network are secure and protected. They can also monitor all the devices, data, and traffic flowing within the network to detect any anomalies and take preventive measures. Furthermore, businesses can set up a central security system to monitor all IoT devices, ensuring that any vulnerabilities are identified and patched in a timely manner. On the other hand, by isolating external networks, businesses can prevent security concerns from spreading from their network to their business partners' or customers' networks. This helps build trust and confidence among customers and partners, demonstrating that the business takes IoT security seriously (Sethi and Sarangi, 2017).

Overall, channel networks are an effective way for businesses to manage IoT security concerns. By isolating internal and external networks, businesses can contain any issues that arise, preventing them from spreading to other networks (see Figure 8.6). This technique also helps businesses protect their IoT devices, data, and

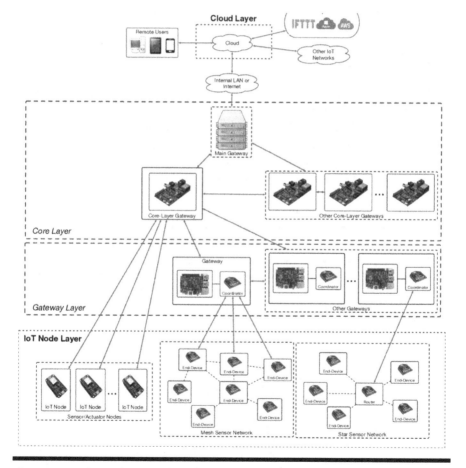

Figure 8.6   Channel Networks.

Source: Fernandez-Carames, 2020.

networks, ensuring they can continue to operate efficiently and productively while maintaining a high level of security (Soldatos, 2017).

8.5 Summarization

In this chapter, first, various challenges are categorized in the integration of the Internet of Things and cloud (IoT-Cloud) and later a suggestive model is proposed that identifies potential security problems related to cloud-assisted IoT and suggests solutions to manage them effectively. This model recommends the use of security measures provided by cloud service providers, such as network communication security, monitoring, and security for IoT devices – IoT data in transit and at rest – and security audits to identify vulnerabilities that information technology (IT) administrators can fix before a security breach occurs. In addition, the cloud can offer further assistance for IoT device security by hosting IoT middleware that acts as a bridge between connected devices and the applications they use, scanning connections for security flaws, and sending quick alerts if an IoT device exhibits unusual behavior that suggests security vulnerability.

Furthermore, this chapter emphasizes the importance of clearly defining the roles and responsibilities of the cloud vendor and enterprise IT teams in a service contract. This contract should specify who is responsible for monitoring all IoT activities, implementing software security updates, encrypting data while it is at rest and in motion, and defining user levels of IoT authorization. By doing so, users can ensure that both the cloud provider and IT teams understand their respective responsibilities and work together to address security concerns effectively.

Finally, the chapter discusses channel networks, which involve keeping the internal corporate network and external business partners' or customers' networks isolated from each other. This approach helps to limit and isolate any IoT security concerns that may develop within a specific network, preventing them from spreading to other networks. By following these recommendations, enterprises can effectively manage the security challenges associated with cloud-assisted IoT, enabling them to take full advantage of the benefits offered by this powerful technology.

References

Atanasova, T. (2019). Methods for Processing of Heterogeneous Data in IoT Based Systems. *Communications in Computer and Information Science, 1141 CCIS* (December 2019), 524–535. https://doi.org/10.1007/978-3-030-36625-4_42

Bhat, M. I., Yaqoob, S. I., & Imran, M. (2023). Engineering Challenges in the Development of Artificial Intelligence and Machine Learning Software Systems. *In* System Reliability and Security (December 2023). 133-142. *Auerbach Publications*. https://doi.org/10.1201/9781032624983-7

Chen, M. Y., & Wu, H. Te. (2021). Real-Time Intelligent Image Processing for the Internet of Things. *Journal of Real-Time Image Processing, 18*(4), 997–998. https://doi.org/10.1007/s11554-021-01149-0

Fernandez-Carames, T. M. (2020). From Pre-Quantum to Post-Quantum IoT Security: A Survey on Quantum-Resistant Cryptosystems for the Internet of Things. *IEEE Internet of Things Journal, 7*(7), 6457–6480. https://doi.org/10.1109/JIOT.2019.2958788

Guillen, G. (2019). Sensor Projects with Raspberry Pi. In Sensor Projects with Raspberry Pi. Apress. https://doi.org/10.1007/978-1-4842-5299-4

Gupta, R., Rana, A. K., Dhawan, S., & Cengiz, K. (2022). Advanced Sensing in Image Procesing and IoT (Vol. 21, Issue 1). http://journal.um-surabaya.ac.id/index.php/JKM/article/view/2203

Kumar, N., Kumar, K., & Kumar, A. (2022). Application of Internet of Things in Image Processing. *2022 IEEE Delhi Section Conference, DELCON 2022.* https://doi.org/10.1109/DELCON54057.2022.9753308

Manyika, J., Chui, M., Bisson, P., Woetzel, J., Dobbs, R., Bughin, J., & Aharon, D. (2015). The Internet of Things: Mapping the Value beyond the Hype. *McKinsey Global Institute, June(2015)*, June, 719–746. https://doi.org/10.4018/978-1-7998-9155-0.ch036

Sethi, P., & Sarangi, S. R. (2017). Internet of Things: Architectures, Protocols, and Applications. Journal of Electrical and Computer Engineering, 2017. https://doi.org/10.1155/2017/9324035

Society, S. C. (2024). IOT security. Recognising Iot Security Issues: 12 Ways You Can Protect Your Devices. www.scs.org.sg/articles/iot-security-how-to-secure-your-devices

Soldatos, J. (2017). Building Blocks for IoT Analytics. https://doi.org/10.13052/rp-9788793519046

T, S., S, C. S., & S, S. (2022). The IoT-Based Real-Time Image Processing for Animal Recognition and Classification Using Deep Convolutional Neural Network (DCNN). *Microprocessors and Microsystems, 95*(September), 104693. https://doi.org/10.1016/j.micpro.2022.104693

Chapter 9

IoT Security with Blockchain Technology in the Financial Sector

Divyashree K. S. and Achyutananda Mishra

Christ University, Bangalore, India

9.1 Introduction

The Internet of Things (IoT) and Blockchain are frequently discussed as major digital transformation technologies. The Internet of Things means physical gadgets that can detect, sense, network, and analyze data and are connected to the Internet. Considering the rise of IoT supporting technologies such as cloud-based computing, wireless sensor networks, Big Data Analytics, and so on, the Internet of Things is spreading at a rapid pace, yet it confronts issues related to privacy and security. Blockchain (BC), a game-changing technology for the Internet of Things, employs a decentralized, distributed, public, and real-time ledger to store transactions between IoT nodes. The Internet of Things connects people, places, and things, making it possible to add value to products and corporate processes in new ways. Sensors and electronics are changing the way we work and supporting the financial industry. Yet, security and scalability is a big worry when adopting this technology on a broad scale.

The chapter explains meaning and working of IoT and Blockchain, and examines how blockchain technology can be used in securing IoT applications in the Financial Sector such as in banking, insurance, enterprise and organizational operations and

DOI: 10.1201/9781003474838-9

product delivery optimization as a part of the Digital Transformation. It is divided into three parts – the first part gives an understanding of IoT and Blockchain. Applications of IoT in the financial sector and its challenges is dealt with in the second part. The last part deals with blockchain solutions for IoT issues.

9.2 Internet of Things (IoT)

The term Internet of Things means everyday things that are connected to the Internet.. During 1990s, software engineers started adding digital sensors and CPUs (Central Processing Unit) into everyday things like cars, television, air conditioning and so forth. The traditional chips were large and heavy, therefore progress was slow at the beginning. Later ,RFID (radio frequency identity) was used in place of large traditional chips, which were much smaller in size and consumed less power. These computer chips were first employed to track costly machinery. These processors slowly evolved through time to become more efficient, smaller, quicker, and smarter as computer devices shrank in size. [1]

The other reason for things getting popular with IoT is that the cost of incorporating processing power into small things has significantly decreased. Example: smart home devices and appliances like Alexa, Google Assistant, Smart Gadgets and so forth. [2] The notion of putting IoT devices in our homes, places of business, and workplaces has given rise to a whole industry. Automatic data transfer to and from the Internet is possible with these cutting-edge gadgets. "Internet of Things" refers to both the network of these "invisible computing devices" and the related technologies.

"Internet of Things" (IoT) refers to both the larger network of networked objects as well as the technology that permits their communication with one another and the cloud. Now that low-cost computer processors and high-bandwidth communication services have been developed, there are billions of devices connected to the Internet. This implies that commonplace devices like vacuum cleaners, vehicles, and robots may employ sensors to gather data and have direct conversations with consumers.

Technologies Enabling the Internet of Things (IoT): The IoT idea as a whole depends on connectivity. Connecting sensors, cloud, and all other physical objects grew simpler as numerous network technologies for the Internet emerged. Some of the technologies which enable IoT are: [3]

1. Cloud Computing Systems
2. Wireless Sensor Network
3. Embedded System
4. Big Data Analytics
5. Communications Protocol

1. **Cloud Computing:** This is a process of giving services through tools and apps like data storage, networking, software and so forth. Rather than storing data in drive and local storage units, businesses can now access the information through cloud-based software and apps. Cloud makes use of the Internet for providing services through different tools.

Some of the Examples of Cloud Computing Are as Follows:

■ **IaaS (Infrastructure as a Service)** Technology as a Service offers pay per usage Internet services such as physical computers, servers, networking, storage, and so forth. Financial institutions make significant investments in security and compliance protocols in order to safeguard their assets and maintain compliance.

■ **PaaS (Platform as a Service):** This offers a cloud-based platform for everything developing and delivering Web-based (cloud) applications without the cost and complexity of buying and managing underlying hardware, software provisioning, and hosting. Hardware, operating systems, libraries, and more are examples of computing platforms. The main thing it does is act as a platform for developing apps.

■ **SaaS (Software as a Service):** SaaS provides the cloud-based application as a service online. By just using online software access instead of installing and maintaining it, you may avoid difficult software and hardware management. The alternatives for SaaS apps include hosted software and Web-based software on demand. On the servers of SaaS providers, SaaS program control security, availability, and performance. For instance, Office, Gmail, Google Docs, and so forth.

■ **Wireless Sensor Network:** Distributed sensor-equipped devices that track physical and environmental traits form a wireless sensor network (WSN). End nodes, routers, and coordinators form a wireless sensor network. Routers are used to transmit data from the numerous sensors that are linked to end nodes to a coordinator. The coordinator serves as the WSN's Internet gateway and link.

■ **Big Data Analytics:** This is a method of analyzing big data, that is, huge amounts of data. Processing huge amounts of data is difficult due to its amount, speed, or diversity. Big Data is obtained from many different sources, such as videos posted on social media, digital photos, sensors, and sales transaction records. Data cleaning, munging, processing, and visualization are only a few of the processes involved in Big Data analysis.

■ **Embedded Systems:** Certain tasks are carried out using systems with embedded hardware and software. It consists of flash memory, storage devices, micro controller, Bluetooth, Wifi, digital cameras and so forth. The data is gathered and posted online. Embedded systems-devices include, but are

not limited to, digital cameras, industrial robots, wireless routers, and DVD (Digital Versatile Disc) players.
■ **Communication Protocols:** The fundamental building block of IoT systems, communications protocols allow for application interfacing and network access. Communication protocols allow data to be sent between devices via a network. There are typically many protocols used to address various parts of a single message. A protocol stack or protocol suite is a group of software-implemented, interoperable protocols.

9.3 Blockchain Technology

A blockchain is a database that keeps track of all information that is cryptographically encrypted in a chronological manner. The data stored in blockchain is immutable and transparent where miners can check the blocks and validate them. All users involved in data input then share them. Each user or node in the system keeps the same ledger as all other users or nodes in the network. Information is preserved and/or published as an immutable public ledger. [4]

A distributed, unchangeable database called blockchain makes it simpler to monitor assets and log transactions in a business network. A blockchain network makes it possible to store and exchange nearly everything of value, which lowers risk and boosts efficiency for all parties. Blockchain is the top information delivery technology because it provides distributed, fully transparent, real-time data that is stored on an immutable ledger and only available to users of a permissioned network. A blockchain network can keep an eye on things like orders, payments, accounts, and production. [5]

Blockchain is the combination of the following three technologies:

■ Cryptographic technology
■ A peer-to-peer network that employs distributed ledger technology
■ A computing method that keeps track of network activity and records/a time-stamped record

Parties must have cryptographic keys in order to complete transactions. These unique keys are used to provide a secure point of reference for each individual's digital identity. These private identities and data are the most important aspect of blockchain technology. The digital signature and peer-to-peer network are combined to reach consensus on transactions and other issues. When a transaction's validity is mathematically validated, it successfully completes as a secured transaction between the two network-connected parties. Finally, users of blockchain technology engage in a variety of digital exchanges utilizing cryptographic keys through a peer-to-peer network. [6]

9.4 Characteristics of Blockchain Technology

A blockchain is a decentralized architecture with built-in security that boosts data reliability and trust. The characteristics of Blockchain technology can be summarized as:[7]

a. **Efficient:** Blockchain technology has improved the capacity of storing data because there are numerous computers working together, which gives more power than a limited number of machines where everything is centralized.

b. **Security:** Blockchain technology is more secure than its competition because it lacks a single point of failure. Data is continuously cycled across a large number of nodes since blockchain relies on a dispersed network of nodes. Thus, even if one node is compromised by a hack or other problems, the integrity of the original data is not damaged.

c. **Immutability:** The generation of immutable ledgers is one of the key characteristics of Blockchain. Since it relies on a third-party mediator for security, any centrally hosted database is subject to fraud and hacking. When a transaction block has been uploaded to the ledger, no one can just go back and modify it. As a result, any network user will be unable to modify, delete, or update it.

d. **Transparency:** Because technology is decentralized, each participant's profile is visible to everybody. The blockchain is more dependable since every update is transparent.

e. **Consensus:** For a transaction to alter its state from one to another, participants must reach consensus. The consensus serves as a form of endorsement. Members agree to carry out the transaction using this means. If agreement is not reached, the transaction remains off the main chain as an orphaned block. Consensus-obtained blocks are the only ones that are added to the main chain. With this procedure, the central authority is removed, and the trust element of the transaction is transferred to the participants.

f. **Decentralized Network:** A decentralized peer-to-peer network serves as the foundation for blockchain technology. Every node is regarded as a peer. The program has determined the permissions and roles that are allocated to the nodes. Decentralization eliminates the requirement for a central authority (server) for authentication. A decentralized network gets rid of the bottleneck caused by a centralized system's single point of failure.

g. **Time Stamped:** The chain serves as a record of the transactions for auditability (provenance). The timestamp aids in establishing the sequence. The Blockchain serves as a storage facility. The blocks' read-only functionality is momentary. As a result, the system always supports Auditability and Provenance.

9.5 Types of Blockchain

We can broadly classify blockchain into 4 types based on its use, they are: [8]

a. **Permission-less Blockchain:** A public blockchain network system is a common term used to describe permission-less blockchain. Real-world participant identification in this type of blockchain technology is pseudonymous, and any participant has the ability to add a new block to the ledger.

b. **Permissioned Blockchain:** Permissioned Blockchain is made to provide access to a single person, an organization, or a group of organizations so they may move data and record transactions with efficiency. With permissioned blockchain, where every member's identity is known to all other members, choosing who may take part in network transactions entails an extra degree of privilege.

c. **Hybrid Blockchain:** Blockchain networks that blend private and public chains combine their advantages. While vulnerabilities are fixed, the advantages of the two blockchain systems are maintained. Businesses can prohibit access to some parts of a hybrid blockchain while keeping the rest of the network accessible. Due to the owner's inability to alter data without the agreement of other nodes, data integrity is greater on a hybrid blockchain. Because all network nodes share a consensus, hybrid networks are also more secure.

d. **Consortial Blockchains:** Similar to public blockchains, it has a peer-to-peer, decentralized structure. No one entity has control over the system, and each member of the network owns a copy of the distributed ledger. Despite the fact that a group rather than a single organization decides who may join the network, a consortium blockchain is still a private network. Collaboration between many organizations aiming for a secure, stable, and effective method of communication usually results in a consortium blockchain.

Blockchain Technology Application Designers will need to establish specific designs that specify the analysis to be done and determine the type and amount of data required for these analyses since participant authorization must be gained and maybe paid for. Designers will need to learn more about the many forms of data that may be utilized in these studies, as well as what distributed ledgers and personal data files do and do not offer.

Applications of IoT in Financial Sector

a. **Automation:** IoT-powered systems are capable of doing a variety of tasks automatically, such as processing requests, opening bank accounts, disabling credit cards, and so forth. This reduces the need for human interaction and, as a result, the likelihood of human mistakes. The ability to make loan-related judgements based on algorithms rather than depending on machines is thanks to automated underwriting procedures in banking. In the financial sector Accounts payable, invoicing, and accounts receivable are all essential aspects of bookkeeping. Tax reporting and compliance, Payroll and expense control can be automated through IoT.

b. **Fraud Investigation:** In order to acquire and analyse user account data to identify fraud and hacker risks, IoT and AI-powered analytics are used. If there is any suspicious behavior, the user may be alerted right away and have their account briefly terminated. IoT technology is used to track and monitor client behavior and transactions in real-time, which may help identify and stop fraudulent conduct. [9] It is also used to safeguard physical assets, such bank branches and ATMs (Automated Teller Machine), and to assist in preventing cyber attacks. [10]

c. **One-Touch Transactions:** Customers may make purchases without directly using their credit or debit cards thanks to the use of wearables and banking IoT technologies. Smartphones and smartwatches feature NFC (Near Field Communication)-enabled contactless payments for rapid financial transactions. Businesses may function more cost-effectively and efficiently with less of a need to manage cash. Moreover, IoT-enabled transactions increase transparency, enabling governments to trace transactions and find tax evaders with ease. NFC is a unique sort of contactless technology utilized in the Internet of Things since it communicates over a very narrow range (0–5 cm) for security. The majority of iOS and Android smartphones have it – the a (no codes, or addresses). [11]

d. **Security:** The Internet of Things (IoT) connects and remotely operates CCTV (Closed Circuit Television) cameras, smart alarm systems, car telematics, and other monitoring technologies to assure continual property and equipment safety. It also alerts consumers when criminal conduct happens. IoT systems enable customers to make payments via mobile applications by utilizing their fingerprints, retinas, or faces as forms of user authentication, which is another important driver of cybersecurity. [12]

e. **Finance for Trade/ Supply Chain Monitoring:** Using real-time data and maintaining awareness of the physical flows they are supporting, IoT enables banks engaged in trade finance to make judgements. Banks may leverage IoT-generated data to better analyse risk across the trade life cycle, distribute money more effectively, and increase their usage of finance methodology. [13] Example, the **Origin Trail:** It favors supply chain management. It resolves issues, including data sharing, inefficient keeping and querying of related data, and poor interoperability of data inside supply chains. [14]

f. **Insurance:** IoT devices monitor the status of insured assets and alert insurers to any irregularities, allowing them to take the required actions and safeguards to reduce risks. Insurance firms use IoT data to predict problems and take preventative actions. An insurer, for example, may be able to detect an asset breakdown and notify the policyholder before it causes harm. This technique minimizes the number of insurance claims while also protecting against insurance fraud. [15]

g. Auditing and Accounting: The link between the customers' payment systems and the CPAs' software, facilitated by the Internet of Things, allows for the automation of basic accounting procedures like data input, reconciliation, invoicing, and other similar processes. (Client Professional Accounting Software, designed with CPAs in mind, will be developed for payroll, expenses, and reporting for a variety of organizations and will also include useful features like auditing, tax preparation, and time-based invoicing.) IoT gives accountants of the ability to track financial data in real-time and get accurate operational insight to improve their advisory duties. IoT also enhances transparency and automation in auditing, enabling CPAs to maintain audit trails and monitor transactions immediately to detect data abnormalities and prevent fraud. [16]

h. Smart Branch: Smart branch IoT solutions improve customer experience by monitoring lineups, advising consumers of how long they will have to wait, and guiding them to an open counter. For operations to run more smoothly and with fewer staff members needed, intelligent branches can communicate user information. [17]

i. Automated Teller Machine (ATM): Banks can track customer behavior, determine ATM usage patterns, and place additional ATM's depending on demand thanks to IoT-enabled data flow for ATM's. Before switching to cost-saving operation modes, IoT sensors are required to collect data about the ATM site environment (room temperature, light, motion, and so forth). [18]

j. Smart Asset Management: With IoT technology, banks may have better control over and remote monitoring of the assets of their clients. The practice of supervising mortgages for real estate, equipment, and other forms of property that are backed by bank loans is known as smart collateral management. For instance, sensors might be used to monitor the status of a structure used as loan collateral. Customers might benefit from a discount if a repair or renovation loan is immediately granted in the event that the moisture detectors reveal any problems. [19]

k. Increased Investments and Visibility of the Capital Markets: Monitoring the market's current condition in real time is essential for making better investing decisions. The Internet of Things will be able to increase capital market awareness for both individual investors and multinational enterprises. The capital market's primary IoT applications are listed below: Scannable real-time data for improved investment analysis; autonomous trade creation; gathering and generation of trading strategies, ideas, and suggestions. [20]

l. Proactive Client Relations: By examining the information gathered during their visits, the Internet of Things can assist banks in anticipating the demands of their clients. The instances of IoT in enhancing customer service are numerous, ranging from data collection to autonomous service start. For illustration: To help customers handle their tasks more effectively, an IoT system can deliver the necessary information to their mobile phones and guide them to a free counter or notify them of the overall waiting time. [21]

m. Chatbots: As a result of the IoT, companies have established a 24/7 customer care experience through the use of chatbots, or virtual assistants. Intelligent chatbots learn from every user contact and utilize natural language processing to provide a more individualized experience over time. [22]

9.6 Challenges of IOT

The Internet of Things is being quickly employed in the financial services industry. Although some institutions made significant investments in the required infrastructure and saw rapid adoption, others are currently testing IoT to see how it can alter the course of the business. These are some of the difficulties that should be taken into account before implementing IoT.

a. **Network Security:** The advancements afforded by 5G networks and the connection they enable, these networks might be a very appealing target for hackers. Potentially insecure IoT devices, since a hacked device might be used to target other network devices. [23]

b. **Data Integration:** Data from several sources must interact and integrate on the same level while maintaining privacy, data ownership, and data security.

c. **Absence of Encryption:** One of the biggest threats to IoT security is the absence of encryption, despite the fact that it is a powerful tool for preventing hackers from accessing data. These drives are used to the processing and storage capacity offered by a standard computer.

d. **Privacy Concerns:** Privacy concerns are problems with the gathering, keeping, using, and sharing of personal data. Concerns regarding who has access to personal information, how it is used, and whether it is shielded from illegal access or abuse might fall under this category. Since personal data is gathered and kept on an unprecedented scale in the digital era, privacy issues have risen in importance. In order to resolve privacy issues, people and organizations must put in place the proper security measures to safeguard personal information, be honest about how it is being used, and respect people's right to privacy control. In order to provide standards and protect people's personal information, privacy laws and regulations have also been formed. [24]

e. **Software Vulnerabilities:** Weaknesses in software code that may be exploited by attackers to obtain unauthorized access, steal sensitive data, or engage in harmful activity are known as "software vulnerabilities." By using out-of-date or unsupported software, flaws or mistakes committed throughout the development process might lead to software vulnerabilities. These flaws can be used by attackers to take over a machine, put malware on it, or steal confidential data. Software users should maintain their software up to date and correctly configured, and software developers should adhere to safe coding techniques to limit the risk of software vulnerabilities. [25]

f. Unsecured Data Transmission: This term describes the transmission of data via a network or the Internet without the necessary security. This may expose the data to hostile entities who could intercept, alter, or steal it. Data transfer across an unencrypted network connection or the usage of insecure protocols can both result in insecure data transmission. It's critical to employ secure protocols, like SSL (Secure Socket Layer)/ TLS (Transport Layer Security) or VPN (Virtual Private Network), and to encrypt data before transferring it if you want to safeguard sensitive data during transmission. Even if the data is intercepted while being sent, this can help to maintain its secrecy and integrity. IoT devices often send sensitive data, which might be compromised if it is not adequately protected. [26]

g. Network Attack: Network attack vulnerability describes the propensity of a network, system, or device to be compromised or abused by cybercriminals. This may occur as a result of flaws in the network architecture, outdated software, careless password management, or an absence of adequate security precautions. Network attacks can lead to data theft, privacy violations, service interruptions, and monetary losses. Strong security measures, including firewalls, encryption, and frequent software upgrades, should be put in place to lessen vulnerability to network assaults, as well as user education about safe Internet usage. IoT devices are susceptible to assaults like denial-of-service (DoS) attacks since they rely on networks. [27]

h. Absence of Established Standards/Regulations: Certain sectors or industries are referred to as a lack of standardization. This may lead to incompatibility between various systems, goods, or procedures, which might result in muddle, inefficiency, or lower interoperability. For instance, in the world of technology, a lack of standardization might make it difficult for various systems and devices to communicate and exchange data. This may be avoided by establishing standards and procedures, which also assure compatibility and uniformity. IoT devices are not standardized, which makes it challenging to consistently protect them. [28]

i. Lack of testing and Upgrading: Internet of Things (IoT) device producers are more eager to create and deploy their product as soon as possible without giving security much of a thought as the number of IoT devices rises. Most IoT goods and devices do not receive adequate testing or updates, leaving them vulnerable to security threats such as hackers. [29]

j. Lack of Skill Set: All of the development challenges mentioned above can only be managed if a qualified resource is engaged on the IoT application development. When creating IoT apps, having the right abilities will always give you an advantage and enable you to overcome the toughest challenges. [30]

k. Cost: Balancing the benefits of an IoT system against the expense of installing and maintaining it. Organizations should employ an organized and well-planned deployment approach, which includes the careful selection of hardware and software components, careful design of the network infrastructure, and the creation of a strong security policy, to overcome these deployment problems. Moreover, they should put into place effective procedures for managing devices and data, and they should aim to optimize return on investment by selecting affordable options.

l. **Interoperability:** Interoperability is the ability of disparate systems, devices, or components to communicate and exchange data successfully. Since there are so many different kinds of linked devices in the Internet of Things (IoT), interoperability is a significant problem. Lack of standards in the IoT can lead to issues with data exchange and device connectivity, resulting in an inefficient and disconnected system. Organizations and industry groups are striving to create standards and protocols to guarantee interoperability across IoT devices in order to address this difficulty. This involves creating standard data formats, communication methods, and security guidelines. Interoperability is essential for the Internet of Things to realize its full promise and for connected devices to work together, effectively providing efficient data exchange and simple communication across diverse IoT devices. [31]

m. **Scalability:** The term "scalability" describes a system's capacity to manage growing user or task demands without noticeably degrading performance. Scalability is a significant issue in the context of the Internet of Things (IoT), because the number of connected devices is expanding quickly and increasing the volume of data and communication. IoT scalability issues include:

■ Data management is the process of efficiently managing and storing the massive volumes of data that IoT devices produce.

■ Ensuring that networks have the resources to manage the growing volume of data and communication.

■ Device management involves effectively overseeing the expanding number of IoT devices and making sure they are simple to set up and maintain. [32]

In order to overcome these scalability concerns, organizations should implement scalable infrastructures, such as cloud computing, which can handle the expanding number of IoT devices and the data they produce,. To deal with the rising volume of data, they also need to install effective data management and storage solutions, such as distributed databases and data lakes. Organizations can guarantee that their IoT systems can manage the increasing number of connected devices and continue to provide great performance and efficiency by giving scalability a high priority.

9.7 Blockchain-Based Solutions for IoT Challenges

Although the Internet of Things offers several prospects for digitalization, IoT systems are also becoming increasingly vulnerable to security assaults and data breaches. There is a demand for safety solutions that work with limited IoT devices. Blockchain technology, with its security features, provides solutions to IoT concerns as:

a. **Blockchain-based Security for IOT:** Data on blockchain is cryptographically protected, and IoT in financial systems ensures data security. Blockchain allows for the safe, transparent, auditable, efficient, and interruption-resistant recording of these digital interactions. Each block timestamps the occurrences and validates that they occurred correctly and without interruption. Anyone wishing to add a transaction to the chain must first get it accepted by everyone else in the network using an algorithm. When a transaction is approved, it is combined into a block and disseminated to each network node. The current block and subsequent blocks are confirmed using a single fingerprint that matches the fingerprint of the previous block. Regardless of the communication methods used, attackers will be unable to target a particular server and corrupt its data since the blockchain is decentralized. [33]

b. **Data authenticity for quality assurance:** Because of its immutability, blockchain technology may give a rigorous foundation to processes to identify data alterations fast and accurately. Data transfer is made easy because of IoT applications. An IoT network may occasionally receive fraudulent information that is inserted and rerouted by attacks like "Man-in-the-Middle." Blockchain can operate as a third party to validate this information before it moves further in a network in order to thwart such assaults. Similar changes are made to the DNS (Domain Name System) table by harmful actions like DNS poisoning. The immutability property of blockchain may prevent DNS poisoning when IoT and the blockchain network are combined. [34]

c. **Device Monitoring to Detect Errors:** Because IoT networks may be massive, failure patterns might be difficult to spot. Blockchain technology assigns a unique key to every IoT endpoint, helping to identify anomalies. [35]

d. **Faster Automation:** IoT technology alone provides automation, but when combined with smart contracts, automatic replies may be approved through this network.

e. **Access and Identity Management:** Blockchain technology goes beyond sensors to track user behavior and reveal who, when, and how a gadget was used. IoT device ownership evolves over time. An IoT gadget may gain a lot when its identification is coupled with a blockchain network. Once it has been sold again, smart contracts can be used to alter or revoke ownership. Therefore, it becomes incredibly challenging for a criminal to alter the identity of an IoT device if it is taken. The approach described for registering ownership and tracking IoT devices is called TrustChain. For devices with limited resources, like IoT, the authorization processes are problematic because of their complexity. Smart contract mechanisms can offer superior authorization methods for both single and many users in place of traditional protocols.

The use of IoT devices may be governed by a number of criteria, including time limits, approval for software updates, and key pair updates, with the use of smart contracts. An IoT network's security may be significantly improved by placing limitations on these types of access methods with the use of smart contracts. [36]

f. **Blockchain-based privacy control:** a blockchain-based system that offers an effective access control mechanism while protecting privacy and is appropriate for financial applications. By using the proper consensus approach, we may improve network security and effectiveness while lowering network costs, such as bandwidth and processing utilization. A fundamental need of many IoT applications is the security and privacy of user data. The ability to conceal the user identity while transmitting user information allows for the anonymity and data privacy to be realized in the event of IoT and Blockchain integration. The difficulty presented by the IoT's data privacy issue is more challenging since it begins from the data extraction to data communication levels. The implementation of cryptographic methods inside the software modules of the device is necessary to secure the data in the event that tampering is done with the device since an IoT is outside the environment and accessible to any unauthorized person. Because of this, the IoT-Blockchain configuration addresses data protection and privacy. To register a user on the blockchain network, certain Blockchains demand KYC (Know Your Customer) papers. These users are then given public addresses in the form of hash functions. The users' true identities may be determined by connecting the public addresses of the users with the KYC when the information is exchanged on the blockchain network. [37]

g. **Blockchain for Reliable and Better Communication:** IoT uses the protocols HTTP (Hyper Text Transfer Protocol), XMPP (Extensible Messaging and Presence Protocol), AND MMQT (Message Queuing Telemetry Transport) to communicate between nodes. For secure communication, such communication methods must be enclosed inside other communication protocols like TLS (Transport Layer Security). Key management for routing is carried out via the PKI (Public Key Infrastructure) protocol. Because each Internet of Things (IoT) item has a unique ID that is originally registered to a blockchain network, using blockchain can eliminate the need for key management. When this occurs, handling and exchanging PKI certificates is no longer required, making it significantly easier to secure communication. [38] Example: IBM Watson IoT Platform is a cloud-hosted solution that enables information to be extracted from the data sent to it by IoT devices. Blockchain and the Watson IoT Platform work together to aid in decision-making for all applications. [39]

9.8 Conclusion and Suggestions

IoT and blockchain technologies are both continually evolving, and their combination holds the key to address many problems of various sectors, including the financial sector across the world. The next generation of smart finance technologies will use this combination. The use of blockchain in IoT has a great deal of potential to not only safeguard the Financial IoT ecosystem but also pave the way for advanced and more extensive business applications.

Blockchain plays a crucial role in the development and proliferation of IoT payments. The combination of IoT and Blockchain will make it possible to perform transactions between two digital object identities using smart contracts, which are self-executing, autonomous, pre-programmed agreements that are safe, tamper-proof, and low-cost transaction fees. The user payment experience will be flexible and simple as IoT devices gain computing capabilities, interoperability, security, and digital identity management. To reap the benefits of these linked technologies, it is important to overcome the following obstacles:

a. **IoT Devices Need to be More Dependable and Secure:** The majority of these centralized IoT infrastructures are now vulnerable to various assaults, necessitating a difficult strategy to reduce these security risks. A decentralized distributed ledger's fundamental concepts for data authentication, permission, and audit may hold the key to solving these security problems. These functions will not be available until we have more secure IoT devices with cryptographic hardware built in and enough processing power to confirm the accuracy of data created by the device itself before it is shared.

b. **Scalability and Verification Time:** These two issues continue to be the key barriers for blockchain technologies. The network's other users must confirm and approve each transaction. Given the millions of "things" linked to the Internet of Things and a payment transaction as a use case, low latency consensus approaches that ensure majority validation is provided in a matter of seconds are critical.

c. **Untrusted IoT Data:** The basic security mechanisms of blockchain are not applicable to the external data that initiates activities; instead, they are only able to confirm the reliability and tamper-proof characteristics of actions done within its network. Oracles, which are reliable outside services and sensors, attest to these real-world events. Securing software and hardware oracles is a substantial barrier for the adoption of smart contracts due to the risk of "man-in-the-middle" attacks providing inaccurate, malicious, or erroneous data.

d. **Current Regulations Issues:** Governments are hesitant to use blockchain technology because they will diminish the central bank's power to manage economic policy and the amount of money. Market risk will develop if authorities don't look into this new problem and immediately create new regulations.

e. **The Integrated Costs Problem:** Undoubtedly, updating an established system has a significant time and financial cost, particularly when it comes to infrastructure. We must make sure that this innovative technology offers financial advantages and complies with legal requirements.

References

1. Poornima, Galiveeti, Vinay Janardhanachari and Deepak S. Sakkari, (2020). "chapter 2 data management for IoT and digital twin," *IGI Global*. www.academia.edu/89826335/Data_management_for_iot_and_digital_twin

2. Emerson, S. et al. (2015). "An OAuth based authentication mechanism for IoT networks," *International Conference on Information and Communication Technology Convergence (ICTC)*, 2015, pp. 1072–1074. IEEE.

3. Nofer, Michael, et al. (2017). "Blockchain," Bus. Inf. Syst. Eng., 59(3), 183–187.

4. Atlam, H.F. and G.B. Wills, (2019). Technical aspects of blockchain and IoT. In *Advances in Computers* (Vol. 115, pp. 1–39). Elsevier.

5. Tyagi, N., S. Gautam, J. Bharadwaj and A. Goel, (2020). B-IoT (Blockchain Internet of Things): A way to enhance IoT applications via blockchain. SSRN Electronic Journal. https://doi.org/10.2139/ssrn.3747476

6. Hoffman, N. (2017). *Blockchain: Everything You Need to Know about Blockchain Technology and How It Works* (G. McAllen, Ed.). CreateSpace Independent Publishing Platform.

7. Sandner, P., J. Gross and R. Richter, (2020). Convergence of Blockchain, IoT, and AI. Frontiers in Blockchain, 3. https://doi.org/10.3389/fbloc.2020.522600

8. Divyashree, K. S. and Achyutananda Mishra, (2023). "*Chapter 15 Blockchain Technology in Financial Sector and Its Legal Implications*," Springer Science and Business Media LLC.

9. Cekerevac, Zoran, et al. (2017). "Internet of Things and the man-in-the-middle attacks–security and economic risks." *MEST Journal* 5(2), 22–23.

10. Sinthan, D.U. and M.-S. Balamurugan, (2013). Identity authentication and capability based access control (IACAC) for the Internet of Things, *J. Cyber Secure Mob.* 1(4), 309–348.

11. Rubinoff, S. (2020). *Cyber Minds: Insights on Cybersecurity across the Cloud, Data, Artificial Intelligence, Blockchain, and IoT to Keep You Cyber Safe*. E-book: Packt Publishing.

12. Gupta, B. and M. Quamara, (2020). "An overview of Internet of Things (IoT): architectural aspects, challenges and protocols," *Concurrency and Computation: Practice and Experience*, 32, 45–69.

13. Uddin, M. A. et al (2021). A survey on the adoption of blockchain in IoT: Challenges and solutions. *Blockchain: Research and Applications*, 2(2), 100006.

14. Mishra, R. and R. Yadav, (2020). Access control in IoT networks: Analysis and open challenges. SSRN Electronic Journal. doi:https://doi.org/10.2139/ssrn.3563077

15. Braeken, A., P. Kumar, M. Ylianttila and M. Liyanage, (Eds.). (2020). *IoT Security: Advances in Authentication*. John Wiley & Sons.

16. Khan, Minhaj Ahmad and Khaled Salah, (2018). "IoT security: Review, blockchain solutions, and open challenges." *Future Generation Computer Systems*, 82, 395–411.

17. Mann, Prince, et al. (2020). "Classification of various types of attacks in IoT environment." *2020 12th International Conference on Computational Intelligence and Communication Networks (CICN)*. IEEE.

18. Manoj Kumar, Nallapaneni and Archana Dash, (2017). "The Internet of Things: An opportunity for transportation and logistics." *Proceedings of the International Conference*

on *Inventive Computing and Informatics (ICICI 2017)*, pp. 194–197, Coimbatore, Tamil Nadu, India.

19. Krčo, Srdjan, Boris Pokrić and Francois Carrez (2014)."Designing IoT architecture (s): A European perspective." *2014 IEEE World Forum on Internet of Things (WF-IoT)*. IEEE.

20. Panarello, Alfonso, et al, 2018. Blockchain and IoT integration: A systematic survey. *Sensors*, 18(8), 2575.

21. *"Advanced Applications of Blockchain Technology,"* Springer Science and Business Media LLC, 2020.

22. Otte, M. de Vos and J. Pouwelse, (2017). TrustChain: A Sybil-resistant scalable blockchain, *Future Gener. Comput. Syst.*, 720–722.

23. Signla, Dipesh and Kr Sudhakar, (2021) Blockchain for data science, *Insights2Techinfo*. https://insights2technoinfo.com/blockchain-for-data-science/

24. Hersent, O., D. Boswarthick and O. Elloumi, (2011) The Internet of Things: Key Applications and Protocols. Wiley-Blackwell. https://doi.org/10.1002/9781119958352

25. Greengard, S. (2015). *The Internet of Things*. MIT Press.

26. *"Advanced Applications of Blockchain Technology,"* Springer Science and BusinessMedia LLC, 2020.

27. Na, D. and S. Park, (2022). IoT-Chain and monitoring-chain using multi-level blockchain for IoT security. *Sensors*, 22(21), 8271. https://doi.org/10.3390/s22218271

28. Pathak, S. et al. (2022). Improvised security of IoT through blockchain. *SSRN Electronic Journal*. doi:https://doi.org/10.2139/ssrn.4027047

29. Sharma, P., W. Wilfred Godfrey and A. Trivedi, (2022). *When Blockchain meets IoT: A Comparison of the Performance of Communication Protocols in a Decentralized Identity Solution for IoT Using Blockchain*. Cluster Computing. doi:https://doi.org/10.1007/s10586-022-03921-8

30. Ajay, Kumar R. and Anuradha, (2019). Security preservation in Blockchain IoT. *Int. J. Comput. Sci. Eng.*, 7(10), 168–173. doi:https://doi.org/10.26438/ijcse/v7i10.168173

31. Ahmed, I., S. Shilpi and M. Amjad, (2018). Internet of Things IoT meaning, application and challenges. *Int J Trend Sci Res Dev*, 2(6), 1056–1064. doi:https://doi.org/10.31142/ijtsrd18773

32. orion_admin (2022). Digital Twins: The Emerging IoT Paradigm. [online] Orion Innovation. Availableat: www.orioninc.com/blog/digital-twins-the-emerging-iot-paradigm/ [Accessed 15 Mar. 2023]

33. Sureshkumar, T. and D. Vijayakumar, (2020). Security in IoT networks using blockchain technology. *J Adv Res Dyn Control Syst*, 12(1), 74–79. https://doi.org/10.5373/jardcs/v12i1/20201010

34. Agung, A. (2022). Blockchain for IoT security issues. *Blockchain Frontier Technology*, 2(1), 36–43. https://doi.org/10.34306/bfront.v2i1.104

35. Sunyaev, A. (2020). "Cloud computing," *Internet Computing*, 12(1), 195–236.

36. Gubbi, Jayavardhana, et. al (2013). Internet of Things (IoT): A vision, architectural elements, and future directions. *Future Gener. Comput. Syst.*, 29(7), 1645–1660.

37. Snyder, David. (2017). *Blockchain Technology for The Internet of Things*, 42TEK, Inc.

38. Minoli, Daniel and Occhiogrosso Benedict, (2018). " Blockchain mechanism for IoT security," *Internet of Things*.

39. NASSCOM Community | The Official Community of Indian IT Industry. (n.d.). Secured method of Waltonchain to handle the Blockchain. [online] Available at: https://community.nasscom.in/communities/emerging-tech/blockchain/secured-method-of-waltonchain-to-handle-the-blockchain.html [Accessed 15 Mar. 2023]

Chapter 10

Self-Adaptive Cyber-Physical Systems in IoT

Nimish Kumar and Himanshu Verma

BK Birla Institute of Engineering and Technology, Pilani (Rajasthan), India

10.1 Introduction to Self-Adaptive Cyber-Physical Systems in IoT

The Internet of Things (IoT) has revolutionized the way we interact with the physical world, enabling us to monitor and control physical systems remotely. However, as the number of connected devices and systems grows, the complexity of managing these systems increases exponentially. This is where self-adaptive cyber-physical systems (SACPS) come in. SACPS are designed to enable systems to adapt to changes in their environment or in their internal state, without human intervention.

The term "Cyber-Physical System" (CPS) refers to a system that integrates physical and cyber elements, such as sensors, actuators, and computational resources. SACPS add a layer of intelligence to CPSs, enabling them to adapt their behavior to changing conditions. SACPS use feedback control loops to continuously monitor the system's behavior and adjust the system's parameters to optimize its performance. The goal of SACPS is to enable systems to operate autonomously, without the need for human intervention.

SACPS have the potential to revolutionize the way we design and manage complex systems. For example, in the context of smart homes, SACPS can be used to optimize energy consumption by adjusting the temperature and lighting based on the occupancy and activity levels in the home. In the context of transportation systems, SACPS can be used to optimize traffic flow by adjusting the timing of traffic lights based on the volume of traffic on the road. In the context of industrial

DOI: 10.1201/9781003474838-10

automation, SACPS can be used to optimize production processes by adjusting the parameters of the manufacturing equipment based on the quality of the output.

Scientific research has been conducted in the field of SACPS for IoT-based systems to address the challenges and opportunities of this emerging field. For example, machine learning and AI techniques have been applied to SACPS to enable them to learn from their environment and to make decisions based on the data they collect. These techniques have been used to develop self-organizing systems that can adapt to changes in their environment or in their internal state.

One approach for SACPS design and development is based on reinforcement learning. A recent study by Zhang et al. (2021) proposed a novel architecture for self-adaptive cyber-physical systems that uses reinforcement learning to optimize the system's performance. The proposed architecture uses a combination of model-free and model-based reinforcement learning to enable the system to adapt to changes in the environment and to optimize its performance.

Another research direction in SACPS design and development is based on the concept of self-healing systems. Self-healing systems are designed to detect and recover from faults and failures in the system without human intervention. A study by Ratasich (2019) proposed a self-healing framework for cyber-physical systems that uses a combination of model-based and data-driven approaches. The proposed framework uses Bayesian network modeling and data-driven learning to detect and diagnose faults in the system, and then uses model-based optimization to recover from the faults.

Control theory and dynamic systems have also been used to design feedback control systems that enable SACPS to adjust their behavior based on changes in their environment or in their internal state. These techniques have been used to develop self-configuring systems that can adapt to changes in their configuration and self-healing systems that can recover from faults and failures.

In addition, research has been conducted to address the scalability, reliability, security, and privacy issues of SACPS for IoT-based systems. For example, techniques such as data aggregation, distributed processing, and edge computing have been used to address the scalability issues of SACPS. Fault detection, diagnosis, and recovery techniques have been used to address the reliability issues of SACPS. Security techniques such as encryption, access control, and authentication have been used to address the security issues of SACPS. Finally, privacy techniques such as anonymization, pseudonymization, and consent management have been implemented to address the privacy issues of SACPS in IoT-based systems, ensuring that sensitive user data is appropriately protected and user consent is prioritized.

Despite the potential benefits of SACPS for IoT-based systems, there are still several challenges that need to be addressed. One of the key challenges is the design and development of SACPS that can operate in a dynamic and uncertain environment. SACPS must be able to adapt to changes in their environment and to operate under conditions of uncertainty. Another challenge is the integration of SACPS with existing systems and technologies. SACPS must be able to interact with existing systems and technologies to enable seamless integration and interoperability.

In conclusion, SACPS have the potential to revolutionize the way we design and manage complex systems in the IoT era. SACPS enable systems to operate autonomously, without the need for human intervention, and can adapt to changes in their environment or in their internal state. The scientific research in the field of SACPS has addressed several challenges and opportunities, including reinforcement learning, self-healing, control theory, scalability, reliability, security, and privacy. However, there are still several challenges that need to be addressed, including the design and development of SACPS that can operate in a dynamic and uncertain environment, and the integration of SACPS with existing systems and technologies.

10.2 Overview of Cyber-Physical Systems

Cyber-Physical Systems (CPS) refer to systems that integrate physical and cyber components to form a tightly coupled network, where physical components interact with cyber components in a feedback loop. CPS are composed of sensors, actuators, controllers, communication networks, and computing devices, and they operate in a physical environment to perform specific tasks or functions. Examples of CPS include self-driving cars, smart buildings, medical devices, and industrial control systems.

CPS have gained significant attention in recent years due to their potential to transform various domains such as transportation, healthcare, energy, and manufacturing. CPS can improve the efficiency, reliability, and safety of these domains by enabling real-time monitoring, control, and optimization. The development and deployment of CPS have been enabled by the advances in computing, communication, and sensing technologies. See Figure 10.1 for Cyber-Physical Systems examples).

However, CPS also pose significant challenges in terms of their design, development, and operation. These challenges include the need for real-time data processing, reliable and secure communication, and the ability to handle uncertainty and dynamics in the physical environment. To address these challenges, various techniques and methodologies have been proposed in the literature, including control theory, machine learning, optimization, and fault diagnosis. The need for real-time data processing and analysis poses a significant challenge in Cyber-Physical Systems. These systems generate substantial amounts of data from various sources, including sensors. To make informed decisions and take appropriate actions, this data must be processed and analyzed in real time. Efficient algorithms and architectures play a crucial role in enabling timely data processing and analysis. Promising techniques, such as deep learning and reinforcement learning, have shown potential in tackling this challenge (Al-Fuqaha et al., 2015).

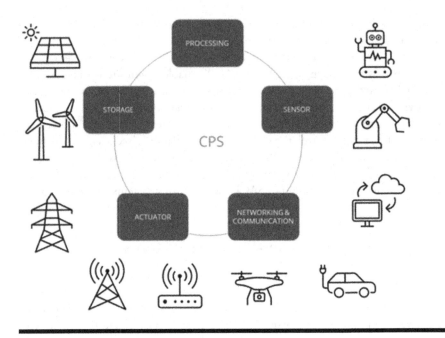

Figure 10.1 Cyber-Physical Systems examples.
Source: Created by the author.

Another critical challenge in CPS revolves around ensuring reliable and secure communication. CPS rely heavily on communication networks to facilitate the exchange of data and commands between physical and cyber components. However, these networks are vulnerable to a range of attacks, including denial-of-service attacks and cyber attacks, which can jeopardize the overall operation and safety of CPS. To address this challenge, the literature has proposed various security mechanisms and protocols such as authentication, encryption, and intrusion detection (Shi et al., 2011).

Additionally, CPS must possess the ability to handle uncertainties and dynamics within the physical environment. Physical environments are often intricate and subject to unpredictable events and disturbances. CPS need to adapt to these changes and operate effectively under conditions of uncertainty. Control theory and optimization techniques have been widely employed to tackle this challenge (Ding et al., 2020). See Figure 10.2 for the evolution of CPS in the industry,

In summary, Cyber-Physical Systems face several key challenges. Real-time data processing and analysis, reliable and secure communication, and the ability to handle uncertainty and dynamics in the physical environment are all critical aspects that must be addressed to ensure the efficient and safe operation of CPS. CPS is an emerging field that has the potential to transform various domains such as

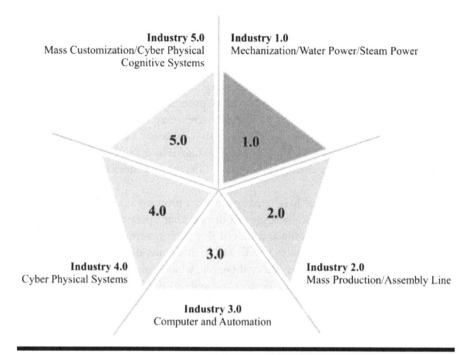

Figure 10.2   The evolution of CPS in the industry 4.0.

Source: Created by the author.

transportation, healthcare, energy, and manufacturing. CPS integrate physical and cyber components to form a tightly coupled network, where physical components interact with cyber components in a feedback loop. CPS pose significant challenges in terms of their design, development, and operation, including the need for real-time data processing, reliable and secure communication, and the ability to handle uncertainty and dynamics in the physical environment. Various techniques and methodologies have been proposed in the literature to address these challenges, including control theory, machine learning, optimization, and fault diagnosis.

10.3 Characteristics and Challenges of IoT-based Systems

The Internet of Things (IoT) is an emerging technology that facilitates the interconnection of physical devices, sensors, and objects with the Internet, allowing for real-time monitoring, control, and optimization. By enabling efficient and effective data collection, analysis, and decision-making, IoT-based systems hold the potential to revolutionize sectors such as healthcare, transportation, and manufacturing. Nonetheless, the design, development, and operation of such systems present notable challenges.

A key characteristic of IoT-based systems is their diversity. IoT devices exhibit variations in form, size, and capabilities, often employing disparate communication protocols and data formats. This diversity poses a considerable obstacle in the creation and implementation of IoT-based systems that seamlessly integrate with diverse devices and platforms. To address this challenge, various standards and protocols have been proposed, such as MQTT, CoAP, and JSON-LD, to facilitate interoperability and data exchange between different IoT devices and platforms (Khan et al., 2019).

The distributed nature of IoT-based systems is a prominent characteristic. These systems consist of geographically dispersed devices that operate in diverse environments and conditions. Managing and monitoring such systems, especially at a large scale, present considerable challenges. To tackle this issue, developers have created various tools like IoT platforms and dashboards, which empower users to monitor the performance and status of IoT devices and systems (Gubbi et al., 2013).

Another characteristic of IoT-based systems is the diversity of devices and protocols involved. These systems encompass a wide array of devices with distinct capabilities, protocols, and communication standards. This diversity can lead to interoperability problems and pose challenges for system integration and management. Efforts, such as the Industrial Internet Consortium (IIC) and the Open Connectivity Foundation (OCF), have been established to address this challenge through standardization (Atzori et al., 2010).

Security and privacy represent significant challenges in IoT-based systems. These systems involve the exchange of sensitive data and commands among devices and networks, making them vulnerable to cyber attacks and data breaches. To ensure the confidentiality, integrity, and availability of data in IoT-based systems, essential security mechanisms include encryption, authentication, and access control (Vikas, 2015).

Furthermore, IoT-based systems need to be capable of handling uncertainty and dynamics in the physical environment. Physical environments often exhibit complexity and dynamism, with unpredictable events and disturbances. Consequently, IoT-based systems must adapt to changes in the physical environment and operate under uncertain conditions. Control theory and optimization techniques have been widely utilized to address this challenge (Bandyopadhyay and Sen, 2011).

In conclusion, IoT-based systems are an emerging technology with the potential to revolutionize various domains by enabling efficient data collection, analysis, and decision-making. These systems bring forth significant challenges in terms of design, development, and operation, including the vast scale of devices and data, device and protocol heterogeneity, security and privacy concerns, and the ability to handle uncertainty and dynamics in the physical environment. The literature offers a range of techniques and methodologies to tackle these challenges, such as machine learning, standardization, security mechanisms, control theory, and optimization.

10.4 Self-Adaptive Systems: Definition and Importance

Self-adaptive systems represent a category of systems that possess the capacity to independently monitor, analyze, and modify their behavior and structure when confronted with alterations in their surroundings or demands (Macías-Escrivá et al., 2013). These systems are distinguished by their capability to adapt to dynamic and uncertain environments, optimize their performance and service quality, and enhance their resilience and dependability. Achieving self-adaptation necessitates the fusion of feedback control, machine learning, and decision-making mechanisms, enabling systems to acquire knowledge from past experiences and make well-informed decisions concerning their future conduct.

The significance of self-adaptive systems lies in their ability to tackle the challenges presented by intricate and fluctuating environments, particularly in the context of IoT-based systems. IoT-based systems frequently operate in uncertain and unpredictable surroundings, where modifications in the physical environment, user behavior, or network conditions can impact their effectiveness and dependability. By adjusting their behavior and structure in response to environmental or requisition changes, self-adaptive systems can effectively address these challenges, ultimately heightening their flexibility and resilience (Macías-Escrivá et al., 2013). See Figure 10.3 for a Self-Adaptive System.

Self-adaptive systems are also important for addressing the challenges of system evolution and maintenance. Systems are often subject to changes in requirements, technologies, or user needs, which can lead to performance degradation, system failures, or high maintenance costs. Self-adaptive systems can address these challenges by adapting to changes in the system and environment, and by optimizing their performance and quality of service. This can reduce the need for manual intervention and maintenance and can increase the longevity and sustainability of the system (Cheng et al., 2019).

In addition to their technical benefits, self-adaptive systems can also provide social and economic benefits. For example, self-adaptive systems can improve the user experience and satisfaction by providing adaptive and personalized services. They can also reduce the environmental impact of systems by optimizing their energy consumption and resource usage. Moreover, self-adaptive systems can provide economic benefits by reducing the costs of system development, operation, and maintenance (Cheng et al., 2019).

To summarize, self-adaptive systems belong to a category of systems capable of independently observing, examining, and adjusting their behavior and structure to

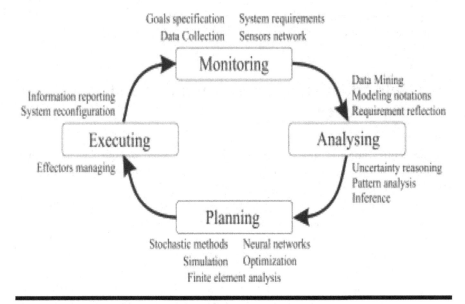

Figure 10.3   Self-adaptive system.

Source: Created by the author.

adapt to alterations in their surroundings or demands. These systems are crucial in tackling the obstacles presented by intricate and ever-changing environments, while also enhancing the performance, dependability, and sustainability of various systems. The technical, social, and economic advantages of self-adaptive systems are substantial, and they are anticipated to assume a progressively significant role in the creation, advancement, and functioning of Internet of Things (IoT)-based systems as well as other intricate systems.

10.5 Autonomic Computing for IoT-based Systems

Autonomic computing is a computing paradigm that aims to create self-managing and self-optimizing systems. It takes inspiration from the biological concept of homeostasis, which refers to the ability of living organisms to maintain a stable internal environment despite changes in their external surroundings. Autonomic computing systems possess the capability to independently monitor, analyze, and control their own behavior and performance without requiring human intervention. In the context of IoT-based systems, the principles of autonomic computing can bring significant benefits. These systems operate in dynamic and diverse environments where alterations in the physical surroundings, network conditions, or user behavior can impact their performance and reliability. Autonomic computing can effectively address these challenges by enabling systems to monitor their behavior, analyze their performance, and optimize their actions and resource allocation in response to environmental changes or requirements.

The autonomic computing paradigm comprises four key components: self-configuration, self-optimization, self-healing, and self-protection. See Figure 10.4 for Autonomic Computing attributes. Self-configuration entails systems automatically adjusting their configurations based on their environment and requirements. Self-optimization involves systems dynamically allocating and managing resources to optimize performance and ensure quality of service. Self-healing refers to systems automatically detecting and recovering from failures or errors. Lastly, self-protection involves systems securing themselves against attacks and intrusions (Kephart and Chess, 2003).

Autonomic computing has found applications in various domains, including cloud computing, cyber-physical systems, and IoT-based systems. In IoT-based systems, autonomic computing can address challenges such as resource management, energy efficiency, and security. For instance, by leveraging autonomic computing, IoT devices can adapt their behavior based on their battery levels, optimize energy consumption, and extend battery life (Cicirelli et al., 2021). Furthermore, autonomic computing can aid in detecting and preventing cyber attacks in IoT networks by automatically identifying anomalies in network traffic and implementing appropriate countermeasures (Zhu et al., 2017).

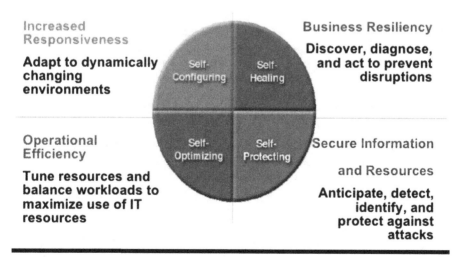

Figure 10.4　Autonomic computing attributes.
Source: Created by the author.

In conclusion, autonomic computing is a computing paradigm that can enable IoT-based systems to become more self-managing, self-optimizing, and self-protecting. Autonomic computing can help IoT-based systems to address challenges such as resource management, energy efficiency, and security. Autonomic computing has been applied to various domains, and its potential for IoT-based systems is increasingly being recognized.

10.6 Machine Learning and AI Techniques for Self-Adaptive Systems

Machine learning and artificial intelligence (AI) methods have emerged as potent instruments for the development of self-adaptive systems across multiple domains, encompassing IoT-based systems. These techniques empower systems to learn from their historical performance, to forecast future behavior, and to make informed decisions based on the available data and knowledge.

Within the realm of self-adaptive systems, machine learning and AI techniques find application in diverse tasks such as anomaly detection, prediction, decision-making, and optimization. For instance, machine-learning algorithms can analyze data obtained from IoT sensors, identifying anomalies or deviations from normal behavior, and subsequently initiating appropriate actions to uphold system performance and reliability. Additionally, machine learning enables predictions of future behavior by leveraging historical data, while optimizing system behavior and resource allocation to accomplish specific objectives like energy efficiency or quality of service (Shi, 2021).

Moreover, AI techniques like reinforcement learning contribute to the development of self-adaptive systems capable of learning from experience and enhancing their behavior over time. Reinforcement learning, a machine-learning technique, involves learning through feedback or rewards received for specific actions taken. It enables the creation of self-adaptive systems that learn from experience, optimize their behavior, and strive towards specific goals like energy efficiency or user satisfaction (Krupitzer et al., 2015).

Machine learning and AI techniques have found diverse applications in various domains, including cybersecurity, cloud computing, and IoT-based systems. In the context of IoT-based systems, they can effectively address challenges concerning resource management, energy efficiency, and security. For example, machine learning can be used to optimize the energy consumption of IoT devices, by predicting their energy requirements and adapting their behavior accordingly (Yang et al., 2020). AI techniques can also be used to detect and prevent cyber attacks in IoT networks, by analyzing network traffic and identifying anomalies or malicious behavior (Saharkhizan et al., 2020).

In conclusion, machine learning and AI techniques have emerged as powerful tools for developing self-adaptive systems in various domains, including IoT-based systems. Machine learning and AI techniques can enable systems to learn from their past behavior, to predict future behavior, and to make decisions based on the available data and knowledge. Machine learning and AI techniques have been applied to various challenges in IoT-based systems, and their potential for developing self-adaptive systems is increasingly being recognized.

10.7 Control Theory and Dynamic Systems for Self-Adaptive Cyber-Physical Systems

Control theory and dynamic systems theory offer a robust framework for the advancement of self-adaptive cyber-physical systems. Control theory focuses on designing and analyzing control systems capable of achieving desired behaviors or performance by manipulating system inputs. On the other hand, dynamic systems theory concerns itself with modeling and analyzing systems that undergo changes over time, such as cyber-physical systems.

Within the realm of self-adaptive systems, control theory and dynamic systems theory serve various purposes, encompassing modeling, analysis, design, and optimization. For instance, control theory enables the creation of controllers that ensure consistent system performance and stability even in the face of evolving conditions, such as fluctuations in loads or disturbances. Dynamic systems theory, on the other hand, facilitates the modeling of cyber-physical system behavior and the analysis of crucial properties like stability, robustness, and performance.

In the context of IoT-based systems, control theory and dynamic systems theory play pivotal roles in addressing key challenges such as resource management, energy efficiency, and reliability. Control theory can be employed to devise controllers that optimize resource utilization, such as energy or bandwidth, in IoT networks (Wang et al., 2018). Similarly, dynamic systems theory aids in modeling the behavior of IoT-based systems and analyzing essential properties like stability, robustness, and performance (Wu et al., 2021).

The application of control theory and dynamic systems theory extends across diverse domains, including robotics, aerospace, and manufacturing. In the realm of self-adaptive systems, these theories have been leveraged to develop adaptable controllers capable of adjusting their behavior in response to changing conditions. Moreover, they facilitate the optimization of system performance and resource allocation. For example, self-adaptive control systems have been developed for autonomous robots, to maintain stability and performance under changing environmental conditions (Švaco et al., 2012).

In conclusion, control theory and dynamic systems theory provide a powerful framework for developing self-adaptive cyber-physical systems. Control theory and dynamic systems theory can be used for various tasks, including modeling, analysis, design, and optimization. Control theory and dynamic systems theory have been applied to various challenges in IoT-based systems, and their potential for developing self-adaptive systems is increasingly being recognized.

10.8 Self-Optimization and Self-Configuration in IoT-based Systems

Self-adaptive systems, particularly in the realm of IoT-based systems, encounter common challenges such as resource constraints, dynamic environments, and diverse device configurations. To overcome these challenges, self-optimization and self-configuration play pivotal roles. Self-optimization entails the capacity of a system to adjust its parameters or configuration to enhance its performance and efficiency. On the other hand, self-configuration refers to the system's ability to automatically discover and configure its components or resources.

In IoT-based systems, the utilization of self-optimization and self-configuration can effectively address concerns like energy efficiency, network congestion, and scalability. For instance, employing self-optimization techniques enables the adjustment of transmission power in IoT devices, minimizing energy consumption while maintaining satisfactory communication quality (Jia et al., 2009). Additionally, self-configuration techniques aid in the automatic discovery and configuration of devices within IoT networks, reducing the need for manual intervention in the configuration and management processes (Ayala et al., 2012).

A range of techniques and approaches has been developed to facilitate self-optimization and self-configuration in IoT-based systems. Machine-learning techniques, including reinforcement learning and deep learning, have proven valuable for self-optimization tasks, such as optimizing resource allocation in IoT networks (Yang et al., 2020). Rules-based approaches, such as fuzzy logic and expert systems, have been successfully applied to self-configuration tasks, such as automatically configuring sensor networks based on environmental conditions (Sobral et al., 2013).

The application of self-optimization and self-configuration techniques extends across diverse domains, encompassing smart homes, industrial automation, and transportation. In the context of self-adaptive systems, these techniques have demonstrated their ability to improve system performance, efficiency, and reliability. For instance, self-optimization techniques have been effectively employed to optimize the configuration of wireless sensor networks in smart homes, leading to enhanced energy efficiency and reduced communication latency (Krupitzer et al., 2016).

To summarize, self-optimization and self-configuration are crucial components of self-adaptive systems in the realm of IoT-based systems. Various techniques and approaches have been developed to address these tasks, and their application spans multiple domains. By leveraging self-optimization and self-configuration techniques, the performance, efficiency, and reliability of IoT-based systems can be significantly enhanced, solidifying their importance in the development of self-adaptive systems.

10.9 Self-Healing and Self-Protection Mechanisms for IoT-based Systems

Ensuring the dependability and security of IoT-based systems relies heavily on the presence of self-healing and self-protection mechanisms. Self-healing denotes the system's ability to autonomously detect and rectify failures, while self-protection involves the implementation of measures to thwart attacks and uphold the system's integrity. Diverse techniques, including redundancy, fault tolerance, and intrusion detection, can be employed to achieve these mechanisms (Diaz et al., 2019). Redundancy is a common technique used to achieve self-healing in IoT-based systems. This involves the duplication of critical components to ensure that if one component fails, the backup component takes over seamlessly. For example, in a wireless sensor network, redundant nodes can be added to ensure that if a node fails, the data can still be transmitted through the other nodes. Fault tolerance is another technique that can be used to achieve self-healing. This involves designing the system to be able to tolerate faults and continue functioning despite them. For instance, in a distributed system, nodes can be designed to detect and recover from faults, thereby ensuring that the system remains operational.

Self-protection mechanisms are essential for ensuring the security of IoT-based systems. One such mechanism is intrusion detection, which involves the monitoring of system activities to detect any unauthorized access or suspicious behavior (Zarpelão et al., 2017). Intrusion detection can be achieved by machine-learning algorithms, which can be trained to recognize patterns of normal behavior and identify any anomalies. Another technique used for self-protection is access control, which involves limiting access to the system to authorized users only. Access control can be implemented using passwords, biometric authentication, and other security measures.

Overall, self-healing and self-protection mechanisms are crucial for ensuring the reliability and security of IoT-based systems. Using redundancy, fault tolerance, intrusion detection, and access control, these mechanisms can be achieved and help to mitigate the risks associated with system failures and security threats.

10.10 Predictive Maintenance in IoT-based Systems

Predictive maintenance refers to the use of data analytics and machine-learning techniques to predict when equipment or machines in a system are likely to fail

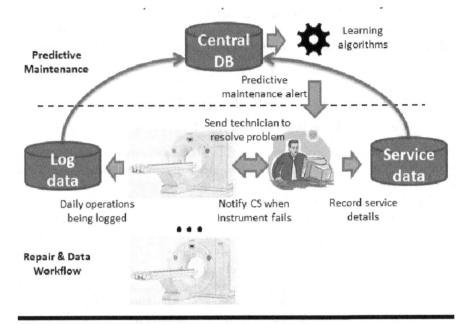

Figure 10.5 Predictive maintenance system.

Source: Created by the author.

and require maintenance. See Figure 10.5 for a predictive maintenance system. In IoT-based systems, predictive maintenance can be used to increase the efficiency and reliability of the system by minimizing downtime and reducing maintenance costs. This is achieved through the continuous monitoring of system components, which enables the detection of anomalies and the prediction of potential failures before they occur.

Predictive maintenance offers a crucial advantage by proactively anticipating failures before they occur, thus minimizing downtime. This advantage holds particular significance in mission-critical systems, where even a brief period of operational interruption can result in severe consequences. Moreover, predictive maintenance helps to optimize maintenance costs by enabling maintenance activities to be carried out based on actual need, rather than following a rigid schedule. This approach not only reduces the frequency of maintenance but also mitigates the risks associated with unnecessary maintenance, which can lead to additional downtime and expenses.

In the realm of IoT-based systems, predictive maintenance can be achieved through a variety of techniques, including machine-learning algorithms, data analytics, and sensor data. Machine-learning algorithms are capable of analyzing historical data to identify patterns that may indicate potential equipment failures. Data

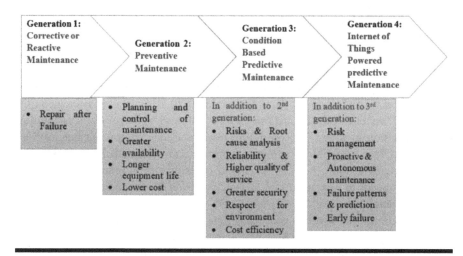

Figure 10.6   Industrial revolution maintenance techniques and objectives.
Source: Created by the author.

analytics plays a crucial role in detecting trends and anomalies within the system data, while sensor data enables continuous monitoring of individual components' performance and early detection of potential failures. See Figure 10.6 for industrial revolution maintenance techniques and objectives

Significant research has been conducted on predictive maintenance in IoT-based systems. For instance, Ran et al. (2019) conducted a comprehensive survey exploring the utilization of machine-learning techniques for predictive maintenance in IoT-based systems. Similarly, Rieger et al. (2019) conducted a detailed review on the application of deep learning in predictive maintenance of machinery within IoT-based systems. These studies emphasize the criticality of predictive maintenance in IoT-based systems and the numerous potential benefits it offers. Overall, predictive maintenance is an important aspect of IoT-based systems, as it enables the early detection and prevention of equipment failures, thereby increasing system reliability and reducing maintenance costs. Using machine-learning algorithms, data analytics, and sensor data, predictive maintenance can be achieved and help to optimize the performance of IoT-based systems.

10.11 Edge, Fog, and Cloud Computing for Self-Adaptive Cyber-Physical Systems

Edge, fog, and cloud computing are three interconnected approaches that can be leveraged to construct self-adaptive cyber-physical systems (CPS) (Sha et al., 2008).

Self-adaptive CPS refer to systems capable of monitoring their own behavior and adjusting it in response to changing conditions. These systems utilize edge, fog, and cloud computing to collect data, analyze it, and derive decisions based on the findings (Mukherjee et al., 2018).

Edge computing entails processing data at the network's edge, in close proximity to the devices that generate the data (Xue et al., 2020). This proves advantageous in CPS since it enables real-time data processing, minimizing latency and facilitating prompt decision-making. Fog computing resembles edge computing but involves processing data in a distributed computing infrastructure situated closer to end-users than the cloud (Bonomi et al., 2012). Fog computing aids in reducing the volume of data that needs to be transmitted to the cloud, thereby enhancing efficiency and reducing latency.

Cloud computing involves processing data on remote servers accessible via the Internet (Mukherjee et al., 2018). Cloud computing is valuable in CPS for its capacity to store substantial amounts of data and perform sophisticated data analysis. This capability allows for large-scale data analysis and machine learning, empowering the identification of patterns and making predictions.

Self-adaptive CPS can employ all three computing paradigms to accomplish their objectives. For instance, edge computing can be utilized for real-time data processing, fog computing can mitigate latency and enhance efficiency, while cloud computing can facilitate large-scale data analysis and machine learning (Xue et al., 2020). By integrating these paradigms, self-adaptive CPS can attain heightened performance, reliability, and scalability.

Developing software architectures capable of accommodating edge, fog, and cloud computing stands as a significant challenge in the realm of self-adaptive CPS (Sha et al., 2008). This requires the integration of different technologies, including IoT, cloud computing, and data analytics. The development of such architectures requires a deep understanding of the underlying technologies and their interactions.

Overall, edge, fog, and cloud computing are important paradigms for building self-adaptive CPS (Mukherjee et al., 2018). By combining these paradigms, self-adaptive CPS can achieve high performance, reliability, and scalability, while also addressing the challenges associated with data processing and decision-making in real time.

10.12 Big Data Analytics for Self-Adaptive Systems

Self-adaptive systems belong to a class of systems that possess the capability to autonomously adapt their behavior and structure in response to changes occurring in their operating environment. The integration of big data analytics is vital for the design, development, and operation of these self-adaptive systems. This section aims to explore the utilization of big data analytics within self-adaptive systems and highlight recent scientific advancements in this field.

Big data analytics encompasses the process of extracting valuable insights from vast and intricate datasets through the utilization of statistical and computational techniques. Within the realm of self-adaptive systems, big data analytics can be employed to analyze diverse data sources, such as sensor data, log files, and performance metrics. The objective is to identify patterns, correlations, and anomalies, which subsequently facilitate improvements in the performance, reliability, and efficiency of self-adaptive systems.

A prominent challenge in designing self-adaptive systems lies in the development of algorithms capable of effectively analyzing and interpreting substantial volumes of real-time data. Machine-learning techniques, including neural networks, decision trees, and support vector machines, have been leveraged to construct predictive models that detect and respond to changes within the operating environment of self-adaptive systems. For instance, Kumar and Singh (2018) employed a neural network-based approach to predict the future workload of a cloud computing system, subsequently enabling the allocation of resources to meet the anticipated demand.

Another significant application of big data analytics in self-adaptive systems pertains to fault diagnosis and prognosis. Fault diagnosis entails identifying the underlying cause of a failure, while fault prognosis involves predicting the probability of future failures. By analyzing data from sensors, control systems, and maintenance records, big data analytics aids in the detection of patterns and anomalies that may indicate the presence of a fault. Yu et al. (2018) conducted a study employing a data-driven approach to diagnose faults in wind turbine systems using sensor and control system data.

In addition to fault diagnosis and prognosis, big data analytics can optimize the performance and energy efficiency of self-adaptive systems. For instance, Shojafar et al. (2016) utilized a machine learning-based approach to optimize the placement of virtual machines in a cloud computing system, leading to notable energy savings.

To conclude, big data analytics assumes a pivotal role in the design, development, and operation of self-adaptive systems. Through the analysis of vast and intricate datasets, big data analytics empowers self-adaptive systems to become more efficient, reliable, and adaptable to changes in their operating environment. As the field of big data analytics continues to progress, further scientific advancements are anticipated in its application to self-adaptive systems.

10.13 Security and Privacy in Self-Adaptive Cyber-Physical Systems

Cyber-physical systems (CPS) encompass the integration of physical and computational components. Within this domain, self-adaptive CPS refers to systems that possess the capability to autonomously adapt to changing environments. While self-adaptive CPS offers a host of advantages, such as enhanced efficiency and resilience, they also present significant challenges concerning security and privacy. This section explores the security and privacy concerns specific to self-adaptive CPS and sheds light on recent scientific advancements in this field.

Self-adaptive CPS encounter a broad spectrum of security threats, including malicious attacks on system components, communication networks, and data. Exploiting vulnerabilities within the system, attackers can gain unauthorized access, manipulate data, or disrupt the system's operation. To counter these threats, various security mechanisms have been proposed, such as access control, cryptography, and intrusion detection. For instance, Settanni et al. (2018) proposed a secure architecture for self-adaptive CPS that employs digital certificates and access control to ensure that solely authorized entities can access the system's resources.

Privacy protection emerges as another crucial concern within self-adaptive CPS. These systems typically amass substantial volumes of data from diverse sources, encompassing potentially sensitive information like personal health records or financial data. Safeguarding this data from unauthorized access, disclosure, or misuse becomes imperative. Privacy protection mechanisms, including anonymization, data minimization, and encryption, can be employed to secure sensitive data. Keshk et al. (2021) proposed a privacy-preserving framework for self-adaptive CPS, utilizing homomorphic encryption to enable secure data processing while upholding data privacy. In addition to security and privacy, self-adaptive CPS also face challenges in ensuring system safety and reliability. Self-adaptive CPS can sometimes make decisions based on incomplete or inaccurate information, which can lead to system failures or safety hazards. To address these challenges, various approaches have been proposed, including formal methods and model-based engineering. In a study by D'Angelo et al. (2020), a model-based approach was proposed for self-adaptive CPS that uses formal methods to ensure that the system's behavior is correct and that safety properties are satisfied.

In conclusion, security and privacy are critical concerns in self-adaptive CPS. The integration of physical and computational components, along with the autonomous adaptation capabilities, make these systems vulnerable to a wide range of threats. However, with the development of new security and privacy mechanisms, such as access control, cryptography, and privacy-preserving technologies, self-adaptive CPS can be designed to be both efficient and secure.

10.14 Case Studies and Applications of Self-Adaptive Cyber-Physical Systems in IoT

Self-adaptive cyber-physical systems (CPS) have emerged as a promising approach to building efficient, reliable, and resilient Internet of Things (IoT) applications. This section, discusses case studies and applications of self-adaptive CPS in IoT and highlight some of the recent scientific advances in this area.

Smart Home Energy Management: A self-adaptive CPS-based energy management system was proposed in a study by Lissa et al. (2021). The system uses a reinforcement learning algorithm to adapt to the dynamic energy demands of smart homes, while minimizing energy consumption.

Smart Traffic Management: A self-adaptive CPS-based traffic management system was proposed in a study by Li et al. (2016). The system uses a multi-agent approach to adapt to the changing traffic conditions and optimize the traffic flow in smart cities.

Agriculture Monitoring: A self-adaptive CPS-based agriculture monitoring system was proposed in a study by An et al. (2017). The system uses wireless sensor networks and machine-learning algorithms to adapt to the changing environmental conditions and optimize crop growth.

Healthcare Monitoring: In a study conducted by Verma et al. (2022), they introduced a healthcare monitoring system based on self-adaptive Cyber-Physical Systems (CPS). This innovative system utilizes wearable sensors and machine-learning algorithms to dynamically adjust to the evolving health conditions of individuals, ensuring the delivery of personalized healthcare services.

Building Automation: A self-adaptive CPS-based building automation system was proposed in a study by Gurgen et al. (2013). The system uses a rules-based approach to adapt to the changing occupancy and environmental conditions in smart buildings, while optimizing energy consumption and comfort levels.

Industrial Process Optimization: A self-adaptive CPS-based industrial process optimization system was proposed in a study by Alaya et al. (2017). The system uses machine-learning algorithms to adapt to the changing process conditions and optimize the process performance in manufacturing plants.

Smart Grid Management: A self-adaptive CPS-based smart grid management system was proposed in a study by Wang and Govindarasu (2020). The system uses a multi-agent approach to adapt to the changing energy demands and supply conditions in smart grids, while ensuring grid stability and reliability.

Transportation Management: A self-adaptive CPS-based transportation management system was proposed in a study by Xiong et al. (2015). The system uses a rules-based approach to adapt to the changing traffic and weather conditions and optimize the transportation network performance.

Disaster Response: A self-adaptive CPS-based disaster response system was proposed in a study by Gunes et al. (2014). The system uses wireless sensor networks and machine-learning algorithms to adapt to the changing disaster conditions and provide real-time situational awareness to emergency responders.

Water Resource Management: A self-adaptive CPS-based water resource management system was proposed in a study by Wang et al. (2015). The system uses a rules-based approach to adapt to the changing water demands and supply conditions and optimize the water resource utilization in smart cities.

Smart City Infrastructure Management: A self-adaptive cyber-physical system for infrastructure management in smart cities that adapts to the traffic and environmental conditions using machine-learning algorithms (Delicato et al., 2020).

In conclusion, self-adaptive CPS has numerous applications in IoT, ranging from smart home energy management to disaster response. These systems can adapt to changing conditions and optimize system performance, while ensuring reliability, efficiency, and resilience.

10.15 Future Directions and Research Challenges in Self-Adaptive Cyber-Physical Systems in IoT

Self-adaptive cyber-physical systems (SACPS) are gaining significant importance within the context of the Internet of Things (IoT), where the interconnection of numerous devices and sensors generates vast quantities of data that necessitate real-time analysis and action. Although SACPS have demonstrated their potential in facilitating more efficient and effective management of IoT systems, there remain numerous challenges and prospects for future research in this domain.

One of the primary obstacles in SACPS involves ensuring their security and privacy. These systems are susceptible to a wide array of security threats, including cyber attacks, data breaches, and insider threats. Moreover, the deployment of SACPS in IoT environments raises concerns regarding privacy, as these systems have the potential to collect and analyze sensitive personal data. Therefore, the development of robust security and privacy mechanisms for SACPS is vital to their successful implementation in IoT. Another significant research direction entails the creation of algorithms that are efficient and scalable for SACPS. With the increasing number of connected devices in IoT systems, the volume of data generated by these devices is growing rapidly. To effectively manage this data, SACPS must possess the ability to analyze and act upon it in real time. Hence, it is essential to develop algorithms that exhibit both efficiency and scalability to ensure the triumph of SACPS in IoT. The development of self-explanatory and interpretable SACPS presents another challenge. These systems must possess the capability to elucidate their behavior and decision-making processes to users and stakeholders, particularly in critical applications such as healthcare and transportation. This necessitates the development of methods and tools for visualizing and interpreting the behavior of SACPS.

Lastly, there is a need for more comprehensive evaluation frameworks for SACPS in the IoT realm. While numerous case studies and applications of SACPS in various domains exist, standardized methods for evaluating the effectiveness and performance of these systems are lacking. The development of such frameworks will enable researchers and practitioners to compare different SACPS and identify best practices for their design and implementation. In conclusion, SACPS have the potential to revolutionize the management of IoT systems, yet numerous challenges and opportunities for future research exist in this domain. Addressing these challenges requires a multidisciplinary approach that combines expertise in computer science, engineering, and other relevant fields.

10.16 Conclusion

To sum up, the advancement of self-adaptive cyber-physical systems (SACPS) within the realm of the Internet of Things (IoT) holds immense potential for revolutionizing the management of intricate systems. This chapter has presented a comprehensive overview of cyber-physical systems, examined the attributes and difficulties faced by IoT-based systems, and emphasized the significance of self-adaptive systems.

The development of SACPS relies on fundamental techniques such as autonomic computing, machine learning, and control theory. These techniques empower SACPS to continuously optimize their performance, configuration, and healing mechanisms in real time. Furthermore, predictive maintenance, as well as the domains of edge, fog, and cloud computing, along with big data analytics, constitute crucial areas of exploration for enhancing SACPS within the IoT context. However, the development of SACPS also presents many challenges, including the need for robust security and privacy mechanisms, the development of self-explanatory and interpretable systems, and the need for comprehensive evaluation frameworks. These challenges require a multidisciplinary approach that combines expertise in computer science, engineering, and other fields. Despite these challenges, many case studies and applications of SACPS in various domains have shown promising results. For example, SACPS have been used in healthcare monitoring, building automation, disaster response, and infrastructure management. These applications demonstrate the potential of SACPS to improve efficiency, reduce costs, and to enhance user experiences.

Overall, the development of SACPS in IoT presents both challenges and opportunities for future research. Addressing these challenges will require continued innovation and collaboration across multiple fields and will be crucial for the successful deployment of SACPS in a wide range of domains.

References

Alaya, N., Dafflon, B., Moalla, N., & Ouzrout, Y. (2017, March). A CPS-Agent self-adaptive quality control platform for industry 4.0. In *Proceedings of the 7th International Conference on Information Society and Technology, Kopaonik* (pp. 12–15). Serbia.

Al-Fuqaha, A., Guizani, M., Mohammadi, M., Aledhari, M., & Ayyash, M. (2015). Internet of Things: A survey on enabling technologies, protocols, and applications. *IEEE Communications Surveys & Tutorials*, 17(4), 2347–2376.

An, W., Wu, D., Ci, S., Luo, H., Adamchuk, V., & Xu, Z. (2017). Agriculture cyber-physical systems. In *Cyber-Physical Systems* (pp. 399–417). Academic Press.

Atzori, L., Iera, A., & Morabito, G. (2010). The Internet of Things: A survey. *Computer Networks*, 54(15), 2787–2805.

Ayala, I., Amor, M., & Fuentes, L. (2012). An agent platform for self-configuring agents in the Internet of Things. *Infrastructures and Tools for Multiagent Systems*, 65, 65–78.

Bandyopadhyay, D., & Sen, J. (2011). Internet of Things: Applications and challenges in technology and standardization. *Wireless Personal Communications*, 58(1), 49–69.

Bonomi, F., Milito, R., Zhu, J., & Addepalli, S. (2012). Fog computing and its role in the Internet of Things. In *Proceedings of the First Edition of the MCC Workshop on Mobile Cloud Computing* (pp. 13–16). ACM.

Cheng, B. H. C., de Lemos, R., Giese, H., Inverardi, P., Magee, J., & Andersson, J. (2019). Software engineering for self-adaptive systems: A research roadmap. In *Software Engineering for Self-Adaptive Systems III. Assurances* (pp. 1–32). Springer.

Cicirelli, F., Guerrieri, A., Mastroianni, C., & Vinci, A. (2021). Emerging Internet of Things solutions and technologies. *Electronics*, 10(16), 1928.

D'Angelo, M., Pagliari, L., Caporuscio, M., Mirandola, R., & Trubiani, C. (2020). Towards a continuous model-based engineering process for QoS-aware self-adaptive systems. In *Software Engineering and Formal Methods: SEFM 2019 Collocated Workshops: CoSim-CPS, ASYDE, CIFMA, and FOCLASA, Oslo, Norway, September 16–20, 2019, Revised Selected Papers 17* (pp. 69–76). Springer International Publishing.

Delicato, F. C., Al-Anbuky, A., Kevin, I., & Wang, K. (2020). Smart cyber–physical systems: Toward pervasive intelligence systems. *Future Generation Computer Systems*, 107, 1134–1139.

Diaz, S., Mendez, D., & Kraemer, R. (2019). A review on self-healing and self-organizing techniques for wireless sensor networks. *Journal of Circuits, Systems and Computers*, 28(05), 1930005.

Ding, D., Han, Q. L., Ge, X., & Wang, J. (2020). Secure state estimation and control of cyber-physical systems: A survey. *IEEE Transactions on Systems, Man, and Cybernetics: Systems*, 51(1), 176–190.

Gubbi, J., Buyya, R., Marusic, S., & Palaniswami, M. (2013). Internet of Things (IoT): A vision, architectural elements, and future directions. *Future Generation Computer Systems*, 29(7), 1645–1660.

Gunes, V., Peter, S., Givargis, T., & Vahid, F. (2014). A survey on concepts, applications, and challenges in cyber-physical systems. *KSII Transactions on Internet and Information Systems*, 8(12), 4242–4268.

Gurgen, L., Gunalp, O., Benazzouz, Y., & Gallissot, M. (2013, March). Self-aware cyber-physical systems and applications in smart buildings and cities. In *2013 Design, Automation & Test in Europe Conference & Exhibition (DATE)* (pp. 1149–1154). IEEE.

Jia, J., Chen, J., Chang, G., & Tan, Z. (2009). Energy efficient coverage control in wireless sensor networks based on multi-objective genetic algorithm. *Computers & Mathematics with Applications*, 57(11–12), 1756–1766.

Kephart, J. O., & Chess, D. M. (2003). The vision of autonomic computing. *Computer*, 36(1), 41–50.

Keshk, M., Turnbull, B., Sitnikova, E., Vatsalan, D., & Moustafa, N. (2021). Privacy-preserving schemes for safeguarding heterogeneous data sources in cyber-physical systems. *IEEE Access*, 9, 55077–55097.

Khan, R., Khan, S. U., Zaheer, R., & Khan, S. (2019). Future internet: The internet of things architecture, possible applications and key challenges. In *2019 International Conference on Frontiers of Information Technology (FIT)* (pp. 185–190). IEEE.

Krupitzer, C., Roth, F. M., Pfannemüller, M., & Becker, C. (2016, July). Comparison of approaches for self-improvement in self-adaptive systems. In *2016 IEEE International Conference on Autonomic Computing (ICAC)* (pp. 308–314). IEEE.

Krupitzer, C., Roth, F. M., VanSyckel, S., Schiele, G., & Becker, C. (2015). A survey on engineering approaches for self-adaptive systems. *Pervasive and Mobile Computing*, 17, 184–206.

Kumar, J., & Singh, A. K. (2018). Workload prediction in cloud using artificial neural network and adaptive differential evolution. *Future Generation Computer Systems*, 81, 41–52.

Li, J., Zhang, Y., & Chen, Y. (2016, August). A self-adaptive traffic light control system based on speed of vehicles. In *2016 IEEE International Conference on Software Quality, Reliability and Security Companion (QRS-C)* (pp. 382–388). IEEE.

Lissa, P., Deane, C., Schukat, M., Seri, F., Keane, M., & Barrett, E. (2021). Deep reinforcement learning for home energy management system control. *Energy and AI*, 3, 100043.

Macías-Escrivá, F. D., Haber, R., Del Toro, R., & Hernandez, V. (2013). Self-adaptive systems: A survey of current approaches, research challenges and applications. *Expert Systems with Applications*, 40(18), 7267–7279.

Mukherjee, M., Shu, L., & Wang, D. (2018). Survey of fog computing: Fundamental, network applications, and research challenges. *IEEE Communications Surveys & Tutorials*, 20(3), 1826–1857.

Ran, Y., Zhou, X., Lin, P., Wen, Y., & Deng, R. (2019). A survey of predictive maintenance: Systems, purposes and approaches. arXiv preprint arXiv:1912.07383.

Ratasich, D. I. D. (2019). *Self-Healing Cyber-Physical Systems* (Doctoral dissertation, Technische Universität Wien).

Rieger, T., Regier, S., Stengel, I., & Clarke, N. L. (2019). Fast predictive maintenance in industrial Internet of Things (IIoT) with Deep Learning (DL): A Review. *CERC*, 69–80.

Saharkhizan, M., Azmoodeh, A., Dehghantanha, A., Choo, K. K. R., & Parizi, R. M. (2020). An ensemble of deep recurrent neural networks for detecting IoT cyber attacks using network traffic. *IEEE Internet of Things Journal*, 7(9), 8852–8859.

Settanni, G., Skopik, F., Wurzenberger, M., & Fiedler, R. (2018). Countering targeted cyber-physical attacks using anomaly detection in self-adaptive Industry 4.0 Systems. *Elektrotech. Informationstechnik*, 135(3), 278–285.

Sha, L., Gopalakrishnan, S., Liu, X., & Wang, Q. (2008, June). Cyber-physical systems: A new frontier. In *2008 IEEE International Conference on Sensor Networks, Ubiquitous, and Trustworthy Computing (sutc 2008)* (pp. 1–9). IEEE.

Shi, J. (2021). *Creating Self-Adaptive and Scalable Wireless Networks for Industrial Internet of Things (Doctoral dissertation*, State University of New York at Binghamton).

Shi, J., Wan, J., Yan, H., & Suo, H. (2011, November). A survey of cyber-physical systems. In *2011 International Conference on Wireless Communications and Signal Processing (WCSP)* (pp. 1–6). IEEE.

Shojafar, M., Cordeschi, N., & Baccarelli, E. (2016). Energy-efficient adaptive resource management for real-time vehicular cloud services. *IEEE Transactions on Cloud computing*, 7(1), 196–209.

Sobral, J. V., Rabelo, R. A., Araujo, H. S., Baluz, R. A., & Holanda Filho, R. (2013, July). Automated design of fuzzy rule base using ant colony optimization for improving the performance in Wireless Sensor Networks. In *2013 IEEE International Conference on Fuzzy Systems (FUZZ-IEEE)* (pp. 1–8). IEEE.

Švaco, M., Šekoranja, B., & Jerbić, B. (2012). Industrial robotic system with adaptive control. *Procedia Computer Science*, 12, 164–169.

Verma, R. (2022). Smart city healthcare cyber physical system: characteristics, technologies and challenges. *Wireless Personal Communications*, 122(2), 1413–1433.

Vikas, B. O. (2015). Internet of things (IoT): A survey on privacy issues and security. *International Journal of Scientific Research in Science, Engineering and Technology*, 1(3), 168–173.

Wang, P., & Govindarasu, M. (2020). Multi-agent based attack-resilient system integrity protection for smart grid. *IEEE Transactions on Smart Grid*, 11(4), 3447–3456.

Wang, W., Yang, H., Zhang, Y., & Xu, J. (2018). IoT-enabled real-time energy efficiency optimisation method for energy-intensive manufacturing enterprises. *International Journal of Computer Integrated Manufacturing*, 31(4–5), 362–379.

Wang, Z., Song, H., Watkins, D. W., Ong, K. G., Xue, P., Yang, Q., & Shi, X. (2015). Cyber-physical systems for water sustainability: Challenges and opportunities. *IEEE Communications Magazine*, 53(5), 216–222.

Wu, X., Wang, J., Li, P., Luo, X., & Yang, Y. (2021). Internet of Things as complex networks. *IEEE Network*, 35(3), 238–245.

Xiong, G., Zhu, F., Liu, X., Dong, X., Huang, W., Chen, S., & Zhao, K. (2015). Cyber-physical-social system in intelligent transportation. *IEEE/CAA Journal of Automatica Sinica*, 2(3), 320–333.

Xue, H., Huang, B., Qin, M., Zhou, H., & Yang, H. (2020, November). Edge computing for Internet of Things: A survey. In *2020 International Conferences on Internet of Things (iThings) and IEEE Green Computing and Communications (GreenCom) and IEEE Cyber, Physical and Social Computing (CPSCom) and IEEE Smart Data (SmartData) and IEEE Congress on Cybermatics (Cybermatics)* (pp. 755–760). IEEE.

Yang, H., Zhong, W. D., Chen, C., Alphones, A., & Xie, X. (2020). Deep-reinforcement-learning-based energy-efficient resource management for social and cognitive Internet of Things. *IEEE Internet of Things Journal*, 7(6), 5677–5689.

Yang, L., Li, M., Si, P., Yang, R., Sun, E., & Zhang, Y. (2020). Energy-efficient resource allocation for blockchain-enabled industrial Internet of Things with deep reinforcement learning. *IEEE Internet of Things Journal*, 8(4), 2318–2329.

Yu, D., Chen, Z. M., Xiahou, K. S., Li, M. S., Ji, T. Y., & Wu, Q. H. (2018). A radically data-driven method for fault detection and diagnosis in wind turbines. *International Journal of Electrical Power & Energy Systems*, 99, 577–584.

Zarpelão, B. B., Miani, R. S., Kawakani, C. T., & de Alvarenga, S. C. (2017). A survey of intrusion detection in Internet of Things. *Journal of Network and Computer Applications,* 84, 25–37.

Zhang, M., Li, J., Zhao, H., Tei, K., Honiden, S., & Jin, Z. (2021, September). A meta reinforcement learning-based approach for self-adaptive system. In *2021 IEEE International Conference on Autonomic Computing and Self-Organizing Systems (ACSOS)* (pp. 1–10). IEEE.

Zhu, X., Badr, Y., Pacheco, J., & Hariri, S. (2017, September). Autonomic identity framework for the Internet of Things. In *2017 International Conference on Cloud and Autonomic Computing (ICCAC)* (pp. 69–79). IEEE.

Chapter 11

The Internet of Things (IoT): Security and Privacy Issues in IoT and Its Solutions

Namita Tiwari,[1] Ashutosh Tripathi,[2] Amit Virmani,[3] and Praveen Kumar Agarwal[4]

[1]Department of Mathematics, School of Basic Sciences,
CSJM University, Kanpur, India

[2]T. Systems, Pune, India

[3]Department of Computer Application, UIET, CSJM University, Kanpur, India

[4]School of Business Management, CSJM University, Kanpur, India

11.1 Introduction

Can you imagine it being possible to connect every physical device to the Internet and they start communicating, sending data, and instructing each other? Yes, that is the power of Internet of Things (IoT), which envisions a world with billions of interconnected objects over the Internet. And on top of that, these objects are well equipped with the capabilities of Artificial Intelligence, which can do work like normal human beings. Think of an IoT plus AI-enabled human-like robot sitting at reception and solving human queries.

The Internet of Things is connecting more devices every day, and we're headed for a world that will have 64 billion IoT devices by 2025. With all these tremendous

DOI: 10.1201/9781003474838-11

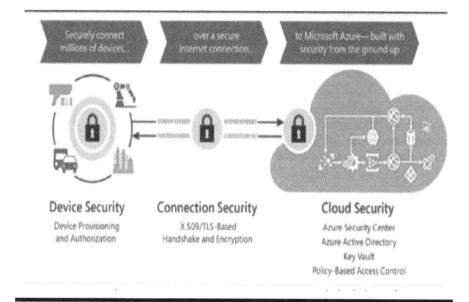

Figure 11.1   Azure IoT Security Architecture.
Source: Saira Afzal (2021).

capabilities, don't you think there would be some security and privacy issues? The moment we connect any device with the Internet, it becomes searchable to the outside world and opens the door for cyber threats. Let's have a look at various levels of security issues in IoT enabled devices (see Figure 11.1).

I would say, IoT is solving amazing problems, however it is still evolving and is not yet completely secure. So, in this chapter we discuss in detail the important issues with respect to security and privacy and then look into the possible solutions to mitigate those threats. Let's develop high-level understanding of those issues and the corresponding solutions.

11.2 Security in IoT

Every technology brings various security threats with it, and if not handled or mitigated on time, they become huge, and technology becomes the curse. You must have heard the popular phrase "Technology, a curse or boon to human society". So, it all depends how we use it. Below you can find some real time examples of IoT security issues:

11.2.1 Nest-Camera Hacker

In a recent event in 2018, a mother living in Texas informed that some third party hacked her whole system of cameras, which this party used to threaten the parents, saying they intended to kidnap their baby.

Ellen Rigney and her husband were awoken by a noise from the Nest-camera that was connected to their baby son's room. The Rigney's jumped out of bed and were startled when another nest-camera in their room switched on, and a voice ordered them to turn off the light. Then the voice threatened that he was going to kidnap their baby and said that he was in their baby's room. They rushed to their son's room, but no one else was there and the baby was sleeping as they had left him. So actually, no kidnapper was there but someone was hacking the camera system. The Rigneys informed the police.

An inquiry from the Nest side involved only random statements, investigations, and a final statement that gave the couple no comfort or recourse Nest camera hacker (nbcnews.com).

11.2.2 A Flaw in Several Chrysler Models

A Chrysler computer flaw can easily give access to hackers to play with the internal systems of the car. For example. they can control the braking system, or even turn off the engine, or control the steering. The core problem? There is a vulnerability in the wireless service, "Uconnect," that links these cars to the Sprint cellphone network, Chryslers-hack,(2015).

Researchers have concluded that the vulnerable Chrysler models are those from late 2013, all of 2014 and early 2015 that are loaded with Uconnect and the full navigation displays.

Clearly, it is important to have security updates in IoT-enabled devices, as we have in smartphones or tablets.

Now, let's examine the different security threats associated with IoT devices and applications.

Data encryption: Most of the IoT devices contain personal data. This data needs to be securely encrypted before being sent over communication channels. In general, IoT devices are equipped with different types of sensors which collect data from surrounding environments and then send it over the Internet to cloud storage for different purposes. One purpose could be simply storing it temporarily or to process this data over the cloud on a high computing environment and then send back to the original device. So in this complete two-way communication when data is over the Internet, all the security threats can come into the picture. For example, you have installed an image processing camera at your smart home main door. Now this door should automatically open when it recognises the family members, or else it does not open and someone has to manually give permission to open the door. So if

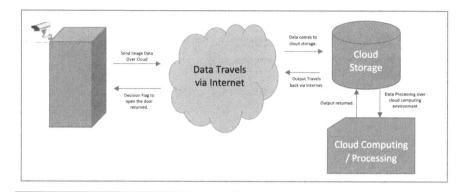

Figure 11.2 **High Level bi-directional Architecture of CCTV Camera Image Processing Application.**

Source: Created by the Ashutosh Tripathi.

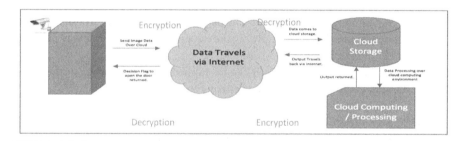

Figure 11.3 **Encryption-Decryption in Cloud Data Travel.**

you try to understand complete flow of this image-processing IoT application (see Figure 11.2).

Data travelling over the Internet has security threats. So, this is the place where an encryption mechanism should be in place (see Figure 11.3).

Data Authentication: Authentication is something that validates the source of the data. Assume there is no proper authentication mechanism in place, so even if data is encrypted, it can be accessed using unverified sources and can be misused.

The authentication mechanism is established over IoT application to make sure that connected devices can be trusted to be what they are claiming to be. Therefore, every connected IoT device should have a unique identity that can be validated when the device wants to connect to other devices via a connected gateway or other communication channel. With this unique identifier in place, any of the devices in the IoT mesh can be tracked throughout its lifecycle and communicate securely

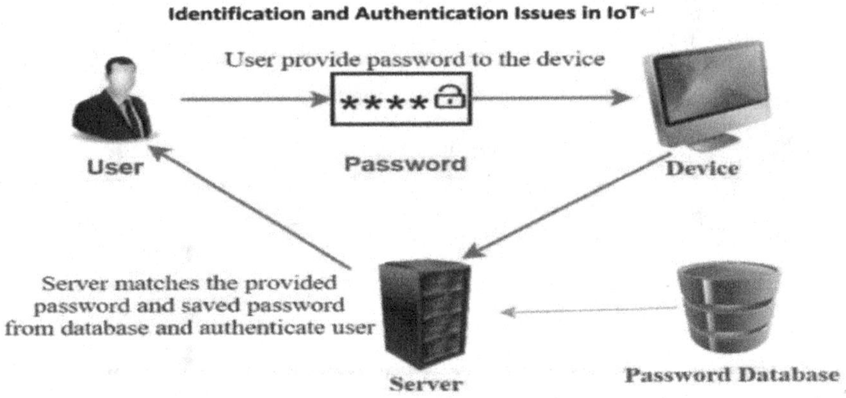

Figure 11.4 Identification and Authentication Issues in IoT.

Source: Created by the Ashutosh Tripathi.

and, hence, unauthenticated intruders can be prevented. If administrators see any unexpected behaviour, they can simply revoke the privileges and in this way possible threats can be mitigated.

There are different methods which can be applied to achieve strong authentication to secure IoT applications and devices connected over the Internet.

1. **One-way authentication:** Here two parties communicate with each other. If only one party authenticates itself to the other, while the other party does not.
2. **Two-way authentication:** If both parties authenticate each other.
3. **Three-way authentication:** If there is a central authority who authenticates the two parties and helps them to authenticate each other.
4. **Distributed:** A distributed straight authentication method works between the parties to the communication.
5. **Centralized:** There is a centralized server who distributes and manages the certificates for authentication. The Top IoT Authentication(2020),and IoT Device Authentication,(2023) (see Figure 11.4).

Below is the high-level diagram explaining the authentication process on a simple card reader (see Figure 11.5).

Device Update Management: Devices that connected over the Internet are prone to the threats and, hence, timely updates to the software and firmware is required. And even the manufacturer offers the most recent updates, devices might encounter new vulnerabilities.

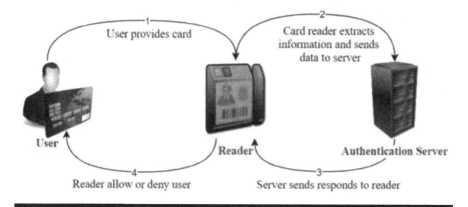

Figure 11.5   Authentication process on a simple card reader.

Source: Identification (2021) and Update management (2023).

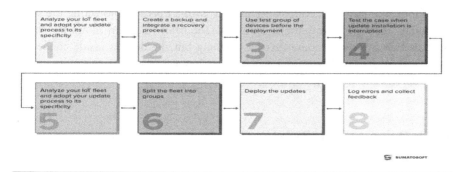

Figure 11.6   IoT update management process.

Source: Update management (2023).

IoT Update Management is the process of managing the IoT fleet by deploying updates to smart devices in order to keep their firmware updated, fix bugs, add new software features, and increase the security level of the entire system.

The typical IoT update process consists of two parts:

1. Download of new updated package
2. Installation of new package on device.

Please refer to Figure 11.6.

Hijacking and Ransomware: Normally Ransomware is a kind of virus that encrypts user's data and prevents its unauthorized access. However, if you have poor security in IoT devices then ransomware can also attack IoT devices. The main problem starts when hackers compromises the device with ransomware and demands ransom money to protect the victim's devices.

Recently at a hacking conference "Defcon" in Las Vegas, two researchers demonstrated that they could inflict anyone's smart thermostat with ransomware from hundreds of miles away and force the victims to pay cash/bitcoins to regain control of the application. Ransomware is a breed of malware that encrypts user's files on the system so that these files cannot be accessed. Finally, they sell a decryption key to decrypt the files to get access back. Ransomware in IoT is relatively new. In the year 2015, experts presented research on ransomware for wearables at the "BlackHat" conference. Subsequently, some experts also raised the issue in healthcare IoT at the institute for critical technology. Unfortunately, ransomware is not yet given much attention IoT ransomware (2023).

Home Intrusion: When we talk about IoT, then the first major use case comes to the mind is Smart Home. This home automation brings the possibility for intruders to find the IP address of the owner, using Shodan searches, and start misusing it. There are various solutions for examples connecting with VPNs and protecting the user's credentials are the two important solutions. The below diagram shows the threat associated with a smart home that has nothing but the devices inside connected using IoT. In that case there are great possibilities for intruders to get access to the inside devices and then use them for various purposes (see Figure 11.7).

11.3 Privacy in IoT

Privacy challenges in Internet of Things devices arise from the collection, storage, and processing of personal data by interconnected devices. These challenges can be attributed to several factors:

1. **Data Collection and Consent:** IoT devices continuously gather vast amounts of data about users and their environments, including personal and sensitive information. Users often lack awareness of the types of data being collected, how it's being used, and who has access to it. Obtaining informed consent becomes crucial, but it can be challenging to provide clear and understandable information to users given the limited interface of many IoT devices.

2. **Data Security:** IoT devices may have vulnerabilities that can be exploited by attackers to gain unauthorized access to personal data. Weak authentication mechanisms, inadequate encryption protocols, and insecure network connections can lead to data breaches. Once a breach occurs, the

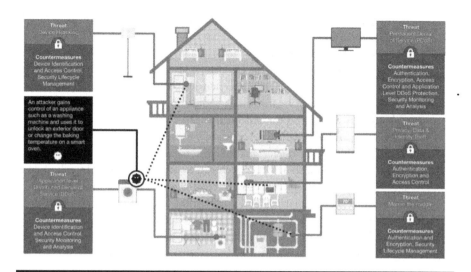

Figure 11.7   Threat associated with a smart home.

Source: IoT ransomware (2023).

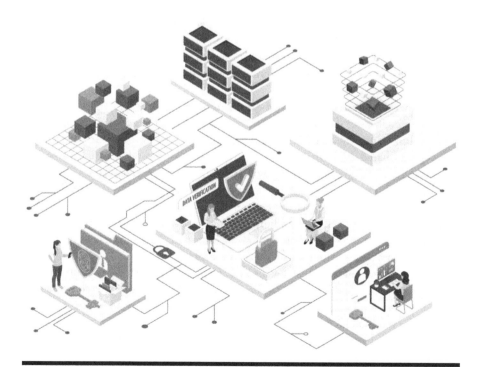

Figure 11.8   IoT Connected Devices. Image by macrovector on Freepik.

compromised data can be misused for identity theft, surveillance, or other malicious activities.

3. **Data Storage and Retention:** IoT devices generate and store vast amounts of data, including historical records. Long-term data retention raises concerns as the data could be used to build comprehensive profiles of individuals or enable unauthorized tracking. Organizations should implement data-retention policies that balance the need for historical analysis with privacy requirements.

4. **Data Sharing and Third-Party Access:** IoT ecosystems often involve multiple stakeholders, including device manufacturers, service providers, and third-party developers. Data sharing between these entities increases the risk of data leakage or misuse. It's essential to establish clear guidelines and agreements regarding data access, sharing, and anonymization, and to ensure that third-party developers adhere to robust privacy practices.

5. **User Tracking and Profiling:** IoT devices can collect data from various sources and create detailed profiles of user behaviour, preferences, and habits. The aggregation of data from multiple devices raises concerns about the potential for intrusive monitoring and targeted advertising. Users should have control over the collection and use of their data, including the ability to opt-out of profiling or to limit data sharing.

6. **Lack of Standardized Privacy Frameworks:** The IoT landscape consists of a diverse array of devices, protocols, and platforms, making it challenging to develop standardized privacy frameworks. Varying levels of privacy protection across different devices and manufacturers can create inconsistencies and confusion for users. Developing industry-wide standards and best practices can help address these challenges.

7. **Inadequate Transparency and Accountability:** IoT devices often lack transparency in their data collection and processing practices. Users may not have visibility into the data being collected, how it's being used, or whether it's being shared with third parties. Organizations should adopt transparent practices, provide clear privacy policies, and establish mechanisms for individuals to access, modify, or delete their personal data.

8. **Data Abundance:** As per the Federal Trade Commission, 10,000 households create approximately 150 million discrete data every day. So, clearly, the possibilities for breaches of privacy in IoT are increased. Thus, hackers have another point of hacking while leaving sensitive information.

9. **IoT Connected Devices:** Let us say an intruder got access to your mobile microphone. And now he can easily listen to each and every conversation of yours. He has every bit information about your daily activities, and you can't even imagine what he can do with this information. He can easily sell it to criminals or even can completely modify the content you consume from mobile devices.

So having a strong privacy system in place is must, and the foremost requirement while implementing IoT in our day-to-day lives.

10. **Eavesdropping:** Consider that a hacker uses someone's smart home appliance to inquire into his/her personal life. To do so, hackers could use a connected device.

    For example, suppose a smart meter device has unencrypted data; researchers are getting success in eavesdropping in IOT by intercepting. This unencrypted data helps hackers to identify that the individual is watching a television show and hacker is free to whatever extent he wishes to use this information.

    The original/uncoded data helps to identify the television show an individual is watching at any particular time. And then it depends on the hackers as to how or to what extent he wants to use this hijacked information.

11. **Unwanted Public Exposure:** As per the Federal Trade Commission, manufacturers could purchase data from consumers to make decisions on employment. The reason is the IoT manufacturers have lengthy documents that can be read completely by anyone. Hence this is also a major privacy issue within the IoT world.

    For instance, an insurance company can find/collect some information from someone regarding his/her habits of driving using a car connected to the Internet. Similarly, life/health insurance agents can also steal data to calculate the rates of insurance. To do so, they use fitness tracker devices connected to the Internet.

11.3.1 Bottom Line

IoT tells us how to recognize devices. Almost, every device could be connected to the Internet. No one can ignore the issues of security and privacy in information technology. Everyone must understand these issues related to IoT for its growth in long term.

Addressing these privacy challenges requires a multi-faceted approach that involves robust security measures, informed consent mechanisms, clear privacy policies, user empowerment, and industry collaboration to establish standards and best practices.

11.4 IoT Security Solutions

11.4.1 Understanding the Architecture

The architecture design for IoT devices security solutions can vary depending on the specific use case and the type of IoT devices involved. However, there are several common components and layers that are typically included in an IoT security solution architecture design. Here is an overview of the typical components and layers of an IoT security solution architecture design (Figure 11.9):

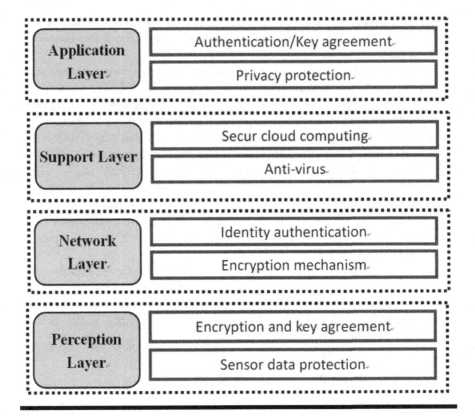

Figure 11.9 Components and layers of an IoT security solution architecture design.

Source: springernature.com

1. **Device Layer:** This layer includes the physical IoT devices that are connected to the network. These devices can include sensors, actuators, controllers, and other types of devices. The security measures implemented in this layer may include device authentication, encryption, and access control.

2. **Communication Layer:** This layer is responsible for managing the communication between the IoT devices and the network. This can include wired or wireless communication protocols such as Wi-Fi, Bluetooth, ZigBee, or cellular networks. The security measures implemented in this layer may include secure communication protocols, encryption, and firewalls.

3. **Gateway Layer:** The gateway layer serves as an intermediary between the device layer and the network layer. It may include IoT gateways, which are devices that aggregate data from multiple IoT devices and provide a single point of entry for data to enter the network. The security measures implemented in

this layer may include device authentication, encryption, access control, and intrusion detection systems.

4. **Network Layer:** The network layer is responsible for managing the flow of data between devices and the cloud. This layer may include local area networks (LANs), wide area networks (WANs), and the Internet. The security measures implemented in this layer may include firewalls, intrusion detection systems, and secure communication protocols.

5. **Cloud Layer:** The cloud layer is where data from IoT devices is stored and analyzed. This layer includes cloud computing platforms, such as Amazon Web Services (AWS), Microsoft Azure, or Google Cloud Platform. The security measures implemented in this layer may include authentication, encryption, access control, and intrusion detection systems.

6. **User Layer:** The user layer is where users interact with the IoT devices and the data generated by them. This can include web or mobile applications that allow users to monitor and control IoT devices or to access data generated by those devices. The security measures implemented in this layer may include user authentication, encryption, and access control (see Figure 11.10).

Overall, the architecture design for IoT security solutions requires a multi-layered approach that addresses the unique security challenges of IoT devices and networks. By implementing security measures at each layer of the architecture, IoT devices can be protected from a wide range of security threats.

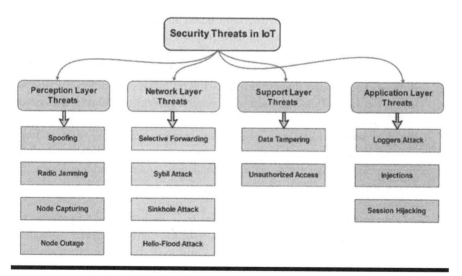

Figure 11.10 Security threats in IoT.

Source: Security, Cybercrime (2020).

11.4.2 Methods Used to Provide Security to IoT Devices

There are several methods used to provide security in IoT devices, including authentication, encryption, access control, and device management. Following is a detailed explanation of each method along with relevant diagrams.

1. **Authentication:** Authentication is the process of verifying the identity of an IoT device or user before allowing access to the network or resources. This can be done through various methods, including passwords, biometric identification, and digital certificates.
2. **Encryption:** Encryption is the process of encoding data in such a way that only authorized parties can read it. In IoT devices, encryption is used to protect data as it moves between devices and over networks. This is especially important in healthcare and financial applications.
3. **Access control:** Access control is the process of limiting access to resources based on the user's identity, role, or permissions. In IoT devices, access control is used to ensure that only authorized users can access the device or its data.
4. **Device management:** Device management involves the processes and systems used to manage IoT devices throughout their lifecycle. This includes configuring devices, monitoring their performance, and updating firmware and software to address security vulnerabilities.
5. **Firewalls:** Firewalls are network security devices that monitor and control incoming and outgoing network traffic based on predetermined security rules. In IoT devices, firewalls can be used to prevent unauthorized access to the device or the network.
6. **Intrusion detection systems:** Intrusion detection systems (IDS) are security appliances or software that monitor network traffic for signs of security threats. In IoT devices, IDS can be used to detect and prevent unauthorized access or malicious activity.
7. **Physical security:** Physical security involves protecting IoT devices from physical threats, such as theft, tampering, or destruction. This can include locking cabinets or rooms, using surveillance cameras, and implementing access control systems.

IoT security is a complex topic that requires a multi-layered approach. By implementing authentication, encryption, access control, device management, firewalls, intrusion detection systems, and physical security measures, IoT devices and networks can be protected from a wide range of security threats (see Figure 11.11).

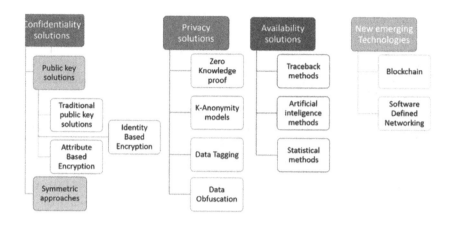

Figure 11.11   Ways of protecting IoT devices and networks from threats.

Source: springernature.com

11.5 Conclusion

In summary, IoT devices' security concerns are complex, and solutions require a multi-layered approach. Manufacturers must implement robust security features and release regular updates, while users should be educated on best practices for securing their devices. Governments and regulatory bodies should also establish standards and guidelines to ensure that IoT devices' security measures are sufficient. By working together, we can minimize the risks associated with IoT devices and make the most of their potential.

Overall, ensuring IoT security requires a concerted effort from all stakeholders, including device manufacturers, service providers, and end-users. By implementing robust security measures and raising awareness, the risks associated with IoT can be minimized, and the benefits of the technology can be fully realized.

References

Nest camera hacker (nbcnews.com), www.nbcnews.com/news/us-news/nest-camera-hacker-threatens-kidnap-baby-spooks-parents-n949251

Chryslers-hack,(2015),https://money.cnn.com/2015/07/21/technology/chrysler-hack/index.html

The Top IoT Authentication (2020), www.keyfactor.com/blog/the-top-iot-authentication-methods-and-options/

IoT Device Authentication,(2023),www.nabto.com/iot-device-authentication-comparison-guide/

Identification (2021), https://securityboulevard.com/2021/12/identification-and-authent ication-issues-in-iot/

Update management (2023), https://sumatosoft.com/blog/internet-of-things-iot-update-management-complete-guide

IoT ransomware (2023), www.iotsecurityfoundation.org/the-iot-ransomware-threat-is-more-serious-than-you-think/

Threats and Countermeasures www.rambus.com/iot/smart-home/

Saira Afzal, Abdullah Faisal, Imran Siddique, Miriam Afzal (2021), Internet of Things (IoT) Security: Issues, Challenges and Solutions, *International Journal of Scientific & Engineering Research*, 12(6), pp 52–61, 2021.

springernature.com, https://media.springernature.com/lw685/springerstatic/image/chp%3A 10.1007%2F978-981-16-1372-2_3/MediaObjects/491641_1_En_3_Fig1_HTML.png

Security, Cybercrime (2020), www.researchgate.net/figure/Security-threats-at-different-lay ers-of-the-IoT-architecture_fig2_337259162

Chapter 12

The Dark Side of Internet of Things in E-Commerce: Uncovering the Misuse of Personal Information

Hannah Divyanka Doss and Achyutananda Mishra
Christ University, Bangalore, India

12.1 IoT, Big Data and Data Mining – Meaning and Application

The Internet of Things (IoT) is known to be a complex network of connected equipment that can exchange information and communicate to achieve smart recognition, positioning, tracing, monitoring and administration (Patel et al., 2016). In layman's terms, IoT is a system of computing or Internet-enabled devices that connect and transfer data to one another. Data can be personal or general. The issue of contention is that protecting one's personal data is a right of an individual. Personal data is defined as any such data that can take away the anonymity of a person in a public sphere. Such data is qualified as information that is directed to an identified or identifiable natural person (General Data Protection Regulation, 2018, Art. 4(1)).

It is self–explanatory and understandable as to why personal information must be protected. It is the property of the individual and must be protected, recognised and enforced by law and its authorities, private or public – apart from this being

DOI: 10.1201/9781003474838-12

a recognised human right under Article 12 of the 1948 Universal Declaration of Human Rights. Theorists have also asserted that every individual has a right to dictate and control their information and the extent to which another person knows about him or her (Ghani and Sidek, 2009).

Data is constantly transferred via the Internet, which makes every user a large contributor to the virtual space data collection. One cannot imagine, if one has multiple devices, the extent of data one is handing over to an unregulated space, be it a Cloud platform or the website itself. The large collection of data, known as big data, acts like an ocean that has to be streamlined by e-commerce websites to find their potential customers. E-commerce utilises this data, transferred to understand the needs of a customer and to respond to it to add to their financial benefit. Data here is used as input to understand, analyse, and profile a consumer thereby to translate their interests and preferences into wants. This helps businesses achieve organisational goals but also means that user data can be employed for unethical, illegal, unlawful and, most importantly, unauthorised reasons.

12.2 Big Data

In today's world, data is regarded to be the life of a business. One cannot identify data as non-productive, non-existent and dead. It is given utmost importance because of its ability to make a business succeed or fail. Data is intentionally or unintentionally submitted by people through routines of various transactions like online purchases and browsing histories, and by undergoing tasks. Big data is a concept that signifies the enormity of data captured by computer systems (Fuller, 2019). It is an outcome of the data available for the purpose of data analysis of consumers.

Data can be any information that, prima facie, does not seem important or imperative. It can include Internet clocks, transactions on Internet-enabled devices, social media interactions, content generated by the user and also information about such as healthcare, finance, and genomics (George et al., 2014). Big data has been of exceeding value to organisations as it is explored, analysed and valued in terms of the needs of individuals and businesses, and private and public institutions.

Apart from making decisions on gauging the needs of consumers, big data has benefited companies in emphasizing consumer intelligence, increased efficiency within a business enterprise, boosting brand loyalty and most importantly, reduces the investment in traditional (extensive) market research techniques (Kumari, 2021).

Big data plays an important role in online marketplace such as Amazon. This online platform is known to be a 'mammoth' that is specialised with connecting customer data to business or organisation objectives. The platform collects information by browsers and clicks to add on to the recommendation engine so far as the activity of customers on their application or website is recorded to keep track of products that one views, reads (Dwivedi, et al., 2021).

The Apple Company infuses its products with the ability to function and respond with the big data it has procured from customers. Such devices are SMART, which means specific, measurable, attainable, relevant, and time-based. In real time, the device collects the information and data of the user, enough for it to be analysed and to respond to the instructions of the user (Bi et al., 2019).

Every piece of data fits somewhere on the puzzle – the puzzle being a human profile. Big data serves this purpose with its large magnitude. It can be structured and unstructured data. Structured data is identifiable, organised, and carries meaning and consists of the same attributes. Such data is easily understandable and can be generated by a machine without human intervention. On the other hand, unstructured data has no similarity and does not carry a single meaning, format or rule (Sagiroglu and Sinanc, 2013).

Big data is useful and an important part in understanding e-commerce and its functioning. As stated, it serves as a fuel in the route that e-commerce websites take in fulfilling their institutional or organizational goal.

12.3 Data Mining

Mining is typically understood as the process to obtain something underground. When one thinks of the concept of mining, it is related to the digging for value. Likewise, data mining is the digging (analysing) of data to get information that makes sense and can communicate a certain meaning. Data on e-commerce websites helps in understanding various possible attributes of the buyer – their interests, age group, and use of related products.

Data mining is initiated when specific input is given to an Internet-enabled computer system. Such input is analysed to compute a large number of derivatives putting the user/consumer in a specific bracket or box. Such data creates patterns where data is simply understood as input and the knowledge derived from it are the outputs. This output is what is needed for businesses to financially benefit or profit them (Diwandari et al.,2018) .

Market Basket Analysis (MBA) is used by every customer product industry that gauges and satisfies the needs of a consumer and in parallel, the profit needs of their own. MBA is a concept and instrument adopted by retailers to analyse the behaviour of customers within a store, online or offline. Such behaviour helps understand purchase patterns, which items are bought as combinations and those products that are fast selling and in high demand. This understanding enables retailer's profit and income factors (Gurudath, 2020).

The concept of MBA is based entirely on the traditional book record system at supermarkets just before the exit. Such information is looked into to find out what has been bought, in what quantity, and what can be paired with it. This information is analysed and understood by sales teams to keep tabs on the stock and also

Figure 12.1 Shopping Basket od A, B & C.

Source: Figure created by author.

to estimate pricing. Such information, though prima facie not personal information, is in fact just that, when one takes a closer look – it can determine a person's age group, their likes and preferences and moreover their next likely product pick (Kurniawan, 2018).

Instacart is a US-based e-commerce application that uses MBA. It deals with grocery supplies and delivery. The application has features common to other websites, like "suggestions for you," and "other people purchase this as a combination". The application highlights what a person has bought, what they can buy in the future on the basis of what they have purchased earlier, and understands the profession, character of a person on the basis of their purchases and products in advance of their requirement (Gurudath, 2020).

To understand the extent of information one can get from basic data is beyond alarming. Data sometimes seems so simple, unrelated and sometimes unimportant. However, if one actually looks at data, it can express a lot more about a consumer, a user and, if in unregulated spaces, can also cause some extent of harm.

Breaking down Figure 12.1 (above), three customers, A, B, and C, at a grocery store have displayed the contents of the shopping basket. From the market research point of view, it is very clear that milk, diapers, and bread are much in demand and a necessity for their household. The supplier can understand that supply of this must be constant and, even if the price is increased, the demand will still be present. A researcher can also understand that a famous combination with milk and bread is jam, eggs and butter, so offers and packages can be made using such products. One can also assume that their customers, A, B and C are in the baking profession.

This is a good and positive way of looking at the information so begotten. However, this information also suggests various other things that can be misused. For example, any unregulated use of this data or data in the wrong hands can also show that in the households of A, B, and C, there are infants, toddlers or newborns because all three baskets consists of diapers.

Therefore, personal information can be any such information that can remove the veil of rightful anonymity of an individual in a public space. Such information must be protected by law but it is also the same information that is foundational to big data and data mining.

12.4 Digital Marketing as a Tool in IoT

Customers are regarded to be the 'Kings of the Market' – a popular belief that is not far from the truth. It is said so for the simple reason that customers have the power to either make or break a business and also an entire market. Marketing and advertising are often used as synonyms, whereas marketing is the aim of allowing people to know about a specific product and advertising is the method through which such aim is established. Nevertheless, both are methods to captivate the desires of the customer and transform them for the benefit of the businesses by allowing them to achieve institutional goals.

Advertising is understood to be the 'official art' of advanced industrial nations (Dyer, 2008). Advertising throws light on a product, good or services, its uses, features and utility. The unsaid aim of advertising is to lure prospective consumers into buyers. This is the instrument on which the market thrives.

Business houses experience consistency only because of the positive actions of consumers. In order for businesses to meet the demands of consumers, they must be alert and responsive to their needs and requirements even before it is recognised in the market. Such psychic ability of businesses is achieved through market research. It is a strategy that allows businesses, in advance, to prepare the needs of the market and execute supply when such needs come into play.

The most accepted definition of market research is the collection and analysing of information about potential purchases of consumers and their feedback on things already purchased (Cambridge Dictionary, 1999). Market research allows an organisation to understand the requirements of the market, consumers along with competitors. Such research enables the organisation in achieving goals and performances (Sarstedt et al., 2019).

Lego, a worldwide toy brand, expressed that it was market research that brought the company out of bankruptcy. Their method of market research was through observations and interviews and directed them to 'innovate' and increase their product portfolio by integrating creative playing and learning (Cong et al., 2021).

Due to the advances in technology and the era of customisation we live in, market research has taken a new meaning and procedure. With the synchronisation of online tools, Internet of Things, digital marketing has become a sought-after concept.

Age-old techniques of market research methods have changed drastically due to the change in consumer communication from telephone communication to then emailing techniques. Social media has created a new space to reach, understand and provide market research in order to achieve goals (Patino et al., 2012).

The world was fast moving and markets had to move digitally, where methods of advertising had to be online. Digital marketing is that response to the needs of the virtual market, an additional channel of advertising that was positively welcomed. Digital marketing does not only involve selling online but it also includes understanding the needs of a consumer, meeting their demands by creating it from scratch, taking away those products that have not helped the market, understanding views, feedback and understanding of a product and most importantly post-sale service (Dwivedi et al., 2021).

Digital marketing can be in the form of e-mail marketing, pay-per-click, SEM, SEO link building (content and keywords), social media marketing (hashtags on platforms) and also online presence. Search Engine Marketing (SEM) is a method of promotion and advertising whereby companies rank above the rest in that product domain. Search Engine Optimization (SEO) is setting up the web in such a way that it responds to keywords. (Burghate, 2018).

Digital advertising has been defined to be activities that are aimed in presenting individuals a non-personal or general, oral or visual, open message with information in regard to a product, service, idea by an identified sponsor. Advertising has the ability to influence human life, intentionally or unintentionally. It may be in the form of newspapers, billboards, handbills, phone calls and since a decade ago, the Internet.

To understand the concept of digital advertising, one can identify it by drawing a distinction or seeing the development with respect to traditional advertising. In the latter, shops did not know what a customer was looking at. The model consisted of advertisements being contextual, where they were out in places where people were expected to be. For example, advertisements were put on billboards along busy roads, popular magazines and catalogues and also during intervals in football or cricket matches where the fan base was enormous. It was a method where targets were made on the basis of expecting large groups of individuals to be the receivers of such information in a specific place (Bhatnagar et al., 2013).

Every advertisement seen on one's platform is thoughtfully constructed and put forward specifically for that viewer. The question is how do businesses know what the customer needs at what time. The answer is that the pieces of a puzzle have been left behind by the user through their clicks, views, downloads and searches on the Internet. Analysing such data, marketers ensure posting such advertisements customised to the need of the user.

For every business to function, decision-making is very important. Marketing has always been keen on making the right decisions to succeed. In digital marketing, the power of making decisions though is powered by data, fueled by the Internet of

Things and Artificial Intelligence. Data analytics, working, studying and acting on data, has given patterns of insights and allowed markets to not only respond to the needs of the consumers but also create one that they never knew they had.

Marketing strategies today ensure the concept of 'Segmentation, Targeting and Positioning' where customers are segmented into their likes, preferences, behavior and patterns. Consumers are put in boxes and frameworks so that they can be targeted in the same way to convert their interest into a sale, which reap benefits to the businesses. This is to enable a customer-centric approach of marketing (Andaleeb, 2016).

The integration of IoT and digital advertising has benefited consumers and producers (companies), the latter more than the former. Companies are able to navigate through and understand the product design that will sell to the market and be appreciated by consumers. Product design includes understanding the needs of the market and what exactly customers expect from certain goods and services with respect to their utility and likeness (Fattahi, 2022). IoT helps achieve operational goals and each device has sensors that collect and exchange data by virtue of the environment it is in thereby creating a customer database. The devices can range from highly sophisticated machines, smartphones, tablets, televisions and even wearable devices.

Patterns and behaviours of an individual are subjective and are variable. However, when it comes to buying patterns, there is a string of similarity that one can notice in individuals in either the same geographical location or age group or financial status category. Since the human is a social animal, they can be influenced easily by their surroundings. For example, bridal emerald jewelry was 'on-demand' when popular Bollywood actresses decided to choose it as part of their wedding attire. This was understood through various clicks on the websites including the product, its price, the manufacturer or designer and other comparable information. Understanding the current mindset and taste, businesses can respond before the excitement dies down.

IoT has facilitated a progressive relationship between consumers and retail businesses, allowing the latter to provide the former with an experience through personalisation. Data fed to an application is sufficient for the application to predict what, how and in which manner to be portrayed to the customer to convert it into a sale. Data on the Internet is like trails of information that lead to a single individual. Such data, when analysed, will be able to remove the anonymity on which individuals expect to work in a public space.

12.5 Obtaining the Right to Personal Data: Theory versus Reality

Data in itself cannot be accredited to computer systems. Data is information that is wholly the property of individuals. One is entitled to understand the plethora of rights they have with respect to data, one of the biggest rights being that of privacy and absolute proportion from the state. Data does not have to be structured or make sense. Any piece of information makes sense when seen through a whole different perspective and has the ability to identify a person. For example, IMEI number on a mobile phone box does not prima facie seem to be important but, when researched, it carries the registered owner of the mobile, their address and payment details.

Many developed countries have understood the importance and priority that must be given to the right of privacy and security needed for data, especially when it is personal data. General data is any such information that by nature is open to the public and cannot be owned by anyone. This data is beyond the purview of protection. Law protects personal data by way of regulations, legislations, orders and by-laws.

The General Data Protection Regulation, 2018 is a legislative initiative of the European Union (EU) in recognition of the need to protect personal data. This regulation has defined the aspects of personal data, sensitive personal data that can be broadened by virtue of the situation. Prior to 2018, through the Charter of Fundamental Rights of the European Union, 2009 and the European Convention on Human Rights, 1953, the EU has continually emphasised and reasserted the rights of individuals with respect to their private life, which envelopes even communications.

Likewise, the United States has the Federal Trade Commission vested with the power to protect data of its citizens. Due to the governmental structure of the country, each state government has devolved the responsibility upon various sectors to protect the privacy of their customers. For example, the California Consumer Privacy Act, 2018, emphasises the protection and control of personal data of consumers when given to businesses for appropriate usage.

However, such protection of privacy is expressly absent in the Indian subcontinent. Though the country well understands the nuances with, and importance of, the right to privacy, India has much to do to provide adequate Internet data protection for her citizens.

E-commerce websites and browsers have been appropriating information and data of its users for their own purposes and profiling customers, inducing them to make unplanned purchases. Online advertising deals with a specific or target audience, showing customers exactly what they want. The question is how can a computer enabled by the Internet find the correct product to show a customer that they have never seen or interacted with before. The answer is a 'Web Cookie'. It is understood to be in the form of "little crumbs" that are placed on one's phone and like devices that follow, track and save web searches, habits, and every click on the Internet. Advertisers are able to understand what one does on their website, whether it is a simple glance or a thorough reading. Cookies are said to be holders of data specific to a computer system or website (Imam and Biswas, 2019).

The concept of cookies and its legality has long been debatable. It was developed in 1994 by Netscape and was viewed through the lens of 'self-regulation' by the

United States. In the European Union, the concept did not survive well because of the popularity and acceptance of the concept of consent. In today's world, Cookies have become a subject matter of privacy concerns rather than for its initial purpose of privacy mechanism (Jones, 2020).

Cookies have allowed advertisers to be specific in their target by utilising one's information through online presence to understand likes, preferences, habits, needs and wants. Every time one uses their Internet-enabled devices, they are leaving behind a track of their data that they do not realise. This data can include personal data that reflects one's behaviour.

Researchers at Carnegie Mellon University were keen to understand if users of websites actually read the privacy policy that they so quickly agree to by the click of the button. It was understood after careful research that 75 most popular websites had policies which required users to spend an average 250 words per minute, which meant that they required 10 minutes of reading the policy before signing the contract. Apart from that, an online study of 212 participants suggested that $781 billion would be the cost for the time spent to read policies (McDonald and Cranor, 2008).

12.6 Lack of Explicit Consent to Transfer Data

Terms and conditions or terms of service is the e-contract, at the beginning of the website to enable usage. Companies online tend to slide in terms relating to data transfers and ownership, knowing fully well that users merely click on 'I Agree' as a procedure to use the website rather than expressly reading and understanding the terms within a website and what they are signing up for (Robinson and Zhu, 2020).

The basis of contractual laws and regulations world over is that what is offered must be accepted by the acceptor in the same terms and understanding as that being offered. This concept has also embodied electronic contracts or contracts over the Internet with a view of securing trade and alike relations over the Internet. However, by users clicking the I agree clause, is rather procedural and obligatory and not intentional to accepting the terms and conditions of the E-contract (Ben-Shahar, 2009).

The clause, 'I Agree', ensures that ratifies lawful data transfer to the businesses which allow them to know your likes, preferences and habits and showcase products, advertisements and services in that field itself. This is a classic way of target audience by deriving the data of the user lawfully but without their express consent of transfer.

For example, Instagram and Facebook are popular social media platforms in today's world, owned by an American multinational company called Meta Platform Incorporation. Both companies' platforms enable socialising with known and unknown individuals, sharing pictures, videos, locations, thoughts, and also utilising it as a marketplace. The terms and conditions provide adequate protection from any sexual abuse, harassment, representation, fraud, threat and stealing, amongst other illegal activities. However, terms and conditions of Meta Platform Incorporation also state that profiles on such platforms when posted, shared or uploaded content, are thereby granting non-exclusive, transferable licence to host, use and distribute such data and transfer the same to service providers (Meta, 2022).

12.7 Profiling

Profiling over the Internet is said to be a method of collecting information through the user's surfs, clicks and behaviour. This allows formulating a profile of the user, including their likes, dislikes, preferences and other such habits (Weidmann et al., 2002). Online Public Network (OPN) as its basic feature tends to take information from users when they either create or link profiles over the Internet. Basic information that includes age, sex, location and other such data will be automatically retrieved, which in itself reflects the psychological and behavioural characteristics (Ali et al., 2017).

The Council of Europe defined profiling to be automatic processing of data with the aim of profiling a person to predict any personal preferences, behaviours, and attributes (Council of Europe, 2010). For the purpose of profiling, technologies have advanced to such a level where data mining automatically takes place in large databases.

Profiling enables advertising to be more individualised and also location-specific instead of standard, general and objective. Profiling has helped businesses to a large extent in achieving their monetary goals (King and Jessen, 2010).

The concepts of 'Suggestions for you' or 'We thought you may like to purchase this' are all gimmicks of profiling. They intend on carrying forward the interests of consumers on the basis of the information so derived to earn monetarily. Recommendation Engines on Netflix, Amazon Prime and even YouTube function on the basis of data derived from users. Data transferred can also direct what a consumer is seeing over the Internet. Content so portrayed is determined by previous watches and searches. These recommendation engines act as advertisements as it shows the user one product or shows over the other. This though prima facie this seems useful, it boxes in the user's freedom of choice.

12.8 Instances of Misuse of Personal Information

Misuse of personal information is equivalent to the infringement of data privacy whereby there is unauthorised use, access or disclosure of personal information. On e-commerce websites, customers give their personal information, without which the mechanism would not function. However, these websites are authorised to use the data for that specific purpose. Any other purpose it is used for comes under the banner of an infringement (Phelps et al., 2000).

One must accept that there can never be smoke without fire. There have been a number of cases where data breaches from e-commerce websites have compromised the information of their customers. Once information is given by the customers, the onus of responsibility lies entirely on the e-commerce website to ensure proper protection over the same.

12.9 Alibaba Group Holdings

Alibaba Group Holdings has been a strong competitor in the market for more than a decade. Their products have made possible the individual expectation of using a variety of goods that may not be available within domestic borders. The e-commerce company, incorporated in China, was thriving until a data breach in 2022. The company has been alleged to have fallen short of basic security standards of personal information of their users. It is regarded to be one of the biggest data breaches in history (Patridge, 2022). In 2022, information concerning one billion Chinese citizens were at stake, including their names, phone numbers, identification, addresses and also criminal records – all of which were stolen from a cloud server owned by Alibaba (Kaur, 2022). It was found in 2023 that two critical flaws from the side of Alibaba's cloud were exploited, which caused the infringement of data privacy rights of the Chinese citizens involved (Lakshmanan, 2023).

12.10 eBay Inc.

eBay has been known to be one of the more popular e-commerce websites where individuals can post, negotiate and sell their goods, new or used, over the Internet. This direct relationship between seller and buyer has made eBay successful and sought after for pre-owned goods. In 2014, 145 million accounts of eBay came under threat by a cyber attack. Information regarding passwords, names, e-mail address and residential addresses, and phone numbers were all part of the attack, taking away full anonymity and security of the users (Reuters, 2014). Account holders were advised to change their passwords and also notified to change them periodically to ensure anonymity and security were maintained (Cutler, 2022).

12.11 Target Corporation

The retail store Target is world-acclaimed for the extensive services, quality and brand value that it carries. In 2013, the company went through a huge attack of more than 41 million customers' credit card details (McCoy, 2017). The cyber attack was on Target's gateway server, which lacked security measures, because of which credentials were stolen from a third-party vendor. Target was required to compensate for their lack in safety measures and were liable for 18.5 million dollars (Reuters, 2017).

12.12 Conclusion

One cannot take away the concept of data from e-commerce. It is the means to attain the goal of businesses that transact over the Internet. With the new age technology, e-commerce is inevitable. However, it is important to also keep intact the *sanctum sanctorum* of data privacy of users.

12.13 Suggestions

Though data is imperative, there can be a curb on the amount of information that is acquired. Information unrelated and unnecessary, or ancillary information can be avoided from being not obligatory on such websites, for example – location on GooglePay

Forgetting information on a server is not an impossible task. Regulations, laws around the world, have accepted the individual's right to be forgotten. Such must also be present in e-commerce, where information can be withdrawn and forgotten by the website when transactions are over.

Proper security measures must be taken to keep information safe considering the extent of risk it can be subjected to. Such measures should be periodically looked into, updated, and tested by way of formal/mandatory assessments.

Government representatives knowledgeable in the field must be appointed to ensure that compliances, standards of security are met with. Such officers must also be accountable to the state and have authority to penalise wrong-doers or any non-compliance. Strict action of taking away licenses and permits must be adopted in order to ensure the strength of subsequent rules.

References

Ali, S., Rauf, A., Islam, N., Farman, H., & Khan, S. (2017). User profiling: A privacy issue in online public network. *Sindh University Research Journal-SURJ (Science Series)*, *49*(1), 125–128.

Andaleeb, S. S. (2016). Market segmentation, targeting, and positioning. In *Strategic Marketing Management in Asia* (pp. 179–207). Emerald Group Publishing Limited.

Ben-Shahar, O. (2009). The myth of the 'opportunity to read'in contract law. University of Chicago Law & Economics, Olin Working Paper No. 415, Available at SSRN: https://ssrn.com/abstract=1162922 or http://dx.doi.org/10.2139/ssrn.1162922

Bhatnagar, H., & Asnani, K. (2013). Online Vs Traditional advertisement media-A Comparative analysis. *Pacific Business Review International*, 6(4), 54–58.

Bi, Y., Wang, P., Wang, Z., & Cheng, S. (2019, February). The architecture design for big data application system in apple industry. In *Journal of Physics: Conference Series* (Vol. 1168, No. 3, pp. 032075). IOP Publishing.

Burghate, D. M. (2018). Digital marketing and its techniques for online businesses. *International Journal of Commerce and Management Studies (IJCAMS)*, 3(4). https://bit.ly/492nOtO

Cambridge Dictionary (online), 1999.

Cong, Y., Liu, C., & Qian, J. (2021, December). Research on Lego Multi-channel development: Success and improvement. In *2021 3rd International Conference on Economic Management and Cultural Industry (ICEMCI 2021)* (pp. 2104–2109). Atlantis Press.

Council of Europe. (2010). *Draft Recommendation on the Protection of Individuals with Regard to Automatic Processing of Personal Data in the Context of Profiling, The Consultative Committee of the Convention for the Protection of Individuals With Regard to Automatic Processing of Personal Data, T-PD-BUR (2009) 02 rev 5 Fin*, pp. 5. (resulting from the 21th Bureau Meeting, Lisbon, 13–15 April 2010)

Cutler, J. (2022). E-Commerce time machine: eBay's Historic 2014 Data Breach, Power Retail. https://powerretail.com.au/hot-topics/e-commerce-time-machine-ebays-histo ric-2014-data-breach/#:~:text=Encrypted%20passwords%20and%20personal%20 details,a%20stunning%20turn%20of%20events accessed on 25.06.2023

Diwandari, S., Permanasari, A. E., & Hidayah, I. (2018). Research methodology for analysis of e-commerce user activity based on user interest using web usage mining. *Journal of ICT Research & Applications*, 12(1), 54–69.

Dwivedi, Y. K., Ismagilova, E., Hughes, D. L., Carlson, J., Filieri, R., Jacobson, J., … & Wang, Y. (2021). Setting the future of digital and social media marketing research: Perspectives and research propositions. *International Journal of Information Management*, 59, 102168.

Dyer, G. (2008). *Advertising as Communication*. Routledge.

Fattahi, A. (2022). *IoT Product Design and Development: Best Practices for Industrial, Consumer, and Business Applications*. John Wiley & Sons.

Fuller, M. (2019). Big data and the Facebook scandal: Issues and responses. *Theology*, 122(1), 14–21.

Genarro, L. (2023). 68 Useful e-commerce statistics you must know in 2023. https://wpfo rms.com/ecommerce-statistics/ accessed on 25.06.2023

General Data Protection Regulation, 2018.

George, G., Haas, M. R., & Pentland, A. (2014). Big data and management. *Academy of management Journal*, 57(2), 321–326.

Ghani, N. A., & Sidek, Z. M. (2009). Controlling and disclosing your personal information. *WSEA-S Transactions on Information Science and Applications*, 6(3), 397–406.

Gupta, A. (2014). E-Commerce: Role of E-Commerce in today's business. *International Journal of Computing and Corporate Research*, 4(1), 1–8.

Gurudath, S. (2020). Market basket analysis & recommendation system using association rules. *Master of Science in Big Data Management and Analytics, Griffith College*, Dublin.

Imam, M. A. Y., & Biswas, M. P. K. (2019) What is Cookie, it's phenomenon and it's private residence overview. *International Journal of Sciences: Basic and Applied Research* (IJSBAR), *46*(1), 188–194.

Jones, M. L. (2020). Cookies: A legacy of controversy. *Internet Histories*, *4*(1), 87–104.

Kaur, D. (2022), Is Alibaba responsible for the largest data heist in China?, Tech Wire Asia https://techwireasia.com/2022/07/is-alibaba-responsible-for-the-largest-data-heist-in-china/ accessed on 25.06.2023

King, N. J., & Jessen, P. W. (2010). Profiling the mobile customer–Privacy concerns when behavioural advertisers target mobile phones–Part I. *Computer Law & Security Review*, *26*(5), 455–478.

Kumari, R. (2021). 10 Companies that uses big data. www.analyticssteps.com/blogs/compan ies-uses-big-data accessed on 25.06.2023

Kurniawan, F., Umayah, B., Hammad, J., Nugroho, S. M. S., & Hariadi, M. (2018). Market basket analysis to identify customer behaviours by way of transaction data. *Knowledge Engineering and Data Science*, *1*(1), 20.

Lakshmanan, R. (2023) Two critical flaws found in Alibaba Cloud's PostgreSQL Databases. The Hacker News. https://thehackernews.com/2023/04/two-critical-flaws-found-in-alibaba.html accessed on 25.06.2023

McCoy, K. (2017) Target to pay $18.5M for 2013 data breach that affected 41 million consumers. USA Today. www.usatoday.com/story/money/2017/05/23/target-pay-185m-2013-data-breach-affected-consumers/102063932/ accessed on 25.06.2023

McDonald, A. M., & Cranor, L. F. (2008). The cost of reading privacy policies. *Isjlp*, *4*, 543.

Meta. (2022). Terms of policy. https://m.facebook.com/legal/terms accessed on 25.06.2023

Partridge, M. (2022). The fallout from Alibaba's huge data breach. *MoneyWeek*. accessed on 25.06.2023

Patel, K. K., Patel, S. M., & Scholar, P. (2016). Internet of Things-IOT: Definition, characteristics, architecture, enabling technologies, application & future challenges. *International journal of engineering science and computing*, *6*(5), 6122–6131.

Patino, A., Pitta, D. A., & Quinones, R. (2012). Social media's emerging importance in market research. Journal of consumer marketing, *29*(3), 233–237.

Phelps, J., Nowak, G., & Ferrell, E. (2000). Privacy concerns and consumer willingness to provide personal information. *Journal of Public Policy & Marketing*, *19*(1), 27–41.

Reuters. (2014). Hackers raid eBay in historic breach, access 145M records, CNBC. www.cnbc.com/2014/05/22/hackers-raid-ebay-in-historic-breach-access-145-mln-records.html accessed on 25.06.2023

Reuters. (2017). Target settles 2013 hacked customer data breach for $18.5 million. NBC News. www.nbcnews.com/business/business-news/target-settles-2013-hacked-custo mer-data-breach-18-5-million-n764031 accessed on 25.06.2023

Robinson, E. P., & Zhu, Y. (2020). Beyond "I Agree": Users' understanding of web site terms of service. *Social Media+ Society*, *6*(1), 2056305119897321.

Sagiroglu, S., & Sinanc, D. (2013, May). Big data: A review. In *2013 International Conference on Collaboration Technologies and Systems (CTS)* (pp. 42–47). IEEE.

Sarstedt, M., Mooi, E., Sarstedt, M., & Mooi, E. (2019). Introduction to market research. *A Concise Guide to Market Research: The Process, Data, and Methods Using IBM SPSS Statistics*, 3rd Edition, 1–9.

Tian, Y., & Stewart, C. (2006). History of e-commerce. In *Encyclopedia of E-Commerce, E-Government, and Mobile Commerce* (pp. 559–564). IGI Global.

Wiedmann, K. P., Buxel, H., & Walsh, G. (2002). Customer profiling in e-commerce: Methodological aspects and challenges. *Journal of Database Marketing & Customer Strategy Management, 9*, 170–184.

Chapter 13

Intrusion Detection in Home Automation in IoT

Pawan Whig,[1] Shama Kouser,[2]
Ashima Bhatnagar Bhatia,[1]
Rahul Reddy Nadikattu,[3] and Yusuf Jibrin Alkali[4]

[1]Vivekananda Institute of Professional Studies-TC, New Delhi, India

[2]Department of Computer Science Jazan University, Saudi Arabia

[3]University of the Cumberland, Williamsburg, Kentucky, USA

[4]Federal Inland Revenue Service, Nigeria

13.1 Introduction

The Internet of Things (IoT) has transformed the way we live our lives. With the ability to connect devices and appliances to the Internet, we have access to a level of convenience and control that was once unimaginable [1]. In particular, home automation systems have gained popularity in recent years, allowing us to manage, through a single app or device, everything from lighting and temperature to home security systems.

However, this convenience comes at a cost. As more and more devices are connected to the Internet, the number of potential vulnerabilities and attack vectors increases. Home automation systems are no exception, and their increasing popularity has made them a target for cybercriminals. Without adequate security

DOI: 10.1201/9781003474838-13

measures, these systems can be compromised, putting the privacy and safety of homeowners at risk [2].

This is where intrusion detection comes in. Intrusion detection systems are a key component of any cybersecurity strategy, and their use in home automation can help mitigate the risks posed by IoT security threats [3]. In this discussion, we will explore the importance of intrusion detection in home automation systems and the challenges and benefits of designing and implementing an IDS for this context.

First, it's important to understand the security threats and attack vectors that are present in IoT systems. Common IoT security threats include malware and ransomware attacks, distributed denial of service (DDoS) attacks, and vulnerabilities in network protocols or encryption standards. In the context of home automation systems, the risks posed by compromised devices are particularly concerning. For example, if a hacker gains access to a smart lock or security camera, they could potentially gain entry to a home or monitor the activities of its occupants [4].

Given the significant risks associated with IoT security threats, it is crucial to incorporate an IDS into home automation systems. An IDS is a tool that monitors network traffic and system activity for signs of intrusion or suspicious behavior. It can detect potential threats in real time and alert homeowners or security personnel, allowing them to take action before any significant damage is done. This is especially important in the case of home automation systems, where the security of a home and its occupants is at stake [5].

Designing an IDS for home automation systems presents unique challenges. The system must be able to monitor a wide range of devices and protocols, while also being able to distinguish between normal and suspicious behavior. Additionally, it must be able to integrate with existing security systems and be easy for homeowners to use and understand. Some key features to consider when designing an IDS for home automation include anomaly detection, signature-based detection, and machine-learning capabilities [6–7].

Implementing an IDS for home automation systems also requires careful consideration. Best practices include deploying the system on a separate network from other devices, using strong encryption protocols, and regularly updating software and firmware. However, there are also limitations to consider. For example, the system may generate false positives or fail to detect certain types of attacks. Additionally, the cost and complexity of implementing an IDS may be prohibitive for some homeowners.

Despite these challenges, there are examples of successful intrusion detection systems in home automation. For example, popular smart home security systems like SimpliSafe and ADT use a combination of traditional security measures and IDS to protect homes and occupants. By integrating an IDS into these systems,

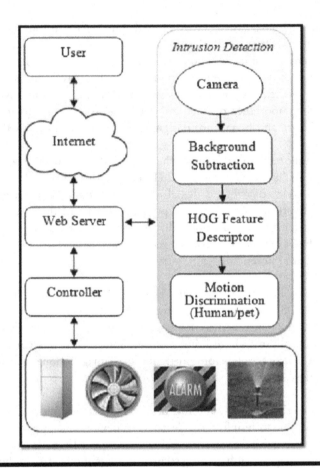

Figure 13.1   Flow of smart home automation.

Source: Created by the author.

homeowners are able to monitor their homes in real time and receive alerts when suspicious behavior is detected [8].

Intrusion detection is a crucial aspect of home automation security; the flow of smart home automation is given in Figure 13.1. As the popularity of IoT devices continues to grow, so too does the need for robust security measures to protect against potential cyber threats. By incorporating an IDS into home automation systems, homeowners can rest assured that their homes and families are protected from malicious actors [9]. However, designing and implementing an effective IDS requires careful consideration of the unique challenges and limitations of this context. As technology continues to evolve, it will be important to stay up-to-date on the latest security trends.

13.1.1 Overview of IoT and Home Automation Systems

IoT is a rapidly growing network of devices and objects that are embedded with sensors and connected to the Internet. These devices can connect with one additional, gather and transmit data, and respond to commands from users or other devices [10]. IoT has a wide range of applications, from smart cities and transportation systems to healthcare and agriculture. One of the most popular and visible applications of IoT is home automation systems.

Home mechanization schemes allow proprietors to control numerous features of their homesteads remotely, such as illumination, heating and cooling, and safety systems [11]. The systems typically consist of a network of smart devices and appliances – such as smart thermostats, smart lights, and security photograph camera, which are associated to the Internet and measured through a central hub or mobile app. Some systems even incorporate voice assistants like Amazon Alexa or Google Home, allowing users to control their homes through simple voice commands. An IoT-based home automation system is given in Figure 13.2

One of the key benefits of home automation systems is convenience. By centralizing control over various home devices, homeowners can streamline their routines

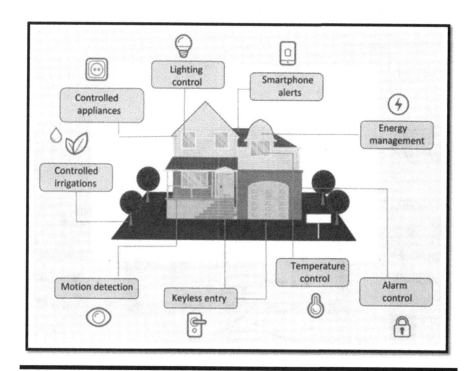

Figure 13.2 IoT based home automation system.
Source: Created by the author.

and simplify daily tasks [12–13]. Home automation can also provide energy savings by optimizing heating and cooling usage and reducing energy waste.

However, as mentioned earlier, the convenience of home automation systems comes with a cost in terms of security risks. As more devices are connected to the Internet, the number of potential vulnerabilities and attack vectors increases. It is crucial to implement security measures to protect against cyber threats and prevent hackers from accessing personal and sensitive data. The effective use of IDS can help provide peace of mind for homeowners and prevent intrusions from malicious actors [14].

Home automation systems are a prime example of the power and potential of IoT. They offer significant benefits in terms of convenience and energy savings. By understanding the benefits and challenges of home automation systems and the importance of intrusion detection, homeowners can make informed decisions about implementing IoT technology in their homes [15–16].

13.1.2 Security Challenges in Home Automation

As home automation systems become increasingly popular, the security challenges associated with these systems are also on the rise. Some security challenges in home automation are given with solutions in Figure 13.3. These challenges can be grouped into several categories:

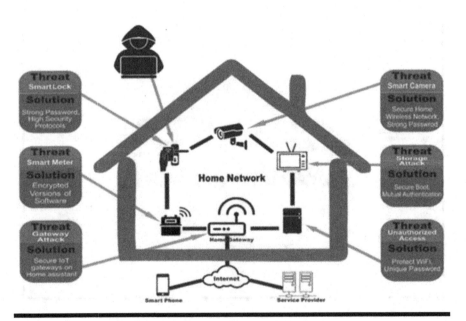

Figure 13.3   Security challenges in home automation.

Source: Created by the author.

1. Network security: Home automation systems rely on network connections, which means that the devices and data are vulnerable to attacks. Hackers can exploit vulnerabilities in routers, modems, and other devices to gain admission to the system and compromise the security of the entire system.
2. Device security: The devices that make up home automation systems can be vulnerable to attacks. Hackers can exploit vulnerabilities in the firmware or software of these devices, allowing them to gain control over the devices or extract sensitive data.
3. Physical security: Many home automation systems rely on physical devices, such as security cameras and door locks. If these devices are not properly secured, hackers can gain physical access to the home and compromise the security of the entire system.
4. Privacy concerns: Home automation systems collect and transmit large amounts of data, including sensitive information such as video footage and personal preferences.
5. Lack of standards: The lack of standardization in the home automation industry makes it difficult to ensure that devices and systems are interoperable and secure. This can lead to confusion among consumers and make it easier for attackers to exploit vulnerabilities.

To address these security challenges, it's important for homeowners to take a proactive approach to security. This includes:

1. Keeping package and firmware up to date: Homeowners should ensure that all devices and software are up to date to address known susceptibilities.
2. Using strong passwords: Strong passwords can help prevent unauthorized access to devices and systems.
3. Segmenting networks: Segmenting networks can limit the impact of a breach and make it more difficult for attackers to gain access to the entire system.
4. Using intrusion detection systems: Intrusion detection systems can monitor network traffic and detect suspicious activity, alerting homeowners to potential attacks.
5. Choosing reputable vendors: Choosing reputable vendors and devices can help ensure that devices and systems are secure and regularly updated to address vulnerabilities.

By taking these proactive steps, homeowners can help mitigate the security challenges associated with home automation systems and enjoy the many benefits that these systems provide.

13.2 Importance of Intrusion Detection

Intrusion detection is an essential component of home automation security, particularly in the context of IoT devices. Intrusion detection systems (IDS) are designed to monitor network traffic and identify suspicious activity, allowing homeowners to detect and respond to potential security breaches in a timely manner.

There are several reasons why intrusion detection is important in the context of home automation:

1. Early detection of security breaches: Intrusion detection systems can help detect security breaches at an early stage, allowing homeowners to respond quickly and prevent further damage. This can help prevent the spread of malware, limit the damage caused by attacks, and reduce the risk of data theft.
2. Protection against unknown threats: Intrusion detection systems are designed to detect both known and unknown threats. This means that they can identify new and emerging threats that traditional security solutions may miss.
3. Mitigation of false positives: This means that they can help reduce the amount of time spent investigating false alarms, allowing homeowners to focus on genuine security threats.
4. Increased visibility: Intrusion detection systems provide increased visibility into the home automation network, making it easier to identify potential vulnerabilities and address security concerns.
5. Compliance with regulations: Implementing intrusion detection systems can help homeowners ensure compliance with these regulations and avoid potential fines and legal issues.

Intrusion detection is critical for ensuring the security of home automation systems in the context of IoT. It can help detect security breaches at an early stage, protect against unknown threats, reduce false positives, increase visibility, and ensure compliance with regulations [17], [18]. By implementing intrusion detection systems, homeowners can protect their homes and personal information against the growing number of cyber threats in today's digital world.

13.2.1 Common IoT Security Threats and Vulnerabilities

The Internet of Things (IoT) refers to the interconnection of various devices, sensors, and machinery through the Internet, allowing them to gather and communicate data, enabling seamless data exchange and automation across a network of physical objects or "things." While IoT technology has immense potential to transform various industries, it also poses security risks that threaten privacy, safety, and financial security. Below are some of the common IoT security threats and vulnerabilities as shown in Figure 13.4:

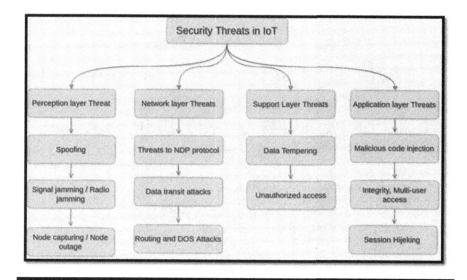

Figure 13.4   Common IoT security threats and vulnerabilities.

Source: Created by the author.

There are a number of common security threats and vulnerabilities that are associated with IoT devices, including:

1. Weak or default passwords: Many IoT devices come with weak or default passwords, making them vulnerable to brute force attacks.
2. Unpatched vulnerabilities: IoT devices often have software and firmware that are not regularly updated, leaving them vulnerable to known vulnerabilities.
3. Lack of encryption: Many IoT devices do not use encryption, making it easier for hackers to intercept and steal data.
4. Insecure APIs: APIs used by IoT devices may be insecure, allowing attackers to gain access to sensitive data.
5. Insecure firmware updates: Insecure firmware updates can lead to the installation of malware or unauthorized software on IoT devices.

13.2.2 Attack Trajectories

These systems can also be vulnerable to various attack vectors, which can compromise the security and privacy of the homeowner [19]. Below are some of the common attack vectors in home automation systems as shown in Figure 13.5:

Home automation systems can be vulnerable to a range of attack vectors, including:

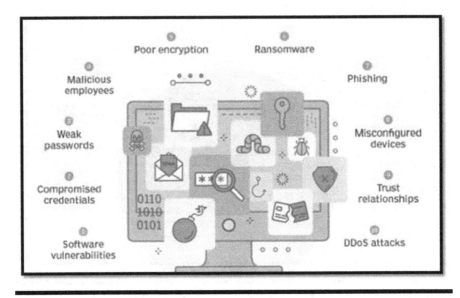

Figure 13.5   Attack vectors in home automation systems.

Source: Created by the author.

1. Network attacks: Attackers can exploit vulnerabilities in routers and other network devices to gain access to the home automation network.
2. Malware: Malware can be installed on IoT devices to gain control over them or to use them to launch attacks on other devices.
3. Social engineering: Attackers may use social engineering techniques to gain access to passwords and other sensitive information.
4. Physical attacks: Attackers may physically access IoT devices, such as security cameras or door locks, to gain access to the home automation system.
5. Man-in-the-middle attacks: Attackers can intercept data traffic between devices, allowing them to gain access to sensitive data or take control of devices.

13.2.3 Risks Posed by Compromised Devices

Compromised devices, such as computers, smartphones, and IoT devices, pose significant risks to users and organizations. When a device is compromised, it means that an attacker has gained unauthorized access to the device and its data, and can use it to carry out malicious activities [20], [21]. Below are some of the risks posed by compromised devices. Risks posed by compromised devices are shown in Figure 13.6

Figure 13.6 Example of risks posed by compromised devices.
Source: Created by the author.

These risks include:

Data theft: Attackers may use compromised devices to steal sensitive data, such as personal information or financial data.

1. Unauthorized access: Compromised devices may allow attackers to gain unauthorized access to the home automation system, including security cameras and door locks.
2. Device hijacking: Attackers may use compromised devices to launch attacks on other devices, such as launching distributed denial of service (DDoS) attacks.
3. Botnets: Compromised IoT devices can be used to create botnets, allowing attackers to launch coordinated attacks on other networks or devices.
4. Physical risks: Compromised IoT devices may pose physical risks to users, such as allowing unauthorized access to the home or disabling security systems.

It is important for proprietors to be conscious of the possible safety threats and susceptibilities related with IoT devices and home automation systems, and to take proactive steps to mitigate these risks [22], [23]. This includes keeping devices and software up to date, using strong passwords, and implementing intrusion detection systems to monitor net circulation and notice possible security breaches.

13.3 Intrusion Detection Systems (IDS) in Home Automation

An Intrusion Detection System (IDS) is a security system that monitors a network or a device for malicious activities or policy violations. In the context of home automation, an IDS is used to detect any unauthorized access or intrusion attempts on the connected devices, such as smart thermostats, smart locks, security cameras, and other smart home appliances.

The IDS typically consists of sensors or agents installed on the smart home devices, which continuously monitor and analyze the network traffic and device behavior for any suspicious activity. The sensors can be either host-based (installed on the device) or network-based (monitoring the network traffic).

The IDS can detect various types of attacks, such as port scans, brute-force attacks, denial-of-service attacks, and malware infections. When the IDS detects an attack or suspicious activity, it generates an alert or notification to the homeowner, informing them of the potential security threat. The alert may also contain information about the type and severity of the attack, allowing the homeowner to take appropriate action.

In addition to detecting and alerting about potential security threats, the IDS can also take automatic actions to mitigate the attack, such as blocking the network traffic from the attacker's IP address or quarantining the infected device.

13.3.1 What is an IDS and How Does It Work?

When the IDS system identifies network activity that matches a predefined pattern, it alerts the homeowner or security team, allowing them to investigate the potential security breach.

The two main types of IDS (Intrusion Detection System) systems are signature-based and anomaly-based. Signature-based IDS systems use predetermined signatures or patterns to detect possible security breaches, while anomaly-based IDS systems utilize machine-learning algorithms to analyze normal behavior patterns and identify any irregularities that may suggest a security breach.

13.3.2 Types of IDS for Home Automation

IDS systems for home automation are specifically created to detect and prevent unauthorized access to a smart home network. Figure 13.7 illustrates several types of IDS that can be employed in home automation.

There are several different types of IDS systems that can be used in home automation, including:

1. Network-based IDS: Network-based IDS systems are designed to monitor network traffic and identify potential security breaches. These systems are typically installed at the network perimeter, such as on a router or gateway.
2. Host-based IDS: Host-based IDS systems are installed on individual devices, such as laptops or IoT devices, and monitor the activity on those devices for signs of a security breach.

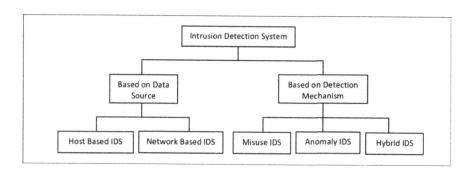

Figure 13.7 Types of IDS for home automation.
Source: Created by the author.

3. Hybrid IDS: Hybrid IDS systems combine elements of network-based and host-based IDS systems.

13.3.3 Benefits of Using an IDS

In today's technology-driven world, security threats are increasing at an unprecedented pace. One way to mitigate these threats is through the use of an Intrusion Detection System (IDS). An IDS is a security tool that monitors network traffic, analyzes it, and alerts system administrators if it detects any malicious or suspicious activity.

The benefits of using an IDS are numerous. First and foremost, an IDS can provide early detection of potential security threats. By analyzing network traffic in real time, an IDS can identify anomalous activity that may indicate an ongoing or impending attack. This early detection allows system administrators to respond quickly and effectively, potentially preventing the attack from causing significant damage.

Secondly, an IDS can help reduce the impact of security breaches. If an attacker manages to breach a network, an IDS can alert system administrators to the breach, allowing them to isolate the affected system and minimize the spread of the attack. Additionally, an IDS can provide valuable information about the nature of the attack, which can help system administrators develop better security measures in the future.

Finally, an IDS can help organizations save money in the long run. By detecting and preventing security breaches, an IDS can prevent costly damage to systems and data. It can also reduce the costs associated with investigating and remedying breaches. The Best Available IDES are shown In Table 13.1

Table 13.1 Best IDEs Available with Bottom Line

Top Intrusion Detection Systems (IDS)		
	Free Trial?	Bottom Line
Solar Winds Security Event Manager	30-Day	A NIDS and HIDS designed to take real-time log data from across your network and enact signature and anomaly-based intrusion. detection SEM is built to perform automatic, customizable intrusion detection actions like disabling accounts or detaching devices.
McAfee	30-Day	Uses signature-based and anomaly-based intrusion detection, alongside emulation techniques, in order to discover and block cyberthreats. This IDS is incredibly scalable and can be integrated, enabling you to grow your intrusion prevention system freely.
Suricata	Free Tool	A free, open-source NIDS designed to apply detection logic to packets and protocols This enables Suricata to differentiate normal behavior from abnormal or malicious behavior. Note that Suricata does not leverage documentation capabilities.
Blumira	14-Day	A SIEM platform that leverages threat detection and response throughout on and off-premises platforms. Automate and schedule reports for compliance, security, and intrusion detection functions You can even address an in-progress attack through this IDS.
Cisco Stealthwatch	14-Day	This NIDS and HIDS is built to use machine learning to establish baselines, which new network activity is checked against. Leverages important contextual information as intrusion detection data, so you can fully understand detected malicious behavior.

Source: Created by the author.

There are several benefits to using an IDS system in home automation, including:

1. Early detection of security breaches: IDS systems can help detect security breaches at an early stage, allowing homeowners to respond quickly and prevent further damage.
2. Protection against unknown threats: IDS systems are designed to detect both known and unknown threats.

3. Reduced false positives: This means that they can help reduce the amount of time spent investigating false alarms, allowing homeowners to focus on genuine security threats.

4. Increased visibility: IDS systems provide increased visibility into the home automation network, making it easier to identify potential vulnerabilities and address security concerns.

5. Compliance with regulations: Implementing IDS systems can help homeowners ensure compliance with these regulations and avoid potential fines and legal issues.

Hence implementing an IDS system in home automation can be an effective way to improve security and protect against potential security breaches. By detecting and responding to potential security breaches at an early stage, homeowners can protect their homes and personal information against the growing number of cyber threats in today's digital world.

13.4 Designing an IDS for Home Automation

13.4.1 Key Features to Consider

When designing an IDS system for home automation, there are several key features to consider, including:

1. Real-time monitoring: An effective IDS system should be able to screen the home automation net in real time and detect potential security breaches as soon as they occur.

2. Machine-learning capabilities: An IDS system with machine-learning capabilities can help identify patterns of normal behavior and detect deviations from these patterns that may indicate a security breach.

3. Customizable rules: An IDS system should allow homeowners to customize the rules used to detect security breaches, to ensure that the system is tailored to the specific needs of the home automation network.

4. Automatic alerts: An IDS system should be able to automatically send alerts to homeowners or security teams when potential security breaches are detected.

5. Centralized management: An IDS system should have a centralized management interface that allows homeowners or security teams to easily monitor and manage the system.

6. Integration with other security systems: An IDS system should be able to integrate with other security systems, such as firewalls, antivirus software, and intrusion prevention systems, to provide comprehensive security coverage.

13.4.2 Integration with Other Security Systems

Integrating an IDS system with other security systems can provide comprehensive security coverage for home automation networks. For example, an IDS system can work alongside a firewall to detect and prevent security breaches, while antivirus software can be used to scan for malware and other threats.

When designing an IDS system for home automation, it's important to ensure that the system is compatible with other security systems and that the integration is seamless. This will ensure that potential security breaches are identified and responded to quickly and effectively.

13.4.3 User Interface and Ease of Use

An effective IDS system should have a user-friendly interface that is easy to use and navigate. The interface should provide real-time monitoring of the home automation network and allow homeowners or security teams to quickly identify potential security breaches.

In addition, the IDS system should be easy to set up and configure, with clear documentation and support available to assist homeowners with any issues or questions that may arise.

Overall, designing an IDS system for home automation requires careful consideration of key features, integration with other security systems, and a user-friendly interface that is easy to use and manage. By implementing an effective IDS system, homeowners can improve the security of their home automation network and protect against potential security breaches.

13.5 Implementing an IDS for Home Automation

13.5.1 Best Practices for Deployment

When implementing an IDS system for home automation, there are several best practices to follow to ensure that the system is effective and efficient:

1. Conduct a security audit: Before deploying an IDS system, conduct a thorough security audit of the home automation network to identify potential vulnerabilities and areas of weakness.
2. Choose the right IDS system: Select an IDS system that is specifically designed for home automation and that has the necessary features to meet the security needs of the network.
3. Configure the system properly: Configure the IDS system according to the specific needs of the home automation network, including setting up custom rules and thresholds.

4. Monitor the system regularly: Monitor the IDS system on a regular basis to ensure that it is working properly and detecting potential security breaches as expected.
5. Regularly update the system: Keep the IDS system up to date with the latest software patches and security updates to ensure that it is protected against the latest threats.

13.5.2 Challenges and Limitations

Implementing an IDS system for home automation can be challenging due to a number of factors, including:

1. Complexity of the network: Home automation networks can be complex, with multiple devices and sensors connected to the network. This can make it difficult to detect potential security breaches and to configure the IDS system properly.
2. False positives: IDS systems can generate false positives, which can be time-consuming to investigate and can result in unnecessary alerts and distractions.
3. Limited resources: Home automation devices typically have limited processing power and memory, which can make it difficult to implement an IDS system that is both effective and efficient.

13.5.3 Examples of Successful Implementations

Despite the challenges and limitations, there are many examples of successful implementations of IDS systems for home automation. For example:

1. Nest Secure: The Nest Secure system includes a built-in IDS system that monitors the home automation network and provides real-time alerts in the event of potential security breaches.
2. Samsung SmartThings: The SmartThings platform includes an IDS system that can detect and respond to potential security breaches, with customizable rules and alerts.
3. Home Assistant: The Home Assistant platform includes support for a wide range of IDS systems, including Snort and Suricata, providing homeowners with a high degree of flexibility and control over their security system.

Overall, successful implementations of IDS systems for home automation require careful consideration of best practices, as well as an understanding of the challenges and limitations of the system. By selecting the right IDS system, configuring it properly, and monitoring it regularly, homeowners can improve the security of their home automation network and protect against potential security breaches.

13.6 Case Study: Intrusion Detection in Smart Home Security Systems

Smart home security systems have gained increasing popularity in recent years as they provide homeowners with the ability to remotely monitor and control their homes' security systems. However, with the growing complexity of these systems, they have also become more vulnerable to cyber-attacks. Intrusion detection systems (IDS) are used to detect and alert homeowners of any unauthorized access or malicious activities in the smart home security system.

One common technique used for intrusion detection in smart homes is anomaly detection. Anomaly detection involves establishing a baseline for the normal behavior of the smart home security system and monitoring for any deviations from that baseline. For instance, an IDS can monitor the number of times a door is opened or closed, and alert the homeowner if there is an abnormal pattern of activity, such as a door opening at an unusual time or when the homeowner is not present.

Another technique used for intrusion detection is signature-based detection. This technique involves comparing network traffic to a database of known attack signatures. If the network traffic matches a known signature, the IDS will raise an alert. For example, if a hacker attempts to log in to the smart home security system using a known username and password combination, the IDS can detect and alert the homeowner of this activity.

Machine-learning techniques are also used in intrusion detection in smart homes. Machine-learning algorithms can learn from the data collected from the smart home security system to detect abnormal activities. The algorithms can identify patterns of behavior that are indicative of a security breach and alert the homeowner accordingly.

13.6.1 Overview of Popular Smart Home Security Systems

Some of the most popular systems include the following:

1. Ring Alarm: Ring Alarm is a DIY home security system that includes a range of sensors, cameras, and other devices that can be customized to meet the specific needs of the homeowner.
2. SimpliSafe: SimpliSafe is another DIY home security system that includes a range of sensors and cameras, as well as a mobile app that provides real-time notifications and alerts.
3. ADT: ADT is a professional home security system that includes a range of sensors, cameras, and other devices, as well as 24/7 monitoring by trained security professionals.

13.6.2 Analysis of How IDS Can Enhance Security

Intrusion detection systems (IDS) can play a key role in enhancing the security of smart home security systems by providing an additional layer of protection against potential security breaches. IDS systems can monitor the network for potential threats and provide real-time alerts and notifications in the event of suspicious activity.

For example, an IDS system can detect when an unauthorized device attempts to connect to the smart home network, or when an authorized device is behaving in an unusual or suspicious way. This can help to identify potential security breaches before they occur, and enable homeowners to take action to protect their network.

In addition, IDS systems can provide valuable insights into the overall security of the network, including identifying potential vulnerabilities and areas of weakness that may need to be addressed.

13.6.3 Real-world Examples of Intrusion Detection in Action

There are many real-world examples of intrusion detection systems in action in smart home security systems.

1. Ring Alarm: Ring Alarm includes a range of sensors that can detect motion, entry, and other potential security breaches. The system also includes a built-in IDS system that can monitor the network for potential threats and provide real-time alerts to homeowners.
2. SimpliSafe: SimpliSafe includes a range of sensors that can detect potential security breaches, including door and window sensors, motion sensors, and glass-break sensors. The system also includes a mobile app that provides real-time notifications and alerts in the event of suspicious activity.
3. ADT: ADT includes a range of sensors and cameras that can detect potential security breaches, as well as a 24/7 monitoring service that can provide real-time alerts and notifications to homeowners and law enforcement agencies.

Overall, the use of IDS systems in smart home security systems can provide a valuable additional layer of protection against potential security breaches. By monitoring the network for potential threats and providing real-time alerts and notifications, IDS systems can help to enhance the overall security of the home and protect against potential security breaches.

13.7 Conclusion and Future Directions

13.7.1 Summary of Key Findings

Intrusion detection systems (IDS) can play a crucial role in enhancing the security of home automation systems by providing an additional layer of protection against potential security breaches. The Internet of Things (IoT) presents many unique security challenges, and home automation systems are particularly vulnerable to attacks due to the wide range of connected devices and the potential for compromised devices to spread malware throughout the network.

Common IoT security threats and vulnerabilities include insecure network protocols, weak authentication and authorization mechanisms, and the use of unsecured devices. Attack vectors in home automation systems include both physical and digital attacks, and compromised devices pose significant risks to the overall security of the network.

Implementing an IDS system can help to address these challenges by monitoring the network for potential threats and providing real-time alerts and notifications in the event of suspicious activity. Key features to consider when designing an IDS for home automation systems include the ability to monitor network traffic, the ability to detect and respond to potential threats in real time, and integration with other security systems.

13.7.2 Future Directions for Research and Development

As the use of home automation systems continues to grow, there is a need for continued research and development in the area of intrusion detection. Future research could focus on developing more advanced IDS systems that can identify and respond to new and emerging threats, as well as improving the accuracy and speed of threat detection.

In addition, there is a need for further research into the use of machine learning and artificial intelligence (AI) to enhance the capabilities of IDS systems in home automation. Machine-learning algorithms can be trained to identify and respond to specific types of threats, and AI can be used to automate the response to potential threats.

13.7.3 Final Thoughts and Recommendations

Intrusion detection is a critical component of any home automation security system, and homeowners should carefully consider the use of IDS when designing their home automation systems. Key recommendations for homeowners include the following:

■ Choose a home automation system that includes built-in intrusion detection capabilities, or consider adding an IDS system to an existing system.

- Work with a qualified security professional to design and implement an IDS system that meets the specific needs of the home and the homeowner.
- Regularly update and maintain the home automation system to ensure that it is secure and up-to-date with the latest security patches and firmware updates.
- Stay informed about the latest threats and vulnerabilities in home automation systems, and take steps to protect against potential security breaches.

Overall, the use of intrusion detection systems can help to enhance the security of home automation systems and protect against potential security breaches. With careful planning and implementation, homeowners can enjoy the benefits of home automation while maintaining a secure and protected network.

References

[1] T. Fritz, and A. Klingler, "The d-Separation Criterion in Categorical Probability," 2023. [Online]. Available: http://jmlr.org/papers/v24/22-0916.html

[2] Y. Alkali, I. Routray, and P. Whig, "Strategy for Reliable, Efficient and Secure IoT Using Artificial Intelligence," *IUP Journal of Computer Sciences*, vol. 16, no. 2, 2022, pp. 1–7.

[3] P. Whig, A. Velu, and R. R. Naddikatu, "The Economic Impact of AI-Enabled Blockchain in 6G-Based Industry," in *AI and Blockchain Technology in 6G Wireless Network*, Springer, Singapore, 2022, pp. 205–224.

[4] P. Whig, A. Velu, and P. Sharma, "Demystifying Federated Learning for Blockchain: A Case Study," in *Demystifying Federated Learning for Blockchain and Industrial Internet of Things*, IGI Global, 2022, pp. 143–165.

[5] P. Whig, S. Kouser, A. Velu, and R. R. Nadikattu, "Fog-IoT-Assisted-Based Smart Agriculture Application," in *Demystifying Federated Learning for Blockchain and Industrial Internet of Things*, IGI Global, 2022, pp. 74–93.

[6] P. Whig, A. Velu, and A. B. Bhatia, "Protect Nature and Reduce the Carbon Footprint with an Application of Blockchain for IIoT," in *Demystifying Federated Learning for Blockchain and Industrial Internet of Things*, IGI Global, 2022, pp. 123–142.

[7] P. Whig, A. Velu, and R. Ready, "Demystifying Federated Learning in Artificial Intelligence With Human-Computer Interaction," in *Demystifying Federated Learning for Blockchain and Industrial Internet of Things*, IGI Global, 2022, pp. 94–122.

[8] P. Whig, A. Velu, and R. R. Nadikattu, "Blockchain Platform to Resolve Security Issues in IoT and Smart Networks," in *AI-Enabled Agile Internet of Things for Sustainable FinTech Ecosystems*, IGI Global, 2022, pp. 46–65.

[9] H. Jupalle, S. Kouser, A. B. Bhatia, N. Alam, R. R. Nadikattu, and P. Whig, "Automation of Human Behaviors and Its Prediction Using Machine learning," Microsystem Technologies, pp. 1–9, 2022.

[10] U. Tomar, N. Chakroborty, H. Sharma, and P. Whig, "AI based Smart Agriculture System," *Transactions on Latest Trends in Artificial Intelligence*, vol. 2, no. 2, 2021, pp. 1–8.

[11] P. Whig, R. R. Nadikattu, and A. Velu, "COVID-19 Pandemic Analysis Using Application of AI," *Healthcare Monitoring and Data Analysis Using IoT: Technologies and Applications*, pp. 1, 2022.

[12] M. Anand, A. Velu, and P. Whig, "Prediction of Loan Behaviour with Machine Learning Models for Secure Banking," *Journal of Computer Science and Engineering (JCSE)*, vol. 3, no. 1, pp. 1–13, 2022.

[13] Alkali, Yusuf and Routray, Indira and Whig, Pawan, Study of various methods for reliable, efficient and Secured IoT using Artificial Intelligence (January 28, 2022). Proceedings of the International Conference on Innovative Computing & Communication (ICICC) 2022, Available at SSRN: https://ssrn.com/abstract=4020 364 or http://dx.doi.org/10.2139/ssrn.4020364

[14] G. Chopra, and P. WHIG, "A Clustering Approach Based on Support Vectors," *International Journal of Machine Learning for Sustainable Development*, vol. 4, no. 1, pp. 21–30, 2022.

[15] G. Chopra, and P. Whig, "Smart Agriculture System Using AI," *International Journal of Sustainable Development in Computing Science*, vol. 4, no. 1, 2022.

[16] M. Madhu, and P. WHIG, "A Survey of Machine Learning and Its Applications," *International Journal of Machine Learning for Sustainable Development*, vol. 4, no. 1, pp. 11–20, 2022.

[17] E. S. Mamza, "Use of AIOT in Health System," *International Journal of Sustainable Development in Computing Science*, vol. 3, no. 4, pp. 21–30, 2021.

[18] Y. Khera, P. Whig, and A. Velu, "Efficient Effective and Secured Electronic Billing System Using AI," *Vivekananda Journal of Research*, vol. 10, pp. 53–60, 2021.

[19] A. Velu, and P. Whig, "Protect Personal Privacy and Wasting Time Using Nlp: A Comparative Approach Using AI," *Vivekananda Journal of Research*, vol. 10, pp. 42–52, 2021.

[20] P. W. Arun Velu, "Impact of Covid Vaccination on the Globe Using Data Analytics," *International Journal of Sustainable Development in Computing Science*, vol. 3, no. 2, 2021.

[21] A. Rupani, P. Whig, G. Sujediya, and P. Vyas, "A Robust Technique for Image Processing Based on Interfacing of Raspberry-Pi and FPGA Using IoT," in *2017 International Conference on Computer, Communications and Electronics (Comptelix)*, pp. 350–353, 2017.

[22] P. Whig, and S. N. Ahmad, "Simulation of Linear Dynamic Macro Model of Photo Catalytic Sensor in SPICE," *COMPEL: The International Journal for Computation and Mathematics in Electrical and Electronic Engineering*, vol. 23, 2014, pp. 1–23.

[23] P. Whig, and S. N. Ahmad, "A Novel Pseudo-PMOS Integrated ISFET Device for Water Quality Monitoring," *Active and Passive Electronic Components*, vol. 2013, 2013, 1–12.

Chapter 14

IoT Performance Assessment

Tawseef Ahmed Teli,[1] Faheem Syeed Masoodi,[2] and Alwi M. Bamhdi[3]

[1]Department of Higher Education, Jammu and Kashmir, India

[2]University of Kashmir, Jammu and Kashmir, India

[3]Computing College Al Qufudah, Umm Al-Qura University, Mecca, Kingdom of Saudi Arabia

14.1 IoT

In terms of heterogeneous systems, IoT (Internet of Things) [1] refers to the blending and interaction of many platforms, networks, and devices, see Figure 14.1. When it comes to hardware, software, communication protocols, and data formats, heterogeneous systems in the IoT [2] entail the collaboration of various technologies, protocols, and so forth. Interoperability, seamless communication, and unified management are all hampered by this variability. But it also offers chances for creativity, adaptability, and scalability. Organizations can bridge the gap between heterogeneous components, promote interoperability, and build a cohesive ecosystem where devices and systems can successfully interact, share data, and collaborate by utilizing gateway devices, middleware, and standardization efforts. IoT provides for the smooth integration of legacy systems, various sensors, and other heterogeneous systems. See IoT architecture [3] in Figure 14.1.

Analyzing an IoT system's performance enables the discovery of potential areas for improvement. Organizations can locate bottlenecks, manage network infrastructure, and enhance system performance by tracking performance indicators including response time, throughput, and resource consumption. Performance

DOI: 10.1201/9781003474838-14

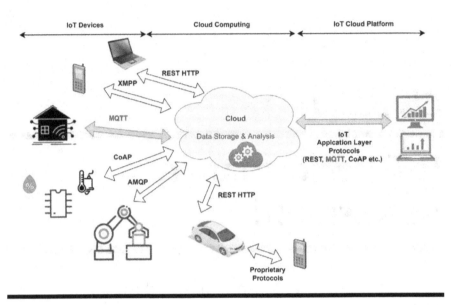

Figure 14.1   IoT Architecture.

Source: [3].

evaluation confirms that an IoT system satisfies the specified quality criteria. Organizations may make sure that the system operates dependably under a variety of settings and scales effectively, as the number of connected devices rises by examining factors including reliability, scalability, and responsiveness. IoT performance has a direct impact on user experience. Users may not be satisfied if there are frequent interruptions, significant latency, or slow response times. Organizations can discover and fix issues through performance assessments that may have an effect on user experience [4–5], ensuring a seamless and easy interaction with IoT gadgets and applications. The battery life and computing power of IoT devices are frequently finite. Performance evaluation aids in resource optimization, reduced power consumption, and increased device longevity. This is crucial for IoT devices installed in remote or difficult-to-reach areas, where battery replacement or device maintenance may be difficult. Security concerns and attacks can affect IoT devices. Organizations can analyze the system's security controls, spot any weaknesses, and put in place the appropriate security measures to guarantee the confidentiality, integrity, and accessibility of data by conducting performance assessments. As more linked devices are added, it is anticipated that IoT systems will expand dramatically. Organizations can better understand the system's scalability and prepare for future expansions by conducting performance assessments. It gives organizations the ability to foresee prospective problems and decide on system architecture, network capacity, and infrastructure changes with knowledge.

IoT performance evaluation is essential for maximizing system effectiveness, assuring quality, boosting user experience, effectively managing resources, addressing security problems, and preparing for future scalability. This makes it possible for businesses to offer dependable, safe, and effective IoT solutions. IoT performance evaluation is crucial for a number of reasons:

14.1.1 Interoperability Evaluation

Heterogeneous IoT systems [6] integrate several platforms, networks, and devices. Measuring performance makes it easier to evaluate how well these parts work together. Organizations can spot any interoperability problems [7] or bottlenecks that impede effective system functioning by tracking and evaluating indicators, including data transmission success rates, compatibility of communication protocols, and seamless device integration.

14.1.2 System Integration and Communication

Devices and platforms from many vendors and technologies must operate together seamlessly in heterogeneous IoT systems [8–11]. Organizations can monitor the effectiveness and dependability of communication between these heterogeneous components by using performance measurement [12–13]. Organizations can uncover communication inefficiencies, troubleshoot connectivity issues, and enhance the system for better data interchange and cooperation by analyzing metrics like latency, message loss, and data synchronization.

14.1.3 Resource Utilization

Organizations can better understand resource usage in a heterogeneous IoT system by using performance measurement. This includes assessing how effectively resources like processor power, memory, and network bandwidth are distributed among various components [14]. Organizations can spot resource bottlenecks, improve resource allocation, and ensure effective resource use to meet the system's various needs by keeping an eye on resource usage data.

14.1.4 Scalability and Flexibility

Heterogeneous IoT systems frequently require the capacity to support the addition or removal of platforms and devices. Organizations can evaluate the system's scalability and adaptability [15] through performance measurement. Organizations can assess a system's capacity to manage increasing workloads, accommodate new devices, and adapt to changing requirements by monitoring performance metrics during changes in system size or configuration. This makes it possible to plan effectively for capacity and guarantees that the system can scale up or down without sacrificing performance.

14.1.5 Problem Detection and Optimization

By finding and resolving performance issues, performance measurement enables enterprises to maximize the performance of heterogeneous IoT systems. Organizations can identify abnormalities, bottlenecks, or departures from expected behavior by tracking a variety of performance measures. To improve system performance and stability, this information can be utilized to diagnose issues, pinpoint their underlying causes, and implement the necessary corrective measures.

14.1.6 Service Level Agreement (SLA) Compliance

In heterogeneous IoT systems, performance assessment is essential for achieving SLA criteria. To maintain compliance and provide the anticipated level of service quality, organizations must track and evaluate performance against set SLA indicators. By tracking critical metrics like response times, availability, and data correctness and comparing them to SLA standards, enterprises are able to take preventative action to meet or exceed customer expectations.

14.2 Technology in IoT

IoT uses pull-based and push-based data propagation techniques for transmitting sensor data to clients. Pull-based techniques involve clients requesting data from a server, while push-based techniques involve the server actively sending data to clients [16]. These techniques can be implemented using TCP, WebSocket, or HTTP connections [16]. There are IoT platforms that are central components in the processing layer of IoT applications. These platforms perform middleware functionalities, such as storing and processing sensor data, fusion, mining, and anomaly detection [16]. IoT platforms can be integrated with cloud solutions, offering unlimited storage and computational resources for handling IoT big data [16]. For communication between IoT devices and platforms, protocols like REST, MQTT, and XMPP are commonly used [17]. The OGC SWE specifications define interfaces and data syntax specifications for retrieving observed data, alerting available sensor data, and tasking for new sensor data [17]. Real-time processing is vital in IoT applications. Many tools like Apache Kafka, Apache Storm, and Spark Streaming can be employed within a cloud to provide real-time processing [18].

Many IoT platforms use semantic-based architectures, where data is transformed into abstract form using rules or metadata. This enables intelligent services and integration with semantic sensor network ontologies [18]. IoT technology encompasses various communication protocols, IoT platforms, cloud solutions, real-time processing tools, and semantic-based architectures that enable the development and operation of IoT applications. Some communication protocols are discussed below.

14.2.1 Representational State Transfer (REST)

REST allows clients to interact with servers by issuing standard HTTP requests (GET, POST, PUT, DELETE) and receiving appropriate data in response. It is commonly used for pull-based data access in service-oriented architectures [16]. RESTful APIs are widely used in IoT platforms and cloud-based solutions for data retrieval and manipulation [19].

14.2.2 Message Queuing Telemetry Transport (MQTT)

A lightweight messaging protocol called MQTT was created for restricted devices and high-latency, low-bandwidth networks. It permits effective and dependable connectivity across IoT platforms and devices. MQTT is commonly used for push-based data propagation in IoT applications [19].

14.2.3 Extensible Messaging and Presence Protocol (XMPP)

XMPP is frequently utilized for the exchange of data in real time. XMPP can be used for push-based data propagation in IoT applications, enabling IoT devices to forward data to clients in real-time [19].

14.2.4 Open Geospatial Consortium Sensor Web Enablement (OGC SWE)

OGC SWE defines terms for hosting IoT platforms and defining interfaces for retrieving observed data, alerting available sensor data, and tasking for new sensor data. It utilizes trivial Web services and REST-based interfaces, with syntactic definitions in XML [19].

14.2.5 Constrained Application Protocol (CoAP)

CoAP is similar to HTTP but optimized for resource-constrained environments. CoAP enables efficient communication between IoT devices and platforms, supporting both pull-based and push-based data access [20].

These protocols play a crucial role in enabling communication, data retrieval, and real-time processing in IoT applications, catering to the specific needs of IoT platforms. Hence the performance assessment of these technologies directly affects the performance of the IoT platform.

14.3 Performance Evaluation of IoT

IoT performance evaluation mainly focuses on measuring the latencies and throughput rate of sensor data message delivery in IoT applications. The evaluation considers various components that impact the overall performance, including communication protocols, message encodings, data processing, and processing graphics over the Web [19]. The total latency time (Ttotal) is equal to the summation of transfer time (Ttransfer), processing time (Tprocess), and rendering time (Trender) [21].

The time needed for message encoding at the server side (Ttransmit) and the time data spends being transmitted from the server to the client (Tdecod) is taken into account by the authors to calculate Ttransfer [21]. Given that it is carried out within the employed library and is a component of the protocol stack, the encoding time might occasionally be challenging to directly measure [21].

The authors in [22] evaluated different technologies like REST, MQTT, XMPP, and CoAP [19]. They analyzed message encodings, including XML, JSON, and binary formats like Google protocol buffers [21]. They compared the latencies of these protocols and message formats in different scenarios. The performance evaluation also considered graphics processing on the Web, as it affects the time required for data interpretation [21].

Other evaluation techniques include the following:

14.3.1 Load Generation

The effectiveness of the platforms is assessed when dealing with various loads of requests from virtual devices. JMeter, a load generator tool, is used to simulate virtual sensors or publishers and generate different rates of requests or messages per second [23].

14.3.2 Metrics Collection

Measurements are collected using Prometheus, which acts as a monitoring platform. Prometheus server and node exporter components are used to collect information such as CPU utilization, active memory, and drop rate [24].

14.3.3 Scalability Evaluation

The scalability of the platforms is measured in terms of throughput and response time. Throughput is calculated as the number of messages received by the platform per second, and low response time indicates fast response and processing of platforms [24].

14.3.4 Stability Evaluation

The system's stability is assessed using CPU usage, active memory, and drop rate variables. The Linux Kernel tracks CPU usage, and active memory shows the pages and instructions that were loaded into memory during the test [24].

Performance evaluation of heterogeneous IoT nodes with differential QoS in IEEE 802.11ah RAW method [25] is just one example of a wide range of performance metrics. These include the following evaluation techniques:

1. Random-access response estimation scheme for IoT communications performance evaluation [26].
2. Power management techniques and the impact of limited on-node storage on MAC layer performance in industrial IoT networks [27].
3. Large-scale cellular IoT applications RACH performance analysis [28].
4. Performance evaluation of NOMA-based RF energy harvesting and information transfer for IoT relay systems with competing signals [29].
5. Exploration of the NB-IoT performance boundaries [30].
6. IoT streaming data prediction system with high performance utilizing Spark [31].
7. Performance programming method and effective estimate optimization algorithm for the SFC orchestra [32].

These evaluation techniques are used to assess the performance of the platforms in terms of scalability, stability, and robustness under different loads and conditions [23–24].

14.4 Case Studies: IoT Platforms

Many researchers [33] have used performance evaluation of different IoT platforms like ThingsBoard, Open Daylight (ODL) platform, Orion, InatelPlat and SiteWhere.

■ Open Daylight (ODL) platform: The study shows that the ODL platform, which utilizes NETCONF and SNMP protocols, demonstrates the greatest results in terms of IoT network and systems management [34].
■ Open Source IoT Platforms: The study mentions the use of open-source IoT platforms for benchmark evaluation and to decrease the difficulties in IoT application development. However, specific platforms are not mentioned [32].
■ Orion: Orion, a project of Firmware, is mentioned as one of the middleware platforms that performed well in a comparative study [35].
■ InatelPlat: InatelPlat is another platform system that performed well in the comparative study [35].

■ An open-source IoT platform called ThingsBoard offers data gathering, processing, visualization, and device management features. For connectivity, it supports common IoT protocols as MQTT, CoAP, and HTTP. Users can register, administer, and monitor various devices using the device management functionality provided by ThingsBoard. Additionally, it offers APIs that server-side programs can use to instruct devices. Data storage and visualization are supported, with options to integrate with databases like HSQLDB, PostgreSQL, and Cassandra. ThingsBoard can be linked with Kafka and Apache Spark for more advanced data processing, and it contains a role engine for the first examination of incoming messages [36].

■ Another open-source IoT middleware platform with service integration capabilities is SiteWhere. For communication, it supports a number of IoT protocols, including Restful, MQTT, AMQP, Stomp, CoAP, Socket, and Web Socket. It provides device management functionalities such as device specifications, device groups, and asset assignment. It supports databases like MongoDB, HBase, and InfluxDB for data storage. Siddhi, a software engine for complex event processing (CEP), and Apache Spark, a software engine for data analytics, can both be linked with SiteWhere. InfluxDB and Grafana can be combined with it for visualization even though it doesn't offer built-in data visualization [37].

The evaluation focuses on scalability, specifically throughput and average response time, as well as stability, including CPU and memory utilization and message drop rate. The platforms are tested under heavy loads of sensor data readings using REST and MQTT protocols. Also, various aspects such as security, congestion control, flow control, and energy consumption efficiency are covered. This performance evaluation offers insights into the performance characteristics and challenges of IoT systems, providing valuable information for researchers and practitioners in the field.

14.4.1 Insights

The outcomes of the performance assessment, various studies show, are as under:

1. Web Platforms: HTML5, Adobe Flash, and Microsoft Silverlight are all capable of running real-time IoT Web applications with similar performance levels. HTML5 is considered a mature platform with better support and performance on mobile devices.

2. Messaging Protocols: MQTT is identified as the most suitable messaging protocol for numerous IoT applications. It offers low latency and high message throughput rates. However, the study found that when using the Mosquitto message broker with a JavaScript client over WebSocket, MQTT's performance may be affected.

3. Message Encodings: JSON messages have the lowest latency in HTML5, while Adobe's AMF encoding performs well in Flash. The choice of message encoding can impact the overall performance of IoT Web applications.
4. Comparison of Protocols: The study compared the performance of different protocols, including WebSocket and long-polling. The results provide insights into the advantages and limitations of each protocol in terms of latency and message sizes.

Overall, the evaluation highlights the importance of selecting appropriate Web platforms, messaging protocols, and message encodings for IoT applications to achieve optimal performance.

The results achieved in the performance evaluation of ThingsBoard and SiteWhere platforms are as follows:

1. Throughput: In terms of throughput, ThingsBoard outperformed SiteWhere in both REST and MQTT APIs. The average throughput of ThingsBoard was 789.6 and 608.8 messages per second for REST, while SiteWhere achieved 285.5 and 265.1 messages per second [36].
2. Response Time: The average response time of ThingsBoard was lower than SiteWhere for both REST and MQTT APIs. ThingsBoard had an average response time of 511 milliseconds for REST, while SiteWhere reached 917 milliseconds [36].
3. Stability: In terms of stability, CPU utilization was higher for ThingsBoard in REST, reaching 77.1 percent with 1,000 publishers. SiteWhere, on the other hand, reached its maximum CPU usage with 500 publishers, recording 62.9 percent [38].

These results indicate that ThingsBoard performed better with respect to throughput, response time, and stability when compared to SiteWhere in the evaluated scenarios [36][38].

ThingsBoard also performs better in both REST and MQTT protocols. However, SiteWhere exhibits better CPU utilization in both protocols. Additionally, ThingsBoard demonstrates better performance with larger message sizes.

14.5 Conclusion

Evaluation of IoT platforms and consideration of different use cases are recommended to gain a more comprehensive understanding of their performance and capabilities. The performance evaluation emphasizes how crucial it is to choose the right IoT platform, reveals its advantages and disadvantages, and offers insightful data on how effectively IoT applications function on the Web. The performance evaluation offers a thorough overview of the components and technologies that affect the Web performance of IoT applications. It provides useful data for software developers to make wise choices and enhance the functionality of their IoT Web applications. It also highlights the characteristics and capabilities of these protocols and their suitability for resource-constrained IoT devices. It also discusses the challenges and trends in IoT communication protocols and identifies research opportunities in this field.

References

[1] D. Evans, The Internet of Things–how the next evolution of the internet is changing everything. *CISCO White Pap.* Apr. 2011. 1–11.

[2] J. Gubbi, R. Buyya, S. Marusic, M. Palaniswami, Internet of Things (iot): A vision, architectural elements, and future directions. *Future Gener. Comput. Syst.* 29 (7) (2013), 1645–1660.

[3] C. Bayılmış, M. Ali, Ü. Çavus, K. Küçük, A. Sevin, A survey on communication protocols and performance evaluations for Internet of Things. *Digit. Commun. Netw.* 8 (2022), 1094–1104.

[4] A. A. Ismail, H. S. Hamza, A. M. Kotb, Performance evaluation of open source IoT platforms. *2018 IEEE Global Conference on Internet of Things (GCIoT)*. Alexandria, Egypt, 2018, pp. 1–5. doi: 10.1109/GCIoT.2018.8620130.

[5] A.A. Mauro, J.P.C. Joel, Arun Kumar, Jalal Al-Muhtadi, Valery Korotaev, Performance evaluation of IoT middleware. *J. Netw. Comput. Appl.* 109 (2018), 53–65.

[6] A.R.S. Hammergren, C. Thomas, 2009. *Data Warehousing for Dummies.* second ed. Wiley, Hoboken, N.J.

[7] G. Fersi, Middleware for Internet of Things: A study, in: Distributed Computing in Sensor Systems (DCOSS). *2015 International Conference on, IEEE*, 2015, pp. 230–235.

[8] T. A. Teli, R. Yousuf, and D. A. Khan, MANET routing protocols, attacks and mitigation techniques: A review. *Int J Mech Eng.* 7(2) (2022).

[9] T. A. Teli, F. Masoodi, and R. Yousuf, "Security concerns and privacy preservation in blockchain based IoT systems: Opportunities and challenges," 2020. [Online]. Available: https://ssrn.com/abstract=3769572

[10] T.A. Teli, R. Yousuf, and D.A. Khan (2022). Ensuring secure data sharing in IoT domains using blockchain. in *Cyber Security and Digital Forensics* (eds M.M. Ghonge, S. Pramanik, R. Mangrulkar and D.-N. Le). https://doi.org/10.1002/9781119795667.ch9

[11] T. A. Teli, and F. S. Masoodi, "IoT implementation in India: A complex decision process using GRA/AHP." *2023 10th International Conference on Computing for Sustainable Global Development (INDIACom)*, New Delhi, India, 2023, pp. 773–778.

[12] A.H.H. Ngu, M. Gutierrez, V. Metsis, S. Nepal, M. Z. Sheng, IoT middleware: A survey on issues and enabling technologies. *IEEE Internet Things J.* 4 (1) Oct. 2016, 1–20.

[13] M.A. Razzaque, M. Milojevic-Jevric, A. Palade, S. Cla, Middleware for internet of things: A survey. *IEEE Internet Things J.* 3 (1) Feb. 2016, 70–95.

[14] L. Da Xu, W. He, S. Li, Internet of things in industries: A survey. *IEEE Trans. Ind. Inform.* 10 (4) (2014), 2233–2243.

[15] L. Wang, S. Hu, G. Betis, R. Ranjan, A computing perspective on smart city [guest editorial] . *IEEE Trans. Comput.* 65 (5) (2016), 1337–1338.

[16] L. Atzori, A. Iera, and G. Morabito, "The Internet of Things: A survey." *Comput. Netw.* 54 (15) Oct. 2010, 2787–2805,

[17] J. Åkerberg, M. M. Gidlund, and M. Björkman, "Future research challenges in wireless sensor and actuator networks targeting industrial automation." in *Proc. 9th IEEE Int. Conf. Ind. Inform. (INDIN)*, Jul. 2011, 410–415.

[18] Z. Babovic, and V. Milutinovic, "Novel system architectures for semantic based integration of sensor networks." *Adv. Comput.* 90, Dec. 2013, 91–183.

[19] A. Al-Fuqaha, M. Guizani, M. Mohammadi, M. Aledhari, and M. Ayyash, "Internet of Things: A survey on enabling technologies, protocols, and applications." *IEEE Commun. Surveys Tuts.* 17 (4) (2015), 2347–2376, 4th Quart..

[20] Z. Shelby, K. Hartke, and C. Bormann, The constrained application protocol (CoAP), document RFC 7252, Jun. 2014, accessed on Jul. 20, 2016. [Online] . Available: https://tools.ietf.org/html/rfc7252

[21] D. Miorandi, S. Sicari, F. De Pellegrini, and I. Chlamtac, "Internet of Things: Vision, applications and research challenges." *Ad Hoc Netw.* 10 (7) Sep. 2012, 1497–1516.

[22] Z. B. Babovic, J. Protic, and V. Milutinovic, "Web performance evaluation for Internet of Things applications." *IEEE Access,* 4 (2016), 6974–6992. doi: 10.1109/ACCESS.2016.2615181

[23] Ala Al-Fuqaha, Mohsen Guizani, Mehdi Mohammadi, Mohammed Aledhari, and Moussa Ayyash. Internet of things: A survey on enabling technologies, protocols, and applications. *IEEE Commun. Surv. Tutor.* 17 (4) (2015), 2347–2376.

[24] Padraig Scully, and Knud Lueth. IOT Platforms: Market report 2015–2021. Technical report, IoT Analytics, 2016.

[25] M. Z. Ali, J. Mišić, and V. B. Mišić, "Performance evaluation of heterogeneous IoT Nodes with differentiated Qos in Ieee 802.11ah Raw Mechanism." *IEEE Trans. Veh. Technol.* 68 (4) Apr. 2019, 3905–3918. doi: 10.1109/TVT.2019.2897127

[26] S.-S. Yoo, S.-H. Lee, S.-Y. Jung, and J.-H. Kim, "Performance evaluation of random-access response estimation scheme for IoT communications." in *2017 IEEE International Conference on Communications (ICC)* (2017), 1–6. doi: 10.1109/ICC.2017.7996507

[27] M. P. R. S. Kiran, V. Subrahmanyam, and P. Rajalakshmi, "Novel power management scheme and effects of constrained On-Node storage on performance of MAC layer for industrial IoT networks." *IEEE Trans Industr Inform.* 14 (5) May 2018, 2146–2158. doi: 10.1109/TII.2017.2766783

[28] H. G. Moussa, and W. Zhuang, "RACH performance analysis for large-scale cellular IoT applications." *IEEE Internet Things J.* 6 (2) Apr. 2019, 3364–3372. doi: 10.1109/JIOT.2018.2883101

[29] A. Rauniyar, P. E. Engelstad, and O. N. Østerbø, "Performance analysis of RF energy harvesting and information transmission based on NOMA with interfering signal for IoT relay systems." *IEEE Sens. J.* 19 (17) Sep. 2019, 7668–7682. doi: 10.1109/JSEN.2019.2914796

[30] B. Martinez, F. Adelantado, A. Bartoli, and X. Vilajosana, "Exploring the performance boundaries of NB-IoT." *IEEE Internet Things J.* 6 (3) Jun. 2019, 5702–5712. doi: 10.1109/JIOT.2019.2904799

[31] H.-Y. Jin, E.-S. Jung, and D. Lee, "High-performance IoT streaming data prediction system using Spark: A case study of air pollution." *Neural Comput & Applic.* Dec. 2019. doi: 10.1007/s00521-019-04678-9

[32] J. Zhang, R. S. Blum, and H. V. Poor, "Approaches to secure inference in the Internet of Things: Performance bounds, algorithms, and effective attacks on IoT sensor networks." *IEEE Signal Process. Mag.* 35 (5) Sep. 2018, 50–63. doi: 10.1109/MSP.2018.2842261

[33] Wasswa Shafik, S. Mojtaba Matinkhah, Melika Asadi, Zahra Ahmadi and Zahra Hadiyan. A Study on Internet of Things Performance Evaluation. *J Commun Technol, Electron Comput Sci.* 28(2020).

[34] P. Solic, Z. Blazevic, M. Skiljo, L. Patrono, R. Colella, and {and} Joel J. P. C. Rodrigues, "Gen2 RFID as IoT enabler: Characterization and performance improvement." *IEEE Wirel. Commun.* 24 (3) Jun. 2017, 33–39, doi: 10.1109/MWC.2017.1600431

[35] T. Yokotani, A. Shimuzu, Y. Sasaki, and H. Mukai, "Proposals for packet processing and performance evaluation of IoT devices." in *2017 Japan-Africa Conference on Electronics, Communications and Computers (JAC-ECC)*, 2017, 5–8. doi: 10.1109/JECECC.2017.8305766

[36] Amy Forni, and Rob Meulen, Gartner hype cycle 2016. www.gartner.com/newsroom/id/3412017 2016. [Online: accessed 28-August-2017]

[37] Jasmin Guth, Uwe Breitenb"ucher, Michael Falkenthal, Frank Leymann, and Lukas Reinfurt, Comparison of IoT platform architectures: A field study based on a reference architecture. in *Cloudification of the Internet of Things (CIoT)*, 1–6. IEEE, 2016.

[38] SiteWhere platform. www.sitewhere.org/ 2017. [Online; accessed 28-August-2017]

Chapter 15

Case Studies on IoT Systems Performance Analysis

Mohini Preetam Singh,[1] Praveen Kumar,[2] and Deepak Singh[3]

[1]Department of ECE, Meerut Institute of Engineering & Technology, Meerut, Uttar Pradesh, India

[2]Fidelity International, India

[3]Matter Vision Mechanics, India

15.1 Introduction

The Internet-of-Things has been in conversations for almost a decade now. It's a network that comprises sensors (physical, optical, analogous, or digital), data conversion mechanisms, technology to communicate the sensed data, and how to react according to the data as per requirements.

15.1.1 Why IoT Is Needed at All?

IoT is needed because humans can't be present everywhere every time, can't do things with the same efficiency in the long run, need to analyze activities to describe, diagnose, predict, and prescribe solutions for the same, for connectivity and data sharing, for automation and efficiency and data collection and analytics.

To make things more understandable let's take an example of a bearing system in any machine.

DOI: 10.1201/9781003474838-15

15.1.2 Case Study 1: Bearing Systems

To predict its time to fail and to suggest the measures to overcome its losses at the lowest cost, one must be able to understand bearing systems' workings, and the possible causes of failure. A particular analysis tool must be designed for the same. And this technology is called Digital Twin.

The faults and defects that may occur in bearing systems include:

Faults in Bearings:

(1) False Brinelling fault
(2) Micro-pitting and macro-pitting faults
(3) Scuffing faults
(4) Axial cracks fault

Defects in Bearing:

(1) Inner-race defect
(2) Outer-race defect
(3) Ball or roller defects
(4) Cage defects

But to fetch data and to analyze it, the data must be sent to systems for analysis. Software like Ansys or MATLAB can be used to draw conclusions based on different loads and rpm for three types of bearings – that is, a good bearing, intermediate bearing and faulty bearing [1].

The same data should be collected from the hardware setup and compared with the simulated results.

Finally, the results of both hardware setup and simulations are matched, then the machine learning can be applied to confirm if the bearing running at present is faulty or not. This can be done by any model for supervised learning [2].

The results of the simulations and hardware dataset collected should be accessible from anywhere, and this is where IoT comes in. Otherwise, the data gathered will stay at a particular machine and cannot be used throughout the industry. For a business model, the information should be available throughout the infrastructure.

IoT's utility for business models has made it a technology giant in today's market. Governments have joined hands with private companies to deliver the best solution in all the fields. The same layout can be implemented.

15.1.3 Importance of Technology in the Life of the Common Man

Whatever technology exists it is because it has been a necessity. Starting from a fan to computers to mobile phones, it's all about comfort. Not everyone can make tools/equipment, but everyone can use them. In today's era, the human is prone to technology, and is comfortable adapting new things if things are there to provide comfort.

Example: A lot of gadgets exist in the market to relieve elderly people from pain of muscles. In fields where engineers, artists and designers are working hard, devices fall under a few major categories:

- Geospatial
- Healthcare Sector
- Robotics
- Image Processing
- Indoor Mapping
- Defense Sector
- Precision Agriculture
- Disaster Management
- Smart Cities
- Smart Villages
- Land Records and Insurance
- Navigation

15.1.4 Case Study 2: From Healthcare Sector

Tremors, such as those caused by multiple sclerosis, stroke, traumatic brain injury, chronic renal disease, and several neurological diseases are among the signs of neurological illnesses. Some specific regions of the brain are damaged or destroyed by these disorders.

Parkinson's disease (PD) is a prevalent neurological ailment marked by slow, trembling movement, rigid limbs and altered gait, including slumped posture, shuffling steps, festination, halting of gait, and falls.

The aging population, which has a high prevalence of PD, frequently displays an increase in cases of gait-slowness brought on by other disorders, such as joint osteo-arthritis or cellular senescence. It can be difficult to correctly identify PD, particularly in the early stages of the disease. Also, another prime condition for observing tremors is in accident cases where, irrespective of age, the patients lose control over their body and fall off suddenly or face imbalance problems [3].

The cause of Parkinson's Disease is unknown, but a demanding or worrying occasion can often cause symptoms. After the demise of a relative member, a massive operation, or a vehicle accident, tremors might also end up becoming very prominent.

Additionally, stress, anxiety, and sleep deprivation constantly make tremors worse. In India, a person's annual medication cost is around 2K USD, while therapeutic surgery abroad can cost up to more than 120K USD. Patients may sustain injuries or even die because of the body's uncontrolled movement. The IoT enabled device can alert care takers and the patient when the patient crosses the limit set by doctor in the device.

15.1.5 Case Study 3: From the Agriculture Sector

India has been an agriculture-driven country for decades and a leader in various crops. A large portion of the Indian population works in agriculture and the whole country depends on this sector.

However, the problem of climate change has made a major impact on the yield of crops, leading to major losses to farmers, especially those who work on small scale agricultural lands. A major investment goes into sowing seeds, and soil preparation is at stake; if the yield is not good, farmers bear the losses.

Moreover, various conditions such as western cyclonic disturbances, have made the rain cycle unpredictable.

A proposed model, with the help of IoT hardware setup and machine learning model, will give an estimate and propose a simulated environment which will be helpful for farmers to reach out to the government and other legal bodies in case of financing through financial models.

The financial model gives a concept for understanding the financial flow of a business or a situation. Budgeting, feasibility, profitability, and the risk-ability analyses allow the farmer to make the best decisions possible for the farming business's future.

This modelling technique will help in the replication of crop cycles and mitigating the losses of farmers as well as improve agricultural techniques. This method will not only optimize the current models but also will ensure the betterment of the overall agricultural sector.

15.2 Existing IoT Infrastructure and Its Shortcomings

The devices connected and technology used for communication and the underlying framework for a system constitutes an IoT infrastructure. The useful data from various sources need to be aggregated to deduce the facts about the process and to monitor and control it. IoT is a technology that enables this monitoring through the Internet from a distance. It has various use cases in industries of all sorts, from farming to manufacturing.

The existing IoT frameworks help in data ingestion, aggregation, and control but lack in data interoperability and provide a database of collected data from the sensors. This unavailability makes the users wait for mass collection, and this delays the analysis process. In the current scenario the databases are mostly available in the form of images.

Example: In case one needs to find out the fault in welding, the data available is in terms of images instead of actual values. The lack of this availability of the database stops the user from referring to the previous feeds that might be useful for prediction tasks.

Another key component of an IoT stack is hardware, which as per technology has been modified, and platforms lack in adaptability of features that could update the simulation models and their functionality for the end user.

Example: One of the freely available IoT platforms with certain restrictions is Thingspeak.com from MATHWORKS. This platform has multiple channel settings for private and public viewing that will allow users to register different fields of interest. The data can be communicated through different API keys for writing and reading to be specific. It also supports GET and POST functions.

Thingspeak.com also support applications like:

(1) MATLAB Analysis, MATLAB Visualization to understand the variation in the data collected.
(2) Plugins, React and talkback to operate/control actuators and output devices, and so forth.
(3) It can also support MQTT protocol-supported devices.

It has no limitation on the type of data fetched. Its current feature now includes the images, too.

To understand, readers may visit this public channel: https://thingspeak.com/channels/1642978

The public data view shows four fields of interest for crop planting and cultivation, namely: temperature, humidity, heat index, and moisture. The data recorded through this project can be seen by visiting export/import tab and downloading the .csv file. The file shows the time stamp and all four fields. Since the setup for different fields was defined at different time periods, the readings in the .csv file for different columns started at different times – that is, the initial few readings for each of the fields are missing but can be visualized later on in the same column.

One advantage of such a data is that it can't be manipulated online. Example, the initial readings of Field 1 are false readings due to the wrong setup, and now they cannot be modified.

The only disadvantage is that the data cannot be guaranteed to be correct. This is because the names of the fields are specified by the account holder, but there is no information about the devices used to collect the data – that is the hardware id and other essentials are not defined. The data can be collected through any sensor and any processor, which means both the accuracy of devices and validation of data, are not confirmed.

15.3 Key Features for IoT Repository to Mitigate the Shortcomings of IoT Infrastructure

The shortcomings of existing IoT frameworks can be rectified by developing an IoT Repository. The repository needs to assure the security of devices, data security collected from devices and IoT devices' registration, certification, and testing. These are discussed below in brief with the risks involved and tasks under each category.

Security for IoT Devices: Risks involved are

(a) Eves dropping attacks during server and IoT devices' communication.
(b) Hack during the maintenance of IoT enabled devices, specially cameras.
(c) Device software bugs.
(d) A physical attack on the computing processor.

The strategy to tackle such problems need 4D approach, that is, Integrity, Availability, Authentication and Confidentiality.

Data Security of IoT Devices in the field of medical health: Risks involved are

(a) Cost factors for ensuring the harmless and tamper-free gadgets for patients/ users.
(b) The data logs of patients should not be tempered with by any third party.
(c) Framework to store all information at a single place.

Registration of IoT devices through framework: Under IoT devices registration, the following tasks must be undertaken

(a) Authentication of Registration of IoT devices under different predefined categories.
(b) Identification of Devices, users/organizations.

IoT devices Certification and Testing:

(a) Certification test designing for IoT components.
(b) Establishing standards for IoT devices testing.

The repository for IoT products:

(a) Currently, all that is available in terms of dataset, is for ML and AI models. Such datasets are mostly in the form of images.
(b) Dataset corresponding to physical sensors is rare and is not maintained on regular basis in all the parts.

15.4 Proposed Solution Architecture

15.4.1 Statement of the Problem

■ The data gathered through sensors by individual users is not shared on a common platform, which restrains the maximum utilization by other target users.

■ The lack of a common platform restricts the advancement that could be made in the field of analytics using IoT, as the only source of information available is either in the form of images due to the popularity of digital media or is owned by individual groups.

■ Also, there is a lack of common platforms that enable language-independent configurations for upcoming hardware.

■ The solution proposed will be to design a software as a service (SaaS) solution repository [4], which holds information about each IoT device deployed in the country, involving several microservices to customize architecture according to the end user.

■ The registration and authentication of user information, using Identity Access Manager. The information will be stored according to customers' persona, IOT device persona, and repository persona.

15.4.2 Objectives

■ An SaaS-based software to onboard the user and enable the authentication mechanism once user is onboarded to the platform. Data communication between server and IOT devices will be readily available; there will be scaling architecture whenever server is down.

■ The repository shall maintain the information about hardware, custom, services used to confirm the authenticity, and confidentiality through JWT Authentication of the data for the IOT devices as per TEC for the entire device module irrespective of its parts/components.

■ REST API's along with microservices for associated services domains such as agriculture. There will be separate endpoints for all the stakeholders in the value chain [5].

15.4.3 Solution Architecture

High level architecture consists of POC (Proof of Concept) components/existing components, and their integration. POC includes physical components, necessary to build the system and its supporting technologies and framework.

To divide the complete layout of a software system in simpler layout, the solution architects present the entire system in two components:

(1) A logical view which represents the flow of information and various processing steps (Figure 15.1).

In Figure 15.1, for the purpose of data loading and advanced analytics, the primary goal is to efficiently extract, transform, and load data from various sources and enable sophisticated analytics capabilities. Here is a short description of the key components and their functions:

Data Sources: These can include databases, files, APIs, streaming platforms, or external sources. Data may be structured, semi-structured, or unstructured, and may reside on-premises or in the cloud.

Data Extraction: The process of extracting data from the various sources mentioned above. This may involve using tools such as data connectors, ETL (Extract, Transform, Load) processes, or data ingestion frameworks to collect the required data.

Data Transformation: Once the data is extracted, it needs to be transformed into a suitable format for analysis. This involves cleansing, filtering, aggregating, joining, or enriching the data. Transformations may be performed using tools such as SQL, data integration platforms, or scripting languages.

Data Loading: The transformed data is loaded into a data repository or data warehouse. This could be a traditional relational database, a distributed big data platform, or a cloud-based storage service. The choice of the data storage solution depends on factors like data volume, velocity, variety, and the desired analytical capabilities.

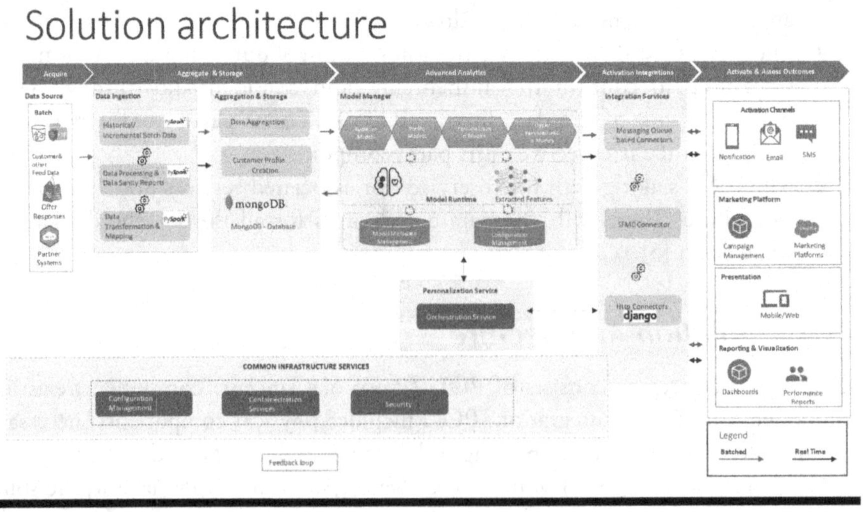

Solution architecture

Figure 15.1 Solution Architecture.

Data Modeling: To enable advanced analytics, the data needs to be structured in a way that supports efficient querying and analysis. This typically involves designing and implementing a data model or schema, such as a star schema or a data cube, which organizes the data into dimensions and facts.

Advanced Analytics: Once the data is loaded and modeled, advanced analytics techniques can be applied. This includes statistical analysis, machine learning, data mining, predictive modeling, or natural language processing. Analytical tools and libraries such as Python, R, or specialized analytics platforms are used to perform these tasks.

Visualization and Reporting: The insights derived from the advanced analytics phase are presented in a meaningful way through visualization and reporting tools. This could involve interactive dashboards, charts, graphs, or reports that allow users to explore and understand the analyzed data.

(2) Deployment view: This includes the technological aspects that will be used for processing the information collected like REST API, and so forth (Figure 15.2).

Both views are categorized under the same heads: Data Acquire, Data Ingestion, Aggregation and Storage, Advanced Analytics, Activation Integration and Activate and Access Outcomes.

Data-acquire and ingestion, although it sounds the same, they have different natures. Data-acquire means collecting data from different sources, whereas Data

Deployment Diagram

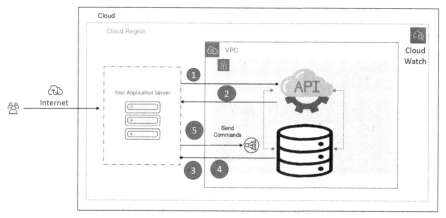

Figure 15.2   Deployment Diagram.

ingestion means transporting the data from one source to another source. Data aggregation is yet another concept of transforming the collected data for protocols acceptable at receiver's end.

In Figure 15.2, The final step is to integrate the data loading and advanced analytics components into the overall system architecture. This may involve connecting with other systems, deploying the solution on appropriate infrastructure, ensuring data security and privacy, and monitoring the system's performance and reliability.

15.5 Summary of the Proposed Solution

The primary focus is to design a repository of IoT, which provides SaaS software solutions.

The vision is to provide the software solution for a complete bundle of IoT repositories. The primary goal is to provide a platform to enable the service to any IoT device and on top of that enable the analytics historical and incremental data stacked.

There will be a defined process where the user can register according to the category and subcategory of IoT devices. Also, some pre-defined stands will be available for certain domains, like Agriculture, Healthcare, Logistics, Telecom, and so forth.

The repository can have profound use cases in agriculture which could be beneficial also for insurance companies and financial model development for farming.

15.6 Technology behind IoT

The case studies mentioned in this chapter so far and in coming write up can be implemented by providing the entire IoT framework, which will need various components:

(1) A sensor node or mobile terminal (mote) is said to be comprised of 4 basic units:

The Sensor (analog or digital), Processor (to process the information after acquiring it and conversion if necessary), battery (for life of product), communication technology (to communicate the data from IoT sensor node to server or between IoT sensor source nodes and sink node or between sink node and the server).

(2) Integrated Development environment for simulating the circuits, development of device software, libraries and Application Programming Interface.
(3) Protocols like MQTT, COAP, and so forth will be needed for IoT framework due to less overhead as compared to HTTP. IoT protocols support

publish–subscribe architecture rather than client server architecture in the rest of the cases [4].

(4) Simulators for processing units like Raspberry Pi etc which will decrease the time to market by indicating the logical problems at the time of simulations rather than implementing everything on hardware and get stuck.

(5) Analysis tools like Machine learning predefined models for analysis of the data collected to reach to a conclusion.

(6) Data storage facility for every user so that the data can be retained for a longer duration.

15.6.1 Some Key Technologies behind IoT

Sensor Technology: Sensors are fundamental components of IoT systems. They gather data from the physical world and convert it into digital signals. Various types of sensors are used in IoT, such as temperature sensors, humidity sensors, motion sensors, pressure sensors, and many more. These sensors detect changes in the environment and provide input for IoT devices to act upon.

Connectivity: IoT relies on different connectivity technologies to enable communication between devices and systems. Some common connectivity technologies:

- **Wi-Fi:** Wireless local area network (WLAN) technology that allows devices to connect to the internet and exchange data over short distances.
- **Bluetooth:** Short-range wireless technology primarily used for connecting devices in close proximity, such as smartphones and IoT devices.
- **Cellular Networks**: IoT devices can utilize cellular networks, such as 3G, 4G, or 5G, to connect to the internet, providing broader coverage and mobility.
- **Low-Power Wide Area Networks (LPWAN)**: LPWAN technologies, like LoRaWAN and Sigfox, are designed for low-power, long-range communication, making them suitable for IoT devices that need to transmit small amounts of data over long distances.
- **Cloud Computing**: Cloud computing plays a significant role in IoT infrastructure. IoT devices can send the collected data to the cloud for storage, processing, and analysis. Cloud platforms provide the necessary computational resources, scalability, and data management capabilities required for IoT applications. Cloud computing allows for centralized data storage and provides a foundation for data analytics and machine learning algorithms to extract valuable insights from the accumulated data.
- **Edge Computing**: Edge computing is an emerging technology that complements cloud computing in IoT deployments. In edge computing, data processing and analytics occur closer to the data source, reducing latency and improving real-time decision-making. Edge devices, such as gateways and edge servers, enable

local data processing, filtering, and storage. This distributed architecture reduces the need for sending all data to the cloud, improves response times, and enhances privacy and security by keeping sensitive data localized.

■ **Data Analytics and Artificial Intelligence**: IoT generates vast amounts of data, and extracting meaningful insights from this data is crucial. Data analytics techniques, including statistical analysis, machine learning, and artificial intelligence, are employed to process and derive actionable insights from IoT data. These technologies enable predictive maintenance, anomaly detection, optimization algorithms, and intelligent decision-making in various IoT applications.

■ **Security**: IoT security is a critical aspect due to the increasing number of connected devices and the potential risks associated with data breaches and unauthorized access. IoT security technologies encompass encryption, authentication mechanisms, access control, secure communication protocols, and regular software updates to mitigate vulnerabilities.

These technologies, combined with ongoing advancements and research, continue to shape the IoT landscape, enabling smarter, more connected environments across industries and everyday life.

15.7 Problem Analysis and Designing a Solution

For any technique to be adopted by masses as a product or service, its value must be perceived clearly by potential customers and end users.

Value perceived by these potential end users has the following five components:

(1) **Utility**: Efficacy, efficiency, functionality, product life and durability which comprises of ingress protection (Ingress protection code like IP65 for prevention from dust and water) to protect the device from tempering and drop strength.

(2) **Usability**: Demographics, cultural anthropometrics (size): this comprises of medical issues like allergy to a certain fabric and hence instructing patient to wear knee pads or massagers, etc.

(3) **Safety and Comfort**: Safety comprises Ergonomics, comfort, forgivable mistakes, injury chances during usage; comfort on the other hand indicates the endurance time for usage in a single go.

(4) **Manufacturing**: Targeting production line: artisanal production, low volume production and mass production.

(5) **Joy and esthetics**: Product design and industrial design.

Basic rule applied by business giants like Apple, is to start with Rule of Joy and esthetics. Later on once they are satisfied by the looks, they push it to engineers to design the machine and customize the hardware to fit in that design. Asking target audiences before giving them any product will lead to failures. Instead, giving a product to the customers and then asking them to use it, will give a valuable feedback based on which, the strategies can be formulated.

(6) **A Big Mistake:** The target audience won't buy a product if it goes above a certain range. In fact, if the product can maintain a supply chain, there can be a possibility that the product cost will go down as the number of products increase and hence it will come under affordable range.

15.8 To Analyze a Problem and Design a Solution for an IoT Project

Define the Problem: Clearly define the problem statement or the specific challenge you want to address with your IoT solution. Understand the context, stakeholders, and objectives associated with the problem. For example, the problem could be inefficient energy usage in a commercial building or lack of real-time monitoring in a manufacturing process.

Conduct Research: Gather information about the problem domain, existing solutions, and technologies related to IoT. Understand the limitations and shortcomings of current approaches. Explore successful case studies and best practices relevant to your problem.

Identify Requirements: Identify the specific requirements and constraints of your IoT solution. Consider functional requirements (what the solution should do) and non-functional requirements (performance, scalability, security, etc.). Involve stakeholders and end-users to gather their inputs and ensure their needs are considered.

Analyze Data Flow: Visualize the data flow in your IoT system. Identify the data sources (sensors, devices, etc.), data transmission paths, data processing points, and data storage requirements. This analysis will help you understand the data lifecycle and make informed decisions about data collection, processing, and storage.

Security and Privacy Considerations: Assess the security and privacy risks associated with your IoT solution. Identify potential vulnerabilities and design appropriate security measures, such as encryption, authentication, access control, and secure communication protocols. Consider privacy regulations and ensure user consent and data protection.

System Architecture: Design the overall architecture of your IoT solution. Determine the components, their interactions, and the communication protocols to be used. Decide on the distribution of intelligence between edge devices and cloud systems. Consider factors such as scalability, reliability, real-time requirements, and power consumption.

Select IoT Technologies: Based on your requirements and architecture, select the appropriate IoT technologies, including sensors, communication protocols, gateways, cloud platforms, and analytics tools. Consider factors such as interoperability, compatibility, availability, and community support when choosing these technologies.

Develop Prototypes: Build prototypes or proof-of-concept implementations to validate your design and test its feasibility. Develop and integrate the necessary hardware, software, and firmware components. Use simulation tools or physical devices to emulate real-world scenarios and evaluate the performance of your solution.

Iterative Development: Adopt an iterative approach to develop and refine your IoT solution. Gather feedback from stakeholders and end-users and incorporate it into subsequent iterations. Continuously test and evaluate the solution's performance, making improvements as needed.

Deployment and Evaluation: Deploy your IoT solution in a real-world environment and assess its performance. Monitor the system, collect user feedback, and measure key performance indicators. Evaluate the solution's effectiveness in solving the identified problem and meeting the defined requirements.

Acknowledgement

The Authors extend their sincere gratitude to Arjun Palawat, Controller, NMRC, India for his time to timely review the manuscript.

References

1. Chirag Agarwal et al., "Fault Prediction and Diagnosis of Bearing Assembly" accepted in *ICMETE2023 7th International Conference on Micro-Electronics and Telecommunication Engineering*.
2. Shagun Chandrvanshi et al., "Bearing Fault Diagnosis using Machine Learning Models" accepted in *ICMETE2023 7th International Conference on Micro-Electronics and Telecommunication Engineering*.
3. Anubhav Agarwal et al., "GUI-Enabled Wearable Solution for Tremor Detection & Fall Prevention" submitted in *2nd International Conference on Robotics, Control, Automation and Artificial Intelligence (RCAAI 2023)*.
4. Mohini Preetam Singh et al.," Blockchain Security for Internet of Things enabled Business Services" accepted in *ICICAT-2023 International Conference on IoT, Communication and Automation Technology*.
5. H. Garg and M. Dave, "Securing IoT Devices and Securely Connecting the Dots Using REST API and Middleware," NIT Kurukshetra, Haryana, India, 2016.

Chapter 16

Privacy and Security Issues in Smart Homes in an IoT Environment

Bazila Farooq

School of Computer Application, Lovely Professional University, Jalandhar, Punjab, India

16.1 Introduction

In the age of globalization, the development of information and communication technology creates substantial hurdles for businesses to maintain development and expansion. In terms of system vulnerability, the development of efficient security systems and the accessibility of diverse security tools both supporting and antagonistic present difficulties. The integrity and accessibility of information can also be impacted by the quality of networks and data transmission medium.

Companies constantly modify their products, services, and marketing plans to be competitive in their particular marketplaces. To preserve stability and increase profitability in the telecommunications sector, outstanding customer service is crucial. Future predictions predict that computers will outperform humans in terms of computational power and play a dominant role. When intelligence is incorporated into the administration and operation of residential environments to improve comfort, healthcare, safety, security, and energy conservation, this is referred to as a "smart home" or "modern application of ubiquitous computing" [1]. This position, which is consistent with the strategy used in this survey report, emphasizes the convergence of two different but complementary perspectives on the functioning of smart homes: system-centric and user-centric [2].

The early twentieth century was the origin of the user-centric approach, which focuses on occupant comfort and has developed over time. On the other hand, with the development of information and communication technology (ICT) and the introduction of smart energy infrastructure, the system-centric approach arose with a focus on building efficiency. The number of "smart" gadgets that can connect to the Internet and be operated remotely through apps has increased dramatically during the past ten years. The Internet of Things (IoT) is a network of devices containing connections, electronics, software, and sensors. A cloud-centric IoT-based method has emerged as a leading option for the development of smart homes in tandem with the growth of cloud computing [3]. With the IoT, functionality will give way to connection and data-driven decision-making, where the interconnectivity of devices will increase their utility. The Internet of Things, however, extends beyond the straightforward tethering of gadgets and sensors to wired or wireless networks.

To facilitate communication between humans and machines, it covers a deep integration of the virtual and real worlds. It may be viewed as a complex web of interconnected networks, each with a different scale, that together make up a massive global web [4]. This covers using technological equipment from a distance as well as making use of the Internet and IoT (Internet of Things) technology. Users may now control and improve electrical gadgets that are connected to the Internet thanks to these developments. As a result, the necessity for face-to-face communication with people will decline as computers and other electronic devices exchange information more often. Additionally, this will result in an increase in Internet users, who will then have access to a variety of online resources and services. The biggest obstacle in the IoT space is bringing the informational and physical worlds together. This entails properly integrating and processing data that has been collected from electronic devices through user-device interfaces (see Figure 16.1).

16.2 Literature Review

An overview of earlier studies on enhancing security and privacy in the Internet of Things (IoT) space is given in this section. A smart home is made up of many different components, such as sensors, appliances, and actuators, some of which may not be naturally intelligent. While a sensor produces data, it does not improve the home environment on its own. Similarly to this, a thermostat cannot be deemed intelligent if the homeowner must manually change the temperature in response to outside conditions. Automation rather than actual "smartness" is simply keeping the temperature steady. When all environmental data is collectively gathered and examined, patterns are discovered, and choices are made without human input: real intelligence develops.

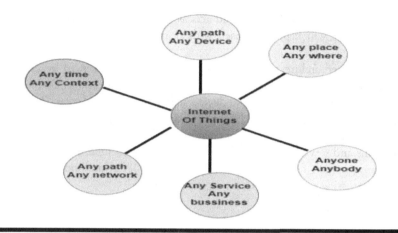

Figure 16.1   Internet of Things (IOT) vision.

Source: Created by the author.

A smart environment is defined by this coupling of data and judgment. The architecture of a smart home is determined by how devices interact with one another, where sensor and appliance usage data is kept, and how this data is processed to spot trends and other factors, and how individuals and gadgets may communicate with one another. Various architectural strategies have been investigated in earlier study investigations. To enable data collecting and action execution, Soliman et al. [5] suggested that system architecture for a smart house requires coupling sensors and actuators to a microprocessor. The microcontroller-based sensors use wireless ZigBee technology to send data to a central server. The data is then uploaded to cloud storage by the server via an application programming interface (API). A front-end application, storage, and a back-end application are all parts of the cloud solution. On the back end, data is specially handled and analyzed using Google App Engine. A Web application allows users to see their surroundings and manage their devices. An architecture including controllers (computer servers), sensors (motion/light/door/temperature sensors), and actuators (relays) at the physical layer was proposed by Cook et al. [6].

The communication layer is made up of wireless communication methods such as ZigBee wireless mesh. A publish/subscribe pattern is the foundation of the middleware layer. By adding a universal interface, Jie et al. [7], established a scalable architectural paradigm. Their design makes it simple to add or remove devices from the smart home infrastructure. The architecture is composed of five layers: the resource layer, which includes end devices, sensors, and appliances; the interface layer, which serves as an abstraction between lower-level layers and the devices; the agent layer, which manages individual resources through RFID tags; the kernel layer, which handles agent management and acts as the primary controller; and the user application layer, which provides users with an interface for managing services and other features.

A cloud-based architecture dubbed CloudThings was presented by Zhou et al. [8] to accelerate the creation and administration of IoT applications. Direct Internet connectivity is made possible by end devices (sometimes referred to as Things) using the CoAP protocol with 6LowPAN. As an online platform, CloudThings serves as a complete application architecture for creating, deploying, and administering Things applications and services. In conclusion, the research presented here provides many architectural models for smart homes, each with a special method for connecting devices, processing data, and interacting with users.

16.3 Architecture

The service platform, smart devices, a home gateway, and a home network are the four components that make up a smart home [9]. The smart home has several linked gadgets that intelligently communicate information through a home network [10]. Figure 16.2 presents a general, cloud-based architecture of a smart home.

Smart devices: A network of wearable gadgets or sensors that are frequently affixed to or integrated into the human body is known as the Body Area Network (BAN). These gadgets may track exercise levels, keep an eye on vital signs, and gather health-related information. Smartwatches, medical sensors, and fitness trackers are a few examples of BAN gadgets. The other elements of the smart home system can connect wirelessly with the BAN devices. The gadgets and appliances that are close to the user, often in a single room or a small area, are included in the Personal Area Network (PAN) [11]. Devices like smart speakers, thermostats, lighting

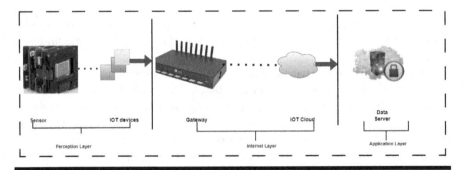

Figure 16.2   Architecture of a Smart Home.

Source: Created by the author.

controls, security cameras, and home entertainment systems are part of this network. PAN devices are connected and exchange information with one another to provide automation, control, and monitoring functions that improve the user's quality of life. A network of wearable gadgets or sensors that are frequently affixed to or integrated into the human body is known as the Body Area Network (BAN). Through a gateway situated at the network's edge, the BAN and PAN networks are linked. Communication between the internal networks and the external Internet is made easier by the gateway, which serves as an intermediate. It acts as a bridge, enabling data to move between smart home appliances and remote or cloud-based applications. The gateway frequently offers Wi-Fi, Ethernet, or cellular network connectivity choices, allowing for easy integration of the smart home system with outside services and remote administration.

Home gateway: Within the ecosystem of a smart home, a gateway device is essential for enabling connectivity between end devices, sensors, systems, and the cloud. The hardware and technology requirements for an effective smart home gateway device are covered in research by Hosek et al. Similar to this, Guoqiang et al. provide a solution for a customizable smart home gateway that can convert disparate sensor data into a standardized format and supports different communication protocols. By supporting several communication protocols, the gateway device acts as a central hub to promote interoperability among disparate devices. It serves as a bridge between end devices and the cloud, enabling smooth data transmission and management. Furthermore, the gateway device has enough processing power to carry out edge computing operations, enabling local data processing before data transmission to the cloud. The gateway device's capacity to increase the security of the smart home network is one of its key advantages. The gateway device filters and keeps track of all incoming and outgoing communication by serving as a communication bridge [12]. With this extra security measure, commands and data are checked before they are sent to end devices, which have fewer resources and are less safe. The gateway device contributes to the improvement of the smart home network's overall availability, dependability, and security in this way. It's more powerful computing capabilities and scalable design provide the opportunity for putting in place reliable security measures. Additionally, the gateway device's cloud integration function enables simple connectivity with other services. Data visualization, smart home device management, and user access and role administration are a few examples of these services. The gateway device increases the functions and opportunities available within the ecosystem for smart homes by using the capabilities of the cloud [13].

Data servers: The National Institute of Standards and Technology (NIST) defines "cloud computing" as an architecture that permits simple, on-demand access to a shared pool of reconfigurable computing resources. These resources, which may be swiftly deployed and delivered with little effort or contact from service providers, can include networks, servers, storage, applications, and services [14]. The cloud is used in the context of smart home design to gather and compile data from many sources, including sensors, actuators, appliances, and other devices. The most sophisticated level of the architecture is the cloud, which provides a reliable infrastructure for storing and processing enormous volumes of data [15]. It has vital traits including high dependability, scalability, and autonomy [16]. It is sometimes referred to as a cloud-based or cloud-centric architecture due to its important position in this framework [15]. Although CPU power has substantially increased, network bandwidth has not, leading to performance problems. This problem is resolved by fog computing, which processes data near its origin before transmitting a compressed version to the cloud. Fog computing takes place on the gateway device in a smart home, minimizing the amount of data transferred to the cloud and speeding up reaction times. Additionally, it prevents single points of failure and permits two-way communication between the gateway and the cloud. Although it uses a different methodology, edge computing is a new computing paradigm with goals that are comparable to those of fog computing. Lopez et al.'s [17] discussion of edge computing in the context of user-driven applications placed a strong emphasis on maintaining privacy and anonymity. Shi et al. [18] performed case studies to examine the difficulties and possibilities associated with this paradigm, while Shi and Dustdar [19] discovered unresolved privacy and security-related problems. By allowing each end device in the smart home to autonomously decide whether data should be kept locally, processed, or transferred to the cloud, edge computing, in contrast to fog computing, advances localized computation. With this strategy, decentralization is improved and the chance of single points of failure is decreased. Tasks involving data processing and decision-making are done on the edge Numerous linked gadgets intelligently share information over a home network in a smart home setting. A home gateway is therefore present to control the information flow between smart devices and the outside network. The service platform is dependent on a service provider who provides the home network with a range of services (see Figure 16.3).

16.4 Security and Privacy in the IoT

IoT security standards are different from those for traditional systems. IoT is a special difficulty since it integrates physical and digital components, adding extra complexity [20–21]. With billions of linked devices producing enormous volumes of data, IoT requires connecting a wide range of heterogeneous smart gadgets. Traditional security solutions are inappropriate for these resource-constrained IoT devices since many of them have little processing power, little memory, and a confined battery supply. Data integrity, availability, and confidentiality are only a few of the high-level security objectives set out by the National Institute of Standards and Technology (NIST). Different technologies, including encryption,

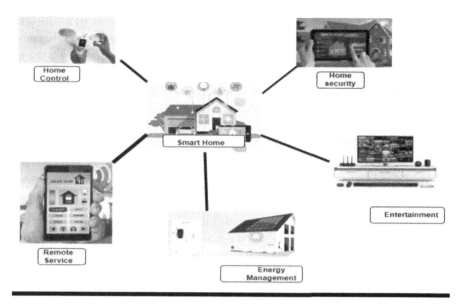

Figure 16.3   Smart Home IOT applications.

Source: Created by the author.

authentication, access control, and key management, are used to accomplish these objectives. However, special security requirements emerge when taking into account the distinctive characteristics of IoT [21].

Confidentiality: The guarantee that only approved systems or people will be given access to data. Data confidentiality is essential to the Internet of Things because it ensures the safe transfer of data while restricting access to authorized parties. Transmissions over the Internet are frequently secured using tools like IPsec [22] and TLS [23]. The overhead associated with these strategies is prohibitive, however, due to the resource limitations of IoT devices. The most important areas of confidentiality sensitivity in the IoT setting are communication, storage, localization/tracking, and identity [24].

Integrity: A smart device becomes subject to security risks when it is linked to a wireless network. By adding malicious software or employing malicious code to change a service's intended functioning, an attacker can take advantage of this vulnerability. Without safeguarding data integrity, this malicious code can spread across the whole smart home system, disrupting services for smart homes. Keeping up the integrity of smart home services is so essential. Employing security mechanisms like hash functions and digital signatures for important information or module instructions is crucial to maintaining the integrity of smart devices [25–26]. These methods offer defense against unauthorized alterations or tampering by assisting in the authenticity and integrity verification of the information and symbols. Keeping data's integrity in IoT systems is essential to prevent data from being altered or modified while being transmitted, especially when taking into account the wireless transmission medium and Low-Power and Lossy Networks (LLNs) that are frequently used in IoT deployments. These settings are vulnerable to attacks that might try to change or tamper with the data being communicated and are prone to data losses. Integrating checksums into each packet is one method of maintaining data integrity.

A checksum is a number that is computed from a packet's contents and added to the packet itself. The checksum is recalculated by the receiver using the data it has just received, and it is then compared to the checksum that was attached to the packet. When the checksums don't line up, it means that the data may have been changed during transmission if the checksums do not agree. Message Integrity Codes (MIC) are another technique for achieving data integrity. A MIC is a type of cryptographic method that enables message integrity to be checked. Using a secret key, the message data is hashed or given a cryptographic signature. The recipient can then compare the newly calculated MIC to the received MIC to confirm the message's integrity. If they line up, it guarantees that the message hasn't been changed. The danger of data modification by attackers is decreased by these measures, which provide an additional layer of assurance that the data is intact and unmodified throughout wireless transmission [26].

Availability: The term "availability" describes a system's or a device's capacity to reliably deliver the necessary information and services at any time. However, because resource-constrained devices are involved in Low-Power and Lossy Networks (LLNs) in the Internet of Things, assuring availability presents difficulties. These weaknesses can be used by attackers to initiate attacks against the network, such as DoS assaults. Strong security methods, like traditional security mechanisms, can improve the security of networks and devices while simultaneously affecting availability. On devices with limited resources, the high overhead brought on by these methods might result in a delay in processing and transmission time. As a result, the device's battery life is reduced and the transmission time is impacted, which eventually affects network availability. The danger of data fabrication and manipulation exists when a smart device communicates with a server or surface through a wireless network while operating offline. The normal operation of smart gadgets may be interfered with by this fictitious data, decreasing user convenience. A decrease in inconvenience can lead to service overflows, financial losses, and significant safety risks, such as higher electrical expenses. Limiting non-essential activities and granting access to just functional operations are vital for ensuring the availability of smart devices. The integrity and dependability of smart devices can be preserved by restricting access and concentrating on crucial features [27–28].

Authenticity: In the context of IoT, authentication is the process of confirming the identity of communicating entities. Whether it is devices communicating with other devices or with humans, it is crucial to ensure that they are legitimate and authorized entities. The purpose of authentication is to prevent unauthorized entities from gaining access to valuable resources. There is a serious risk due to the various gadgets' disregard for security. The entire smart home environment may be compromised if malicious code or a modified module is inserted into a smart device, opening the door for the device to be used for malicious activities like launching distributed denial of service (DDoS) or denial of service (DoS) attacks or leaking confidential information. Furthermore, if an attacker passes off a changed module as a genuine one, it may operate as a backdoor for unlawful acts, reducing the usefulness of the genuine module and decreasing overall availability. Implementing authentication techniques for smart devices is therefore essential. Using certificates as a method of authentication is one option [29–30].

Authorization: It is crucial to make sure that the access privileges for each entity in a smart home system are accurately established to preserve security. According to their identities and responsibilities, entities (people, devices, or services) are either granted or denied permission through the process of access control. To elaborate on this, access control entails creating and overseeing the policies that specify what operations each entity is permitted to carry out within the system. The amount of access provided to various entities is specified by these policies, which also identify the resources they may use and the activities they can carry out on them. These regulations are enforced by access control systems by authenticating and authorizing entities. Verifying an entity's identification helps to confirm that it is, in fact, who it says it is. This may entail security measures like biometrics, digital certificates, and usernames and passwords. The permissions and privileges that the entity has are determined through authorization, which takes place after the entity has been authenticated. Role-based access control (RBAC), attribute-based access control (ABAC), and discretionary access control (DAC) are just a few of the strategies that may be used to create access control. RBAC gives entities roles and bases permissions on those roles. ABAC makes access decisions based on factors related to entities, such as their location or job title. DAC enables a resource's owner to manage access to that resource [31–32]

Non-repudiation: Establishing procedures that offer unquestionable proof or evidence to back the veracity of such claims is necessary to maintain the integrity and verifiability of claims made by entities within a smart home system. Non-repudiation is the term used frequently to describe this idea. To elaborate, non-repudiation makes sure that a party cannot retract its deeds or assertions once they have been stated. It gives reassurance that there is solid proof establishing the sincerity and reliability of the entity's activities or communications. Non-repudiation may be accomplished in the context of a smart home system using a variety of techniques, including audit trails and digital signatures. To produce a distinct digital fingerprint of a communication or document that can be confirmed by anybody using, digital signatures require cryptographic techniques [33–34]. This guarantees that the message or document is authentic and that the purported sender sent it. On the other hand, audit trails document all system-related activities and events in chronological order. This comprises details like who carried out an activity, what action was carried out, and when it happened. The actions of entities inside the smart home system may be tracked and verified by keeping a strong audit trail, giving a clear and unquestionable record of their activities. An effective smart home system will include non-repudiation methods to improve responsibility and trust between parties. It assures that all assertions or acts made by system participants may be supported by incontrovertible evidence, minimizing the possibility of disagreements, fraud, or malicious activities [35]

16.5 Concerns with IoT Privacy Protection

The privacy risks to the Internet of Things may be divided into two primary groups: those that violate user privacy and those that violate device/network security. Both of these groups are depicted in Figure 16.4.

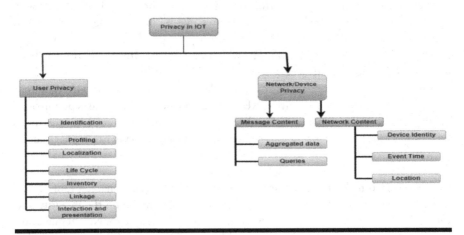

Figure 16.4   Privacy issues in IOT.

Source: Created by the author.

16.5.1 User Privacy Violation Threats

The prevalence of smart gadgets in our environment has increased the number of privacy intrusions. These gadgets record and monitor many facets of our life, such as our habits, activities, and even health. Consider the smart home setting, where it is now feasible to record a person's departure and arrival times as well as their exercise routines, sleeping habits, and other activities. These invasions of privacy include the following:

1. By associating an individual entity with a particular identifier, such as a name and location, identification creates a risk.
2. Localization and tracking entail the risk of figuring out and keeping track of someone's movements using a variety of tools, such as GPS, Web traffic, or tracking their mobile position.
3. By connecting user activities, such as surfing patterns, website visits, and product purchases with their identities, profiling poses a hazard. Businesses may determine people's interests using this aggregated data.
4. The growth of smart gadgets and creative ways to interact with systems and provide consumers feedback are all included under interaction and presentation. When private information is shared between the system and users, this constitutes a privacy risk.
5. When something is sold or ownership is changed, there are lifecycle transitions that might expose private information from the prior owner, such as personal images and movies that were left on a mobile phone. The likelihood of privacy breaches as a result of ownership transitions is predicted to increase with the planned expansion of connected devices.
6. Attacks on inventories entail unauthorized entry and the gathering of information about the presence and characteristics of personal property. Inventory data may be used by thieves to assess a place and determine the best times to commit thefts.
7. Linkage entails the integration of several systems, however, when systems are connected to integrate various information sources, there is a higher risk of unauthorized access and data leakage.

16.5.2 Network/Devices Privacy Violation Threats

Content-oriented, often referred to as data-oriented, and context-oriented are the two main areas of protecting device privacy. Protecting the privacy of data gathered from the network is a key component of content-oriented techniques. On the other hand, context-oriented techniques place a higher priority on safeguarding contextual data, including the whereabouts of the source and destination nodes and the moment at which messages are sent. Data can be compromised in content-oriented privacy preservation through data-analysis attacks, where attackers try to decipher the transmitted communications' encrypted data. In contrast, attackers are unable to decipher the conveyed messages in context-oriented privacy preservation. Instead, they eavesdrop on wireless conversations and examine traffic patterns to obtain data, such as the locations of important nodes (such as the source or destination node).

16.6 Security Attacks

The previously described essential security objectives are frequently the target of security threats in the context of smart homes. These dangers may be roughly divided into two categories. The first class of assaults, referred to as "passive attacks," focuses on data gathering or information exploitation from the system without directly affecting its resources. The objective of passive assaults is information acquisition without modification, often accomplished by eavesdropping or traffic analysis [36]. While traffic analysis examines traffic patterns to glean important information, eavesdropping is unlawfully collecting ongoing communications. Since these attacks don't change data, it might be difficult to identify them, which emphasizes the necessity for preventative measures rather than detection. The second kind, referred to as "active attacks," includes attacks that seek to alter system resources or obstruct its operation. Data alteration or the introduction of false data into the system are two examples of active assaults. Masquerading, replay assaults, message alteration, denial of service, and malicious software are typical types of active attacks. Masquerading happens when an intrusion attempts to get unauthorized privileges by pretending to be a genuine entity. To create an unauthorized effect, replay attacks entail collecting and retransmitting signals. Attacks involving message modification involve changing the text of lawful communications or interfering with the time and delivery of messages to accomplish unauthorized results [37] A cyberattack known as a denial of service (DoS) attempt aims to stop or restrict the use of a system's communication resources. The goal is to temporarily or permanently block the intended users from accessing the targeted system. These assaults overload the system with requests, or they exhaust its resources to the point that genuine users are prevented from using it. Malicious software assaults, on the other hand, are cyberattacks that make use of flaws in a system to alter, obliterate, or steal data as well as obtain unapproved access to system resources. Viruses, worms, Trojan horses, ransomware, and spyware are just a few examples of malicious software or malware. These assaults can be started via software flaws, social engineering tricks, or deceiving people into downloading or running malicious programs. Attacks by malware try to jeopardize the targeted system's availability, confidentiality, and integrity. Important files could be altered or deleted, data might be corrupted, backdoors for unauthorized access might be installed, or private data might be stolen. Malware may be created to take advantage of certain flaws in software or operating systems, or it may spread through email attachments, nefarious websites, or infected files. In conclusion, malicious software attacks target internal weaknesses to alter, delete, steal information, or obtain unauthorized access to system resources, whereas denial of service attacks concentrate on stopping or suspending the availability of communication resources. To reduce the dangers posed by these assaults on system operation, stability, and security, effective security measures are required [38].

16.7 Impact Evaluation

This study makes use of the impact level assessment criteria specified in FIPS 199 [39] to determine the relevance and sensitivity of certain interactions as well as the level of effect presented by threats inside the smart home/smart grid context. Threats' potential effects are divided into three categories by FIPS 199: low, moderate, and high. In the context of this evaluation, the possible impact is denoted by the number [40].

1. **Low (L):** If it is anticipated that a breach of one or more of the security objectives listed above will only have a little negative impact on the operations, the assets, or the occupants of smart homes. Limited negative impacts might include a decline in an entity's capacity to effectively carry out its core responsibilities, modest asset damage, minor financial losses, or slight human injury.

2. **Moderate (M):** If it is anticipated that a breach of one or more of the security objectives outlined above would significantly harm the operations, assets, or occupants of smart homes. Major adverse effects include, but are not limited to, the loss of life or injuries that are life-threatening, major injury to persons, significant asset damage, large financial losses, or severe impairment to an entity's capacity to effectively carry out its principal responsibilities.

3. **High (H):** If it is anticipated that the breach of one or more of the security objectives listed above would have a severe or catastrophic negative impact on the operations, the assets, or the inhabitants of smart homes. Serious degradation or loss of an entity's capacity to carry out its essential tasks, significant injury to assets, significant financial losses, or serious harm to people are all examples of severe or catastrophic adverse impacts.

Technology breakthroughs and the blending of different technologies have changed the way people view the Internet of Things (IoT) since 2014. These technologies include Internet connectivity, embedded systems, wireless communication, and microelectromechanical systems (MEMS). As a result, every industry has the potential to aid in the development of the IoT [41]. While IoT-based smart homes have many advantages, they are also open to a variety of assaults [42]. By taking advantage of its network or local communication interface, an attacker can directly target a field device or an interconnection device, such as a gateway. Additionally, insecure devices can be impersonated by attackers who take advantage of them. Through the home gateway, household appliances are often linked to a wired or wireless network. The viewpoint on the Internet of Things (IoT) has changed since 2014. As the entrance point for external connections, the home gateway can have instantaneous effects on the entire household network [43]. The device or perception layer, the network layer, and the applications layer make up the usual architecture of an IoT-based smart home. Figure 16.5 shows a typical IoT-based smart home setting as well as the security threats that have been discovered and their accompanying mitigation strategies. It's vital to remember that the IoT architecture might include security issues at many stages. For instance, while trying to access the primary system settings, the IoT gateway, or the login procedure for smart home apps, there is a danger of unauthorized access. A strong authentication technique should be used at these places to reduce this danger. Using biometric technology as a component of a multi-factor authentication system is one strategy.

16.8 Security Challenges Smart Home Environment

Due to the lack of end-to-end encryption across IoT components in smart home environments, bad actors can intercept communication and obtain unauthorized access to critical information. The lack of encryption in core protocols like SSDP makes this vulnerability much worse by allowing adversaries to locate and use functional smart hubs [42]. A major challenge in IoT architectures is defending against Denial of Service (DoS) and its distributed counterpart, DDoS. It is even more difficult to effectively defend IP-based services at the moment due to the lack of robust security infrastructures. Additionally, many low-cost IoT manufacturers overlook the implementation of mechanisms for validating firmware integrity during installation, upgrades, and operation. Due to the lack of trusted boot processes, IoT devices are susceptible to software flaws [43]. The frequent usage of default settings in IoT installations is a serious risk.

1. Compatibility: There is currently no widely recognized standard for the interoperability of tagging and monitoring technology. Manufacturers would need to agree on a universal standard, such as Bluetooth or USB, to overcome this drawback.
2. Complexity: The Internet of Things is no different from other complex systems in that it has a greater failure rate by nature. You may have an excess, for instance, if both you and your spouse learn that your milk has run out and decide to buy new milk separately. Software flaws can sometimes have unforeseen repercussions, such as ordering ink cartridges automatically in the event of a power outage and resulting in wasteful expenditure
3. Security and privacy: IoT data storage and transfer increase privacy concerns. Concerns are raised about protecting and securely transmitting sensitive

information. It is crucial to think about who could have access to this information and if you want anyone, including neighbors or employers, to know specifics about your financial or physical condition.

4. Trespassing: If a smart door lock has security holes or is infected with malicious code, an attacker may enter a house without leaving any obvious indications of force. Life and property are at risk from this menace. In addition, sensors that are meant for purposes like fire detection, burglary monitoring, or baby monitoring may be compromised and utilized for continuous house surveillance.

5. DoS/DDoS: Unauthorised users can access smart home networks, flood connected devices with unsolicited messages, interfere with their operation, or infect target devices with malicious software, resulting in DoS (Denial of Service) attacks on the network.

6. Falsification: Attackers can modify routing tables in gateways to intercept packets sent by smart devices to application servers. Despite the implementation of Secure Socket Layer (SSL) encryption, hackers may use fake certificates to reroute or alter data, thus jeopardizing its integrity and secrecy.

16.9 Result and Discussion

Security personnel and inhabitants can monitor the area with the help of the security system used in a smart home environment. Its goal is to reduce the possibility of illegal involvement, whether it comes from outside sources or the environment itself [44–46]. A component of ubiquitous and pervasive computing, smart homes improve quality of life by automating home helpers and appliances. Based on context knowledge gleaned through home environment monitoring, this automation. Even when on the way home, users may remotely operate their household appliances, such as turning on the air conditioner or managing the water heater. The usage of default passwords in IoT devices that are difficult for users to alter is one of the security issues with these devices. Due to this flaw, hackers can use the devices to launch Distributed Denial-of-Service (DDoS) attacks [47]. The Mirai botnet, which has infected millions of IoT devices globally, is one example of such malware. IoT devices with poor security, especially those that utilize default usernames and passwords, can be scanned for and targeted by Mirai [48]. These devices link to a command and control server after becoming infected and start carrying out the attacker's commands. While restarting the computer will temporarily protect it from Mirai assaults, it does not remove the infection entirely [49]. Another defense against Mirai attacks is changing the default passwords on IoT devices. It is increasingly challenging to lessen the impact of Mirai since its designers anticipated the rising understanding of security precautions. Other IoT-related security risks besides Mirai include the Bricker Bot attack and Key Reinstallation Attacks (KRACKs) [50]. Other botnets like Hajime and Mirai try to hijack and use

IoT devices for diverse reasons, in contrast to the Bricker Bot assault, which tries to deactivate unprotected IoT devices. These assaults draw attention to the dangers presented by unsecured IoT devices and their potential effects on vital infrastructure and the digital economy [51]. The use of default passwords must be avoided, and remote access (WAN) to IoT devices must be disabled, to address IoT security vulnerabilities in the smart home setting [52]. Users of IoT devices should adopt these precautions as best practices. Although botnet growth has been slowed by antivirus software and detection methods, IoT security still needs to be improved. The IoT industry has paid close attention to the Smart Home concept, and many businesses and startups are working to build it. There can be conflicting standards and continuous arguments over closed systems and open frameworks as the IoT ecosystem develops further compliance issues and regulation can arise, notably in sectors like healthcare and applications for assisted living [53]. The broad deployment of IoT technology may face difficulties as a result of these worries.

16.10 Conclusion

It is anticipated that the broad adoption of Internet of Things (IoT) applications would significantly affect human life, from smart homes to cutting-edge healthcare solutions. IoT applications are significant, but they also raise issues, notably security-related ones. To manage the complexity of IoT and support multiple business models, the general public needs new, flexible, interoperable, and secure solutions. Many IoT devices currently do not have adequate security procedures, making them easy targets for assaults that occur without the device owners' awareness. Confidentiality, integrity, and authentication are all part of the security requirements for IoT applications. Low-level, medium-level, high-level, and extremely high-level assaults are divided into several groups, each with its character and behavior. There is also a discussion of potential defenses against these attacks. Implementing security measures in IoT devices and communication networks is essential given the importance of security in IoT applications. Users are recommended to thoroughly check the security requirements before using their devices and not to rely on the default passwords for them. Security threats can be prevented by turning off unnecessary functionality. It's also critical to understand the various security protocols employed by IoT networks and devices. Privacy worries are on the rise as more sensitive data is collected and processed by IoT devices, particularly those used in smart homes and healthcare. More work is needed to solve these problems as the chance of possible vulnerabilities rises with the introduction of new IoT devices and protocols. Lack of security knowledge frequently leads to inadequate security settings, insecure cloud and online services, and other issues. Additionally, given the limitations and interconnectedness of IoT features, attackers are more likely to target system and application vulnerabilities in the future. These results point to the need for industry standards, research, and device makers to better match privacy features with consumer expectations and desires.

References

[1] Weber, R., & Weber, T. (2014). Smart homes and the Internet of Things. In *Architecting the Internet of Things* (pp. 23–47). Springer, Berlin, Heidelberg. (Line 16).

[2] Ullberg, J., & Femenias, P. (2018). Smart homes: From technology to impact. In *Smart Homes and Their Users* (pp. 23–39). Springer, Cham. (Line 17).

[3] Han, S. Y., Kim, Y. S., & Lee, C. G. (2014). Building smart home IoT (Internet of Things) system based on cloud computing. In *2014 Eighth International Conference on Complex, Intelligent, and Software Intensive Systems* (pp. 117–122). IEEE. (Line 27).

[4] Ashton, K. (2009). That 'Internet of Things' Thing. *RFID Journal*, 22(7), 97–114. (Line 33).

[5] Soliman, A. S., El-Tawab, S., & Abdelkader, T. M. (2013). An IoT-based architecture for smart home systems. In *2013 IEEE International Conference on Control System, Computing and Engineering (ICCSCE)* (pp. 420–425). IEEE. (Line 22).

[6] Cook, D. J., Augusto, J. C., & Jakkula, V. R. (2009). Ambient intelligence: Technologies, applications, and opportunities. In *Pervasive and Mobile Computing* (Vol. 5, No. 4, pp. 277–298). Elsevier. (Line 30).

[7] Jie, Y., Zhong, Y., Xie, L., & Yu, Z. (2011). A scalable architectural paradigm for a smart home. In *2011 IEEE International Conference on Industrial Engineering and Engineering Management* (pp. 196–200). IEEE. (Line 39).

[8] Zhou, Z., Zhang, Q., Chen, H., Yu, Q., & Zhang, X. (2012). Cloud Things: A common architecture for smart city applications. *IEEE Network*, 26(4), 34–41. (Line 47).

[9] Lee, J., Kim, J., & Kang, S. (2015). A smart home application using a cloud-based residential service platform. *International Journal of Smart Home*, 9(2), 221–232.

[10] Ray, P. P. (2016). A survey on Internet of Things architectures. *Journal of King Saud University-Computer and Information Sciences*, 28(3), 291–319.

[11] Akyildiz, I. F., Jornet, J. M., & Pierobon, M. (2015). Nanonetworks: A new frontier in communications. *Communications of the ACM*, 58(11), 56–68.

[12] Hosek, J., Dolinay, M., Frnda, J., & Misurec, J. (2017). Smart home gateway design. In *2017 18th International Carpathian Control Conference (ICCC)* (pp. 354–359).

[13] Guoqiang, H., Xiaolin, C., Wenxian, Y., & Hua, G. (2016). Research on smart home gateway based on the Internet of Things. *Journal of Chemical and Pharmaceutical Research*, 8(3), 180–185.

[14] Mell, P., & Grance, T. (2011). The NIST definition of cloud computing. *National Institute of Standards and Technology, Special Publication*, 800(145), 7.

[15] Patel, S., & Patel, S. (2015). A review on cloud computing: Design challenges in architecture and security. *International Journal of Advanced Research in Computer Science and Software Engineering*, 5(7), 352–355.

[16] Zhang, Q., Cheng, L., & Boutaba, R. (2010). Cloud computing: State-of-the-art and research challenges. *Journal of internet services and Applications*, 1(1), 7–18.

[17] Lopez, J., Moreno, V., & Muñoz, L. (2015). An overview of the Internet of Things for smart homes. *Journal of Wireless Sensor Networks*, 7(4), 221–248.

[18] Shi, W., Cao, J., Zhang, Q., Li, Y., & Xu, L. (2016). Edge computing: Vision and challenges. *IEEE Internet of Things Journal*, 3(5), 637–646.

[19] Shi, W., & Dustdar, S. (2016). The promise of edge computing. *Computer*, 49(5), 78–81.

[20] Carullo, A., Kayhan, S., & Lampe, M. (2018). Internet of Things (IoT) security: Current status, challenges, and future research directions. *Journal of Reliable Intelligent Environments*, 4(2), 81–93.

[21] Alrawais, A., Alhothaily, A., & Hu, C. (2017). Security and privacy challenges in the Internet of Things for smart homes. *Future Generation Computer Systems*, 76, 446–454.

[22] Kent, S., & Atkinson, R. (2005). Security architecture for the Internet Protocol. IETF RFC 4301. Internet Engineering Task Force (IETF).

[23] Dierks, T., & Rescorla, E. (2008). The Transport Layer Security (TLS) Protocol Version 1.2. IETF RFC 5246.

[24] Roman, R., Zhou, J., & Lopez, J. (2013). On the features and challenges of security and privacy in distributed Internet of Things. *Computer Networks*, 57(10), 2266–2279.

[25] Li, S., Da Xu, L., & Zhao, S. (2015). The Internet of Things: A survey. *Information Systems Frontiers*, 17(2), 243–259.

[26] Jin, X., & Lin, X. (2014). Security and privacy in the Internet of Things: A survey. *IEEE Internet of Things Journal*, 1(5), 301–317.

[27] Carminati, B., Ferrari, E., & Goldoni, L. (2014). Security and privacy in the Internet of Things: Current status and open issues. In *2014 IEEE 10th International Conference on Wireless and Mobile Computing, Networking and Communications (WiMob)* (pp. 544–549). IEEE.

[28] Fernández-Caramés, T. M., & Fraga-Lamas, P. (2018). A review on the use of blockchain for the Internet of Things. *IEEE Access*, 6, 32979–33001.

[29] Jiang, X., & Li, Q. (2018). IoT security techniques based on authentication mechanisms. *Journal of Physics: Conference Series*, 1064(1), 012004.

[30] Biswas, K., Misra, S., & Banerjee, S. (2017). Security and privacy issues in IoT-based smart devices. In *2017 IEEE International Conference on Recent Trends in Electronics, Information & Communication Technology (RTEICT)* (pp. 1969–1973). IEEE.

[31] Sundmaeker, H., Guillemin, P., Friess, P., & Woelfflé, S. (2010). Vision and challenges for realizing the Internet of Things. *The cluster of European Research Projects on the Internet of Things–CERP-IoT. European Commision*, 3(3), 34–36.

[32] Konomi, S. (2019). Internet of Things and edge computing for smart cities. In *The Internet of Things and Edge Computing for Smart Cities* (pp. 43–67). Springer.

[33] Atzori, L., Iera, A., & Morabito, G. (2010). The Internet of Things: A survey. *Computer Networks*, 54(15), 2787–2805.

[34] Ziegeldorf, J. H., Morchon, O. G., & Wehrle, K. (2014). Privacy in the Internet of Things: Threats and challenges. *Security and Communication Networks*, 7(12), 2728–2742.

[35] Li, S., Da Xu, L., & Zhao, S. (2015). The Internet of Things: A survey. *Information Systems Frontiers*, 17(2), 243–259.

[36] Kounelis, I., et al. (2017). Security and privacy challenges in the Internet of Things. In *The Internet of Things: Principles and Paradigms* (pp. 317–350). Wiley.

[37] Yaqoob, I., et al. (2017). Internet of Things (IoT) security: Current status, challenges, and prospective measures. In *The Internet of Things From Hype to Reality* (pp. 229–248). Springer.

[38] Lloret, J., et al. (2015). Security framework for the Internet of Things in smart homes. *Future Generation Computer Systems*, 49, 128–137.

[39] Priyambodo, T. K., & Prayudi, Y. (2015). "Information security strategy on a mobile device based e-government," *ARPN Journal of Engineering and Applied Science*, 10(2), 652–660.

[40] Ukil, A., Bandyopadhyay, S., & Pal, A. (2015). "Privacy for IoT: Involuntary privacy enablement for smart energy systems," In *2015 IEEE International Conference on Communications (ICC)*, pp. 536–541.

[41] Vermesan, O., & Friess, P. (Eds.) (2013). *Internet of Things: Converging technologies for smart environments and integrated ecosystems*. River publishers.

[42] He, J., Xiao, Q., He, P., & Pathan, M. S. (2017). "An adaptive privacy protection method for smart home environments using supervised learning."

[43] Ali, B., Awad, A., Ali, B., & Awad, A. I. (Mar. 2018). "Cyber and physical security vulnerability assessment for IoT Based smart homes," *Sensors*, 18(3), 817.

[44] Varshney, U. (2017). Smart homes and their users: A systematic review of the literature. *Journal of Ambient Intelligence and Smart Environments*, 9(4), 355–376.

[45] Borgia, E. (2014). The Internet of Things vision: Key features, applications, and open issues. *Computer Communications*, 54, 1–31.

[46] Gupta, S., Pandey, B., Mehta, M., & Singh, D. (2020). Security and privacy challenges in Internet of Things (IoT) enabled smart home systems: A comprehensive review. *Journal of Network and Computer Applications*, 159, 102607.

[47] Mahmood, Z., & Najam, A. (2018). Internet of Things (IoT) enabled smart homes: A systematic review of architecture, framework, and future directions. *Journal of Ambient Intelligence and Humanized Computing*, 9(6), 1845–1866.

[48] Nouh, M., Shirmohammadi, S., & Mahmoud, M. (2017). Security and privacy in IoT-based smart homes: A survey. *IEEE Internet of Things Journal*, 4(1), 754–767.

[49] Stojkoska, B. R., & Trivodaliev, K. V. (2017). A review of Internet of Things for the smart home: Challenges and solutions. *Journal of Cleaner Production*, 140, 1454–1464.

[50] Ramachandran, G. S., Khare, A., Singh, A., & Sharma, S. (2018). Security challenges in IoT-based smart home systems: A review. *International Journal of Computers and Electrical Engineering*, 66, 147–157.

[51] Srdanović, G., & Vasković, V. (2018). Security and privacy in smart home systems: A survey. *Journal of Ambient Intelligence and Humanized Computing*, 9(4), 1081–1097.

[52] Alaba, F. A., & Akande, M. A. (2020). Internet of Things (IoT) and smart homes security: A review. *IEEE Access*, 8, 160482–160498.

[53] Djenouri, D., Khelladi, L., & Mahmoudi, T. (2017). A survey of security issues in mobile wireless sensor networks. *IEEE Communications Surveys & Tutorials*, 19(2), 973–997.

Chapter 17

Enhancing Security: Detecting Intrusions in IoT-Based Home Automation

Himanshu Verma and Nimish Kumar

BK Birla Institute of Engineering and Technology, Pilani (Rajasthan), India

17.1 Introduction to Home Automation and IoT

Home automation is a swiftly advancing domain that is transforming the residential experience. It involves the integration of technology to enhance the comfort, convenience, and efficiency of households. Home automation is a key component of the Internet of Things (IoT), which encompasses an extensive ecosystem of interconnected devices, appliances, and objects capable of communicating via the Internet (see Figure 17.1).

This chapter will provide an introduction to home automation and IoT, including their benefits, challenges, and the technologies that are driving their growth.

17.1.1 Benefits of Home Automation and IoT

Home automation offers several advantages, primarily enhancing convenience and comfort for residents. For instance, smart thermostats can automatically regulate the temperature according to individual preferences and schedules. Likewise, programmable smart lighting systems can be set to activate or deactivate at designated times

DOI: 10.1201/9781003474838-17

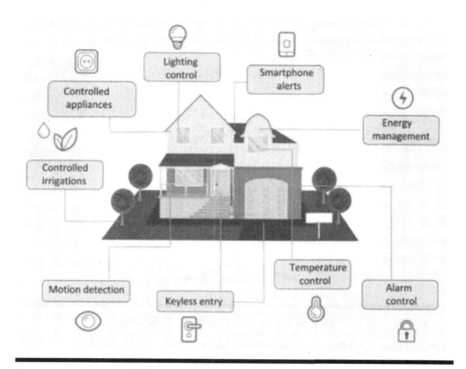

Figure 17.1   IoT-enabled Smart Home that Utilizes Intelligent Sensing Devices for Various Functions.

Source: Figures are based on relevant industry reports, and reputable sources in the fields of cybersecurity, IoT security, and home automation.

or in response to motion sensors. Home automation can also make homes more energy-efficient, which can lead to cost savings for the occupants. For example, smart home energy management systems can monitor energy usage and make adjustments to reduce waste and lower bills. In addition, home automation can improve home security and safety. Smart locks and security cameras can be controlled remotely, while sensors can detect unusual activity and alert the occupants or emergency services [1].

17.1.2 Challenges of Home Automation and IoT

Although home automation and the Internet of Things (IoT) offer numerous advantages, they come with certain hurdles. One significant obstacle revolves around the compatibility of devices sourced from various manufacturers. Numerous smart home gadgets employ distinct communication protocols, which can complicate their ability to interact seamlessly (See Figure 17.2). Consequently, this can result in a fragmented system that poses challenges in terms of administration and regulation.

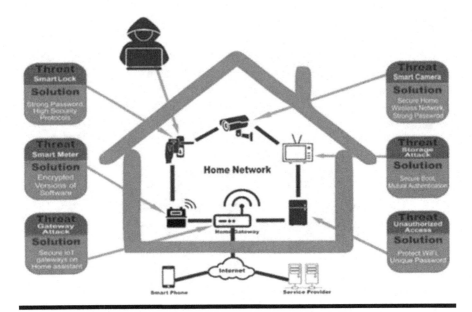

Figure 17.2 An IoT-based Smart Home Security and Challenges.

Source: Figures are based on relevant industry reports, and reputable sources in the fields of cybersecurity, IoT security, and home automation.

Another challenge is privacy and security. Smart home devices collect and store a lot of data about their users, which can be vulnerable to hacking and other security breaches. In addition, many smart home devices are always listening or watching, which can raise concerns about privacy.

17.1.3 Technologies Driving the Growth of Home Automation and IoT

The expansion of home automation and IoT is being propelled by various innovative technologies. One of the main technologies is wireless communication, which allows smart devices to communicate with each other without the need for wires or cables. Home automation relies on two widely adopted wireless communication technologies: Wi-Fi and Bluetooth. Another technology driving the growth of home automation is voice control.

Voice-activated assistants like Amazon Alexa and Google Assistant have revolutionized the way people interact with their smart home gadgets, providing an intuitive and user-friendly method for controlling these devices through vocal commands.

Artificial intelligence (AI) and machine learning (ML) play significant roles within the realm of home automation and the Internet of Things (IoT). These technologies can help smart home devices learn the habits and preferences of their users, making them more efficient and effective over time.

Home automation and IoT are rapidly growing fields that offer many benefits to homeowners. Smart home devices offer a myriad of advantages, ranging from heightened convenience and enhanced comfort to superior energy efficiency and elevated security. These innovations have the potential to elevate the overall comfort, efficiency, and safety of our homes. However, these technologies also present some challenges, including interoperability, privacy, and security concerns. By leveraging technologies such as wireless communication, voice control, AI, and ML, the home automation and IoT industries are poised for continued growth and innovation [2].

17.2 Overview of Intrusion Detection Systems (IDS)

The rapid growth of network-based systems has resulted in an increase in cyber attacks on these systems. Intrusion Detection Systems (IDS) are security mechanisms that detect and respond to unauthorized access to computer systems or networks. They are designed to monitor network traffic and identify potential security threats by analyzing patterns of activity. This chapter provides an overview of Intrusion Detection Systems (IDS) by describing their types, functions, and architectures, and their strengths and weaknesses.

17.2.1 Types of IDS

IDS can be classified into three types: host-based, network-based, and hybrid IDS. Host-based IDS are installed on individual computers or servers and monitor local activity. Network-based IDS, on the other hand, analyze network traffic, and can detect attacks that target multiple computers on a network. Hybrid IDS combine both host-based and network-based IDS to provide comprehensive security coverage.

17.2.2 Functions of IDS

The central role of an Intrusion Detection System (IDS) revolves around the identification and mitigation of security risks (see Figure 17.3). IDS is adept at recognizing various forms of security breaches, encompassing activities like port scans, denial-of-service assaults, and instances of malware infiltration. Moreover, IDS has the capability to pinpoint internal threats and the misappropriation of computing assets. When an IDS identifies a security breach, it promptly notifies security personnel, enabling them to initiate essential countermeasures to curtail the breach's impact and thwart any further harm. In addition, IDS maintains comprehensive logs and conducts in-depth analysis of security incidents, aiding in the determination of the attack's origin, the method employed, and the extent of the resulting damage.

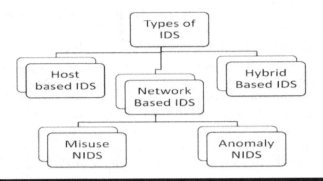

Figure 17.3 Types of IDS.

Source: Figures are based on relevant industry reports, and reputable sources in the fields of cybersecurity, IoT security, and home automation.

17.2.3 Architectures of IDS

There are two primary architectures employed in Intrusion Detection Systems (IDS): signature-based and anomaly-based IDS. The signature-based IDS operates by identifying attacks through the examination of network traffic, comparing it with a database containing a repository of recognized attack signatures. In contrast, the anomaly-based IDS detects intrusions by closely inspecting network traffic and identifying patterns of behavior that diverge from the anticipated or standard norms (see Figure 17.4). For comprehensive security coverage, a hybrid IDS amalgamates both signature-based and anomaly-based methodologies. By doing so, it combines the strengths of both methods to provide comprehensive protection against potential threats [3].

17.2.4 Strengths and Weaknesses of IDS

IDS have several strengths that make them an essential component of network security. IDS can detect known and unknown attacks and can alert security personnel to take necessary actions to contain the attack. IDS can also provide logs of security incidents that can be used to investigate the source of the attack and prevent future attacks. The IDS can be tailored to fulfill unique security demands and seamlessly incorporated with complementary security measures like firewalls and antivirus software. However, IDS also have several weaknesses that make them vulnerable to attacks. The generation of numerous false positives by IDS can pose a significant challenge, overwhelming security personnel and resulting in alert fatigue. IDS can also be vulnerable to evasion attacks, where attackers modify their activity to avoid detection by IDS. It can also be resource-intensive, requiring significant computing power and storage. IDS can also be expensive to deploy and maintain, making them less accessible to smaller organizations [4].

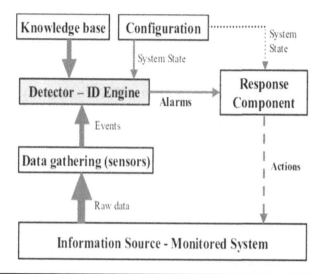

Figure 17.4   Basic Architecture of Intrusion Detection System (IDS).

Source: Figures are based on relevant industry reports, and reputable sources in the fields of cybersecurity, IoT security, and home automation.

In contemporary network security, Intrusion Detection Systems (IDS) hold a vital role. IDS can detect and respond to security breaches and provide logs of security incidents that can be used to investigate the source of the attack and prevent future attacks. IDS can be customized to meet specific security requirements and can be integrated with other security mechanisms such as antivirus software and firewalls. However, IDS can generate a large number of false positives, be vulnerable to evasion attacks, be resource-intensive, and be expensive to deploy and maintain. Therefore, it is important to carefully evaluate the strengths and weaknesses of IDS before deploying them in a network security architecture [5].

17.3 Intrusion Detection in Home Automation Systems

In recent years, the rise of Internet of Things (IoT) technology has led to a surge in the adoption of home automation systems. These systems empower users to conveniently manage different facets of their domestic surroundings, including lighting, climate control, and security, through mobile applications or voice-activated assistants. However, as these systems become more prevalent, they also become more vulnerable to cyber threats, such as hacking and data theft. Therefore, intrusion detection is essential to protect home automation systems and ensure their secure operation.

This chapter provides an in-depth overview of intrusion detection in home automation systems, including the types of intrusions, challenges in detecting intrusions, and existing intrusion detection approaches.

17.3.1 Types of Intrusions in Home Automation Systems

There are several types of intrusions that can occur in home automation systems, including the following:

Unauthorized access: This form of intrusion entails an unauthorized individual acquiring access to the home automation system, thereby potentially enabling them to manipulate different elements of the household setting, including the security system and door locks.

Physical Intrusions: Physical intrusions are one of the most common types of attacks on Home Automation Systems. These attacks involve unauthorized access to the home devices by physically gaining access to the home or the devices. An intruder can manipulate the devices, change their settings, and even steal them. Physical intrusions can also involve the installation of malware on devices that can cause significant damage to the Home Automation System.

Network Intrusions: Network intrusions occur when an unauthorized individual gains entry into the Home Automation System via the network. This malicious actor may take advantage of weaknesses in the network or devices to obtain unauthorized access to confidential data or take control of the devices. Network intrusions can also involve the installation of malware on devices through the network.

Malware attacks: Malware is a distinct type of software intentionally designed to cause harm to computer systems or networks. In the realm of home automation systems, malware incidents can result in unauthorized system access or the theft of valuable, confidential information.

Denial of Service (DoS) attacks: A Denial of Service (DoS) attack entails inundating a system with an excessive volume of traffic or requests, leading to its unresponsiveness or potential crash. In the realm of home automation systems, a DoS attack has the potential to obstruct a user's ability to access the system or manage different facets of their home environment.

Man in the Middle (MitM) Attacks: A Man in the Middle (MitM) attack refers to the act of intercepting and modifying communication between two entities without their knowledge or consent. In the context of home automation systems, a MitM attack could allow an attacker to eavesdrop on the user's communication with the system, or even alter the commands being sent to the system.

Password Attacks: Password attacks involve the use of brute force techniques to guess the password or credentials of the Home Automation System. Attackers can use automated tools to guess passwords or exploit vulnerabilities in the authentication process to gain access to the system. Password attacks can cause significant damage to Home Automation Systems by allowing unauthorized access to the devices or stealing sensitive information.

Social Engineering Attacks: Social engineering attacks encompass tactics designed to manipulate Home Automation System users in order to obtain sensitive data or control over their devices. These tactics encompass various forms, such as deceptive phishing emails, fraudulent phone calls, or misleading text messages, all aimed at coercing users into disclosing their login credentials or other confidential information. The consequences of social engineering attacks on Home Automation Systems can be severe, as they can lead to unauthorized access to devices or the theft of sensitive data. Home Automation Systems have become an integral part of modern homes, providing convenience, comfort, and energy efficiency to users. However, with the increasing adoption of these systems, the risk of cyber threats and attacks has also increased significantly. Home Automation Systems are vulnerable to various types of intrusions that can compromise the security and privacy of users. Therefore, it is essential to understand the different types of intrusions in Home Automation Systems to develop effective security solutions. The types of intrusions discussed in this article include malware attacks, physical intrusions, network intrusions, DoS attacks, MitM attacks, password attacks, and social engineering attacks. These attacks can cause significant damage to Home Automation Systems by disrupting their functionality and causing data loss. To protect Home Automation Systems from these intrusions, it is crucial to implement effective security measures such as intrusion detection systems, firewalls, and authentication mechanisms. Intrusion detection systems based on machine-learning algorithms have shown promising results in detecting and mitigating various types of intrusions in Home Automation Systems [6].

17.3.2 Challenges in Intrusion Detection for Home Automation Systems

There are several challenges in detecting intrusions in home automation systems, including the following:

Diversity of Devices and Standards: One of the major challenges in intrusion detection for home automation systems is the diversity of devices and standards used in these systems. There are several manufacturers and vendors of home automation devices, and each may use a different protocol or standard for communication. For example, one device may use Zigbee, while another may use Z-Wave. This diversity makes it difficult to develop a standardized intrusion detection system that can work with all devices and standards. Additionally, the lack of standardization in home automation systems can make it difficult to identify anomalous behavior, which can be a sign of intrusion.

Complexity of the System: Home automation systems are complex and involve multiple devices and components, such as sensors, controllers, and actuators, which are interconnected and communicate with each other. This complexity makes it difficult to detect intrusions, as it is challenging to determine which component or device has been compromised. Furthermore, the complexity of the system makes it difficult to monitor all the components in real-time, which can result in delayed detection of intrusions.

False Positives and False Negatives: One of the key dilemmas within intrusion detection for home automation systems involves the potential for erroneous alerts and missed threats. False positives emerge when the system erroneously categorizes regular activities as intrusions, creating frustration for homeowners due to unnecessary alerts or interventions. Conversely, false negatives transpire when the system overlooks actual intrusions, posing a severe risk as they could enable unauthorized access to the system, jeopardizing homeowners' security and privacy.

Privacy Concerns: Intrusion detection for home automation systems can raise privacy concerns, as it involves monitoring and analyzing the behavior of individuals in their homes. Homeowners may feel uncomfortable with the idea of their activities being monitored, even if it is for security purposes. Additionally, the data collected by intrusion detection systems can be sensitive, and homeowners may not trust the third-party vendors who develop and maintain these systems.

Limited Resources: Implementing efficient intrusion detection in home automation systems can be a daunting task due to their inherent constraints in terms of memory, processing capabilities, and battery life. Intrusion detection systems demand substantial resources for real-time monitoring and behavioral analysis of devices, potentially exerting excessive pressure on the limited resources of home automation systems. Furthermore, intrusion detection systems may require additional hardware or software components, which can further reduce the resources available for other functions of the home automation system.

17.3.3 Existing Intrusion Detection Approaches for Home Automation Systems

There are several existing intrusion detection approaches for home automation systems, including the following:

Signature-based detection: This method entails generating distinctive signatures or recognizable patterns associated with known attacks, and subsequently analyzing them in conjunction with network traffic or device logs to identify potential security breaches. Nevertheless, it's worth noting that this strategy may prove less efficacious when confronted with novel or previously undisclosed attack vectors.

Behavior-based detection: This method entails a thorough examination of the actions performed by both devices and users within the realm of home automation systems to identify irregularities that could potentially signal a security breach. While this approach exhibits enhanced efficacy in countering novel or previously undisclosed attack vectors, it may also lead to an increased occurrence of false positive detections.

Machine learning-based detection: This approach involves training machine-learning algorithms on network traffic or device logs to identify patterns that may indicate an attack. This approach may be more effective than signature-based or behavior-based approaches but may also require a large amount of training data and computing resources that may not be available on all home automation devices.

Anomaly detection: This method entails the recognition of irregular behavior or network traffic that diverges from established patterns. Anomaly detection can be implemented through a range of methods, including statistical analysis, clustering, or neural networks.

Hybrid approaches: Several intrusion detection strategies incorporate a fusion of various techniques, including both signature-based and behavior-based detection, with the aim of enhancing their overall efficacy while minimizing the occurrence of false positives. Intrusion detection is essential for securing home automation systems in the IoT era. Various types of intrusions can occur in home automation systems, including unauthorized access, malware attacks, DoS attacks, and MitM attacks. Detecting these intrusions can be challenging due to the diversity of devices, resource limitations, dynamic environment, and privacy concerns. Numerous intrusion detection methods are applicable to home automation systems, encompassing signature-based detection, behavior-oriented detection, machine learning-driven detection, anomaly detection, and hybrid strategies. However, each approach has its strengths and weaknesses, and selecting the most appropriate approach requires a comprehensive analysis of the system's requirements, characteristics, and limitations [7].

17.3.4 Strengths and Weaknesses of Existing Approaches

Signature-based detection is proficient in identifying familiar attack patterns; however, it falls short when facing novel and unidentified threats. Additionally, it tends to produce false alarms, leading to alert fatigue and undermining the Intrusion Detection System's (IDS) overall efficacy. On the other hand, anomaly-based detection excels at spotting emerging and uncharted attacks but also grapples with the issue of false positives. Furthermore, it's less adept at recognizing well-known attacks, as it lacks a signature database. A hybrid detection approach bridges these gaps effectively, as it can identify both known and unknown threats while mitigating false alarms, a common issue with anomaly-based systems. However, it demands a more intricate setup and greater resource allocation compared to the other two methods. Machine learning-based detection, like hybrid detection, proves highly capable of detecting both familiar and novel attacks while minimizing false positives arising from anomaly-based detection. Nevertheless, it demands substantial volumes of data to train the machine-learning algorithm, making it susceptible to adversarial attacks that manipulate the training data [8].

When selecting an intrusion detection system for a home automation setup, it is crucial to thoroughly evaluate the merits and drawbacks of each approach. For example, a signature-based detection approach may be suitable for systems with a limited number of devices and known attack vectors, while a machine learning-based approach may be more suitable for larger and more complex systems.

17.3.5 Challenges in Intrusion Detection for Home Automation Systems

There are several challenges that need to be addressed when implementing an intrusion detection system for a home automation system:

Resource Constraints: Home automation systems frequently come equipped with restricted resources, such as limited processing capabilities and memory capacity. Intrusion detection systems need to be designed to work within these constraints to ensure they do not impact the performance of the system.

Network Complexity: Home automation systems are often comprised of multiple devices that are interconnected via a network. This network can be complex and may include wireless connections, which can increase the risk of unauthorized access. Intrusion detection systems need to be designed to handle the complexity of these networks to ensure they can detect attacks that target multiple devices.

Lack of Standardization: The absence of uniformity in home automation systems poses a challenge when attempting to deploy intrusion detection systems that are compatible with various platforms. Intrusion detection systems need to be designed to work with different types of devices and protocols to ensure they can detect attacks on all devices in the system.

False Positives: False positives pose a notable challenge for intrusion detection systems since they can lead to alert fatigue and diminish the system's overall efficiency. To ensure the effectiveness of intrusion detection systems, it is imperative to craft them with a focus on minimizing false positives while maintaining their ability to effectively detect attacks. The realm of intrusion detection holds significant importance in bolstering the security of home automation systems. Various detection techniques, including signature-based, anomaly-based, hybrid, and machine learning-based approaches, can all prove to be proficient in identifying attacks within home automation systems. However, it's crucial to recognize that each approach comes with its unique set of strengths and weaknesses. When choosing an intrusion detection system for a home automation system, the specific needs of the system need to be carefully considered, and the intrusion detection system should be designed to work within the resource constraints of the system while still detecting attacks effectively [9].

17.4 Machine-Learning Techniques for Intrusion Detection in Home Automation Systems

In recent years, there has been a widespread application of machine-learning techniques in the field of Intrusion Detection Systems (IDS). These techniques harness the power of large datasets containing network traffic or system activity to recognize patterns and deviations that might indicate malicious actions. Machine-learning methods for IDS can be categorized into two primary types: supervised learning and unsupervised learning. Supervised learning necessitates the availability of a labeled dataset containing network traffic or system activity samples, where each data point is tagged as either "normal" or "malicious." Through training on such labeled data, the machine-learning algorithm acquires the ability to classify new data points based on the patterns it has learned from the training set. While supervised learning can achieve high accuracy, it comes with the significant requirement of having access to a sizable and diverse labeled dataset. On the other hand, unsupervised learning operates without the need for pre-labeled data. Instead, it autonomously identifies underlying patterns and anomalies within the dataset, devoid of prior knowledge regarding what constitutes normal or malicious behavior. Unsupervised learning is particularly adept at uncovering previously unknown attack patterns and can trigger alerts for any anomalous behavior it identifies. However, it does carry the potential drawback of generating false positives if the system's typical behavior is not precisely defined [10].

17.4.1 ML Techniques for IDS in Home Automation Systems

Home automation systems are complex and heterogeneous, consisting of various devices and services that communicate through different protocols and interfaces. IDS in home automation systems face several challenges, including high dimensionality, class imbalance, and limited computing resources. ML techniques can overcome these challenges and improve the accuracy and efficiency of IDS in home automation systems [11].

Supervised learning methods, including decision-tree algorithms, support vector machines (SVM), and neural networks, have found application in the realm of Intrusion Detection Systems (IDS) within home automation systems. These techniques require a labeled dataset of network traffic or system activity that includes normal and malicious behavior. Decision trees are simple and interpretable models that can handle categorical and continuous data. Support Vector Machines (SVM) represent a robust method adept at managing high-dimensional datasets and capturing non-linear associations. Meanwhile, neural networks, renowned for their adaptability, excel at discerning intricate data patterns and relationships. These techniques have achieved high accuracy in detecting attacks in home automation systems [12].

Unsupervised learning methods, including clustering and anomaly detection, have found applications in Intrusion Detection Systems (IDS) for home automation systems. These approaches operate without the need for labeled data and can detect unusual activities without prior knowledge of what constitutes normal or malicious behavior. Clustering techniques group similar data points together based on their characteristics. Anomaly detection techniques identify data points that deviate significantly from the norm. These techniques have shown promise in detecting unknown attacks and generating alerts for anomalous behavior in home automation systems [13].One of the hurdles when employing unsupervised learning methods for Intrusion Detection Systems (IDS) within home automation systems lies in the task of establishing a precise definition of what constitutes normal system behavior. Home automation setups are profoundly individualized, and what is considered normal for one system might markedly differ from another. Consequently, it becomes imperative to construct a bespoke model for characterizing the normal operation of each distinct home automation system.

Deep-learning techniques, such as deep autoencoders and convolutional neural networks (CNN), have also been applied to IDS in home automation systems. Deep-learning techniques can learn complex patterns and relationships in the data, and they can automatically extract features from the data, reducing the need for manual feature engineering. Deep autoencoders are unsupervised learning techniques that can learn a compressed representation of the input data. Convolutional neural networks are supervised learning techniques that can handle high-dimensional data, such as images and time-series data. These techniques have shown promising results in detecting attacks in home automation systems [14]. Addressing the utilization of deep-learning methods for Intrusion Detection Systems (IDS) within the context of home automation systems presents a noteworthy obstacle due to the constrained computational capabilities of the devices involved. Typically, home automation devices exhibit limitations in terms of available memory and processing capacity.

Consequently, the imperative lies in the creation of streamlined deep-learning models capable of seamless execution on these resource-restricted devices while upholding their operational efficiency.

Another challenge in applying ML techniques to IDS in home automation systems is the class imbalance problem. In IDS, the number of normal data points is often much higher than the number of malicious data points. This class imbalance can lead to biased models that prioritize accuracy on normal data at the expense of detecting malicious data. To address this problem, techniques such as over-sampling and under sampling can be applied to balance the classes in the dataset. Machine-learning techniques have shown promising results in detecting attacks in home automation systems. Supervised learning, unsupervised learning, and deep-learning techniques can be applied to IDS in home automation systems to improve the accuracy and efficiency of the system. However, there are still several challenges that need to be addressed, including defining the normal behavior of the system, developing lightweight models that can run on resource-constrained devices, and addressing the class imbalance problem. Future research can focus on developing personalized models of normal behavior for home automation systems, developing lightweight models that can run on resource-constrained devices, and exploring the use of reinforcement learning for IDS in home automation systems. Overall, ML techniques have the potential to enhance the security and privacy of home automation systems and protect homeowners from cyber attacks.

17.5 Intrusion Detection System Designed for Home Automation

IDS specifically designed for IoT systems are essential in addressing the security challenges faced by these networks. In order to effectively safeguard IoT networks, proactive methods capable of identifying new attacks are highly suitable. Hence, a robust IDS that possesses the capability to detect emerging threats within IoT-based smart environments becomes imperative. Comparison between Traditional Intrusion Detection and IoT-Based Intrusion Detection is given in Table 17.1 and Table 17.2 provides an overview of the IDS proposed for IoT systems. This chapter focuses on the features of all IDS methods for IoT that are applicable in smart environments, as recommended by recent surveys on the subject [15, 16]. Traditional IDS do not offer the specific security measures required by IoT systems, which possess unique characteristics.

Liu et al. [17] introduced a specialized Intrusion Detection System (IDS) tailored specifically for IoT networks. This innovative IDS showcases remarkable adaptability within the IoT environment, and it possesses the capacity for autonomous learning when it comes to identifying emerging attack vectors. It employs a dual approach, combining machine-learning techniques with a signature-based model, all inspired by the principles of artificial immune systems. The overarching goal of this network IDS is to

Table 17.1 Comparison between Traditional Intrusion Detection and IoT-Based Intrusion Detection

Feature	Traditional Intrusion Detection	IoT-Based Intrusion Detection
Sensor Types	Typically limited to motion sensors or door/window sensors	Can incorporate a wide range of sensors including motion sensors, door/window sensors, cameras, smoke detectors, temperature sensors, etc.
Connectivity	Wired or wireless (limited range)	Wireless (Wi-Fi, Bluetooth, Zigbee, etc.)
Scalability	Limited scalability due to wiring constraints	Highly scalable due to wireless connectivity and ease of adding new devices
System Integration	Often standalone systems with limited integration capabilities	Can be integrated with other smart home devices, home automation systems, and security systems for enhanced functionality
Real-Time Monitoring	Provides real-time monitoring and alerts	Provides real-time monitoring and alerts
Data Analysis	Relies on pre-defined rule-based analysis	Can utilize advanced data analytics, machine learning, and AI algorithms for more accurate intrusion detection
Remote Access	Limited remote access capabilities	Offers remote access and control through mobile apps or web interfaces
Automation and Response	Limited automation capabilities, may trigger alarms or notifications	Can automate responses such as activating security cameras, locking doors, turning on lights, etc.
Customization and Flexibility	Limited customization options	Offers customization and flexibility through programmable rules and settings
Cost	Generally lower upfront cost	May have higher upfront cost due to the need for IoT devices and sensors
Maintenance	Requires periodic maintenance and battery replacements	Requires periodic software updates and may require occasional device replacement
Privacy and Security	Generally limited security features	Requires robust security measures to protect against IoT vulnerabilities and ensure data privacy

Source: Tables are based on relevant industry reports, and reputable sources in the fields of cybersecurity, IoT security, and home automation.

bolster the security of IoT networks. Its key attributes include the ability to autonomously adapt to new environments and continuously learn and adapt to evolving attack patterns.

In the realm of IoT networks, Kasinathan et al. [18] put forth an IDS with a primary focus on detecting Denial of Service (DoS) attacks, particularly in the context of 6LoWPAN. Their DoS detection framework comprises three integral components: an IDS probe, a DoS protection manager, and the Suricata IDS [19]. The architecture of this system stems from a meticulous examination of vulnerabilities that are commonly found in IP-based Wireless Sensor Networks (WSN). Notably, the Suricata IDS operates on a host computer, addressing crucial concerns related to power consumption and resource conservation within WSN.

Furthermore, Kasinathan et al. [20] presented an enhanced IDS for the identification of DoS attacks in 6LoWPAN-based IoT networks. This IDS builds upon the foundation established in their earlier work [18], and it introduces two innovative elements, namely, a frequency agility manager (FAM) and a security incident and event management system (SIEM). The integration of these components forms a robust monitoring system, capable of effectively overseeing large-scale networks.

Jun and Chi [21] proposed an IDS that seamlessly incorporates complex event-processing (CEP) technology. The adoption of CEP technology equips this IDS with the capability to identify intricate intrusion patterns in real-time. The event-processing IDS architecture comprises four essential units: an event filtering unit, an event database unit, a CEP unit, and an action engine unit. This system relies on a rule-based approach within its event-processing model to detect and respond to potential intrusions (see Table 17.1).

The paragraph outlines distinct characteristics of the described system. Firstly, it operates in real-time and excels at identifying intrusions within an IoT system, thanks to its utilization of an event-processing mechanism. Krimmling and Peter [22] introduced a Network Intrusion Detection System (NIDS) that harnesses machine learning for both anomaly-based and signature-based intrusion detection. Their system framework is explicitly tailored for smart public transport applications that utilize CoAP. Remarkable aspects of this system include its compatibility with CoAP applications and its reliance on an efficient lightweight algorithm.

Similarly, Butun et al. [23] proposed a NIDS customized for Wireless Sensor Networks (WSN), which amalgamates both statistical and rule-based intrusion detection models. This system operates within a hierarchical structure of WSN, employing both downward-IDS and upward-IDS. The former identifies abnormal behavior among member nodes, while the latter focuses on spotting anomalies among cluster heads. Noteworthy attributes of this system encompass its suitability for hierarchical WSN and its reliance on WSN clustering.

Surendar and Umamakeswari [24] introduced a constraint-based specification IDS intended for IoT networks employing 6LoWPAN. This IDS effectively identifies sinkhole attacks while upholding Quality of Service (QoS) metrics efficiently.

It accomplishes this by isolating malicious nodes and restructuring the network without their presence. The IDS relies on behavioral rules and employs the protocol model approach. Key features of this system encompass its capability to detect sink-hole attacks, maintain QoS, and isolate malicious nodes.

Additionally, Le et al. [25] proposed a specification-based IDS for IoT networks using 6LoWPAN, with a specific focus on detecting various topology attacks against the IPv6 Routing Protocol for Low-Power and Lossy Networks (RPL). These attacks comprise sinkhole, rank, local repair, neighbor, and destination-oriented directed acyclic graph (DODAG) information solicitation (DIS) attacks. The IDS analyzes protocol behavior from trace files to learn the procedures for establishing and maintaining a stable topology. It excels in efficiently detecting RPL topology attacks in an energy-efficient manner, making it a suitable choice for large-scale networks.

Furthermore, Bostani and Sheikhan [26] proposed a hybrid IDS for IoT networks using 6LoWPAN to identify various RPL attacks. This system incorporates both specification-based intrusion detection modules, functioning as IDS agents in router nodes, and an anomaly-based intrusion detection module serving as the primary IDS in the root node. Notable aspects of this system include a reduction in communication messages due to the absence of additional control messages or monitor nodes in the IDS design, as well as its applicability to large-scale networks.

Garcia-Font et al. [27] introduced a Network Intrusion Detection System (NIDS) for Wireless Sensor Networks (WSN) that integrates machine learning and signature modeling. Their approach combines a signature-based detection engine with an anomaly-based detection engine, resulting in enhanced detection rates and a low False Positive Rate (FPR). The system is designed to aid smart city administrators in detecting intrusions by employing the IDS alongside an attack classification schema. Importantly, this system is well-suited for deployment in large-scale WSN (see Table 17.2).

Table 17.2 Descriptive Statistical Analysis of IDS for IoT Systems

IDS Method	Description	Key Features
Liu et al. [17]	Artificial immune IDS tailored for IoT networks. Incorporates machine learning and signature-based model. Enhances security and adapts to new environments.	Self-adaptation to new environments Self-learning of emerging attack patterns
Kasinathan et al. [18]	IDS focused on detecting DoS attacks utilizing 6LoWPAN. Utilizes an IDS probe, DoS protection manager, and Suricata IDS. Suitable for IP-based WSN.	Effective detection of DoS attacks Suricata IDS for power conservation

Table 17.2 (Continued)

IDS Method	Description	Key Features
Jun and Chi [21]	IDS integrating complex event-processing (CEP) technology. Real-time identification of intricate patterns. Rule-based approach for intrusion detection.	Real-time intrusion detection Identification of complex patterns
Krimmling and Peter [22]	NIDS utilizing machine learning for anomaly-based and signature-based intrusion detection. Designed for smart public transport applications using CoAP.	Suitability for CoAP applications Reliance on lightweight algorithm
Butun et al. [23]	NIDS tailored for Wireless Sensor Networks (WSN) combining statistical model and rule model approaches. Detection of abnormal behavior in member nodes and cluster heads.	Compatibility with hierarchical WSN Effective WSN clustering
Surendar and Umamakeswari [24]	Constraint-based specification IDS for IoT networks using 6LoWPAN. Detects sinkhole attacks and maintains QoS metrics.	Sinkhole attack detection QoS preservation Malicious node isolation
Le et al. [25]	Specification-based IDS for IoT networks using 6LoWPAN. Detects topology attacks against RPL. Efficient detection in energy-efficient manner.	High efficiency in detecting RPL topology attacks Energy-efficient detection
Bostani and Sheikhan [26]	Hybrid IDS for IoT networks using 6LoWPAN. Combines specification-based and anomaly-based intrusion detection. Applicable to large-scale networks.	Reduction in communication messages Applicability to large-scale networks
Garcia-Font et al. [27]	NIDS for Wireless Sensor Networks (WSN) using a combination of machine learning and signature modeling. Improved detection rates and low False Positive Rate (FPR).	Enhanced detection with machine learning Applicability to large-scale WSN
Fu et al. [28]	NIDS utilizing signature-based and protocol-based anomaly detection methods. Standardized intrusion detection method for IoT networks.	Classification of attacks into three categories Graphical user interface (GUI) tool for intrusion identification

(continued)

Table 17.2 (Continued)

IDS Method	Description	Key Features
Deng et al. [29]	NIDS utilizing fuzzy c-means clustering (FCM) and PCA algorithms. Lightweight system with low False Positive Rate (FPR).	Lightweight and low False Positive Rate (FPR) Improved detection efficiency
Amouri et al. [30]	NIDS based on the protocol model approach and machine-learning techniques. Local and global detection stages. Low computational complexity and minimal resource requirements.	Local and global detection stages Low computational complexity
Liu et al. [31]	NIDS relying on suppressed fuzzy clustering (SFC) and PCA algorithms. Efficient detection in high-dimensional spaces. Frequency self-adjustment algorithm for improved efficiency.	Adaptable to high-dimensional spaces
Abhishek et al. [32]	NIDS utilizing packet drop probability (PDP)	Statistical model approach for anomaly-based intrusion detection Reliance on theoretical foundations instead of requiring training data Real-time detection of malicious gateways
Oh et al. [33]	Lightweight IDS with malicious pattern matching	Auxiliary Skipping (AS) algorithm Early Decision with Boundary Searching (EBS) algorithm AS-EBS combination algorithm Reduced memory size and workload on smart objects Improved processing speed and scalability

Table 17.2 (Continued)

IDS Method	Description	Key Features
Summerville et al. [34]	Ultralightweight IDS with deep packet anomaly detection	Leveraging bitwise AND operation Payload model approach for anomaly-based detection Low latency and high throughput
Gupta et al. [35]	HIDS combining signature-based and rule-based detection	Traditional signature-based technique Snort-rule-based intrusion detection Simplicity and self-learning capability
Arrignton et al. [36]	HIDS utilizing machine learning and artificial immune systems	Machine-learning approach based on artificial immune systems Behavioral modeling IDS (BMIDS) Enhanced detection sensitivity by eliminating environmental noise
Gupta et al. [35]	Computational intelligence-based IDS for wireless communications	Three-tier architecture with information storage, computation intelligence, and clustering units Machine-learning approach based on swarm intelligence (SI) paradigm Suitable for both NIDS and HIDS

(*continued*)

Table 17.2 (Continued)

IDS Method	Description	Key Features
Raza et al. [37]	Hybrid-based IDS for detecting RPL attacks in 6LoWPAN	SVELTE IDS with 6LoWPAN mapper, intrusion detection, and mini-firewall units Accommodates distributed and centralized IDS placement strategies Lightweight nature and energy efficiency
Khan and Herrmann [38]	Trust management algorithms for IoT networks	Neighbor-based trust dissemination (NBTD) for NIDS in border routers Tree-based trust dissemination (TTD) for HIDS in small networks Clustered neighbor-based trust dissemination (CNTD) for distributed NIDS Lightweight, energy-efficient, and applicable in healthcare environments

Source: Tables are based on relevant industry reports, and reputable sources in the fields of cybersecurity, IoT security, and home automation.

Fu et al. [28] introduced a novel Network Intrusion Detection System (NIDS) that harnesses the power of both signature-based and protocol-based anomaly detection techniques. This NIDS framework specifically targets the identification of threats within IoT networks while efficiently managing the challenges posed by network heterogeneity.

The core detection mechanism involves a meticulous analysis of abstracted action flows found in data packets, which are compared against three distinct databases: a standard protocol library, an abnormal action library, and a normal action library. This innovative approach incorporates several essential components, including an event monitor, event database, event analyzer, and a responsive unit, thereby providing a standardized intrusion detection methodology for IoT networks rooted in automata theory.

Key highlights of this system encompass the classification of attacks into three distinct categories and the development of an intuitive graphical user interface (GUI) tool. This tool serves to visually represent abstract action flows, aiding in the swift identification of potential intrusion attempts.

Deng et al. [29], on the other hand, put forth an NIDS solution that relies on the robust combination of the fuzzy c-means clustering (FCM) algorithm and Principal Component Analysis (PCA). Their system seamlessly integrates machine-learning and data-mining approaches to significantly enhance the accuracy of intrusion detection in IoT networks.

The PCA algorithm is ingeniously employed for feature selection and dimensionality reduction, while the FCM algorithm takes center stage as the clustering method. The system's performance was rigorously evaluated using the KDD-CUP99 dataset [39]. Notable attributes of this system include its lightweight design and the notable achievement of reduced False Positive Rates (FPR), which greatly enhances the efficiency of intrusion detection.

Amouri et al. [30] have proposed an innovative NIDS hinging on the protocol model approach alongside machine-learning techniques. This system comprises two distinctive detection phases: local detection and global detection. In the initial local detection stage, network behavioral data is meticulously collected by dedicated sniffers. These data are then utilized to generate a set of correctly classified instances (CCI) using a supervised learning approach based on decision trees.

In the subsequent global detection stage, the CCI are aggregated by supernodes to create time-based profiles known as accumulated measures of fluctuation (AMoFs), separately for both malicious and normal nodes. Key characteristics of this system include its low computational complexity and minimal resource requirements, making it an efficient choice for IoT networks.

Lastly, Liu et al. [31] introduced a sophisticated NIDS that relies on the suppressed fuzzy clustering (SFC) algorithm in conjunction with PCA. This system amalgamates machine-learning and data-mining techniques to significantly enhance the accuracy of intrusion detection, especially in high-dimensional spaces.

The PCA algorithm plays a pivotal role in feature extraction, while a novel prejudgment-based intrusion detection method, utilizing PCA and SFC, is applied to categorize dimension-reduced data into high-risk and low-risk segments. Impressively, this system showcases adaptability to high-dimensional environments such as IoT. Moreover, it optimizes the efficiency and effectiveness of the IDS through reduced detection time and increased accuracy, courtesy of a frequency self-adjustment algorithm.

Abhishek et al. [32] proposed a Network Intrusion Detection System (NIDS) designed to monitor gateways and identify malicious ones by utilizing the packet drop probability (PDP) in IoT devices. Their approach employs statistical modeling for anomaly-based intrusion detection, employing a likelihood ratio test to pinpoint malicious gateways disrupting communications between IoT devices and access points. Notably, this system specializes in detecting malicious gateways affecting downlink packets but does not extend its coverage to those affecting uplink packets from IoT devices. Key aspects of this system include its reliance on theoretical foundations rather than a need for extensive training data and its ability to operate in real-time.

Oh et al. [33] introduced a lightweight Intrusion Detection System (IDS) that prioritizes malicious pattern matching. They emphasized the challenges of applying traditional IDS to smart objects due to constraints such as limited memory and battery life. To address these issues, Oh et al. proposed three algorithms: the auxiliary skipping (AS) algorithm, the early decision with boundary searching (EBS) algorithm, and a combination of both called AS-EBS. These algorithms efficiently reduce the number of required matching operations [33]. The system relies on a pattern-matching approach centered on signature detection, making it well-suited for smart objects with limited resources. Its standout features include reduced memory usage for matching operations, reduced workload on smart objects, enhanced processing speed, and scalability for handling a large number of patterns.

Summerville et al. [34] introduced an ultralightweight approach to deep packet anomaly detection, specially tailored for implementation on small IoT devices. This system leverages the bitwise *and* operation and adopts a payload model approach for anomaly-based intrusion detection. Noteworthy attributes of this system comprise low latency, high throughput, and ultralightweight design.

Gupta et al. [35] proposed a Hybrid Intrusion Detection System (HIDS) that combines signature-based and rule-based anomaly detection. This system employs a traditional signature-based technique alongside Snort-rule-based intrusion detection, enabling it to detect both known and unknown attacks. However, it's important to note that privacy concerns arise due to the utilization of deep packet inspection for attack detection. Key features include simplicity and self-learning capabilities.

Arrington et al. [36] presented a HIDS employing a machine-learning approach for anomaly-based intrusion detection, specifically utilizing artificial immune system mechanisms. Their Behavioral Modeling IDS (BMIDS) assesses behavior acceptability and improves detection sensitivity by filtering out environmental noise.

Gupta et al. [35] addressed the pervasive threat of attacks in IoT systems by proposing a computational-intelligence-based IDS for wireless communications and IoT systems. Their three-tier architecture forms the foundation of an intelligent IDS suitable for wireless networks, consisting of an information storage unit, a computational intelligence and optimization unit, and a clustering and intrusion reporting unit. This system relies on a machine-learning approach based on the swarm intelligence (SI) paradigm. However, it's essential to note that it is primarily applicable to regions of Wireless Sensor Networks (WSN) using the TCP/IP protocol. Its standout feature is its dual functionality as both a NIDS and a HIDS.

Raza et al. [37] introduced a hybrid-based IDS tailored for IoT networks using 6LoWPAN, with a specific focus on detecting various RPL attacks. Their proposed SVELTE IDS comprises a 6LoWPAN mapper unit, an intrusion detection unit,

Table 17.3 Descriptive Statistical Analysis of Surveyed IDS for IoT Systems

IDS by author	Performance Metrics	Adaptability	Learning Capability	Power Consumption	Scalability
Liu et al. [17]	Artificial immune IDS	High	High	Moderate	High
Kasinathan et al. [18]	DoS detection with 6LoWPAN	High	Moderate	Low	Moderate
Kasinathan et al. [20]	Enhanced DoS detection	High	High	Low	High
Jun and Chi [21]	CEP-based IDS	High	High	Moderate	Moderate
Krimmling and Peter [22]	Machine learning-based NIDS	Moderate	High	Low	High
Butun et al. [23]	Hybrid IDS for WSN	High	High	Low	Moderate
Surendar and Umamakeswari [24]	Constraint-based IDS	High	High	Low	Moderate
Le et al. [25]	Specification-based IDS	High	High	Moderate	High
Bostani and Sheikhan [26]	Hybrid IDS for 6LoWPAN	High	High	Low	High
Garcia-Font et al. [27]	NIDS with machine learning	High	Moderate	Low	High
Fu et al. [28]	Signature and protocol-based NIDS	High	High	Moderate	High
Deng et al. [29]	Fuzzy clustering-based NIDS	High	High	Low	High
Amouri et al. [30]	Protocol model-based NIDS	High	Moderate	Low	Moderate
Liu et al. [31]	PCA and SFC-based NIDS	High	High	Low	High
Abhishek et al. [32]	Statistical model-based NIDS	High	High	Low	Moderate
Oh et al. [33]	Lightweight IDS	High	High	Low	High
Summerville et al. [34]	Deep packet anomaly detection	High	High	Low	High
Gupta et al. [35]	HIDS with signature and rule-based detection	High	High	Moderate	Moderate

(continued)

Table 17.3 (Continued)

IDS by author	Performance Metrics	Adaptability	Learning Capability	Power Consumption	Scalability
Arrington et al. [36]	Anomaly-based IDS with artificial immune systems	High	High	Moderate	Moderate
Gupta et al. [35]	Computational intelligence-based IDS	High	High	Moderate	High
Raza et al. [37]	Hybrid IDS for RPL attacks	High	Moderate	Low	High
Khan and Herrmann [38]	Trust-based IDS	High	High	Low	High

Source: Tables are based on relevant industry reports, and reputable sources in the fields of cybersecurity, IoT security, and home automation.

and a mini-firewall unit. The 6LoWPAN mapper unit collects information about the RPL network, while the intrusion detection unit analyzes the data from the mapper unit to identify intrusions. The mini-firewall unit filters unwanted traffic. This system accommodates distributed and centralized IDS placement strategies. Key attributes of this system include its lightweight design and energy efficiency.

In their work, Khan and Herrmann [38] introduced three algorithms that rely on the protocol model approach and incorporate a trust management mechanism for IoT networks, each offering distinct functionalities and characteristics.

The first algorithm is called neighbor-based trust dissemination (NBTD). It is designed to enable the implementation of a Network Intrusion Detection System (NIDS) within a border router, employing a centralized approach. NBTD facilitates the dissemination of trust information among neighboring nodes. The second algorithm, known as tree-based trust dissemination (TTD), is tailored for implementing a Host Intrusion Detection System (HIDS) in small networks with high communication costs. It utilizes a distributed approach and employs a tree structure to disseminate trust information. This algorithm is particularly suitable for networks with limited resources. The third algorithm proposed by Khan and Herrmann is clustered neighbor-based trust dissemination (CNTD). It is specifically designed for implementing a NIDS using a distributed approach. CNTD aims to reduce the number of packet exchanges compared to the NBTD algorithm by clustering neighboring nodes. This approach improves efficiency in large-scale networks. These algorithms share several key features. Firstly, they are lightweight, ensuring minimal resource consumption. Additionally, they exhibit energy efficiency, optimizing power usage in IoT networks (see Table 17.3). Lastly, their applicability extends to healthcare environments, making them suitable for securing sensitive medical systems and data.

17.6 Conclusion

Intrusion detection in Home Automation systems is crucial for maintaining the security and privacy of users in the IoT environment. The emergence of the IoT technology and its widespread deployment in various domains has opened new opportunities for attackers to exploit security vulnerabilities. As Home Automation systems rely on a range of IoT devices such as sensors, controllers, and actuators, securing these systems has become more complex than ever before. Intrusion detection systems (IDS) have been used as a defense mechanism to detect and respond to several types of attacks in Home Automation systems.

With the growing number of IoT users, services, and applications, there is an urgent requirement for a robust and lightweight security solution that is specifically tailored for IoT environments. The security of IoT networks is of utmost importance as they form the foundation of smart environments. Any vulnerabilities in the security of these networks can have a direct impact on the overall functionality of the smart environments they support. Attacks such as DoS, DDoS, probing, and RPL attacks pose significant threats to the services and applications offered in IoT-based smart environments, emphasizing the criticality of ensuring security in IoT environments. An Intrusion Detection System (IDS) emerges as a potential solution to address this issue. This chapter presents a comprehensive survey of IDS designed explicitly for IoT environments and discusses recommendations for designing a robust and lightweight IDS. The survey encompasses an examination of various papers that primarily focus on the design and implementation of IDS for IoT paradigms applicable in smart environments. The features of all IDS methods presented in these papers are consolidated and summarized. Additionally, the paper puts forward key recommendations that must be taken into account during the design process of an IDS for IoT. These recommendations emphasize the necessity of developing a powerful and lightweight system with a well-planned placement strategy that does not compromise the integrity, confidentiality, and availability of the IoT environment. This chapter underscores the requirement for an integrated IDS that can be effectively deployed in IoT-based smart environments. To ensure its effectiveness, the proposed IDS design needs to undergo rigorous testing on a unified IoT database. Furthermore, the question of the optimal placement strategy must be thoroughly addressed within this design framework.

17.7 Future Work

Improving the efficacy of Intrusion Detection Systems (IDS) in Home Automation systems entails delving into several key domains. Initially, it is imperative to advance IDS methodologies, enabling them to identify hitherto undiscovered security breaches. The majority of current IDS strategies rely on established attack patterns, rendering them susceptible to zero-day attacks. The application of machine-learning and deep-learning methodologies has demonstrated considerable potential in uncovering novel, uncharted attacks and warrants further investigation.

Second, the integration of IDS with other security mechanisms such as access control, encryption, and authentication is necessary to provide comprehensive security solutions for Home Automation systems. Access control mechanisms can prevent unauthorized access to the system, while encryption can ensure that the data transmitted between devices is secure. Authentication techniques can play a crucial role in verifying the authenticity of both users and devices before granting access to the system.

Third, the evaluation of IDS techniques in real-world Home Automation systems is essential to validate their effectiveness and performance. Many prior investigations have relied on simulations or laboratory-based experiments, potentially failing to capture the intricacies of real-world settings. Conducting experiments in real-world environments can provide more realistic results and help identify the limitations and challenges of IDS techniques.

Fourth, the development of IDS techniques that can operate in resource-constrained IoT devices is essential. Many of the current intrusion detection system (IDS) methods predominantly depend on centralized architectures. However, these centralized approaches may not be well-suited for IoT devices due to their constrained processing capabilities and limited memory. Thus, it becomes imperative to investigate distributed IDS techniques capable of decentralized operation, specifically designed to be deployed on resource-constrained IoT devices.

References

1. Sovacool, B. K., & Del Rio, D. D. F. (2020) Smart home technologies in Europe: A critical review of concepts, benefits, risks and policies. *Renewable and Sustainable Energy Reviews*, 120, 109663.

2. Asadullah, M., & Raza, A. (2016, November) An overview of home automation systems. In *2016 2nd International Conference on Robotics and Artificial Intelligence (ICRAI)* (pp. 27–31). IEEE.

3. Heidari, A., & Jabraeil Jamali, M. A. (2022) Internet of Things intrusion detection systems: A comprehensive review and future directions. *Cluster Computing*, 26(6), 3753–3780.

4. Prajapati, N. M., Mishra, A., & Bhanodia, P. (2014, March) Literature survey-IDS for DDoS attacks. In *2014 Conference on IT in Business, Industry and Government (CSIBIG)* (pp. 1–3). IEEE.

5. Jose, S., Malathi, D., Reddy, B., & Jayaseeli, D. (2018, April) A survey on anomaly based host intrusion detection system. *Journal of Physics: Conference Series*,1000(1), 012049. IOP Publishing.

6. Gassais, R., Ezzati-Jivan, N., Fernandez, J. M., Aloise, D., & Dagenais, M. R. (2020) Multi-level host-based intrusion detection system for Internet of Things. *Journal of Cloud Computing*, 9, 1–16.

7. Zarpelão, B. B., Miani, R. S., Kawakani, C. T., & de Alvarenga, S. C. (2017) A survey of intrusion detection in Internet of Things. *Journal of Network and Computer Applications*, 84, 25–37.

8. Soliman, H. H., Hikal, N. A., & Sakr, N. A. (2012) A comparative performance evaluation of intrusion detection techniques for hierarchical wireless sensor networks. *Egyptian Informatics Journal*, 13(3), 225–238.

9. Zarpelão, B. B., Miani, R. S., Kawakani, C. T., & de Alvarenga, S. C. (2017) A survey of intrusion detection in Internet of Things. *Journal of Network and Computer Applications*, 84, 25–37.

10. Sugi, S. S. S., & Ratna, S. R. (2020, December) Investigation of machine learning techniques in intrusion detection system for IoT network. In *2020 3rd International Conference on Intelligent Sustainable Systems (ICISS)* (pp. 1164–1167). IEEE.

11. Tabassum, A., Erbad, A., & Guizani, M. (2019, June) A survey on recent approaches in intrusion detection system in IoTs. In *2019 15th International*

Wireless Communications & Mobile Computing Conference (IWCMC) (pp. 1190–1197). IEEE.

12. Begli, M., Derakhshan, F., & Karimipour, H. (2019, August) A layered intrusion detection system for critical infrastructure using machine learning. In *2019 IEEE 7th International Conference on Smart Energy Grid Engineering (SEGE)* (pp. 120–124). IEEE.

13. Park, S. T., Li, G., & Hong, J. C. (2020) A study on smart factory-based ambient intelligence context-aware intrusion detection system using machine learning. *Journal of Ambient Intelligence and Humanized Computing,* 11, 1405–1412.

14. Sharma, B., Sharma, L., & Lal, C. (2022) Feature selection and deep learning technique for intrusion detection system in IoT. In *Proceedings of International Conference on Computational Intelligence: ICCI 2020* (pp. 253–261). Springer, Singapore.

15. Gendreau, A. A., & Moorman, M. (2016) Survey of intrusion detection systems towards an end to end secure Internet of Things. In: *2016 IEEE 4th International Conference on Future Internet of Things and Cloud (FiCloud)* pp 84–90). IEEE, Vienna.

16. Zarpelão, B. B., Miani, R. S., Kawakani C. T., & de Alvarenga, S. C. (2017) A survey of intrusion detection in Internet of Things. *Journal of Network and Computer Applications,* 84, 25–37.

17. Liu, C., Yang, J., Chen R., Zhang Y., & Zeng J. (2011) Research on immunity-based intrusion detection technology for the Internet of Things. In: *2011 Seventh International Conference on Natural Computation, vol. 1. IEEE* (pp 212–216). Shanghai.

18. Kasinathan, P., Pastrone, C., Spirito, M. A., & Vinkovits, M. (2013) Denial-of-service detection in 6LoWPAN based Internet of Things. In: *2013 IEEE 9th International Conference on Wireless and Mobile Computing, Networking and Communications (WiMob)* (pp. 600–607). IEEE, Lyon.

19. *Suricata the Next Generation Intrusion Detection System.* https://oisf.net/ Accessed 5 Dec 2017

20. Kasinathan, P., Costamagna, G., Khaleel, H., Pastrone, C., & Spirito, M. A. (2013) DEMO: An IDS framework for Internet of Things empowered by 6LoWPAN. In: *Proceedings of the 2013 ACM SIGSAC Conference on Computer; Communications Security,* CCS '13 (pp. 1337–1340). Berlin.

21. Jun, C., Chi, C. (2014) Design of complex event-processing IDS in Internet of Things. In: *2014 Sixth International Conference on Measuring Technology and Mechatronics Automation* (pp. 226–229). IEEE, Zhangjiajie.

22. Krimmling, J., Peter, S. (2014) Integration and evaluation of intrusion detection for CoAP in smart city applications. In: *2014 IEEE Conference on Communications and Network Security* (pp. 73–78). IEEE, San Francisco.

23. Butun, I., Ra, I-H., Sankar, R. (2015) An intrusion detection system based on multi-level clustering for hierarchical wireless sensor networks. *Sensors* 15(11), 28960–28978.

24. Surendar, M., Umamakeswari, A. (2016) InDReS: An intrusion detection and response system for Internet of Things with 6LoWPAN. In: *2016 International Conference on Wireless Communications, Signal Processing and Networking (WiSPNET)* (pp. 1903–1908). Chennai.

25. Le, A., Loo, J., Chai, K. K., Aiash, M. (2016) A specification-based IDS for detecting attacks on RPL-based network topology. *Information* 7(2), 1–19.
26. Bostani, H., Sheikhan, M. (2017) Hybrid of anomaly-based and specification-based IDS for Internet of Things using unsupervised OPF based on MapReduce approach. *Computer Communications*, 98, 52–71.
27. Garcia-Font, V., Garrigues, C., Rifà-Pous, H. (2017) Attack classification schema for smart city WSNs. *Sensors*, 17(4), 1–24.
28. Fu, Y., Yan, Z., Cao, J., Ousmane, K., Cao, X. (2017) An automata based intrusion detection method for Internet of Things. *Mobile Information Systems* 2017, 13.
29. Deng, L., Li, D., Yao, X., Cox, D., Wang, H. (2018) Mobile network intrusion detection for IoT system based on transfer learning algorithm. *Cluster Computing*, 21, 1–16.
30. Amouri, A., Alaparthy, V. T., Morgera, S. D. (2018) Cross layer-based intrusiondetection based on network behavior for IoT. In: *2018 IEEE 19th Wireless and Microwave Technology Conference (WAMICON)* (pp. 1–4). IEEE, Sand Key.
31. Liu, L., Xu, B., Zhang, X., Wu, X. (2018) An intrusion detection method for internet of things based on suppressed fuzzy clustering. *EURASIP Journal on Wireless Communications and Networking* 2018(1), 113.
32. Abhishek, N. V., Lim, T. J., Sikdar, B., Tandon, A. (2018) An intrusion detection system for detecting compromised gateways in clustered IoT networks. In: *2018 IEEE International Workshop Technical Committee on Communications Quality and Reliability (CQR)* (pp. 1–6). IEEE, Austin.
33. Oh, D., Kim, D., Ro, W. W. (2014) A malicious pattern detection engine for embedded security systems in the internet of things. *Sensors*, 14(12), 24188–24211
34. Summerville, D. H., Zach, K. M., Chen, Y. (2015) Ultra-lightweight deep packet anomaly detection for Internet of Things devices. In: *2015 IEEE 34th International Performance Computing and Communications Conference (IPCCC)* (pp. 1–8). IEEE, Nanjing.
35. Gupta, A., Pandey, O. J., Shukla, M., Dadhich, A., Mathur, S., Ingle, A. (2013) Computational intelligence based intrusion detection systems for wireless communication and pervasive computing networks. In: *2013 IEEE International Conference on Computational Intelligence and Computing Research* (pp. 1–7). IEEE, Enathi.
36. Arrington, B., Barnett, L., Rufus, R., Esterline, A. (2016) Behavioral modeling intrusion detection system (BMIDS) using Internet of Things (IoT) behavior-based anomaly detection via immunity-inspired algorithms. In: *2016 25th International Conference on Computer Communication and Networks (ICCCN)* (pp. 1–6). Waikoloa.
37. Raza, S., Wallgren, L., Voigt, T. (2013) SVELTE: Real-time intrusion detection in the Internet of Things. *Ad Hoc Network*, 11(8), 2661–2674.
38. Khan, Z. A., Herrmann, P. (2017) A trust based distributed intrusion detection mechanism for Internet of Things. In: *2017 IEEE 31st International Conference on Advanced Information Networking and Applications (AINA)*. IEEE, Taipei. pp. 1169–1176.
39. KDD Cup. 1999 Data. http://kdd.ics.uci.edu/databases/kddcup99/ kddcup99.html Accessed 6 Oct 2018

Index

Printed in the United States
by Baker & Taylor Publisher Services